ALWAYS ANOTHER DAWN

Always Another Dawn

By

Albert Crossfield and Clay Blair

The P-47 Press
2018

Published by The P-47 Press, Los Angeles.

FIRST PRINTING 2018.

ISBN: 978-1-387-90648-2.

CONTENTS

A Note on Speed

Mach 1.0 is the speed at which sound travels through the air. On an average day at sea level, the speed of sound, or Mach 1.0, is about 760 miles an hour. At higher, colder altitudes on the same day, it is less. For example, at 35,000 feet it might be only 660 miles an hour. Since most of the flying described in this account is at high altitude, Mach 1.0 is, on an average day, about 660 miles an hour.

The speed is also expressed in terms of fractions of a Mach number. Thus Mach .5 is half of Mach 1 or half of 660 miles an hour, about 330 miles an hour. Speeds above Mach 1.0 are also expressed in whole Mach numbers and fractions of Mach numbers. For example, Mach 1.5 is the equivalent of one and a half times the speed of sound, or about 1,000 miles an hour. Mach 2.0, or twice the speed of sound, is twice 660 miles an hour, or about 1,320 miles an hour. Mach 2.5 is about 1,650 miles an hour. Mach 3 is about 2,000 miles an hour.

1: A Modern Day Lindbergh

A MISTY RAIN, TYPICAL OF SEATTLE IN THE SPRING, fell across the lush green campus of the University of Washington that afternoon. It was 1947. I don't recall the exact date because that whole period of my life remains fixed in my mind as a steady, uninterrupted blur of work and study. I do remember that as I drove through the narrow streets setting apart the ivy-smothered Tudor-Gothic buildings, I proceeded with caution. My car was a veteran of many campaigns in Seattle weather and traffic. It was barely hanging together. When I pulled into my special parking place behind the University's wind tunnel, I was quietly angry.

I had just come from an advanced class in aeronautical engineering under Professor Frank K. Kirsten, a brilliant but crotchety old martinet. He had devoted the lecture to a discourse on the jet engine, which, he held, had no future because its fuel consumption was too great. I had challenged his assertions and argued forcibly, concluding, with some heat, that other experts in aviation had made such dogmatic statements, only to have them later completely disproved.

"Take Monteith," I had said actually quoting the Professor. "He predicted the cantilever wing would not be practicable. Yet almost every airplane flying today has a cantilever wing."

In the aviation world, as anywhere, I concluded, everything is subject to change. We must believe this. I walked through the power room to a door marked: CHIEF WIND TUNNEL OPERATOR, stashed my textbook and notes in a desk drawer, and then scanned the bulletin board. Posted over the tunnel's Schedule-of-Operations sheet was a photograph of a smashed-up automobile, with 'Guess Who?' scrawled underneath. It was an earlier car I owned, a veteran of several brief but devastating engagements. It occurred to me then, for the first time, that both my problem cars had been painted green. I recalled an old race-track superstition against green cars. That was the trouble, I was sure. Overdriving my car and its brakes in Seattle streets couldn't be the reason, of course.

The wind tunnel of the University of Washington was one of the first (and finest) modern wind tunnels built in the United States. Many major aircraft companies, such as Boeing and McDonnell, contracted work to the tunnel. The tunnel tests and analyses were carried out by students under faculty supervision. I had worked in the tunnel part-time since returning to the University in the spring of 1946. We were then engaged in tests on the Boeing B-47 bomber. Many years later the plane, bought in vast quantity, would become the backbone of the Strategic Air Command, and a direct descendant, the Boeing 707, would become the first U.S. commercial jet airliner. In 1947 the plane's concept—sharply swept cantilever wings, six jet engines slung on pods beneath the wing—was controversial and exciting.

I joined a fellow student, Joe Tymczyszyn, near the tunnel control panel and greeted him above the noise, the great rushing of wind, and the steady humming of electric generators. Through a glass port mounted on the bottom of the big wind tube, I could see a silvery model of the B-47 rigidly fixed on a pylon. Sensitive force-measuring devices supporting the pylon below the chamber showed the effects of the blast on a row of meters on the control panel. 'Tym' photographed the meter readings every few moments on a special recorder. The panel was marked SECRET since Boeing and the Air Force considered the data classified.

I plopped into a chair and lighted a cigarette. Then Tym and I fell into avid conversation on the topic that bound us as friends and co-workers: aviation. Tym had a wide acquaintance in aviation. He always had some bit of gossip or vital news to impart.

"Did you hear about Slick Goodlin?" he began. "They say he's reluctant to fly the X-1."

Slick was a Bell Aircraft test pilot. The X-1 was then the sensation of the aviation world—a tiny, bullet-shaped craft fitted with a rocket engine. It was built for research purposes, to provide high-speed flight data so that we, and others in aviation, could get information we then could not get from wind tunnels. In those days, when we pumped air through a tunnel close to the speed of sound, strange things happened. The air 'choked' and the flow was distorted. As a result, most wind-tunnel data near the speed of sound were suspect at a time when they were vitally needed. The X-1 had sufficient power to fly faster than the speed of sound.

"He's reluctant to fly it?" I asked.

"Yeah," Tym said. "They say he wants a lot more money."

Few could blame him. The rocket engine of the X-1, a complex device which burned a fuel combination almost as explosive as dynamite, had never been flown wide open. Engineers were split about fifty-fifty over what would happen structurally when the X-1 reached the speed of sound. Some said the plane would disintegrate; others, especially engineers at Bell, said it would not. In any case, it might be a risky flight. But the rewards, other than money, would be great.

"Hell," I said. "The man who flies that plane through the sonic barrier will be a modern-day Lindbergh." Tym nodded agreement and returned to his log.

For the rest of the afternoon I was busy putting together the data from the wind-tunnel meters. But my mind was fixed on the X-1 and I let my imagination soar. For a test pilot, the X-1 was the absolute ultimate. There was nothing like it in the past; it would be years before anything else surpassed it.

I was still thinking about the plane when I got home that evening. Before dinner, when my wife, Alice, and I sat down for our usual martini, I was lost in thought.

"What's eating you?" she asked. Alice is a native of Seattle. Like many people from that part of the country, typical of Norwegian descent, she is usually quiet and straight to the point. After four years of marriage she had come to terms with my obsession for aviation and rarely questioned either my progress or my mood. I didn't encourage it.

"Oh, nothing," I said. I was mentally composing a letter I intended to write to Bell Aircraft proposing that I be named the new test pilot of the X-1. After dinner, while Alice was washing the dishes, I sat down to my battered portable typewriter and carefully pecked out the letter, stressing my qualifications: Age: 26. Flying time: 2500 hours, single-engine, World War II Navy instructor and fighter-pilot. Special flying: lead pilot, Seattle Naval Reserve stunt team (which could be matched against any stunt team in the country, I added). Education: Prewar: three quarters, University of Washington, basic freshman engineering. Postwar: five semesters, aeronautical engineering (aimed at a Master's degree). Practical experience: prewar, production expediter, Boeing plant, Seattle; postwar, partner in aircraft accessories firm (ashtrays; serving tables); University of Washington wind tunnel. Temperament: reliable, family-man type; even disposition, cool in emergencies. Salary? I would fly the X-1 for nothing, if necessary.

It occurred to me, as I reflected on this letter, that anyone outside the aviation world would have viewed this brief summary of my life as the work of a single-minded zealot. This was not precisely so. My interests ranged wide enough, from philosophy to farming. Yet it was a fact that, since boyhood, almost every waking moment had been devoted, directly or indirectly, to the single purpose of scoring a mark in the aviation world. It was not a spectacular record I sought; around the world flight, a speed dash, or a new altitude. Mine was a more serious bent. I wanted to follow in the footsteps of the aviation giants: Boeing's Edmund ('Eddie') Allen and the Air Force's James H. ('Jimmy') Doolittle, and the like. They were both serious scientists and superb pilots, a rare combination and, in these days of specialization, a rapidly disappearing breed. More specifically, my goal was to participate in the design and construction of the most advanced craft man could conceive and then take it into the air and fly it.

Aeronautic pioneer Edmund Turney Allen (1896-1943), an inspiration to many young pilots, designed cutting-edge planes and test-piloted the prototypes himself. Ironically, and tragically, Allen was on the ground when he died in an airplane crash. The second version of the XB-29 exploded in a fireball on take-off, causing an inferno at a Boeing installation which killed Allen and 27 others

This may strike many as a heady ambition for so young a man. It never seemed that way to me. On this earth, at least, I believe man is master of his own fate. Within his God-given physical and mental limitations, he can do what he wants to do. I believe the secret is to work intelligently, economically, and steadily toward a set goal. I must have been about six years old when I made up my mind what I wanted. Shortly after that, I was struck by a disease that kept me bed-ridden, off and on, for almost five years. As a result, I was told I would never fly. My mind shut out these predictions and stubbornly plotted the future. There are many hurdles along the way. I am scaling them, one way or another. Anyone with determination can do the same, I think.

That night when I drafted the letter to Bell I was still far from completing what I believed to be an adequate foundation. For one thing, my education, interrupted by the war, was considerably short of my design. Yet I must admit that at heart I am also a gambler. If I were lucky enough, I knew, the X-1 could catapult me directly toward the very position I sought. The advanced education could come later, with experience. Besides, who could resist the temptation to fly the X-1, if there was a chance?

Bell must have received many such letters from adventurous pilots. I imagine they were all passed on to the public relations department and from there to a handy waste-paper basket. I never received a reply. Unknown to me, and to others who may have written, the Air Force had already picked Goodlin's replacement. Shortly after I mailed my application, I read in the papers that Air Force Captain Charles Yeager was assigned the job. In October, 1947, he flew the X-1 through the sonic barrier with ease—and overnight became the new Lindbergh of the aviation world.

I felt not the slightest tinge of envy over Yeager's feat. On reflection I considered it just as well that my letter had not been answered. My time had obviously not come. Not for one minute, however, did I doubt that it would. I buckled down at the University, working doggedly toward my Master's degree. I supplemented my meager G.I. stipend with the small returns from the aircraft accessories business and my work in the wind tunnel, where, in time, I was named student boss of operations. I kept my flying sharply honed in exercises with my Naval Reserve unit. So as not to tempt fate further on the streets, I painted my battered car bright blue with gratifying results.

2: The Gypsy Caravan

In the spring of 1950, a few months before Commencement, I began to lay final plans for my move into the aviation world. The way the deck was stacked, it did not appear a ripe time for aspiring aeronautical engineers. The Pentagon's post-World War II economy drive had severely deflated the giant aviation industry. There were a few jets in production—Boeing's B-47, North American's F-86, Lockheed's F-80, Republic's F-84, McDonnell's 'Banshee'—and many others in the experimental test stage. Crack aeronautical engineers were, as usual, rare; but new graduates were a dime a dozen, breaking into the industry at less than $300 a month. Many able experimental test pilots were killing time in routine jobs. But as the cards were played out, my timing couldn't have been better. No one could then foresee the outbreak of the Korean War. In a few months this war changed the atmosphere in the aviation industry one hundred and eighty degrees. This change provided me with my great opportunity.

That spring, as I reviewed the chances open to me, I concluded the best stepping stone was a Civil Service job with the government as an 'aeronautical research pilot' for the National Advisory Committee for Aeronautics (NACA). Unknown to the general public, NACA had for years been the vital cauldron in which new ideas in aeronautical engineering were brewed and sampled. The agency was founded in 1915 by President Wilson, after the U.S. had lagged considerably behind Europe in the exploitation of the airplane for civilian and military purposes.

The members of the committee, then the grandees of the U.S. aviation world, were charged with keeping close tabs on all domestic and foreign aviation developments, and to serve as a kind of clearing house for U.S. engineers. The committee was supposed to encourage officially any U.S. aviation development which held promise. As the airplane grew in importance and complexity, NACA grew in size. Langley Laboratory was founded at Hampton, Virginia, to test seaplane hulls, new propeller designs, and important airfoils. It was soon equipped with wind tunnels and other tools of the aeronautical engineers. Much later, in 1940, NACA founded a second aeronautical research laboratory—Ames—at Moffett Field, near San Francisco. Shortly before World War II, a third laboratory, Lewis, was built in Cleveland, Ohio, to work on problems of propulsion. While some NACA engineers dealt with hardware, much new basic theory—some of it sound, some of it impractical—emanated from the ivy-covered, college-like atmosphere of its laboratories. This theory, combined with that from universities such as Washington, and considerably more theory generated by the highly competitive aviation industry, served to keep the U.S. abreast.

The X-1 rocket plane was, in a way, a product of NACA. During World War II, NACA was frantically busy 'fixing' design shortcomings on production military airplanes. In 1944, when the country stood on the threshold of the jet age, NACA engineers came face-to-face with the problem of the suspect data provided by wind tunnels near the speed of sound. Seeking a substitute solution, the Air Force's Ezra Kotcher and a few NACA engineers, including Hartley Soule and John Stack, together with Bell engineer Robert Woods, conceived the idea of building a full-scale rocket-powered research plane that could actually be flown through the speed of sound to get the necessary data. It was a bold, indeed, daring move for the conservative agency, and it paid handsome dividends in the long run.

During the course of modern aviation history, NACA has been alternately praised and damned. In 1935 the British Journal of the Royal Aeronautical Society huffed: "It is notorious that many of our most capable design staffs prefer to base their technical work on the results of the NACA." After World War II, when the complete picture of the astounding Nazi achievements in the field of aeronautics came to light, NACA was severely criticized for the U.S. lag. Much later it was blamed for permitting the U.S. to fall behind in the field of ballistic missiles. These shortcomings, I believe, were more the result of a national attitude than a specific research or policy failure on NACA's part. By and large, considering its shoestring budget, NACA had performed ably. With only occasional exceptions, the U.S. aviation industry has held NACA in high regard. One reason is that the agency served as a training ground for many U.S. aeronautical engineers. For example, my childhood hero, Eddie Allen, was one of NACA's first and best test pilots.

From my point of view in 1950, NACA seemed a likely starting point. I knew that NACA kept a small stable of test pilots at each of its three major laboratories. Most of them were engineers, too; able to translate a deficiency encountered in the air into precise engineering terminology. A close association with these men for a period would be valuable experience. Thus, without knowledge of a specific vacancy, I mailed off a general application form to the government.

There were no openings, the government replied. I wrote again and again without results. When graduation exercises were only a few weeks away, I felt I had to take some kind of direct action. I decided to pay an unannounced visit to Lawrence Clousing, NACA's chief test pilot at Ames. Clousing, I knew, was one of the best in the business. If he did not know of a job, his advice alone would make my trip worthwhile.

I remember everything about that day. It was remarkable not only because it was a turning point in my life, but also because it was filled with coincidences, minor but eerie. The first of the latter happened the moment I walked into Clousing's office—unexpectedly, so I thought.

"Hello, Crossfield," Clousing said. He was a tall man with a deceptively shy manner. He seemed to me more like a college professor than a test pilot. He thrust a friendly hand toward me.

"We've been waiting for you. Your wife called a few minutes ago."

I was very surprised by his greeting. I had told Alice only that I was going to see a "guy named Clousing down near San Francisco." That she had been able to track me down to his office at the big NACA facility amazed me. This feeling soon gave way to concern. I was sure Alice would not call unless there was urgent news.

"Is somebody ill?" I asked Clousing.

"No," he said. "She wanted to pass along the word that you received a reply this morning to your civil service application. You're invited to Edwards for an interview. We have no openings here at all."

The most surprising fact of all in this news was that Alice had opened the letter. Not in seven years of marriage had she so much as touched a letter addressed to me. Well, I thought, it's lucky she did. I turned to Clousing.

"Edwards?" I asked. "Isn't that Air Force?" At that time I knew only that Edwards was a desert test-center for experimental airplanes in Southern California. It was at Edwards that Chuck Yeager had flown the X-1 through the sonic barrier. Industry test pilots from the Los Angeles area used the base for first flights of new planes.

"NACA has a small experimental test group at Edwards," Clousing said. "Two or three pilots and a few engineers and mechanics. They came out with the X-1 back in '46. They're doing some work there with other planes. It was supposed to be a temporary group but they've made it a permanent station now. Walt Williams runs the unit. The chief test pilot is John Griffith. Do you want to go down and see them?"

I wasn't too keen on Edwards. Clousing's brief comments brought to mind a picture of a gypsy caravan from NACA camping in tents on the edge of the Air Force base. What a contrast to the scholarly atmosphere of the massive Ames installation! To me Ames was a known quantity but Edwards a big question. But Clousing had made it clear he was not hiring. Edwards, at least, was a foot in the door. I thought it might be worth a gamble. When I said yes, Clousing put through a call to Walt Williams to arrange a rendezvous. Soon I was on a train, chuffing slowly over the coastal mountains toward the great, desolate Mojave Desert. Today Edwards, like the rest of Southern California, has grown to spectacular proportions. It is a well-organized military base, manned by some 10,000 men, with a neat base-housing area, crosshatched by streets named for pilots who have died in the course of duty at Edwards. It has a Base Exchange, an Officers' Club, gigantic hangars, and all the rest. But on that day when I saw it for the first time, it was little more than a runway scratched out of the desert. The handful of pilots lived in "tarpaper" shacks and drank whiskey in a roadhouse run by an aging but colorful aviatrix named Pancho Barnes.

John Griffith met my train in Mojave, a frontier town not far from Death Valley, once a stopping-off place for the famous twenty-mule teams which labored across the desert hauling borax. The brown wastes of the desert were harsh to my eyes, which had looked for so long on the green of the Northwest. I was not sure Alice would like it. Even in May the heat was stifling. Griffith, a stocky, powerfully built man about thirty-one years old, was appropriately dressed for the climate—slacks, sport shirt, dark glasses. I felt out of place in my blue serge suit, but John quickly put me at ease with his friendly smile and easy manner. We climbed into his car and drove along an arrow-straight, black-top road toward the base. It was hard to believe that this primeval environment was the center of aviation's most advanced flying.

On the way to the field I learned a little of the history of the NACA pilots at Edwards. The original group had consisted of Herbert Hoover, and Howard Lilly, both fine pilots. Lilly was killed when an experimental plane blew up on take-off. Hoover was killed later, when a B-45 jet exploded in the air; his co-pilot, John Harper, escaped. He subsequently went to work for Lear, Inc. To replace them, Griffith came from Lewis Lab and Bob Champine from the Langley Lab to be number two man. An able, sharp-eyed pilot, but not a very experienced one, Champine soon developed a distaste for experimental flight tests. He transferred back to Langley, leaving the opening for which I was to be interviewed. Griffith was the sole pilot, a World War II veteran. He flew for the Air Force in the Solomons and later joined NACA. Superior to him was Joe Vensel, chief of Flight Operations, then came Walt Williams, chief of the station.

The NACA High Speed Flight Test Station occupied one of two small hangars in the sand bordering the runway. As we drew closer, I saw there was just one building, a combination hangar and office. I was soon to learn that the NACA operation was, as I had envisioned it, completely parasitic. It leaned on the Air Force for water, communications, fuel, fire protection—everything but salaries, pilots, and engineers. But the primitive facade was deceptive. Inside there was a highly contagious, pioneering spirit. The NACA group at Edwards was ready to perform big deeds; even more spectacular plans were in the works. The principal reason for this spirit, I soon found, was the boss, Walt Williams, a thirty-one-year-old engineer from New Orleans. A cocky, hard-working operator, Williams had cut his teeth in NACA's Langley Laboratory during the war. In 1946 he had come to Edwards with twelve men under his command, to supervise the research phase of the X-1 program. The plan then was that when Bell had finished the initial flight tests of the plane, Williams and his group would move in. They would fit the ship with instruments and begin recording scientific data on each flight. This scheme had been unavoidably delayed when Goodlin bowed out.

After Chuck Yeager flew the plane through the sound barrier, other Air Force pilots moved in to take the controls and set new records. One of these was Major Frank K. ('Pete') Everest, who zoomed to an altitude of 73,000 feet. Others followed: Captain Jack Ridley and Colonel Albert Boyd, who was then commander of the Edwards outpost, and the epitome of a service test pilot. Herbert Hoover of NACA flew the X-1 and became the first civilian to penetrate the sound barrier.

There were actually three X-1s, I discovered. The first, Yeager's plane, which he nicknamed Glamorous Glennis after his beautiful wife, had been shipped off to the Smithsonian Institution. The second X-1 had been turned over to NACA. The third X-1 was still at the Bell plant in Buffalo, New York, being fitted with a new low-pressure fuel system which would enable it to go higher and faster. But many, many months would pass before X-1 number three was ready for flight. It held a grim surprise. I talked first with Joe Vensel, chief of Flight Operations. He was a man cautious in decision but quick in physical movement. He bore the scars of a rough life of flying: shattered sinuses. At 40, he wore a hearing aid. Vensel had little to say or to ask.

Griffith then took me directly to Williams' office, a makeshift area in one end of the hangar. Williams met me with a firm and enthusiastic handshake. He bounced around the room impatiently, pausing frequently to run his hand through his crew-cut brown hair, or to doodle violently on a scratch pad. It was immediately clear that Williams was a man of action. I liked him on first sight. He and Griffith probed my background.

"How is it you have so much single-engine time?" Griffith asked.

"I like to fly," I said. "I got my private license before the war. During the war I was an instructor at Corpus Christi, Texas. We were very busy. Lot of students. Lot of hours. I took extra students when I could. After the war I was active in the Naval Reserve."

"What about this stunt team?" Williams asked.

And so it went. As the interview progressed, I learned there were two other pilots being considered for the opening, each with about half my flying experience. This competition, unsuspected until then, sharpened my senses. I talked earnestly about my desire to make a serious contribution to aeronautical science.

Before the session drew to a close, Williams made it clear that the job was mine if I wanted it. I didn't want to appear overly eager. I parried for a while, seeking answers to a few questions of my own.

"What kind of flying would I be doing here?" I asked. "It looks to me as though Chuck Yeager and Pete Everest and the other Air Force pilots have a corner on the market." It was a deliberate needle and it obviously touched Williams on a sore spot. He responded with a spiel which sounded as though it had been drafted for a congressional committee.

"The research airplane was conceived at NACA's Langley Laboratory. The funds are provided principally by the Air Force and the Navy. NACA has technical jurisdiction over the flight programs, which are designed to provide maximum data within a given time. Under the new concept, civilian test pilots of the companies concerned in the design and construction of the research airplanes make initial test flights, verifying established design and structural points, engine reliability, and so on. The Air Force pilots then take over and fly them with an eye to military application, under NACA cognizance. After that, so the plan goes, the ships are turned over to us here at NACA for detailed flight research. The ... ah ... the Air Force has been somewhat slow in turning over the planes, that's true, but we have encountered one unpredicted technical problem after the other ..."

"I suppose ..." I broke in. But Williams had not finished. He lunged out of his chair and paced back and forth, warming to his subject.

"We are blazing new trails in aeronautical science out here. The data we are producing are fed directly into the aviation industry through NACA reports available to all. Industry engineers are applying the data to concepts for the next generation of jet fighters, a family of supersonic fighters. We're testing everything here: straight wing, swept wing, tailless jobs. We're running into all kinds of phenomena. Some of them have been predicted in theory and tunnel test; some are brand-new."

"What planes are you working with now?" I asked.

"We've got an X-1 out there in the hangar now, and the X-4. Hell, come on out and I'll show you."

Williams boomed out of the office into the hangar space. I followed, looking in detail for the first time at the collection of weird and fascinating planes. The hangar was busy. Mechanics swarmed over the little hot-rods, removing plates, pulling long snarls of wire from their insides, shoving calibration carts here and there. The whine of a pneumatic drill, accompanied by the staccato of a rivet gun, echoed through the high-beamed, arched ceiling. The scene reminded me of the feverishly busy pits at the Indianapolis race track a few hours before the 500-mile Speedway race on Memorial Day. The analogy is not far-fetched. These planes were nearly comparable to temperamental, overpowered, dangerous, finely-tuned racing cars. Edwards, in reality, was an Indianapolis of the air.

A few of the planes, such as the X-1, were familiar to me; others were new. We stopped alongside the X-4, a tailless plane powered by two jet engines. It had just been turned over to NACA by the Air Force, Williams said, patting the side of the ship. It was a metallic white, like an icebox.

"She was supposed to go Mach 1," he said. "But she can't make it. It's a little tricky to fly. The engines flame out at altitude. She pitches a bit at Mach .9. British lost a couple of DeHavilland Swallows of similar design. Mystery why they crashed. Maybe we can find out with this baby."

Williams rattled on in this fashion as we moved about the hangar. We came to another beautiful ship which looked somewhat like the X-1.

"This is the Douglas Skystreak, the D-558-I," Williams said. "It's a Navy project."

"Oh, yes," I said. This was the model that killed Lilly. I recalled a few of the details of the program. "Gene May also flew that one, didn't he?" May was a Douglas test pilot.

"That's right," Williams said. "We have two of these left. This one is just like the X-1 only it has a jet instead of a rocket engine. We had another D-558 version here, swept wing with a jet using JATO for take-off, called the Skyrocket. Then there also is another swept-wing version with a jet engine and a rocket engine. It's back at the Douglas plant now being modified to an all-rocket version. We'll air-launch it from a mother plane like we do the X-1."

All-rocket, air-launch, swept-wing. I turned these phrases over briefly in my mind, little realizing then the impact this airplane would have on my future.

"What do you expect from that?" I asked.

"Well, the figures are classified, frankly. But in round numbers and stretching, we think she might reach Mach 2, and maybe 90,000 or 100,000 feet," Williams said. He spoke in a low, confidential tone.

"Who is the pilot going to be?" I asked. "Gene May?"

"No." Williams said. "Douglas has a new pilot, an ex-Navy type named Bill Bridgeman."

"The Air Force doesn't get this one?"

"No. This is a Navy project. They do it differently. They'd just as soon have the manufacturer establish the limits of the airplane. Good, sharp outfit to do business with. They don't mind racking up a few records, but it is not their first order of business."

The way Williams spoke of 'records,' he conveyed clearly the impression that at NACA records per se were unimportant, if not frowned upon. We wandered back to his office and sat down.

"Now," he said, "there are about four other types in the works. Bell's got a souped-up version of the X-1 coming out which will easily exceed Mach 2, or better. They also have a swept-wing rocket plane, the X-2, which is designed for nearly Mach 3 and about 150,000 feet. Then there's the X-3, a straight-wing job by Douglas. It is way behind schedule and very complicated. It might turn out to be a dud. Then we'll have the Bell X-5, a jet-powered ship with an in-flight variable-sweep capability."

My head was swimming with figures and visions of these fantastic airplanes. My top speed in an airplane then was maybe five hundred miles an hour, clocked in a dive in a Corsair. Williams talked of 1500 and 2000 miles an hour as if those speeds were routine. I was sold.

"I would have a shot at those airplanes?" I asked.

"If everything works out," Williams said.

"The X-2 as well?"

"If everything works out," Williams repeated.

"When do I start?"

"We'll let you know," Williams said. He glanced at his watch. "You going back into Mojave to catch a train? Why don't you hitch a ride with Drake and Carmen?"

Hubert M. Drake and L. Robert Carmen together made up the 'advanced' design group at NACA's Edwards installation. They were the 'dreamers,' paid to look far into the future and scheme new ways to fly higher and faster. I didn't know it then, and they didn't discuss it, but Drake and Carmen were doing work at night in their homes on an airplane to put the best of dreamers to shame. It was a rocket-powered craft that would fly four thousand miles an hour and to an altitude of 500,000 feet. Five years later, after a tortuous journey through a jungle of bureaucracy, and endless modification, this craft became the X-15. Looking back now, I regard the fact that these two men were picked to give me a lift to Mojave as something of a coincidence.

Of pressing concern to me at that moment was the fact that I was almost flat broke. I had hitch-hiked down to the Ames Laboratory on a Navy airplane and had intended to return to Seattle that same day by the same means. The plane had long since returned; I was stranded in the desert without nearly enough cash for a train ticket to Seattle. There was no money in my checking account. However, by the time I climbed out of Drake's car at the bleak, dusty Mojave railroad station and bid my hosts farewell, I had a plan.

I checked with the station master. There was a north-bound train scheduled to pass through Mojave at midnight. The day-coach fare to Seattle, via San Francisco, was about $20, and this was about $10 more than I had.

"What' the next stop beyond Mojave?" I asked.

"Martinez," the station master said. He eyed me curiously.

"Okay," I said, "give me a ticket to Martinez." It was about $7.00. I then placed a telephone call, collect, to my sister, Elena Ruth ('Babe') Brown, who lived in Sierra Madre, just outside Los Angeles. When she answered, considerably surprised to hear from me, I told her I was taking the midnight train to Martinez and asked her to wire me $25 in care of the station master there. I had not often borrowed money in my life, but I didn't mind asking her. Many years before, when she was a student at Berkeley, I had hocked my camera in order to lend her $40 for flying lessons, for which my father refused to pay. After Babe assured me the money would be sent immediately, I hung up and retired to a corner to count my remaining fortune.

I spent another dollar at the Silver Dollar Cafe for dinner, then blew the rest on a ticket to the local movie. By still another coincidence, the picture was about a test pilot and Humphrey Bogart was the star. I plumped into a seat and watched while he wrestled with a rattling control stick, braving the frontiers of flight. Hours later I was still deeply absorbed, not in that turkey of a movie but in what I had seen and heard that day, when I felt a hand on my shoulder. A voice spoke:

"Are you Mr. Crossfield?"

Startled, I broke out of my supersonic reverie and spun around. It was the theater usher.

"Yeah. I'm Crossfield."

"There's a gentleman out front to see you."

I followed the usher up the aisle wondering who it could be. No one on earth knows where I am, I thought. To my astonishment, I found Babe's husband, Claude, and behind him, my mother, Lucia, waiting in the lobby. My mother had been visiting my sister when I called. After I hung up she talked my brother-in-law into making the three-hour drive to Mojave to surprise me.

"But how did you know I was in there?" I asked.

"Well, I cased every bar in town first, while your mother waited in the car. I didn't see you in any of them so I figured in a town of this size the only place left was the movie."

We laughed and made our way to a nearby restaurant. At midnight, $25 richer, I boarded a day coach on the train.

Back in Seattle, I collected my Master's degree in aeronautical engineering, resigned from my Naval Reserve unit, packed up the family—Alice, Becky, age two, and our new addition, Tommy—traded my 1941 Ford for a '49 Ford, and drove to the desert to begin a new life.

Three weeks later many of my Naval Reserve comrades were mobilized and shipped off to Korea.

3: A Sense of Urgency

A HARSH, BITTERLY COLD DECEMBER WIND, gathering momentum over miles of flat desert, lashed the ramp behind the NACA hangar. I buttoned my jacket close and bowed my head as I pushed against it toward the airplane. Here and there I saw that the small puddles were frozen to solid ice. The desert warms up during the day, but on a winter night it is like the North Pole. Sometimes it snows at Edwards.

I climbed into the cockpit and pulled on my crash helmet, grateful to be shielded at last from the frigid blast. Ralph Sparks, who, on that blue-cold morning, looked as though he was born before the Wright brothers, closed the canopy and removed the aluminum boarding ladder. I smiled and waved my hand sharply. Sparks claimed personal authorship of most of aviation's achievements, but there were few mechanics at NACA, or anywhere for that matter, more able than he. He stood by while I wound up the engines. They caught, and I taxied out for my first X-4 flight, the first of a series of hurried checkouts in NACA's stable of thoroughbreds.

My first six months at Edwards had been a tumultuous time of hurry and change. Walt Williams, as a matter of routine, kept a fast pace. When the Korean War broke out, our outfit, like all of the aviation world, worked with a new sense of urgency. At the climax of the dramatic shift, NACA's top pilot, John Griffith, resigned to take a job at Chance-Vought. In the new climate of the industry, journeyman test pilots were desperately needed. I checked out in a couple of jets, the F-84 and the Douglas Skystreak.

Then, in the final days before Griffith's departure, I gathered what information I could about the foibles of our temperamental champions. Suddenly, then, I was completely on my own. The entire NACA Edwards test program was dumped in my lap.

Actually, I couldn't have been more pleased. Looking back, I believe now that the months that followed were, professionally speaking, the happiest days of my life. I was then too new and too young to concern my mind seriously with government and industry politics. My approach to the job was completely starry-eyed. I could move at my own pace, always fast. I flew morning, noon, and afternoon in the strangest and most unpredictable airplanes man had ever devised. These flights were never long. Experimental airplanes are like powerful rockets. They blaze furiously for a few moments, during which the pilots strive to probe an unknown area, and then they sputter and die. The one big difference between the manned plane and the missile is that the pilot brings the multimillion-dollar plane back to earth for another flight. Usually.

Before my flight in the X-4 that morning, Walt Williams and Joe Vensel clucked around the hangar like two old maids grooming their niece for a grand debut. I had read all the flight reports on the X-4 and had picked Griffith's brain thoroughly. I knew the weak points of the airplane: its two engines were erratic above 30,000 feet; at Mach .88 the plane became unstable; it broke into a steady porpoising motion, like an automobile cushioning over a washboard road. Beyond that, nearer the speed of sound, no one knew what would happen. The X-4 had never been flown there. Williams and Vensel added a fact I knew quite well: the plane was equipped with barn-door-sized speed brakes. If popped in flight they would slow the X-4 abruptly and allow her to withdraw from any zone of trouble.

The X-4, by then, was a veteran of Edwards. The plane was conceived in the postwar years by Jack Northrop, an imaginative inventor and an unyielding advocate of the 'tailless' concept. The X-4 was first flown by Northrop's renowned test pilot, Charlie Tucker, in 1949. After considerable modification, it had been turned over to the Air Force. Chuck Yeager, Pete Everest, Colonel Richard Johnson, and Al Boyd flew it. Thirty flights later, NACA inherited the plane and its mechanic, Ralph Sparks, who had been with the project from the outset.

I pushed the twin throttles forward and as the fuel surged into the burning chambers, the X-4 leaped toward the runway. In the distance I could see a plane leaving Air Force Fighter Ops, headquarters for the military test-pilot group. Pete Everest was the pilot of the Air Force craft, an early-model F-86. He would join me to fly 'chase,' observing the performance of the X-4 and watching for danger signals from close quarters.

Officially, no rivalry existed between the pilots of the Air Force and the NACA group. As Williams had said, the two jobs were poles apart. Once contractor pilots, such as Tucker, had demonstrated that the plane could fly, the Air Force flew it to evaluate military applications. Then NACA pilots put the plane through an exhaustive aerodynamic dissection, learning every new fact possible.

In fact, there was a natural rivalry between the test pilots. Each day at Edwards, the pilots played out a kind of small scale Olympic Games of the air. Occasionally these were major battles to break records, staged by rival Navy and Air Force.

More often, they were small but significant demonstrations of a new flying technique or a daring maneuver into the unknown, a step beyond the previous pilot of the airplane. For example, some of the planes had vicious weaknesses. If, on a given flight, the pilot was able to skirt these, he had achieved a minor triumph, worth a toast at Pancho's. Edwards was not the place to attract non-competitive pilots.

Some of the reason for the keen rivalry lay in the Air Force's approach to flight test. Along with its triumphs in the X-1, the Air Force, first at Wright

Field, later at Edwards, had set out to create a cadre of schooled engineering test pilots on a par with the best in NACA and industry. For example, Yeager was not an educated engineer. He was an intuitive engineer, one of the best. He could feel in an instant a deficiency in an airplane and come close to pinpointing its fault technically. A rare pilot, born to fly, like a figure-skater born to skate, Yeager set standards of conduct in the air that were emulated for years afterward at Edwards. The pilots adopted even his understated West Virginia drawl, and ever afterward the radio talk at Edwards reflected this. The pilots at Edwards—to judge by the radio talk—were raised on hominy grits and corn fritters.

But Yeagers are rare. Later the Air Force sent vast numbers of its pilots back to college to study aeronautical engineering and, still later, founded a full-blown test-pilot school at Edwards, which in recent years has graduated a fine group of young, educated test pilots. But before this ambitious, challenging program, many Air Force pilots, resisting the engineering approach, died needlessly. We gave them little reverence: "Hell, he was dead before he took off."

I was not a member of the 'inner circle' that morning in early December. I had met Yeager, Everest, Jack Ridley, Boyd, and the rest, but I had yet to prove my ability in the air. I knew that the moment Everest locked wingtips, he would be watching every move. He had flown the X-4. He would know when I goofed, and the word would soon get back to the others. Conceivably, some leeway might be allowed for the first flight, but it was not likely. Yeager gave little quarter in the air. On his first flight in the X-1, he says, he had been tempted to roll the ship in front of the Edwards tower, scant feet above the ground.

When I received radio permission to take off, I firewalled the throttles. As the X-4 wobbled down the long, bumpy runway, I gingerly felt out the controls. Then the churning jets took hold, and the small X-4 abruptly lunged into the air. Backing off the stall point, I nosed her over gently and leveled out. Then I eased back on the stick and the tiny, tailless craft zoomed skyward like a winged rocket. Behind me, Everest had opened his F-86 wide, trailing a long, black snake of soot, but he could not keep up. I waited for him at altitude, rolling and stalling the plane, getting to know its special strengths and weaknesses. When Everest locked wingtips, I opened the throttle wide, once again leaving him far behind. As predicted, at Mach .88 the X-4 broke into its gentle but potentially dangerous porpoising motion. I opened the air brakes, and the X-4 slowed instantly, throwing me forward against my shoulder restraint straps. Everest hurtled by, chortling on the radio.

The Edwards base now lay far below us, nearly obscured in the vast wilderness of the Mojave wastes. Here and there on the desert floor I could make out the mottled outlines of the curiously shaped 'dry lakes.' These 'lakes' are stretches of fine, closely packed silt, left behind eons ago by the retreating seas and bleached almost white by the hot desert sun. The soil of the lakes is quite unusual. When mixed with water, it becomes slimy like oil. Industrialists mined the soil as a lubricant for well drills. When the lakes are completely dry, the surface is hard and flat, like concrete, and thus ideal natural landing areas for airplanes.

When it rains in the desert, the lake beds are temporarily put out of commission. The water, unable to penetrate the fine, self-sealing surface soil, collects on top in small pools, or sometimes, after a hard rain, in vast, shallow, real-life lakes. This water is swept back and forth by the brisk desert winds until it evaporates. The gentle movement of the water smooths the surface of the lake beds, eliminating bumps and ruts. During this 're-paving' process, the surface becomes mushy and slick, dangerous for a heavy airplane. There is sometimes a little rain in July which temporarily closes the lakes. But the hard rainy season usually begins in mid-December. Frequently, but not always, the intermittent rains keep the lake beds either flooded or soft until March or April. No one can predict the capricious desert weather.

The Edwards base was set directly alongside one of these lakes—Rogers Dry Lake—which in earlier times, appropriately enough, had, like the great salt flats of Utah, been an automobile race track. During the rainy season, at times, I have seen the water on the lake so deep that it was lapping at the edge of the parking ramps, and so penetrating that shrimp eggs of some pre-historic age worked loose from the soil and came to life, mysteriously attracting sea gulls from the distant California coast. To maintain year-round operations, the Air Force had built a normal concrete runway at the base, butting against the dry lake. In the dry season, if required, the lake bed, marked by parallel black lines, could be used as an extension of the concrete runway. For the rocket planes, which required long take-off and landing ar-eas, another runway, lying in the opposite direction and seven miles long, had been painted on the lake bed. Still other nearby lakes—Rosamond, Harper, Three Sisters, Cuddeback—were designated emergency landing areas. When flying experimental planes at Edwards, the pilots always kept within easy reach of one of the dry lakes.

After about fifteen minutes in the air, I felt at home in the X-4. The plane responded so well, in fact, that it was hard for me to keep in mind that I was piloting a marginally stable, experimental racehorse. Had all that talk of dan-ger been the product of some public relations mill? I was beginning to feel my oats now, and a determination that hardly struck me as daring at the time seized me. I would loop the X-4.

Heading back toward Edwards, the check-out virtually complete, flying wing to wing with Everest, without warning I pulled back hard on the stick. The X-4 climbed rapidly, leaving Everest far below. The desert disappeared from my windshield, replaced by the deep blue of the clear sky. In a few sec-onds the X-4 was flat on its back at 27,000 feet. Suddenly all hell broke loose.

A noise like the sound of a fifty-caliber machine-gun exploded through the cockpit. My maneuver had disrupted the smooth flow of air into the two engine intakes. Starved for air, and sensitive anyway at my altitude, the engines had rebelled, and after a flash of uneven running they gave up completely. I righted the plane and sheepishly called Pete Everest on the radio.

"Lost both engines."

"Rog," he said. Then I heard him calling Edwards Tower to report an emergency. I could visualize the reaction there: sirens screeching, fire trucks racing out to the runway, NACA's Walt Williams and Joe Vensel perched on the edge of their chairs. Now working desperately to restart the engines in the air, and mentally locating the position of the emergency dry lakes, I silently cursed my boldness. I could imagine the talk that night: "That new fellow, Crossfield, down at NACA. Pretty green . . ."

I managed at last to win half the battle. One engine coughed to life. If it kept running (a big if, indeed, at that point), I would have sufficient power, at least, to reach the Edwards base runway. Without the engines the X-4 would come in with a low lift over drag (L over D)—in other words, it would glide like a brick, but I would be spared the ignominy of landing on a lake remote from the base. Vensel was taking no chances. By radio he ordered me to land on the lake.

As we lined up for the approach, I could see the emergency trucks parked along the edge of the lake; quite embarrassing. The X-4, already sluggish, began to settle toward earth. As we descended, I was further chagrined when Everest began to call altitude readings, interspersed with occasional helpful hints on how to fly a plane. He was ribbing and I had it coming, so when, finally, the X-4's tires screeched on the lake, I switched off the radio receiver.

Joe Vensel was waiting anxiously on the NACA ramp when I rolled to a stop in front of the hangar. I climbed down the ladder.

"Well," Vensel said, "what happened?"

"I looped it and lost both engines," I said. "Got an air start on one and stop-cocked the other."

"Damn," Vensel muttered. He stalked back to his office.

4: Excitement and Frustration

"You might as well try a rocket flight," Joe Vensel said.

We were sitting in his office, which faced the NACA hangar workshop. His tone lacked enthusiasm. His whole attention seemed focused on the pencil he was twirling between his fingers. It was the day after Christmas, twenty days since my first X-4 flight. The Chinese Communists had entered the Korean War, splitting and decimating our armies on the peninsula. The President had declared a state of national emergency. In the Pentagon the economizing Secretary of Defense, Louis Johnson, had been replaced by General George Marshall. The aviation industry, now overwhelmed with money, was gearing for a future freighted with uncertainty, perhaps a global war with the Soviet Union. Its engineers desperately needed data. Wind-tunnel results from scale models of the newly designed, supersonic, Century Series jet fighters—the F-100, the F-101, F-102, and F-104—had foreshadowed critical instability at high speed. Every man at NACA was anxious to press ahead.

"Okay," I said. "I'll tell them to get 945 ready."

The number 945 was our mundane designation for the Douglas D-558-II Skyrocket, a research airplane with an impressive background and a sensational future. It requires much time and planning to prepare a rocket plane for a test flight. This was especially true in those pioneering days. Rocket engines are complicated and temperamental, something like the engines of expensive high-speed racing cars. They burn a powerful, dangerous fuel combination of liquid oxygen (Lox) and water-alcohol, and sometimes even more exotic fuels, which eat into the pipes and fittings, corroding or unsealing joints. The fuel is pumped into the engine through a complex maze of plumbing, which forever leaks and loses pressure.

The liquid oxygen is very cold, approaching minus 300 degrees Fahrenheit. This intense cold forms a coating of ice on the outside of the tanks and the plane, and permeates everything, sometimes freezing systems not designed for extreme temperatures. The preparation of a rocket engine for flight was always an adventure for our mechanics. I made my way into the hangar to pass on the word to Eddy Layne, our crew chief on 945.

"How about it, Eddy?" I said. "Can we fly tomorrow?" The skin of 945 lay about the hangar floor. The bare skeleton was under siege by half a dozen mechanics, who appeared to be devouring the plane like so many piranha fishes. It hardly seemed possible that it could all be reassembled in one day.

"Sure thing, Scotty," Eddy said. "Got a leaky regulator in the fuel tank, but we'll get it squared away in a while. Go ahead and plan on it. Is this a speed run?"

"No, just a check flight," I said.

"I think Bridgeman and the Douglas people will be flying 943 in the morning. You might want to touch base with them."

"Right," I said. It was obvious that I had not yet scored among the mechanics. What Eddy meant was that I had better check with Bridgeman and find out how to fly the 945. I had already done that. I remained in the hangar for some time, looking over the ship and recalling the plane's history.

In late 1944, when the Air Force and NACA launched the X-1, the Navy, as part of the overall research airplane program, began a separate project of its own, referred to as the D-558. (In the Navy's hopelessly confusing aircraft terminology, the 'D' stands for Douglas, the manufacturer.) The D-558 'Skystreak' was similar to the X-1 in shape; the main difference was that the plane was powered by a jet instead of a rocket engine. The X-1, which was intended to be launched in the air from a mother plane, would fly fast in brief bursts. The D-558, which was designed to take off conventionally from a runway, was slower, but it could stay aloft longer. Between the two designs, it was thought, the aerodynamics in the trouble area at, or just below, the speed of sound could be thoroughly blanketed.

Three of the original jet-powered D-558 Skystreaks were built. In August, 1947, a couple of months before Yeager flew the X-1 through the sound barrier, Navy Commander Turner Caldwell, flying the first D-558, set a speed record of 640.7 miles an hour. Five days later Marine Major Marion Carl pushed the same plane to 650.6 miles an hour, a speed considered sensational at that time. In May, 1948, the 'time bomb' engine in one D-558 blew up on take-off, killing NACA test pilot Howard Lilly. The second airplane became a Hangar Queen and was cannibalized for parts. The third Skystreak was still at NACA gathering data. I had flown it before my first hop in the X-4.

From the outset the D-558 program grew into a second generation of airplanes. To distinguish these from the earlier models, we called the later ones 'Phase Two' airplanes, which was short for D-558-II. The plane was popularly called the 'Skyrocket.' Three Phase Two airplanes were built, all with the new swept wing. In 1946 there was then much controversy, but little swept-wing flight data except those which we had obtained from the Nazis. In each of the Phase Two airplanes, the power-plant or launch scheme was deliberately varied to cover a wide range of research possibilities. The first Phase Two model was, like the 558-I, powered by a single jet engine. Designed to take off conventionally, it was fitted with two small jettisonable rocket bottles (JATO) to help boost it into the sky.

The second model, also intended for conventional ground take-off, was powered by a jet engine and a rocket engine, similar to the rocket engine in the X-1. The third model (945), built to be dropped from a mother plane like the X-1, was also equipped with a jet and rocket-engine combination. Its maximum speed was about Mach 1.2, somewhat slower than the X-1's top of Mach 1.4. Douglas test pilots John Martin and Gene May first flew these tricky

Phase Two's, taking off from the ground, burning the rocket barrel, the jet engine, or both at once. The adventures they logged would make a book in themselves. Ex-Navy pilot Bill Bridgeman of Douglas was later recruited to make the Phase Two air-launched demonstrations. By the time I arrived at NACA, the Phase Two Skyrocket was a familiar sight on the Edwards runway, and Bill Bridgeman was on his way to the Hall of Fame.

Bridgeman flew the jet-rocket ground take-off version of the plane fairly regularly at Edwards. The jet-only JATO-boosted version never really panned out. The Navy ordered it shipped back to the factory for changeover to an all-rocket version, designed for an air-launch (causing even more model confusion). It was this plane that Walt Williams, in our first interview, hinted might reach Mach 2 and 100,000 feet. NACA—I, to be specific—would get a crack at it after Bridgeman had worked out the bugs. The third Phase Two airplane, the air-launched jet-rocket combination, had been delivered to NACA in the fall of 1950, after Bridgeman had made three test air-launches. No NACA pilot had yet flown this model. This was ship number 945, my next challenge. In the long run it turned out to be a very useful and worthy research airplane in the trans-sonic zone, a work horse as well as a race horse.

On the following day, when I reported to the flight line, lugging my parachute and crash helmet, the ground crews were ready. The Skyrocket had already been 'mated'—snugged up like a bomb in its special nesting place in the belly of the B-29 mother plane. The Skyrocket's fuel tanks, for both the jet and the rocket engine, were brimming. The B-29 mother-plane pilot was George Jansen, a top man for Douglas, and experienced in air-launch.

Douglas intended to keep the mother plane until Bridgeman had checked out the all-rocket version of the Skyrocket. I spotted the tanned bald dome of Bill Bridgeman towering above the knot of men clustered near the boarding ladder of the B-29. He was dressed in a flying suit. A crash helmet dangled loosely from his right hand. I walked over.

"You going along, Bill?"

"Yeah. Might be able to help out a little," he said with that wonderful friendliness that was his hallmark.

"Fine. Fine."

We climbed aboard and made our way back to the bomb-bay compartment, into which the top of the Skyrocket fuselage protruded. The Skyrocket cockpit canopy was erect. A maze of wires and tubes—the umbilical cords—was plugged into the back of the Skyrocket, supplying power from the B-29 en route to the launch point. At the proper time I had only to climb into the cockpit, close the hatch, and fall away.

Jansen lost no time. Through my earphones in the bomb-bay compartment, I heard him contact Edwards tower, and the two chase pilots, Fitzhugh Fulton and John Konrad, both Air Force types. In the following years, Fulton became something of a legend at Edwards. I think he must have spent three or four tours at the base, specializing in mother-plane operations. He launched most of the rocket pilots and was back again in 1959 to launch me in the X-15.

Soon we were airborne, straining for altitude. I sat beside Bridgeman on a bench, going through the long pre-flight check-list. At 10,000 feet the crew went on oxygen and I started to board the Skyrocket.

I climbed down into the tiny cockpit, connecting my oxygen hose to the supply inside the Skyrocket. As Bridgeman towered over me, helping to cinch up my shoulder harness straps, I wondered how that long drink of water had ever managed to squeeze into the Skyrocket cockpit. Bridgeman and the launch operator slammed the canopy shut. The floodlights inside the bomb-bay compartment spilled through my windshields, affording enough light for me to see the instrument panel. At twenty minutes prior to launch, Jansen called the time. Following an item on the check-list, I lit off the jet engine. This added thrust would help the B-29 through the thin air and provide the Sky-rocket with flying speed when I dropped.

Now all hands in the air kept a sharp watch for signs of danger. They could come from a hundred points. At that time we had not yet lost a rocket-powered airplane, either in the air or on the ground. But it could happen at any moment—and did, in later months. The B-29s were something of a prob-lem, too. They were fire-prone.

A few minutes before drop I primed the rocket engines. Chase pilots Ful-ton and Konrad, who were flying alongside the B-29 beyond my view, reported routinely:

"Prime looks good."

As we bore down over the dry lake at 35,000 feet, seconds before launch, I glanced one last time at the instrument panels and made ready. Launching a rocket plane and lighting off the engine properly is an exacting task. Improper observation of the numerous gauges and their reactions, or a small mistake in their analysis, can bring failure, possibly fatal. To gain maxi-mum performance from the engines—the basic purpose of any research airplane flight—they should be touched off before the plane has dropped too far into the thick atmosphere. The plane must also be maintained at a precise angle of attack. If it noses down too steeply, precious rocket fuel is expended, regaining lost altitude. If the plane is overly nose-high, the increased drag con-sumes fuel needlessly.

In theory, the jet-rocket Skyrocket gave the pilot a nice edge. He could launch with the jet engine going full blast. This would help him maintain the plane's equilibrium during the rocket-engine light-off.

The next sixty seconds were crowded with excitement and frustration. Jansen, keying his radio mike, droned a brief countdown: "Five . . . four . . . three . . . two . . . one . . . DROP."

I heard a rattle as the two bomb shackles holding the Skyrocket in its metallic perch were disengaged. Suddenly, then, brilliant sunlight poured into the Skyrocket cockpit, blinding me. I was falling like an elevator and flying!

I pulled the nose up and climbed; there was not much time. The jet engine, fed by scoops that were far too small and inefficient, would soon starve for want of air. My fingers had flicked across the separate switches for the four rocket barrels. I felt a gentle forward surge, indicating a successful light-off. Chase pilot Fulton drawled on the radio:

"All four going."

I glanced momentarily at the rocket pressure-gauges. They were in the green—I think. My eyes were still adjusting to the glare of the sunlight. Five . . . ten . . . fifteen seconds. My Mach meter and altimeter seemed to be running a clock-like race. Speed: Mach .9 and increasing. Altitude: 40,000 feet and increasing. My chase planes were far behind, left in a cloud of rocket dust. Altitude: 43,000 feet.

In the next second, fifteen events—all of them bad—took place simultaneously. In the first brief instant, I was suddenly thrown forward against my shoulder straps, almost to the face of the instrument panel. I heard the jet engines popping crazily, then the rockets burned out, followed by eerie silence. I knew what had happened: the balky jet had flamed out; the sudden loss of thrust had sloshed the rocket fuel forward in the tanks, shutting down all four barrels. Suddenly my chest felt as though it were supporting the weight of a platoon of soldiers. The engines were out; cabin pressure was seeping off. The battery, which should have supplied ship's power in the event of engine failure, responded slowly. Everything was out: radios and electrical instruments.

In that particular airplane, the windshield defogging system was hooked directly into the electrical system. With no power to supply defogging air to the windshield, a coat of ice quickly formed, shutting off my vision. Now the emergency was complete; no power, no instruments, no cabin pressure, iced-over windshields. Breathing heavily under the strain of the decompression, I leveled the plane and then banked until the sun beamed directly on the windshield. I knew, at least, that I was pointed in the general direction of the lake, which lay to the west of my position.

By strange coincidence, it happened that the same critical sequence of events had taken place on Bridgeman's Skyrocket flight that morning. When I suddenly left the radio circuit, he guessed immediately what must be taking place in the Skyrocket cockpit. He yelled on the radio for chase pilots Fulton and Konrad to pull up and lock wingtips with my plane—to guide me, if possible, back to the landing area. My battery came on the line at last and began to pump power. To conserve it, I switched off all but the most important instruments. As I descended, the ice began to thaw and the breathing became easier. I reached up and scratched a small hole on both sides of the windshield. Now I could see Fulton and Konrad sitting on my wingtips. They flew formation on me until 10,000 feet, where the ice became so slushy that I could brush it off with my hand. I never wore gloves. Flying a sensitive airplane with gloves is like playing a piano with gloves.

I brought the Skyrocket in deadstick and made a normal landing on Rogers Dry Lake. The mechanics towed the powerless craft to the NACA hangar with a tractor.

"Scotty," Walt Williams said later, "if we can just get you through these first check-out flights, I think we've got it made."

5: An Unusual Heritage

"Getting it made" was very important to me, and always will be. The quest for perfection is a compulsion with me, and has been since boyhood. One reason may be my unusual heritage.

Another, without doubt, was my father. Then, as always, it would seem, there were those twinges of adversity, and stern compressions of circumstance, in early life, which Winston Churchill writes "are needed to evoke that ruthless fixity of purpose and tenacious mother-wit" which drive men to unusual endeavor. There was, too, an element of denial, an important factor in a man's motivation, I believe.

My family tree has always intrigued me. One reason may be that while I was growing up I was very conscious of it. There was a strong sense of 'family' in our house, no matter how the luck ran. There was a Crossfield mold which we children—my two sisters and I—were expected to fit. We were constantly reminded that we were entrusted with a tradition that spanned almost the entire history of the New World. And because of the unusual mixture of our blood we were acutely aware of matters of race and prejudice. I know it is popular today to scoff, as decadent, at Southern traditions, and mock the proper Bostonians who cling to family ties, and to trumpet the dope-crazed sputterings of beatnik derelicts who, given complete head, would destroy all concept of God and family. Perhaps here, in this increasingly mobile society, this is one place we have failed. I cannot be held responsible for my family, but I am proud of it.

My mother, for example, fiercely proud and uncompromising, was half Mexican. The other half was pure Irish, and a more fearsome combination one is not often likely to encounter. She was a direct descendant of a Spaniard named Holguin, a Conquistador who served under Cortés during the Conquest of Mexico. Every inch a lady in the most severe Spanish tradition, my mother demanded extreme standards of conduct and discipline in our home. These were seldom relaxed, no matter how low our material circumstances, which at their nadir were very low indeed. I inherited a great deal from my mother: jet-black hair, dark eyes, a swarthy complexion, an insatiable curiosity, a touch of the romantic, an appreciation of music, and a flair for drawing and working with my hands. I profited even more by her example.

My mother's side of the family is a little complicated. What I know of it comes not from books and historical documents, but by word of mouth from my relatives. For this reason it is not precise but may be close. To describe it best I should begin with my maternal great-grandfather, Thomas Aloysius Dwyer, who from all accounts was an amazing character. Born in Ireland, he was one of the youthful cadets who figured in the great Irish insurrection of

1848. He married a Lady Crocker who was, so the family story goes, a lady-in-waiting to Queen Victoria. Just how this politically incongruous match came about is lost in the mists of love and history, but no doubt it accounts, at least in part, for the somewhat adventurous, peripatetic aftermath. Thomas and Anne Dwyer immigrated to Boston. Soon thereafter they moved on to Corpus Christi and San Antonio, Texas, where Thomas Aloysius Dwyer, an educated man, became a judge and sired six children, including Thomas Aloysius, Junior.

Judge Dwyer, remembered as a distinguished-looking man with a carefully manicured beard and pince-nez, was evidently not totally dedicated to the law. He developed a good many side business interests, including the shipment of various goods and supplies by railroad from El Paso to small towns in Mexico. He sent his son, Thomas Junior, my maternal grandfather, then sixteen years old, to Mexico to oversee these shipments. Tom Junior was a curious blend of hard-headed businessman and romantic. He reported to his father in beautifully scripted letters (some of which I have seen), and sometimes enclosed drawings and sketches stroked with skill and talent. In Jimenez, Mexico, the youthful, talented Tom Junior branched out. He became, successively, a Wells Fargo agent, the proprietor of a general store, a streetcar magnate (the cars were pulled by mules), a lumberman, and a distributor for the ubiquitous Singer sewing machines. In Mexico, Tom Junior met, admired, and married a seventeen-year-old senorita named Paula Holguin, my maternal grandmother. Paula, both an artist and a musician, was truly gifted, stubborn, and proud. I enjoyed her piano-playing in later years, but communications between us were difficult: as a matter of personal pride she refused to speak any language except Spanish. In her ladylike way she was also quite fearless.

The marriage between Tom Dwyer and Paula Holguin produced fifteen offspring, ten of whom survived childhood. One of these was my mother, Lucia. For a while the large family lived in happiness on a great, prosperous ranch. My grandfather's businesses expanded. As new mines were developed in Parrall and Terron, Mexico, he sent men to open general stores and to establish wagon-train routes.

Then in about 1910, the Mexican bandit Madero, who preceded Pancho Villa, rose up to strike down the prosperous. Americans especially suffered in this period of anarchy, and for a long while it was touch-and-go for my grandparents. As a child I listened in awe to the tales of how my mother stood off groups of marauding Mexican banditos with a bull-whip. When the United States President declared he could no longer guarantee the safety of Americans in Mexico, Tom and Paula Dwyer sent the ten children by train to El Paso. My mother, Lucia, then 19, was one of the first to go. She was followed in time by the others, now virtually destitute, having lost everything in the retreat. Lucia, who was educated by nuns in a convent in Mexico, inherited much of her mother's talent for music and art. She dabbled briefly at writing and then took a job teaching elementary Spanish in an American school in El

Paso. A year or so later, in 1914, she went to the University of California at Berkeley to study for the summer. There she met my father.

The Crossfields came from England; I have never been able to determine just when, but it was probably seven or eight generations ago. They settled in New England. There is a court record noting the marriage of a Crossfield before the Revolution. One branch of the family moved to Kentucky. The Scott in the name comes from the same family as does General Winfield Scott, who was, I'm told, a distant relative. Scott has been a middle name on the Crossfield side of the family for generations. My paternal grandfather, Amasa Scott Crossfield, was a lawyer from New England who married Louise Brown, a direct descendant of Governor William Bradford. I am certain of the latter point, because some of the Governor's furniture was passed along in the family. It was traced to us and later asked for by a museum. We still have a highboy which I believe is authentic Governor Bradford.

About 1885 someone conceived a plan to build a canal in Minnesota connecting Big Stone and Traverse Lakes to provide a direct water route between the Hudson Bay and the headwaters of the Mississippi. Somehow my grandfather Crossfield became interested in that project and moved from Boston to Browns Valley, Minnesota. (The Brown was no kin to my grandmother.) When the canal project fell through, my grandfather entered local politics. He was an Indian Reservation Agent and later he ran for and won a seat in the state legislature. I'm told that he won his first election when he bested his political opponent at knuckle-bending before a large crowd of voters. My father, Albert Scott Crossfield, one of three children, was born in Browns Valley. From all the family stories I've heard, I surmise that my grandfather Crossfield was a rugged, pioneering type, a two-fisted drinker with a restless soul, seeking new frontiers to conquer. In any case, he didn't stay in Browns Valley long. Soon he turned up in the Philippine Islands as Chief of the Customs Department under the colonial administration of Governor William Howard Taft. My father, his brother, who later died, and a sister were raised in the Philippines. My father's sister, Ruth, married Peter A. Drakeford, a brother of Sir Arthur Drakeford, Australia's Air Minister in World War II.

The move to the Philippines brought prosperity and success to my grandfather. He built up a coconut and hemp plantation, the Kumassie Plantation Company, on the Bay of Davao on Mindanao, which still exists, I believe. In time he became a pillar of the Philippines. He was appointed a judge of the Supreme Court in the Philippines. Contemporary with him was a woman journalist, Bessie Dwyer, an editor of the Manila newspaper, a daughter of Judge Dwyer of San Antonio, Texas, and my great-aunt on my mother's side. Judge Crossfield and Bessie Dwyer were close friends in the Philippines.

My father was a conscientious young man who took his schooling seriously. He was a scientist by nature, especially interested in chemistry. He took most of his secondary education in the Philippines, then graduated from high school in Berkeley, California, where he lived with his mother, who had temporarily returned to the States to give the children a U.S. education. Later he studied chemistry at the University of California and was a graduate Fellow at the Mellon Institute in Pittsburgh.

Bessie Dwyer wrote to her niece, Lucia, then studying at the University of California, suggesting that she get in touch with the family of her good friend Judge Crossfield, then residing in Berkeley. By then my father was a graduate student taking advanced work in chemistry. When the two met, love bloomed and they were married in 1916. One chemical result of this union was me, Albert Scott Crossfield, Junior, one-quarter Mexican, with a sprinkling of pure English, Irish, Boston Brown, and the good Lord only knows what else.

My father was slow and deliberate, a man who patiently looked at all sides of an issue and was forgiving, yet in his quiet, detached way quite demanding. As I think about it, he was a very unusual person. I have a lasting and profound respect for him.

He was basically a chemist, a scientist, if you please, one whose natural bent leaned to theory but whose life led him into the practical application of science, or as we call it today, development, as opposed to pure research. When World War I broke out, he took a commission in the army and worked for the Chemical Warfare Department trying to perfect bizarre new weapons. After the war he turned to the petroleum industry. He was a pioneer in the then new field of extracting oil deposits from shale. This work ultimately led to an executive position with the Union Oil Refinery in Wilmington, at that time a small waterfront and refinery town in Southern California.

Outwardly my father was the coolest man I have ever known. He used to tell me: "A gentleman never laughs, but he may chuckle. Nor does he cry." When he punished me, he never displayed anger or emotion. He was completely detached about it, as though analyzing some chemical compound. I don't think I ever heard him raise his voice. He was not altogether without personal fear, but I never saw any signs of it and, believe me, I searched diligently.

He took great pains to disguise his courage. During the first World War, he was a leader of a small group of chemists who developed a new and effective gas mask, an urgently needed item in those days. My father was one of those who entered gas chambers to test the mask. The tests apparently were not always successful; the repeated exposures to gas in the chamber robbed him of much of his hair—my earliest recollection is that he was bald—and left a grim reminder on his body—white splotches where the gas had discolored his skin. I was quite old before I was able to worm out of him the fact that he had taken part in this hazardous experimental work.

My father routinely worked seven days a week and eventually he rose to be superintendent of the Union Oil Company in Wilmington. On Sundays, when there was no school, he sometimes took me to the plant with him. In those days, as in these, the men kept a careful watch for fires; a refinery fire is a vicious and terrible catastrophe. One Sunday while we were walking through the 'cracking plant' a fire broke out. My father ordered everyone to keep back. As I looked on, he draped a blanket over his head and asked the firemen who had answered the alarm to douse him thoroughly with water. Then, quietly and calmly he walked into that roaring inferno and closed off some valves in order to keep the fire from spreading. His burns were severe and he was confined to a hospital for days. Not a word about the fire ever was mentioned in our house.

Dad was infinitely polite and proper. He was neither aloof nor snobbish, yet I think it is a fact that he was little understood by his friends and co-workers, perhaps because of his studied emotional detachment. Perhaps it was because of his granite-like principles about right and wrong. He was unyielding in this respect. On one occasion he clung to his principles so tenaciously that it cost him his position at the refinery and changed the whole course of his life and ours as well.

The oil refinery in those days, around 1930, imported many Mexican laborers for the dirty work. They were paid, I believe, fifty cents a day, and they lived in shacks around Wilmington; the area soon became pretty much of a Mexican community. My parents had a natural sympathy and pity for these people and my father was outspoken at the refinery about this 'exploitation' of alien labor. With time these feelings grew deeper and more pointed.

When the depression struck Southern California, these imported workers were the first to lose their jobs at the plant. It was my father's duty to fire them. A number were shipped back to Mexico, but a good many remained, out of work and penniless and, because they were aliens, not entitled to the usual governmental or community relief. Feeling responsible to some degree for the distress of these people, my father set aside a good deal of his own money for their support. My mother spent the money for food, scouring the markets for day-old bread and rejected vegetables which she cooked and passed out to the Mexicans. She was running a soup kitchen, really, and at times it seemed as though we fed half the population of Wilmington.

As the depression worsened, the firing went on at a more rapid and ruthless pace. One day one of my father's bosses pointed out to him that there were still people on the roster with Spanish and Italian names. That was true, my father replied, but those people were not aliens: they were Americans, born on the soil of the United States, and many of them excellent workers. Never mind that, they must be fired before the ones with Anglo-Saxon names, was the order from the boss. This my father refused to do, and he was thus forced to resign. He left the oil industry entirely. I do not believe there are very many men who would have given up a top position at the height of the depression for the sake of a principle.

Our family was not destitute—far from it. Dad was not frugal, but he was not a spendthrift either, and during his years at the refinery he had managed to lay aside a healthy nest egg. He used most of this money to buy a small creamery. Like many chemists he was fascinated by the challenge of producing some unusual substance—a plastic, for example—from the waste-products of milk. I think his plan was to operate the milk company as a livelihood and spend his evening hours experimenting with the casein waste-products in a laboratory.

He never realized this goal. Not long after he bought the creamery, a vicious price war erupted in Southern California, and in time it wiped us out completely. The trucks were overturned and the men were beaten up. When Dad began in the business, he bought the raw milk for six cents a quart and after it was processed sold it for about eleven cents a quart delivered to the home. At the peak of the milk war the raw-milk cost remained fixed by the NRA but the price on delivery fell as low as one and a half cents a quart. Caught in the squeeze, Dad trimmed the business to the bare bones, but his capital dwindled rapidly.

The final days were grim. The whole family rushed to the rescue. My mother collected money on the milk routes, then being served by several trucks which were driven by my father and a man named Harold Babb. I often rode the trucks and ran up to the houses with the milk bottles. Later in the day I ran the bottle-washing machine, which cleaned about 7,500 bottles a day, all of which had then to be put into crates and stacked. I was not in the best of health. Often, in the midst of the grueling work, I was so tired that I hid behind the crates—where my father, who never seemed to tire, couldn't see me—and bawled. Typically, my father refused to give up on that milk business until he ran through his last dime. When the business finally collapsed, he must have been hurt deeply, but he showed no outward signs of his feelings.

There was one noteworthy facet of Dad's character, which in retrospect seems important, and perhaps contradictory. Although he certainly held a tight rein on us children, at the same time he allowed us great individual responsibility. We were given complete freedom, for example, in our choice of courses in school.

"What you make of your schooling is your own business," he said. On the question of learning, he was not didactic, but had what was probably a shrewdly calculated way of spurring us on. At the dinner table, where we had the closest contact with him, he would never say, "Well, why don't you know that?" about some subject. Instead he would say, "That's strange. I thought you knew that." This, of course, made us feel like idiots and soon after dinner we were all flying to the encyclopedia.

My father's unusually severe and unyielding spirit dominated our home, where I can remember no emotional scenes. Every family problem was discussed with judicial calm, and the solution arrived at was not an expeditious one, but a just one as my father saw it. Mother was a full and enthusiastic partner in these discussions. She was treated by my father, and by us children as well, with regal respect. This atmosphere might have seemed to some outsiders as oppressively dull. I am certain it had a profound impact on me, a pint-sized kid who might otherwise have grown up to fear his own shadow.

6: An Isolated Environment

I BELIEVE THE FACT THAT I WAS TOLD I WOULD NEVER be physically able to fly was the single greatest spur in my life. I was a healthy baby, but all this changed rather abruptly one day.

In Wilmington we lived in a big pink stucco house on the corner of Lakme and L streets. There was a huge eucalyptus tree in the parkway, so large that its roots had tunneled beneath our house and disturbed the foundations. We were fond of that tree, but my father decided after painful consideration that it would have to go. Its removal was an enormous task, requiring many men, bulldozers, and other pieces of earth-moving machinery. The job took a whole day. I was five years old. There were no boys my age living on the block, so I usually played alone, or with my older sister, Elena Ruth, then eight. My younger sister, Mary Ann, was a toddler, going on three. The day the men removed the tree was a big one for all three of us. The weather was cold and damp, but we stayed outside from dawn to dusk watching as the bulldozer gouged the earth from the yard.

This prolonged exposure left Elena and me with bad cases of pneumonia. She recovered quickly, but I was seriously ill. My lungs were severely damaged and my heart was affected. For a while my parents thought I was going to die. They sent for our priest, Father Skiperelli. I can still remember the moment he entered my room. The walls were covered with pictures of airplanes.

Father 'Skip' joshed: "But what about the Lord?" My mother led him to a picture of the Sacred Heart, almost obscured by the montage of airplanes. He administered the last rites. It was touch-and-go for days on end. My mother smothered me in mustard plasters. I was in a coma for some time. Our family physician, Dr. E. J. Rowan, knew a man at the University of California who was trying to develop a new serum for pneumonia. He injected some of this serum into my blood. Finally I began to recover, but the illness had left its mark. For years I was sickly and small—and would always be the smallest boy in my class.

A year or so later, perhaps as an aftermath of the pneumonia, I came down with rheumatic fever. I was not strong and the fever struck me harder than it does most people. I was in bed, flat on my back, for at least four months, possibly longer. Then for the four years following—until I was about ten years old—every so often for weeks at a time I was made to lie down and rest until dinner-time. My mother and father thought I might be crippled for life. They didn't tell me this. My father's strategy was to feign complete indifference lest I feel sorry for myself. Not once did anyone ever say to me that I might be a cripple. On the contrary, my parents used to joke about my having developed 'rheumatism' at so young an age. But I sensed that from a physical standpoint I was lacking.

I grew to adolescence in an unusual, isolated environment, finding things to pass the long hours at rest that few other boys do.

Although it now pains me to recall it, my mother taught me how to sew and knit, and I became quite adept at embroidering. I also became skilled at drawing. I had once withdrawn from school for a while, but my fifth-grade teacher, Mrs. Paymiller, came to my house to award me the class prize for art. My main interest, however, was aviation, and most of these long, lonely hours were devoted to it.

This interest was stimulated originally, I am certain, by a close friend and neighbor of my father's named Charles ('Carl') Lienesch, a pilot for the Union Oil Company. The company maintained one airplane, a wire and fabric Eagle Rock (or 'Eagle Brick,' as Lienesch used to call it). This was probably one of the very first 'executive' airplanes. Lienesch, who was also a chemist, visited at our home frequently. He was a colorful character, quite a story-teller. I believe his rambling air stories bored my father and mother. But in me he had an eager one-boy audience. Lienesch brought fascinating word pictures into my restricted life, and I always looked forward to his visits.

He gave me my first airplane ride. It took place in 1927, when I was about six years old. Oddly, I can remember but a few details of the flight, although it was undoubtedly the high point of my childhood. Lienesch remembers that after flying 45 minutes or so in the front cockpit of the biplane, I fell sound asleep. This, too, strikes me as odd—if not inconceivable, though my own youngsters today do this. It may be the lulling effect of the engine.

In those times, everyone involved in aviation was a walking public relations man for the trade. I don't know why Lienesch singled me out for a special pitch. It couldn't have been simply the fact that I was an eager listener. In any case, my earliest recollection is that this generous friend was determined that someday I should be an aviator. Although he knew I was not too strong physically, he urged me on and continued to do so for many years.

I really didn't need much urging. Lienesch had captured me from the outset. When I was old enough to realize that my health was shaky, and told by some doctor that I could probably never pass a flight physical, I was more determined than ever to be a pilot. I leaned heavily on my imagination in those days. When I was about nine, during the time I had to rest each day after school, my mother set aside a special wicker chair for me in our small lattice-work 'summer house' in the back yard. The chair had deep, downy pillows and broad arm-rests to hold my books and drawing board. To this chair I rigged some special devices of my own: an airplane control stick and rudder pedals. With the books lying open on the arm of the chair, I 'flew' hour after hour, carefully following the instructions. In that chair I learned the correct stick and rudder motions for every conceivable airplane maneuver. My imagination took me across oceans, into deep valleys, and above the mountains. I dreamed of flying from California to New York non-stop and setting a new record!

Meanwhile, I had become a model airplane addict. I built models of many airplanes then in the air. The models were not hastily or sloppily made. They were near-professional, I hoped. As I grew older, I sought absolute perfection. This work led, in turn, to considerable research into the theory of flight and aircraft construction. I read everything available on the subject and wrote away, for example, to NACA, for reports on various wing air-foils and aircraft structures. I kept meticulous files. Soon I was designing my own model airplanes. Later I helped some boys build Southern California's first model airplane powered by a (hand-built) gasoline engine.

Flying was then a sports rage in Southern California. I think there were at least a hundred small airports in and around Los Angeles. When I could manage it, I used to hang around these places. I was impressed by any pilot. But I was especially fascinated when I heard about pilots who flew air races, which in those days were frequent and dangerous events. A boyhood hero of mine—heroine, rather—was 'Pancho' Barnes, the aviatrix who later built the ranch near Edwards. In those days she was idolized locally, something like the way Amelia Earhart was nationally. 'Pancho' had a new airplane known as the Travelair Mystery Ship. She swaggered around in boots and flying jacket and won nearly every race she entered.

For several years Los Angeles, or more specifically Burbank Airport, was the starting point for the 1500-mile Transcontinental Bendix race to Cleveland. Carl Lienesch took me out to Burbank to watch the start. I can still remember the frenzied last-minute preparations by the ground crews, and the high-pitched whine as the ridiculously tiny, stubby-winged, man-killing planes took off into the darkness with no radio and no instruments. I saw and worshiped all the great pilots: Roscoe Turner in his Weddell-Williams Special, Jimmy Weddell in another Weddell-Williams, and Benny Howard in Ike, Mike, and Pete, and Mr. Mulligan, the plane that nearly killed him. I built models of all these planes, and followed air racing around the country, from long distances, as some people follow baseball games and players. I was aware of the most obscure racing pilots, and every new racing design that emerged from their garages and workshops.

From one side of the family or the other, I must have inherited a broad stubborn streak. I did no special exercises or took no special medicines; but somehow, by sheer will power and the help of God, I began to regain my strength. I firmly believe that if the spirit is willing, the flesh will keep pace. I think my father's example—his refusal to display physical or emotional weakness—influenced me tremendously in this regard. You can't be around a man like that very long and feel sorry for yourself. I think, too, the fact that Carl

Lienesch treated me like a normal, healthy boy who would obviously some-day be a pilot, had a strong psychological impact on me. By the time I was twelve years old I was well on the road to recovery, and as a result of my long years of confinement a dedicated airplane fanatic.

About that time I took over a newspaper route for the Long Beach Press-Telegram from a boy named Norman Laird. By coincidence, or maybe it wasn't coincidence, one delivery point on the route was the Wilmington Air-port, a small grass field in a slough, operated by a great colorful aviator named Vaughn McNulty. McNulty had an Inland Sportster, a high-wing mon-oplane, which he used to teach people to fly and to take up passengers. There were a few other planes on the field—an old C-3 Cub, an Eagle Rock, and a Travelair.

Those were tough days for small airport operators. The depression had hit Southern California and few people had dollars to shell out for airplane rides; fewer still had money for flight instruction. McNulty was ripe for the deal I proposed to him.

The newspaper delivered at the airport cost him sixty-five cents a month. I offered to supply the paper free (I always had a couple of extras) in return for one half-hour of flight instruction a month.

McNulty agreed, I think, not because it was an equitable business, but because he was moved to help a starry-eyed kid get a start in aviation. I was tremendously grateful and performed odd jobs around the airport for McNulty: sweeping out the hangars, cleaning mud from the airplanes, and so on. My association with McNulty and the Wilmington airport was a very per-sonal secret.

My parents did not know I was taking flying lessons. By my thirteenth birthday I had logged several hours in McNulty's Inland Sportster. I wasn't yet ready to solo, but McNulty had taught me some of the basic rudiments of fly-ing, how to handle an airplane in flight. For me each practice minute in the air was a fantastic, wonderful experience, and a tonic as well.

Each minute removed me that much further from the possibility of backsliding into illness, and took me closer to my dream. I continued these flights, off and on, until my father became involved in the milk-price war and I was recruited to help wash those 7,500 bottles every day.

In sum, the seed of my life's ambition had sprung from a twinge of ad-versity and it grew boldly and intensely in the face of denial. By the time I was thirteen it was clear to me that nothing could stand in the way. Moreover, what had begun as ambition had, perhaps because of the stern compression of circumstances, subtly been transformed into an urgent drive toward perfec-tion. I would be not only a pilot but the best damned pilot in the world. My father's ill-timed move into the milk-processing business had certainly proved to be one of the "stern compressions of circumstances."

He was left at the depth of the depression jobless, virtually penniless and wounded in spirit, I think, although typically he showed no outward flicker of unhappiness or distress. I know the experience moved him profoundly. He broke all ties with the past. He gave up his chosen field of chemistry, at which he had excelled for eighteen years or more, and moved all of us to a new and totally different environment. It is idle, perhaps, to probe too deeply for motivation in matters of this kind for, as we know, nothing is so clear-cut as it may appear. My own belief is that in starting life anew he responded to what I believe is a basic and fundamental urge in all of us to return to the soil whence we come and where we shall return in death. He sold our house in Wilmington and bought a heavily-mortgaged, run-down 120-acre farm in the rich but remote Boistfort Valley near Chehalis, Washington, about midway between Seattle and Portland, Oregon. He got it for $50 an acre.

I was both pleased and stunned when I first saw the farm. The setting was beautiful. Boistfort Valley was lush green and stayed that way the year round. It was a land of rich, virgin timber—towering Douglas fir trees—lovely grape arbors, and rushing, salmon-filled streams. A river ran right next to our property. About sixty acres of our farm lay along this river. There were twenty more acres under cultivation and these lay higher, on a hill overlooking the river. It was a clean, silent country, full of wild fruits and berries.

Apart from the setting there was not much about the farm I could admire. The main house was a rambling, drafty, thirteen-room monster, with detached toilet facilities: a two-seater privy, which in the deep of winter was less than comfortable. Out back there was also a tottering barn, built in 1884, and a wobbly chicken shack, the whole enclosed by a broken-down, zig-zag wooden fence. Then in the winter there was mud, more mud than I ever dreamed existed on the face of the earth. The barnyard, the grounds, the paths, the driveway—all were a bottomless sea of mud.

My father's approach to this new challenge was somewhat startling. From the outset he was determined to transform that bruised and battered piece of ground into a show place. He was an intelligent man and his method was intelligent. He studied farming. He sought advice from other farmers. He consulted often with the county government farm agent. He stretched every dime to the breaking point. Typical, I think, was his scientific handling of the chickens. He despised chickens. Yet he became the champion chicken farmer in the valley. He did it by keeping greatly detailed, endless records. He logged every egg that was laid. He carefully analyzed the results of different feed combinations on the chickens, noting if a new type increased or retarded the laying rate, how frequently the chicken house had to be cleaned, and so on. Everyone laughed, until in due time his painstaking research began to pay off handsomely.

He followed the same system with the cattle. His objective was to build up a dairy herd, the best in the valley. He couldn't afford to buy good cattle:

purebreds cost four or five hundred dollars. Instead he bought grade cattle for $50 apiece or less. Then when he found a good cow, he bred her. Again he kept unending records. By trial and error, and trading cows left and right, he built up a herd of twenty-five, which produced a much greater return than the pure-bred herds.

As I think back on it, my father had soon organized everything on that farm to perfection. The work was limitless. Every morning and night for seven days a week we milked those twenty-five cows. In the spring we did the plowing, a brutal, grueling, seemingly hopeless task. We couldn't afford tractors or even good draught horses. We used cayuses, worn out from years of labor in the nearby logging camps. It was usually my fate to draw the walking plow. Near the river on the bottom land, the soil was a thick, black loam. We plowed two acres a day, moving at a fast clip, and worked several cayuses to death. In the fall we harvested the hay, wheat, and oats—a hundred tons, cured to a 'T'—and stored them in the barn, after the appropriate and detailed data on the crop had been drawn up and filed away for study.

After a year or so the farm was still a long way from a show place. But I do remember one evening when my father closed his account books with a smile. He said: "We're now one dollar in the black, the net result of twenty years of work." In the curious way that life unfolds, as the farm grew so grew Scott Crossfield. This parallel has never occurred to me until now. I arrived there weak and puny and not fully recovered from my childhood illness. But as the months passed—months of hard labor and good healthy food—I no longer pooped out easily or noticed any shortness of breath. I gradually became as strong as an ox.

Consciously or unconsciously my father was transforming his own son, as well as a patch of earth. Perhaps somewhere in the unfathomable depths of his mind, my father knew what he was about. I will never know. I never came near reaching perfection, but from the moment I landed on that farm, with one exception, I never again became ill.

As my own strength grew, so did my determination to achieve my life's ambition. In one sense, the farm was also a denial, a greater one than my illness in Wilmington. I had been transplanted from the center of aviation to a remote outpost. Here in this isolation I developed a great thirst and craving for any news of my interest. This craving, I think, inspired resourcefulness and a sense of independence, which in turn fostered a boldness that might not otherwise have sprouted. I was not trapped in the routine of my interest, nor influenced by mediocrity, nor bound by the usual conventions. My mind was free to try anything that occurred to it.

My room was on the second floor of our big house. After the day's work, the last chores, I retired there not to dream but to work on model airplanes, or to read magazines and books on aviation, or to go through my files, which, after seven years, had grown to great proportions. I hung a blanket over the window so that my parents could not see the light reflecting on the ground below. There, alone with my thoughts, I worked until two or three in the morning.

Out of this room emerged what I thought was a new and brilliant idea for making a radio-controlled model airplane. Such models are common now, but in those days the concept was fairly avant garde. Proudly I revealed my new idea to the son of a friend on the adjacent farm, a young man who was a Doctor of Physics at the University of Washington. He said it would never work. He followed this comment with a general lecture on sizing up and working within one's capabilities. This lecture served only to convince me that nothing would stand in the way of building that model.

Everything about the model was new and different. My greatest problem was to devise a lightweight structure to carry the enormous radio 'payload.' For the fuselage I selected a new and radical method of construction known as 'geodetic,' which had been devised and published by a British aeronautical engineer. (Later I learned that the British used this construction to build the World War II Lancaster bomber.) The finished fuselage weighed about half as much as with the usual methods.

The development of the special radio gear, and the devices which would translate a radio signal into a movement of the model's control surfaces, took months. Knowing little of radio circuits or the theory of radio, I had to start from scratch and teach myself everything—with the help of some ham operator friends. The result, if I may brag, was ingenious. It was as good as, or better than, the units I have recently seen in current radio-controlled models, with transistors and 'printed circuits.'

The final product of my labors, a graceful, gull-winged model, weighed a total of seven pounds and was capable of lifting a seven-pound payload of radio gear. In any man's league this is very efficient aerodynamics. The model flew like a dream and the radio worked perfectly. Then one day during a flight the plane dipped behind a tree which interfered with the radio signal.

The ship crashed and was destroyed.

7: "TAKE HER UP AND TRY A SPIN"

I WENT TO BOISTFORT HIGH SCHOOL, A CONSOLIDATED country school about nine miles from our farm. There were fifty-six pupils in the whole school, quite a contrast to the big 3000-student schools in Southern California. The superintendent of Boistfort School, Carl Aase, was a most unusual man and to me, at least, a very generous one. Intelligent and resourceful, Aase became a good friend of my father's. He visited our farm frequently, but he didn't let this friendship stand in the way of doing his job, or of administering discipline to incorrigible boys. In this respect, he was quite like my father. Mr. Aase never displayed anger or emotion. Like the other farm boys, when I reached the age of fifteen I was a tough, scrappy youngster. We boys used to fight often, and occasionally Carl Aase would suspend me from school. He was very calm and matter-of-fact about it.

"Scott," he would say, "don't wait for the school bus today. Just walk on home right now."

At first I was not an exceptional student. My grades averaged about 'B.' They improved later when I was seriously preparing for college. But at sixteen my interests were many and my time too limited for concentrated study on anything but aviation, for which I was not given credit in school. I joined in 4-H Club work and raised several prize dairy animals. I was also intrigued by photography. I converted one of the unused rooms on the second floor of our home to a dark room. I took all the photographs and made the woodcuts for the school yearbook. I had no time for sports such as football, tennis, or swimming, and I haven't found time for them yet.

The farm and the school absorbed most of my hours. I got up early to do my chores, spent most of my day at Boistfort, in the evening returned to my chores, and then to my private room on the second floor. But there was one other spot to which I was drawn like a metal filing to a magnet: the Chehalis municipal airport. I didn't get there as frequently as I wanted to. When I went, it was in secret. I didn't want to trouble my parents with my ambitions to be a pilot. Although he never mentioned it directly, I believe my father hoped I would study law or medicine. A professional education, he thought, was a necessary part of a gentleman's preparation for life.

The Chehalis municipal airport was a cow pasture adorned with two skeletal airplane hangars, a tiny CAA weather shack, and a tattered windsock. It was home for about a dozen old wire-and-fabric airplanes, several of them derelicts and veterans of the first World War, which had then been over for eighteen years. The field was operated by a man named Donahoe, who somehow managed to stay one step ahead of the sheriff. The people who hung about that airport were, I think, typical of the depression era, young and old who almost on faith alone stuck with aviation, consciously and un-consciously knowing its future. Some, like me, were called 'airport bums.' Chehalis Airport was a Garden of Eden to me. The pilots to a man were my special heroes.

Whenever I had the money, which was seldom, although the amount re-quired was ridiculously small, I took flight instruction from anybody and everybody. I was lucky to squeeze in one hour a month; many months went by during which I received no instruction at all. It was slow going and I'm not certain that the instruction was top quality. But I was learning, inching to-ward my first solo flight. It finally came quite unexpectedly, and it turned out to be rather exciting.

"Why don't you try it by yourself?" one of the pilots said to me one day at the airport. At this time I probably had accumulated about seven or eight hours of flight instruction. A solo flight was technically illegal: I had no student permit. But at Chehalis there was a sort of devil-may-care attitude about rules and regulations. A small knot of airport hangers-on gathered around us. "Yeah, Scotty, take her up and try a spin." The crowd broke up with laughter.

I crawled into the cockpit of the Curtiss Robin. It was a high-wing mono-plane powered by a cranky OX-5, the engine that was used in World War I. Someone spun the prop and soon I was bumping over the cow pasture to-ward the end of the strip. Without fear or hesitation—indeed, very happily—I gunned the engine and horsed the Robin gracefully into the air. The deep green Chehalis Valley spread out below me. The engine, laboring heavily, took me to 4,000 feet, which was about the ceiling of that airplane.

I flew about over the valley for ten or fifteen minutes, turning, twisting, and tracing lazy eights in the sky. This, I thought, was it, the absolute ulti-mate! Here man had a new view of his life and the world. He was detached, removed from the detail of it—the mud, the privy, the school fights, the chicken house, the slights and denials. Here, high in the sky, man's vision was unobscured. He could see far and wide, the whole picture of God's world, a model of grace and perfection. At the same time there was challenge: a man, a brain, some muscle, and a machine pitted against the air, a basic and im-portant element of that earthly perfection.

I was an ace now, zipping low over the battlefield returning to my aero-drome in France. Then I was Lindbergh, passing over wild Nova Scotia, eight hours out of New York, ready to bank over the cold gray Atlantic. Then I was Benny Howard, poised on the end of the runway at Burbank Airport in tiny Mr. Mulligan, ready for an incredible 1500-mile non-stop flight to Cleveland. Then I was Scott Crossfield, setting off in a new plane of his own design to break the Los Angeles-to-New York record.

The long years of denial made these moments far more endearing and meaningful than I can possibly describe. I wondered: did more denial lie ahead? Maybe I had better squeeze every drop out of this flight. Maybe I had better see how far I could go: find out where nerve left off and fear began. Find out, in one fell swoop, if I had it.

"Try a spin," the crowd had said. Well, while I'm about it, why not? The crazy thought absorbed my attention. I climbed higher. I deliberately pulled the nose up steep and stalled out. The Robin's right wing dipped. Earth and sky alternated in the windshield. I was spinning. Suddenly I was aware of a strange and startling noise, a kind of banging, foreign to the ordinary noise of the plane. What was it? Quickly I pushed the stick forward and the rudder pedal hard left and brought the Robin to normal, level flight. The noise disappeared. Was I imagining something? What happened?

I climbed back to altitude and dropped the Robin into a second spin. Once again the fearful racket began. Again I brought the Robin to normal flight. No, I definitely was not imagining the noise. It was not my nerves. It happened when I put the ship into a spin. Curiosity overwhelmed me. What was it?

For the third time I climbed and spun the Robin. This time when the clattering began, I strained and looked behind me, searching for the answer. Then I found it: the rear door of the plane was loose. In ordinary flight the slipstream kept it firmly in place. But in the spin gyrations it was banging open and shut.

I laughed aloud at my concern.

Time was running out. I had to land. I banked in a large circle and lined up on the cow pasture. The Robin ghosted down. Her wheels struck the soft grass and she clung. I taxied toward the knot of people near one of the hangars, shut off the engine and climbed out, showing not a trace of excitement or elation. I was as dead-pan as an undertaker.

"How'd it go?" someone asked.

"Good," I said. I knew they had watched the three spins. There was no need to brag about it.

"No trouble?" Then with a start I realized I was the subject of a practical joke. The crowd knew what happened to the Robin's door in a spin. I was being hazed, like a college freshman. But I was determined to give them no satisfaction.

"None at all," I replied. I read disappointment on all their faces.

I returned to the farm and my chores. At the dinner table that night I felt very proud. But I dared not say why.

Carl Lienesch visited us from time to time on the farm. He no longer worked for the Union Oil Company. He had moved to Seattle, where he took a job as a Civil Aeronautics Board inspector. One day he proposed that I go up to Seattle with him to watch the first flight tests of Boeing's new Clipper.

Compared to anything I had seen, the flying boat looked huge, squatting on Lake Washington, on the eastern edge of Seattle. It had four powerful engines mounted high on the metal wing, and a towering single tail. The test pilot was Eddie Allen.

Eddie Allen would have been quite surprised, I'm certain, to know how much the young man standing on the Lake Washington dock knew about him. By then my files on test pilots matched or surpassed my files on racing pilots and other famous characters in aviation. Jimmy Doolittle was far and away the most famous U.S. test pilot. On the East coast the top dog was James Taylor, who flew mostly for Grumman. On the West coast the top dog was Eddie Allen, who was also Boeing's Chief Engineer. As I have said, he began his career with the old NACA shortly after World War I. At Boeing his word was considered law. He participated in the design of the airplane he would fly. If he didn't think a piece of equipment ought to be on an airplane, it wasn't put on the airplane. There was no great gap between Allen and the airplane designers. He was an airplane designer.

I watched as Allen taxied the mammoth plane through the water. The engines roared to life and the plane plowed through the water gaining speed. Allen lifted it a few feet into the air and splashed it back down again. A short while later he returned to the dock. The Clipper lacked fin area. Allen directed that two additional fins be added to the airplane.

As we were driving back to Chehalis, Lienesch, visibly impressed by the flight, was garrulous. His expensive Auburn was making nearly a hundred miles an hour.

"Now, Scotty," he said, "if you're going to get into the aviation business, Allen's job is the one you want to shoot for. That's the top of the ladder. You don't want to be a barnstormer, or a racing pilot, or a military pilot. Get a degree. Be an engineer. Help build the airplanes. Then fly them and find out what you did wrong. Then fix it. That's a real profession. It has dignity as well as excitement and challenge. You can combine all your energies and focus them toward one single objective: to improve the airplane. Who knows, maybe you might contribute something in this never-ending, restless urge of man to do better."

I was profoundly impressed.

My father's limitless energy and meticulous research—his drive for perfection—had a telling effect on the farm as the months rolled by. It was still far from a show place, but it was no longer bruised and battered. The herds were growing and producing. The chickens were profitable and were pointed to as examples by the County Agents. The barn had a new addition. We had stemmed the sea of mud somewhat with gravel walkways. The main house was equipped with an indoor toilet.

The farm produced enough money to support us and to send my older sister, Elena Ruth, to the University of California in Berkeley.

Although it appealed to me not at all, I was caught up in the rural way of life and naturally influenced by the people. As the son of an increasingly successful farmer, and naturally competitive, I took some pride in contending with the sons of other farmers. I became a leader in our 4-H Club. My pure-bred Guernsey bull, which I had nursed to a beautiful showpiece, won many prizes at county livestock fairs and brought me an invitation (which I accepted) to represent the State of Washington in the International Livestock Show in Chicago. I was also assured of a scholarship to Washington State College provided I majored in agriculture.

None of this gave me any real satisfaction. My basic interest lay elsewhere and was deeply rooted. I liked to pal around with the farmers' sons, but they were not my closest friends. Indeed, my really close friends seem a strange lot to me now. I probably fitted in perfectly. One of my friends was a ham radio operator, Art Beal, who was about forty years old. I first met him when he came to the farm to investigate my weird radio-transmitter signals which were disturbing the airways. He taught me a great deal about radio and helped me build the radio-control model. Through him I met Elden Reed, about twenty-five years old, and Bill Young, about twenty-eight, and blind from birth. All three were avid hams; they never seemed to sleep. All of us, together with a tomboy about four years older than I, Louise Wilrich, became fast friends. Art, Elden, and Louise all learned to fly at Chehalis.

Bill Young was an extraordinary person. He lived on a small pension, alone except for his seeing-eye dog, and picked up extra money tuning pianos. In Nature's strange way, having denied Bill sight, she developed his ears to perfection. Bill was often the only operator who could pick up signals from North Africa. During the war the Air Force used his cheap home-made gear and sensitive ears to communicate with North Africa when military radio could not get through. I remember the time when a thief broke into Bill's house, robbed him, and killed his seeing-eye dog. I think that if the rest of us had caught the thief we would have killed him.

When we went to the Chehalis airport to fly, or just to shoot the breeze with Donahoe and the other pilots, Bill always came along. However, the airplane was something of a mystery to him.

He walked about, feeling the wings, the fuselage, and the propellers. But it was too big and complex and he couldn't 'see,' as he said, the whole concept of the plane. I think this distressed him considerably because in that crowd we talked of little else besides radio and airplanes. Bill's inability in this regard touched me, because to me Bill was a kindred spirit, a piece of nature's bruised fruit. I helped him to understand the airplane by bringing along my models. With these miniature versions he could 'see' the airplane as a whole.

It was about this time that I began building my own life-size airplane. The idea came to me one day when I read in one of the many aviation publications I subscribed to that a French company, LeBlonde, had produced a very lightweight, efficient gasoline engine of 15 horsepower. One of these engines successfully powered a small plane. There on the farm, over six thousand miles from France and the nearest LeBlonde engine, the seed took root and sprouted. An engine that small ought to be pretty inexpensive, I thought. If I built the airplane, I would find a way to buy the engine.

As my father lacked enthusiasm for my flying, so he viewed with less enthusiasm my plan to build an airplane. I suppose any rational father would try to talk his son out of a scheme like that. But in spite of my father's advice to the contrary, I was determined to carry the idea through. I worked late at night, drawing up the plans and designing my vehicle, the sum product of a 17-year-old's aeronautical know-how and skill with a pencil.

I had long talks with my school principal, Carl Aase, about the material for the airplane. One problem was that the spruce I intended to use in the wing, tail, and fuselage was very expensive. Aase suggested that I substitute Port Orford cedar, which in the old days the Indians used to build canoes. It was strong and flexible, a good inexpensive local substitute. I saved my money and sent away for the cedar. Since I had little money, I spaced the orders far apart.

I enjoyed building anything. This full-scale airplane that could take me into the boundless sky turned into an intense work of love. I doubt that ever in history an airplane was built with such painstaking care for detail. Each piece of cedar—one-inch square strips—was handled like a piece of gold. After steaming it into shape, I sanded it carefully and then laid it in place. Then I tacked it down with glue-coated nails (which I ordered as required, with no allowance for surplus) and mortised each individual joint. As with my models, I strove for perfection. It was slow going. It took months and months to complete the fuselage. Then I saved for more cedar, built some jigs and laid out the wing spars.

Though I worked on the airplane only after my chores were finished, I always felt guilty about the time it took. In a way it was like waving a red flag in my father's face. He was becoming very attached to his piece of the earth and its mounting production. I believe he hoped I would share his enthusiasm and in time take over. Perhaps because it was a symbol of my conflicting ambition, annoying to my father, I never finished the airplane. It became a kind of unfinished Hangar Queen—in this case Barn Queen. I would meet other Hangar Queens later.

Carl Lienesch convinced me that my approach to my chosen profession should begin with a solid college foundation in engineering. Upon graduation from high school in June, 1939, my plan was to go straight to basic freshman engineering at the University of Washington. But this well-laid plan went astray. I was delayed a whole year by a variety of factors. In January of 1939, several months before I was to graduate, my younger sister Mary Anne, fourteen years old, was stricken by polio, and after a brief but severe illness she died in an iron lung. She was a pretty girl, already determinedly planning a career on the stage. Her sudden death was a stunning blow to my parents and me. It brought us closer together than ever before. To leave for college then, to leave my mother and father alone on the farm, seemed to me like deserting them. (My older sister was still enrolled at the University of California.)

The farm was simply too big for my father to operate alone. For several years he employed a boy named Harold Jones, who lived nearby, to help with the heavy work. Over the years Harold became another son in the Crossfield home. But in 1939 Harold went away to college to study agriculture, and my father could not afford to hire a full-time employee to replace him. A year later it would be a different story. But now my father obviously needed my help.

After turning these facts over in my mind, I decided to stay home on the farm for one year. At the time it seemed a dreadful decision, an agonizing delay, a frustrating denial. Yet I probably gained by it. In 1940, through the combined efforts of my father and myself, the farm was a going concern. We were able to afford automatic milking equipment and—believe it or not—a tractor. I traded my old Oakland jalopy (bought in high school for $26) for a 1935 Chevrolet and tuned the engine to near-perfection. I filled in some lacking school credits by taking correspondence courses in math, physics, and chemistry from the University of Nebraska. I logged an increasing number of flying hours at Chehalis airport with my constant companions, Art Beal, Elden Reed, Louise Wilrich, and Bill Young.

8: CHANGE AND CHALLENGE

IN RETROSPECT, THE BRIEF TWENTY MONTHS OF MY LIFE from September, 1940, when I left the farm, to May, 1942, seem a disjointed period, a tumultuous time of change and challenge. Perhaps because of this it was in some ways the most fruitful. I was about eighteen when it began; by the time I was twenty I had entered the University, graduated from a civilian aviation school, officially soloed, and obtained my private pilot's license, withdrawn from the University, worked for Boeing Aircraft Company, quit to join the Air Force briefly, worked for Boeing again, quit again to join the Navy. My course was solidly set straight toward the aviation world. During that important transition in my life, however, new and sharp influences disturbed my compass, causing it to 'hunt.' One towering influence was the outbreak of World War II, which in one way or another disturbed the lives of all my contemporaries as well as my elders.

When I left the farm in September of 1940, I marched upon the University of Washington with determined strides, as though I had only a few weeks in which to absorb all it could provide. Thumbing through the catalogue, I signed up for twenty hours of college courses per quarter; this was about twenty-five per cent above the average load. When my counselor discovered that I had to work to pay my way, he advised me to cut my schedule. He might just as well have been talking to a sphinx.

I explained that I was accustomed to working long hours and sleeping only a little. He protested again and again, but eventually I won the argument. He gave up to let me find out the hard way.

I was not used to many luxuries, but I must say I had a tough time of it during the first year in Seattle. I lived in depressing boarding houses which served up a monotonous diet at meal-times, and I worked at odd jobs that I found through the University employment bureau. The first of these was an agonizing experience for a lad fresh from the farm. I was a glorified butler in a snooty sorority house. I tended the furnace, put on a white jacket to serve tables at dinner-time, and washed the dishes—all for twenty-five cents an hour. Later I found a job mowing lawns; then I worked in a gas station; then I became a chauffeur.

Finally I turned my skill with a pencil to profit as a part-time draftsman, tracing radio circuits. The University was a fantastic well of knowledge and intelligent people, and my appetite to devour this knowledge was insatiable. I had neither time nor inclination to make many new friends or to join in the heavy college social life. (For a short time I shared an apartment with two Dekes, one a member of the University crew, but this didn't work out at all.) I was a lone wolf on a special mission, moving steadily from class to class and part-time job to part-time job. It took hard study to overcome some of the gaps from Boistfort Consolidated School, which was seldom called on to provide college preparatory courses. At the end of three quarters my grades were averaging B. But in one year I advanced one and a quarter years in college.

I went back to the farm for the summer of 1941. It was reaching perfection and the yield was enough so that my father could afford full-time workers. I helped harvest the hay and grain and did other chores, and still found time to smooth out and advance my flying.

As part of the general defense preparedness the government was in the process of converting the old CAA pilot-training program to something new called Civilian Pilot Training (CPT), designed to encourage a great number of young people into aviation. The new program, affiliated with colleges and universities, amounted to a government subsidy for aviation ground school and flight training. Through normal channels it then cost about $200 to get a private license. Under CPT it was free. For me this bargain-basement offer couldn't have come at a better moment. That summer I promptly enrolled in CPT at Centralia Junior College near Chehalis. Art Beal, Elden Reed, and Louise Wilrich joined me. Unfortunately Bill Young could not join us; but in the evenings he got much of what we had learned second hand.

The flight instructor of our small, almost informal CPT class was a man of about fifty named Elvin V. Puckett, a one-time Montana cowboy with a weather-beaten face and large, strong hands. Years before, having tired of 'riding fences' on a horse, Puckett bought a plane and taught himself to fly, thus patrolling the huge ranch boundaries the easy way. He went on to barnstorming, finally settling down in Washington State. Puckett 'sat' an airplane as I'm sure he sat a horse, easy, relaxed, natural.

Maybe he wasn't the best instructor in the world, but he taught me one lesson that stuck: the pilot of a plane is captain of his ship and fully responsible for its operation at all times. "No one else should ever be allowed to interfere with the pilot's controls or to overrule the pilot's judgment," he told us.

As luck would have it, it fell to me to stick by that rule to my possible disadvantage on one of the biggest days in my early flying life. Having completed flying with Puckett's class, now came time for the big test. A Civilian Aeronautics Administration inspector, G. S. Buchanan, climbed into my airplane to pass me or fail me for my private license. When we reached altitude, Buchanan leaned over and pulled the engine throttle to idle.

"You've just lost your engine," he said.

Puckett's rule ran through my mind. Yet, I thought, here certainly is the exception. I debated. But no, a rule is a rule. There should be no exceptions to rules in the air.

I stared at Buchanan and said: "Keep your hands off the controls of this airplane."

He stared back.

"When I'm flying this airplane, you are a passenger," I said.

"The passengers don't handle the controls. If you want to simulate a lost engine, you tell me and I will pull the throttle back to idle." I pushed the throttle forward to regain air speed, thinking well, that's that and I fail. As it turned out, Buchanan found the episode amusing and yielded.

"All right," he said. "You win. You lost an engine."

I pulled the throttle back and followed through with emergency procedures for a lost engine. When we got on the ground, Buchanan gave me an 'upcheck,' meaning I passed. Officially then I 'soloed' in the summer of 1941 and got my license. But at that point I probably had more than fifty hours in the air. Quickly I moved up the grade, accumulating more time and passing official government tests for larger and more powerful airplanes. I bought a one-third interest in a Taylorcraft, but it cracked up on take-off at Tacoma and killed my two partners. It was a funeral pyre. The coins in their pockets were melted.

I returned to the University in the fall of 1941 with my mind made up to stay off the sorority-house butler circuit. My search for a better-paying and more interesting job soon led to Boeing's Seattle plant, which had just secured enormous contracts to build bombers for the U.S. Air Force and the British. Boeing was desperate for new people. The word was that they were hiring anything that walked. I applied for a job, planning to schedule my college courses around my work. But when I hired on for the seemingly fabulous wage of sixty-two cents an hour as an assembly page clerk—making certain the stockroom numbers were kept up to date—that plan went out the window.

When I got my first look inside the Boeing plant I was fascinated. Everything about it thrilled me: the rattle of rivet guns, the heavy thumping of the presses, the shrill grinding of the saws, the whirling of the lathes. But greatest of all was watching an airplane grow in shape and perfection all in one room: from the confused beginnings of the production line to the end product which rolled out the door. In this environment thoughts of the ivy-smothered buildings at the University were lost. This was action. This was it!

The pace in the plant is best described as frantic. The war was coming fast and the Air Force wanted airplanes yesterday. My job, as it turned out, couldn't have been better suited to my purposes. I was not tied to any specific point; the whole factory was my domain. As an assembly page clerk, I was called or sent to every part of the plant and production line. Where there is strong interest there is strong retention. Quite soon all the apparent confusion made eminent sense to me, and I became intimately familiar with the problems and techniques of building real airplanes. In this job I was an observer with a free ticket to a great show.

Some time around my twentieth birthday I was promoted to the position of production expediter, a glorified title for a bottle-neck-breaker. In my new job I was to chase down certain parts that were not available in time and hand-carry or expedite them through their many processes so that they arrived at the assembly line in the right quantity at the right time. This work led to greater responsibility. Having noted my talent with a pencil, my boss assigned me the task of drawing up special change-orders and engineering change-orders for various small airplane parts. Most of this was 'emergency' work, trying to salvage a part from damaged material, or devising a substitute for a part for which no material was available. This job, too, took me to all corners of the plant. I think that in a few months I learned as much as many men who work for years in an aircraft plant assigned to a specific detail. I worked long hours seven days a week and occasionally slept on the drafting table through the remaining hours of the night.

When the Japanese struck Pearl Harbor, my duty was clear. I would have to lay aside my personal ambition and go win the war—in an airplane, of course. The week following Pearl Harbor I visited an Air Force cadet recruiting center and filled in all the papers. A few days later, I reported for a physical examination. I flunked it. My pulse rate, possibly an aftereffect of my childhood illness, was too high. It might also have been the result of the long hard hours at Boeing. The Air Force doctor told me to rest up a few days and come back for a second try.

The years of discipline from working on the farm and training under my father paid off. The disappointment was short-lived. I would do something about this. I would not be denied my life's determination.

I looked up a private physician in Seattle. Everyone, I suppose, was feeling patriotic in those days and they all wanted to help any boy get into the service. The doctor gave me a handful of pills—probably sedatives—and told me to take one before retiring, one on arising, and one just before the physical. The pills did the trick. I passed the physical.

For a long time I was plagued with this high pulse rate on physicals. In due time I learned to control my pulse—to hold it down—almost by yoga. Once I tried the traditional trick of using the depression of a hangover to pass a physical. It worked, but it wasn't worth it. Certainly this annoyingly high pulse rate never in any way hampered or restricted my endurance and flying ability, which may or may not prove something about the accepted routine of flight physicals.

My boss at Boeing was greatly put out when he learned I had been 'called up.' First he offered to get me a draft deferment, and then he insisted on it, declaring I was essential to the war effort. I couldn't make him understand that I wanted to go.

Finally, to preclude drastic action on his part, I simply told him I was in the Reserves and there was nothing he could do about it. My friends at Boeing gave me a small farewell party, and off I went to the wars. I was back at Boeing a week later working at the same job. The Air Force shipped me from

McChord Air Force Base near Tacoma to Williams Field, a processing center in Arizona. Williams was a madhouse. Evidently every recruiting office in the nation was swamped by boys eager to join the Air Force. The base was saturated with starry-eyed kids. There were no living quarters nor places to feed all these people. The officers in charge shipped me back to McChord. There I was told to go home and wait until there was an opening in a cadet class. While waiting, I returned to my old job.

I waited and waited, wondering if the war would be over before I could get into the service. In the second week of February, with still no word from the Air Force, I went down to a Navy recruiting station. The requirement then for Naval Aviation cadets was at least two years of college. The Naval officers examined my record at Boeing, my University credits, my private flying background (some three hundred hours now), and waived the two-year college requirement. Frankly, I think they were overjoyed to snatch an Air Force cadet. I took three more pills, passed the Navy physical, and was sworn in on February 21, 1942, in Seattle. I then resigned from the Air Force.

The Navy was giving primary training to some of its aviation cadets at Sand Point Naval Air Station in Seattle, a fact that pleased me no end, having briefly glimpsed the parched-earth and desolation at Williams Field in Arizona. I was scheduled to join a Cadet Class at Sand Point on the day I was sworn in, but I was delayed by a ridiculous but, to the Navy, vital matter. I am a 'junior,' and that fact was duly published on my birth certificate. I never used the junior in my signature. Thus I filled out my Navy papers 'A. Scott Crossfield.' When the discrepancy was spotted, the officers, following meticulous Navy regulations, insisted that my papers be returned and corrected. Because of this I missed my class. My reporting date was postponed until the next class convened on May 7th, two and a half months later. While waiting, I kept on at my job at Boeing. As before, I worked seven days a week, never hesitating to accept greater responsibility. When I think about it now, I laugh at some of the quick and (to me) awesome decisions I made there. Actually, I suppose, the mind functions pretty clearly between the ages of nineteen and twenty-five. It is not yet encumbered by experience and mistakes, or corralled by conservatism, which is the product of fear of making a mistake. It is bold and aggressive, and difficult to deny.

I believe those nine furious months at Boeing were among the most valuable in my life.

9: Manhood and Maturity

I served in the Navy four years, until I was twenty-four. I never achieved my goal of engaging the enemy plane-to-plane over the Pacific. After winning my wings I was waylaid as a flight instructor for eighteen months. I very nearly made it. When the war ended, I was in training in Hawaii with a carrier air group for the invasion of Japan.

My Navy tour laid the groundwork for the contribution I made to aviation and the nation years later in a different land of war. In the Navy I became a professional, disciplined aviator. Ironically, I almost flunked at the outset. It happened during my two months of 'elimination' service in Seattle in May and June of 1942. Like many men who already knew how to fly when they entered the military services, I found my past experience in the air not a help but a hindrance. A civilian pilot is an individualist. In the military a pilot is part of a closely meshed precision team. The adjustment is difficult to make. Civilian pilots learn many bad habits. One day my instructor said:

"Crossfield, I don't think you're going to make it."

I did make it. In fact I never got a 'down-check' although there was one close call.

It was a glove that almost did me in. One of our final checks at Seattle was an emergency landing in a small tree-bordered field. My airplane was an old N3N or 'Yellow Peril' biplane, built in about 1933. While flying near this field one day my instructor gave me the signal to simulate an engine failure. I throttled back all the way and aimed for the field, calculating my glide-path, intending to make a perfect approach and landing. I miscalculated. We were quite low when I realized I had undershot the field and would have to open the throttle. My instructor reached this conclusion about the same instant. He moved his gloved left hand to the throttle. As I pushed forward a split second before him, his glove caught and jammed in the throttle bracket. He tried to pull the throttle back momentarily to disengage the glove. Unaware of this mishap, all the while I was pushing the throttle hard forward, wondering what was holding it.

The ground was rushing up fast. I had to land. There was a hole between the trees that looked large enough to squeeze through. We grazed over a barbed-wire fence and penetrated the hole. It was too small. The right wing brushed the top of a tree, making a fearful racket on the taut dope-covered fabric of the wing. The plane bounced on the grass strip and rolled out. My instructor crawled out of the front cockpit, lit a cigarette, and paced about the plane, inspecting the broken ribs in the wing and the torn fabric. I sat in the cockpit awaiting the inevitable. Soon, I knew, I would be headed for a ship as a seaman second class.

I wondered why my instructor was delaying. Then it dawned on me. He was worried that we had damaged the plane so badly that it would fall apart in the air. "As long as we're here," he said, "I'll just stay on the ground and watch while you make a few precision landings between the markers over there." This was the next phase of my test, scheduled to be carried out at another field. It was true that it would save time to do these maneuvers at this field. But I had a hunch the real reason was that the instructor wanted me to take that plane up and test-fly it—alone.

Very well, I thought, I'll do it. I got us into this fix. I gunned the engine and took off. The plane held together and I made the precision landings without further incident. The instructor climbed in and we flew back to main base. He gave me an up-check, but I believe I earned it by default—because he was ashamed to report the glove snafu and because I had tested the airplane for him. Thereafter, in the way some men respond to error, I was determined never to repeat that fiasco. In time and with exacting practice, landings became the strongest point of my flying.

We moved from Seattle to the Naval Air Training Center in Corpus Christi, Texas—the big league. What a sight! It was the Boeing plant all over again. The Navy was just gearing for the instruction of aviators on a mass scale. Thousands of people were pouring into Corpus Christi each week. Everywhere new outlying flying fields were being scratched out of the dry, ugly Texas soil. Hangars, maintenance shops, barracks and officers' clubs, it seemed, were sprouting all across the great expanse of Texas. It was semi-organized confusion on a grand scale. For the next six months, along with the fifteen other members of my cadet class from Seattle, I lived, studied, and flew hard while this transformation was taking place. We paid it scant heed. Our minds were set on learning our profession and going on to war, to the Pacific, where Naval aviators were desperately needed.

The skies over Texas were black with airplanes flown by young inexperienced pilots, feeling their oats, frozen in the grip of that infantile phase all pilots must go through: flat-hatting, or buzzing the ground. I don't know how or why all pilots get this disease. Maybe it's simple showing-off, or some kind of deep-seated craving for the sensation of speed, or a reaction to the highly disciplined military formation flying. It is very dangerous. But a lot of fun.

We had several special flat-hatting tricks calculated to stretch any pilot's nerves to the breaking point. First there was windmilling. The surface of Texas is a forest of windmill-driven water pumps. We used to dive at these lazily turning windmills, scream across the ground, lift the wing as we passed over the tower, and kick the rudder. When the plane's slipstream hit the blades of the windmill, they would turn at tremendous speed, gushing water in a torrent, and probably grinding up the pump gears.

Another trick was the rare sport of playing leapfrog with automobiles. We would spot a lone car driving on a long, straight Texas road. Then we would ghost down and land behind him. We would clip along, waving at the awestruck kids in the back seat, their noses pressed against the rear window. We'd gun the engine and hop over the moving car, taxiing on down the road at high speed. I saw one pilot do this to a moving van. When the plane's slipstream hit the broad side of the van it knocked the truck into a ditch.

Then there was the railroading. What better sport than to fly down a railroad track at night, directly toward an oncoming train, and at the last second turn on the plane's landing lights and pull up steeply, all the while enjoying the vision of the engineer grinding his brakes into steel filings, wondering what he was about to smash into.

Bridges, of course, held the greatest fascination to the youthful, inexperienced pilot. There was a bridge up near Smithville on the Colorado River that loomed as my greatest flat-hatting challenge. It was tricky because there was a little turn involved just before passing under the bridge. Flying below the river banks, the drafts and winds were confusing and I had to take care that the plane didn't drift into one of the bridge foundations. I made several tries before I finally plunged under. As it turned out, there was plenty of room— fully twenty feet clearance between the bottom of the bridge and the water. My dream was to loop around that bridge, but for some reason I never did. No guts, I guess, or maybe I had a little sense, at that. These were rare diversionary moments in a rigid schedule of work and study. Mostly we flew in formation under strict observation. We advanced steadily in our profession, on the ground and in the air, learning about engines and propellers, navigation, night flying, bombing, gunnery, and the niceties of being a Naval officer. I learned one special discipline. On the night before a special check-flight, I would mentally fly the complete trip from take-off to landing, going through every motion of the controls and relating the movement of the plane to the geography. At Edwards many years later I was still able to commit a complicated experimental airplane flight to memory the night before flight. This left my mind free to concentrate not so much on flying but on gathering the aeronautical data we sought.

In December, 1942, one year after Pearl Harbor, we graduated as ensigns and full-fledged pilots. I had just turned twenty-one. Of the twenty-five men who were commissioned that day twenty-three got orders to the fleet. Two drew orders to remain at Corpus Christi as flight instructors. I was one of the two. At the time it seemed the blackest day of my life. I partially offset my deep disappointment by thinking that I had been selected for the job because I was an outstanding pilot. But I am sure they just picked my name out of a hat. I came to this conclusion when I saw what poor pilots some of the instructors were.

For six weeks I attended a school to learn how to be an instructor in advanced bombing and gunnery, then I was assigned to Kingsville Naval Air Station—a desolate outlying field. There I soon learned that instructors are not the infallible monarchs I had considered them when I was a cadet. Instructors are men like all other men, full of imperfections, contradictions, and uncertainties. Most of us were very young—twenty-one or twenty-two. We lived in dirty BOQs, engaged in seemingly endless cycles of new students, parties, poker games, graduation, new students, parties, poker games, graduation, new students, and so on. The pace we kept would defy all aero-medical studies on pilot fatigue—especially my own. I slept hardly at all. I flew probably four and sometimes six flights a day, with occasional time off during brief periods of bad weather. I never missed an assigned flight.

The second stage of infantilism in an airplane comes when the pilot learns aerial acrobatics and can be sure of a captive audience. As instructors we had such an audience in our students. One sure way to get a rise was to make a series of barrel rolls around a tight formation of student airplanes. This was one of my specialties until one of the new instructors, a former student of mine, tried to imitate it. Evidently he had not first practiced the maneuver behind the student formation. He miscalculated and smashed into a student plane, killing himself, the student, and another student in the rear seat. After that, I was far more conservative in the air when students were around.

I don't mean to overdramatize this incident. Death is the handmaiden of the pilot. Sometimes it comes by accident, sometimes by an act of God. Over the years I have tried to become calloused about death. This attitude began at Corpus. Twelve out of the sixteen members of my original class at Seattle were eventually killed in airplanes. Hundreds of students, many of whom I knew well, passed through Corpus to a quick death in the Pacific. Eleven men in my training squadron were killed at Corpus.

Indeed, come to think of it, three-quarters of all the pilots I ever knew are now dead.

There was a camaraderie among the instructors, and a sharp sense of competition. Teaching bombing and gunnery week in and week out eventually turned us into pros. One reason was that we shot and bombed far more than anyone else, including pilots in combat. When a new class reported in, we instructors began with a 'demonstration' of bombing and gunnery, each with a student in the back seat of the plane. For us this was a moment of high drama. Instructor was pitted against instructor. We laid huge money bets for high score. In our eagerness to win we very nearly drove our planes into the ground or into the target sleeves. It must have been quite an indoctrination for the students. Some of them resigned after the demonstration flight.

We felt pretty good about our gunnery records until 'Bogie' Hoffmann, a senior Navy pilot, came up from DeLand, Florida. A mustang from the famed Fighting 2 off the Lexington, Hoffmann, with Captain John ('Jimmy') Thach, had developed a new gunnery technique. It was astounding in its simplicity and it greatly improved our scores. Alongside Hoffmann we instructors, supposedly the pros, felt like amateurs. I made every effort to hitch a ride in the back seat of Hoffmann's plane when he made a demonstration. I strove to imitate him. The results were gratifying. From that point on, I met few men in the Navy who could seriously challenge me in aerial gunnery, but I could never touch Hoffmann's shooting.

Flying over Corpus shepherding my flocks amid the hundreds of planes milling about, both in daylight and at night, and with a near-crisis every ten minutes, I learned the value of stern discipline in the air. Too often in times of trouble I witnessed tragedies which could have been averted had the participants remained at least outwardly cool. Too many times I heard people shouting conflicting advice—and orders—into radio circuits. I saw then the advantage of my father's detached, emotionless attitude. I deliberately emulated it, striving never to raise my voice but to take positive command in times of emergency and do what I thought was right. Some people—those who knew only this calculated glacial exterior—thought I was a cold fish. No matter. The technique paid off.

One day, for example, I was leading a group of my students on a 'tail chase'—a sort of follow-the-leader of aerial acrobatics, including loops, rolls, Cuban Eights, chandelles—the works. Somehow one of the pilots fell out of place and the prop of his plane chewed into the tail of the plane in front of him. The first word I had of impending catastrophe was a blast on the radio:

"Jones. Land immediately. Your tail is chopped off."

The first thought of inexperienced aviators who get into trouble is to get back to earth quickly. They get down low only to find out the plane is no good and it is too late to bail out. The proper course is to keep all possible altitude until someone can find out how badly the airplane is damaged. I broke in on the radio circuit, my voice deliberately held low: "Jones. Remain at your present altitude until we check your airplane."

Jones started to argue back.

"Shut up," I said calmly. I moved in and took a look at his plane. Quite a bit of the tail was missing. "Head for base," I ordered. I flew alongside, coaching him through gentle maneuvers to feel out the plane. One of these showed that if he slowed to ordinary landing speed, the plane would not fly. If he had followed the first advice on the radio, he would have been killed. "Okay," I said. "You land that plane about ten or fifteen knots above normal speed."

Just then someone else broke in and radioed the base tower:

"We've got a crash coming in! Emergency! Emergency!"

This yelling only served to rattle the pilot of the stricken plane. Holding back my rage, I spoke on the radio: "Defer the emergency. We don't need any special equipment. Jones, remember to land fast."

The pilot landed the plane, saving his own life and a piece of expensive government equipment. Experiences like these drove home the lesson never to permit foolish, though well-meant, interference to supplant a pilot's responsibility in the air. The lesson is documented by a long roll of dead pilots. As the months rolled on the flying was hard, endless, and gratifying. Life in the BOQ at night was soft, endless, and boring.

Night after night we gathered in one room or another and drank until the bottle was empty, hangar-flying and telling endless, untrue sea stories. I tried correspondence courses to pass the time, but the insidious magnetism of that fun-loving bunch of troops shot down that effort. It did not take keen observation to see this was not doing some of us any good. In a few it was reflected by poor flying which made me wonder about my own flying. Here I would not compromise in the slightest—this nonsense had to stop. I had to get off that circus wagon.

I was engaged to a twenty-two-year-old girl from Seattle named Alice Knoph, a beautiful blonde who worked as a long-distance telephone operator. I met Alice on a double date back in the days when I worked at the Boeing plant. She was a vivacious Nordic type with a talent for singing, and she quickly became the delight of my life. She was engaged to a friend of mine, a picture I was determined to change. On our first date I told Alice I would marry her someday. She laughed, but six months later she was wearing my ring. Very sensibly we decided not to marry until the war was over.

But one day in April, 1943, I called Alice on the telephone and asked her to come down to Corpus Christi and marry me. The call cost $56.00, but this and the money I sent her for train fare was the best investment I ever made. Her sudden answer to my call for help naturally dismayed her family. But in the end they became reconciled. Alice lost her luggage on the trip down.

When we were married by a Justice of the Peace in Corpus Christi she wore one of my shirts as a blouse. A cab driver was best man. Alice and I rented an apartment in Corpus. Inevitably it became a hang-out for my bachelor friends among the instructors. There were too many parties. In that wartime atmosphere it was not quite possible to avoid a party even if we wanted to, which was not always the case. But when Alice came, it was as though I gained a balance wheel. My entire outlook changed.

I was always profoundly conscientious about my students. Slipshod instruction in gunnery and bombing could cost a combat pilot his life. But now I took on a new, voluntary chore. I became a specialist at saving the pilots slated for washout—the imperfections of our factory. In a way it was faintly comparable to my job at Boeing, when I redesigned parts that would otherwise have been scrapped.

I'm not certain just how or why I was moved to do this work. It may have started one day when I learned that an entire flight of cadets was about to be washed out. I looked into it and discovered that their instructor was a former student of mine. Had some imperfection in my own teaching caused this chain reaction? In any case, to my regular flights I added hundreds of hours of overtime work with these bruised pieces of fruit. To me this work, an attempt to mold these wayward men and their machines into perfect fighting units, was the most trying, and in some ways the most rewarding, of all. I tackled the job with missionary-like zeal.

Most of the work amounted to patient tutoring, simply building confidence first, then teaching technique. Occasionally, however, it was a matter of using common sense. I remember one case. The cadet was an ex-theology student. He stopped at our apartment one morning after church.

"Mr. Crossfield," he said. "What can I do? I don't want to give up."

He came in and sat down while Alice rustled up some coffee. This was a very sad case. The cadet had been before three different boards. Each board failed him. For some reason he simply could not make precision landings, which were crucial to flying on and off an aircraft carrier.

While we sat waiting I looked at him, trying with him to ferret out his lack. Then I noticed his legs. They were the shortest I had ever seen on a man. An idea flashed in my mind.

"Can your feet reach the rudder pedals?" I asked.

"Yes, sir," he said. But as I thought about it and mentally measured his legs in the cockpit, I knew he wasn't being completely frank. He probably reached the pedals, but with difficulty.

"Tell you what you do," I said. "I'll get you another flight and tomorrow when you go up I want you to put a pad—two pads—behind your back. This will bring you forward and closer to the rudder bars."

Next day the student flew with two pads behind his back. From then on the precision landing was a cinch. It was that simple, after over two hundred hours of apparently indifferent instruction. The flying board reversed its decision and he went on to fight in the Pacific. I don't know what happened to him. The best way to learn anything thoroughly, I believe, is to teach the subject to others. This is no new thought: college professors and scientists have known it for centuries. With each new student you begin all over, retracing the same fundamental course, each time exposed to a fresh, inquiring, and often challenging mind, and sometimes superlative ability. During my eighteen months at Corpus I logged 1,400 hours of single-engine time. Thus in one sense I learned to fly a thousand times, repeating the same familiar steps over and over and over, but each time adding a little knowledge and polish.

I think that this single tour of duty, more than anything else, honed my flying to a point of near-perfection.

10: No Penalty for Being Late

THE LAST FOURTEEN MONTHS OF MY ACTIVE NAVY service amounted to a determined but futile endeavor to get to war. This crazy-quilt travelogue took me from Corpus Christi to Jacksonville, Florida, back across the country to San Diego, to Seattle, to Klamath Falls, to Seattle, to Pasco, to Arlington, to Seattle, to Hawaii, to Philadelphia, to Norfolk, and back again to Seattle. Along the way, intense operational training improved and broadened my flying considerably.

The rat race began in September, 1944, when at last I was sprung from my duties as instructor in gunnery and bombing at Corpus and issued orders to the fleet. I was told to report to the Naval Air Training Center in Jacksonville, Florida, for a brief operational transition course. Alice and I packed our worldly belongings in our 1940 Mercury and set out. When I reached the new base and checked in, I was again forced to acknowledge that the Navy was not run for my express benefit.

I had drawn an assignment to dive bombers. To a fighter pilot, being a fighter pilot is very important. Fighters are the avant garde, the lancers, the agile fencing foils of the fleet, the spearhead of offense and defense in any pitched air-and-sea battle. The forte of the fighter pilot is individuality, perhaps erroneously, but nevertheless romantically, inspired by two wars. I had connived to be assigned to fighters when I was a cadet at Corpus Christi. With mixed feelings of adherence to duty and instructions, I decided to try again to bend the course of events more to my inclinations. If I didn't try, I thought as a salve to my feelings, what a waste of two years of intensive training!

"Can't I get fighter orders?" I asked the officer at the desk.

"We don't have any fighter-plane orders," he said.

"Well, in that case, consider me on leave." I had about twenty-two days coming, as I had foregone leave since I was commissioned. My thought was to postpone my reporting date until some fighter orders came in. Alice and I rented a cottage on Jacksonville Beach. Each day for three weeks I drove eighty miles to the Naval Base to see whether any fighter orders had arrived.

During this time—it was October 20, 1944, to be precise, and I don't know why I remember the specific date because I remember few others—a hurricane struck the beach where we were living. This incredible unleashing of nature's power was without doubt the most impressive thing I have ever seen in my life. The pounding sea ripped up the concrete seawall and stove in cottages. It swept over automobiles, including ours. I tried to save it, and others besides, feverishly working on the drowned-out engines while the wind-driven rain pelted me like BB shot.

It was useless. I pushed the Mercury against a fence which I hoped would prevent the car from drifting out to sea. Then Alice and I caught the last Coast Guard rescue truck, which took us to a brick schoolhouse in an emergency housing area for the displaced people. Before that storm hit us I never quite realized the awesome force the earth has cached in its storehouses. When this model of perfection goes awry it is a sight to behold. Against this force man's efforts seem feeble indeed. Against the U.S. Navy this man's efforts were feeble, too. I was assigned to dive bombers, along with eleven other instructors from Corpus. Our instructor was a Marine and a wonderful aviator. He greeted us thus:

"Boys, bombing is my business. If any of you want to put a little money on the bombing competition, I'll be glad to match it."

Without telling him we had been bombing instructors too, we all laid bets. Dive bombing turned out to be far easier than the glide bombing we were doing in Texas every day for eighteen months. We won in a walk. The result was really to our benefit. In the strange way that a competent pilot shows his respect for other competent pilots, our instructor worked us night and day with no quarter, and gave us, rather than a transition, a post-graduate course in the finer points of dive-bombing tactics.

As a result of my desire to be a fighter pilot, I found my rear-seat man an annoyance through no fault of his own. To this day I find it hard to justify a flight crew of more than one in almost any airplane. The additional crew encumbers the pilot and compromises the performance of the airplane with added weight and duplication. Most of the new rear-seat men remembered all the horror stories they heard in training school about target fixation on a dive. So whether the pilot liked it or not, the men insisted on calling out the altitudes during the dive. The only cure for this was for the pilot to recover at such high G that the rear-seat man blacked out. Sooner or later he'd get the point. But my man stumped me. He never gave up. Once I dived almost into the ground and pulled out viciously.

On the way down the rear-seat man called the altitudes: "10,000 . . . 5,000 . . . 2,000 . . . 1,500 . . . 1,200 . . . 1,000 . . . 800 . . ."

And from there on I was blacked out. Coming to in the climb, I could almost hear him shaking off the black-out, foggily picking up where he left off, calling altitude as we climbed. I gave up. A few weeks later came the last straw. Sometimes on our flights we carried aloft a three-pound bag of powdered gilt-paint pigment. If the usual floating targets were engaged by other flights, we tossed the bag of paint out of the cockpit. When it splashed into the ocean, it spread out and made a good substitute target. I handed my rear-seat man the paint bag and told him to drop it if and when I so instructed. It was an unforgettable take-off. By regulation we kept the greenhouse canopy open, and the cockpit was always very windy.

About midway down the runway my rear-seat man got curious and opened the bag. Then he dropped it. The bag burst. The rushing wind caught the powdered paint and swirled it through the cockpit—a regular blizzard of gold. I was almost blinded. The gold flecks coated everything, including our faces and hands, sticking to the oil film that usually covered us on those flights. I cleared my eyes somehow and landed. The cockpit, the instruments, everything—and both of us—were beautifully gold-plated El Dorados. Weeks went by before I got all the flecks out of my hair. Incidents like this strengthened my desire for the lonesome fighter cockpit.

Fate intervened favorably. After a couple of months, I was ordered to report to San Diego for fleet orders—without my rear-seat man. I packed the car again and we set off cross-country. Alice was about two months pregnant.

We were leaving Shreveport the next morning when suddenly I recalled all the stories I had heard at Corpus about the bigness of the State of Texas. "I'm going to cross Texas the long way in one day," I said to Alice. It was 986 miles to El Paso. We made it, but the cost was high. A little further along, in New Mexico, Alice had a miscarriage.

My orders required me to report in "on or before" a certain day that January of 1945. Time was short. If I took Alice to a hospital I would have to leave her there alone in New Mexico, an unthinkable desertion. But I knew the long drive remaining would be dangerous for her. Trying to make the best of an impossible situation, we decided to push on as rapidly as possible to leave Alice in the care of my sister, Elena Ruth, who lived near Los Angeles.

I drove on swiftly, without sleep, completing the cross-country drive from Jacksonville to Los Angeles in eighty-eight hours. When we reached my sister's house, Alice was very ill. She almost died. It was a sobering lesson for a young man. I made up my mind then that no matter what challenge loomed in my life I would never tackle it at the risk of involving her or anyone else. I would go it alone—all the way. From that time on, Alice, with my encouragement, drew a protective cocoon around her life. She never inquired about what new Mount Everest I might be scaling, and in fact until she read this book she had little idea of the flying at Edwards. I've pointedly ignored it, both with her and the children. I've lived in two different worlds: in hers with our family, and in the world of my other love, aviation. This separation is a boon. It removes the insidious and encumbering influence of expressed day-to-day concern so common in the lives of pilots. And to some degree—to a great degree, I hope—it has spared her the anguish of waiting for the telephone call so many of her friends have received when their men bought the farm.

When I was certain Alice was in good hands, I raced on to San Diego, reporting in twenty minutes before the deadline. Good news was waiting for me at the end of that mad journey. When I got there, the last man to report, some of the other pilots had been assigned to dive bombers, torpedo planes, and so on. But at the very last minute a request came through for a few fighter pilots for Air Group 37, based in the Seattle area, of all places. I snatched up the orders and hurried north to Seattle, then to Klamath Falls, Oregon. As soon as she was well, Alice joined me.

We had time to visit with her family and to spend a few days on the farm in Boistfort Valley. I found my father and mother—like most farmers during the war—short-handed but more prosperous. My father's research and diligence were bringing handsome returns. He was laying plans to build a modern barn with an automatic milking line, and to buy new power tools and tractors.

He was reconciled to my chosen profession by then, but he openly urged me to do more. "A pilot," he said, "is nothing more than a glorified chauffeur. Use your skill and talent in flying as a tool to help accomplish something lasting and significant for mankind."

From Air Group 37 at Klamath Falls I was re-assigned to Air Group 51 at Seattle. We recommissioned that famed squadron and moved to Pasco, Washington. Air Group 51 prepared for war. We flew morning, noon, and night. Our skipper, Commander William Lamb, an Annapolis graduate, was one of the ablest men I have ever met. He rated others strictly by performance. Although I was a senior lieutenant, with many more flying hours than most of the pilots, I flew last man Charlie until I proved to him in the air that I knew what I was about. After that he assigned me to command a division. All Naval officers must assume a collateral duty, and as I had been with every squadron, I was assigned as an Engineering Officer. When we changed a wing, or conducted a major overhaul of an airplane, it was my job to take the plane into the air for the first test hop, to make sure it had been put back together properly. This was not flight-test work in its purest sense, but as close as I could come. I took keen satisfaction in squeezing longer life from some of those tired old birds and tried to keep them in near-perfect mechanical order, just as I did my automobile.

One man I especially admired in that outfit was a boot ensign named Smith. He was a natural hunter like Sergeant York, or Gabreski, or Chuck Yeager. No matter how hard I tried—and I went full-bore—he could always top my score in aerial gunnery. He was eventually transferred to another outfit, but of all the men I knew in the Navy this Ensign Smith stands out in my memory like a sore thumb—or an unsealed Mount Everest. I don't know what ever happened to him.

We were scheduled to ship out on the aircraft carrier *Cabot*, but she broke a shaft, so our group sailed to Hawaii, plane-less, on an LSV that burned out a bearing and so proceeded at a top speed of six knots. It was one of the longest voyages of the war, I'm sure. The ship was crowded with aviators and soldiers. I remember it as one long Acey-Deucy tournament, which in the end I lucked out and won (the pot was $28.00). In Hawaii we were assigned to the aircraft carrier *Langley* and given brand-new, 400-mile-an-hour F6F airplanes.

And that was as close as I came to the war. In Hawaii we moved down to the island of Maui and for several months trained with the Second Marine Division, preparing for the invasion of Japan. The training was quite realistic, with live ammo and bombs. We were assigned a specific landing point on the coast of Japan, and on Maui we practiced our invasion role on terrain similar to it. Then the scientists unlocked the power of the atom and ended the war. We boarded the Langley, lashed down our planes, and steamed to Philadelphia via the Panama Canal. We based in Philadelphia for a few weeks at Mustin Field. From there we moved to Norfolk for decommissioning. Alice had been waiting on the farm ever since I shipped off to Hawaii.

For a while, I considered remaining in the Navy after the war. It had many appeals for me. I met some of the finest men in my life in the Navy. It was a good life if you approached it from the right point of view in the right frame of mind. It was an opportunity to do my country a service in my chosen endeavor. The Naval Air Test Center at Patuxent River, Maryland, where new Navy planes are flight-tested, had just opened up, and I thought of applying for a test pilot's job there. In fact I talked to Commander Lamb about it at length. He gave me little encouragement to buck the Academy men and those with technical training with my 'trade school' background. I decided then to return to college for a sound engineering education. I was well grounded in aviation, but too many people, such as Commander Lamb, clearly held an advantage over me. If I had known then that the Navy would send many of its officers to college after the war to obtain engineering degrees, I might have stayed on and thus avoided the tight financial squeeze that soon followed.

A lunatic episode, the maddest race of all, climaxed my Navy career. I'm not certain how it began. I think that the separating officer at Norfolk resented reservists who were deserting the Navy. "Okay," he said, "we'll separate you in Seattle, the point closest to your home, and fast, too. You're due at the separation center there not 'on or about' but 'on or before' five days from now. You'll have no transportation priority."

"But how do you expect me to get to Seattle in five days with no priority?" I asked. It was November 1, 1945, and the entire transportation system of the nation was staggering under the load of returning servicemen. Without a priority, commercial airlines were out of the question. All military airplanes were jammed. Trains were packing people in like sardines and running days behind schedule.

"That's your problem," the officer said. He handed me my orders.

This return trip to Seattle suddenly and curiously emerged as a great game. I don't know why. I guess it was because the officer implied that I could never make it. All right, I thought, if that's the way it is, that's the way it is.

And I'm not about to report in late for the first time in my Naval career and spoil a perfect record. I packed a few clean clothes in a suitcase, sealed and shipped my foot-lockers (which arrived months later), and set off.

From beginning to end the trip was insane. I left Norfolk on a train, standing in the aisle. We chugged north for a thousand years and then south for another thousand, then east, I think it was, and finally arrived in Washington, D.C., which is about a hundred miles from Norfolk—fourteen minutes by fighter plane. I made up my mind right then that I would get back on a train only as a last resort, after trying a mule. Incidentally, I still feel that way about trains. I checked in at Military Operations in Washington and by great luck got a hop almost immediately to Olathe, Kansas. I waited patiently there for a ride farther west, or north, or northwest, but the few planes that came through were jammed with priority passengers. The time was ticking by rapidly.

When I heard that I might have better luck in Chicago, I wormed my way on board a military plane going there. In Chicago I felt richer: I was now far ahead of the train. I could have boarded a train in Chicago that day and made it to Seattle with ease. But the thought of that prolonged trip was enough to make me gamble. Heavier air traffic was moving across the South so I jumped on another military airplane and wound up in Fort Worth, Texas. This move put me behind the train schedule. I had to make it by air, or else ...

In Fort Worth I waited. Without a priority it seemed hopeless. But luck is where you find it. I discovered very late that night that the Naval officer dispatching people on the airplanes was an old student of mine from Corpus Christi days. As a favor to a buddy, he stamped my orders with the lowest possible priority. Still it was a priority and it moved me ahead of about a hundred people in the line. Hurrying now, for I was far behind the train schedule, I scrambled aboard a plane heading for Oakland, California, with an intermediate stop in Phoenix, Arizona. If I didn't get bumped in Phoenix, I knew I had it made.

I got bumped in Phoenix. I then had less than twenty-four hours to make it to Seattle. I paced the floor of the waiting room. The clock ticked on. Then a minor miracle happened. Completely unexpected, an airplane came through Phoenix headed for San Francisco. It was an old R4-D, converted to a hospital plane, manned by a flight crew and a staff of male and female nurses, flying back and forth between the East and West coasts, hauling the wounded to hospitals in the East and caring for them along the way. They were returning for more. I have never seen people so dead tired. I don't think any of them had slept in a bed for a month. Yet they immediately turned their thoughts to my comfort. They gave me a sleeping bag, some hot coffee, and a ride to San Francisco. This little touch of humanity made me feel like a new man. Moreover, this hop to the Coast made up much lost time and put me ahead of the train again.

In San Francisco I boarded an Air Force plane bound for Seattle. As fate would have it, just then some luckless pilot drove an airplane into a mountain nearby. The plane I was on was diverted from its destination to help in the search for survivors. They dropped me off at the end of the world—Medford, Oregon. I might have made it to Seattle by train yet—a ten-hour trip—but having come that close, I refused to give up, although I was getting pretty tired at this point and was badly in need of a bath and clean clothes.

The next morning I met an Air Force colonel who had flown down to Medford in a B-17 bringing a ground rescue crew. At that moment he was debating with himself whether to return in heavy weather to his base at McChord Field, Tacoma, about thirty miles south of Seattle. I got into the debate, urging that the weather wasn't so bad and that he return to McChord with me as his passenger. At about three in the afternoon we took off into a raging snowstorm. I sat shivering in the Plexiglas nose turret.

When we got to Tacoma about dusk the snowstorm was still in full fury. I think the Colonel would have sought another field then—probably any pilot would have—except for the expression on my face which plainly said: "It doesn't look so bad to me."

Coming from a Naval aviator, it was a challenge to this Air Force type, perhaps. He lowered the gear and we threaded our way up the river through the storm groping—and I do mean groping—for McChord Field. It was dark and snowing hard when we landed. The runway lights were on, the tower was manned, but otherwise there was not a soul to be seen. No jeep came out to the plane; hell, the weather was too lousy. My clock was running out. Without so much as a thank you to the Colonel, I plowed through the deep snow to a road where I hitched a ride in a truck that happened along. The truck dropped me at the base gate. I then moved out onto the main highway and thumbed a ride—I believe it took two rides—to Seattle. I arrived at the Processing Center at eleven o'clock that night, one hour before my deadline, November 6, 1945.

I have recounted these last days and hours of my active Naval service in some detail for special reasons. For one thing, the recollection of that trip has always astonished and amused me, especially the way those Florence Nightingales just happened along in Phoenix in the hospital plane and took pity on a forlorn traveler engaged in a restless, disjointed journey, a crazy race against time. That was the denouement of the trip; that hop really let me win. And to those people, whose names I cannot recall, I shall be forever grateful. Another thing: I think this screwball tale tells a lot about the workings of the feeble clot of gray matter which I call my mind.

I should close this account by adding the significant fact that there would have been no penalty whatsoever if I had arrived late. Even a couple or three days late.

11: How Dark the Clouds

During my four years at the University of Washington in Seattle after World War II, I kept strong ties with Naval aviation. In early 1946 I helped organize a reserve squadron, VF-74, a group of mature 'Weekend Warriors.' The pilots were experienced aviators, mostly married men and veterans of the war. Under Navy supervision we trained hard to achieve a high degree of readiness, prepared for instant mobilization in the event the nation went to war again. We flew drills two days a month and spent two weeks on active Navy duty every year. Our squadron was consistently among the leaders in Naval reserve gunnery scores, but we could never claim a trophy because our maverick pilots were indifferent to paperwork. For me personally, my tour with this hard-flying outfit provided not only the most rewarding moments in the air but also in one instance the most humiliating.

The rewarding moments came during the months and months of weekend flights around Seattle. Our squadron was furnished a mixed bag of F-6-F and F-4-U Corsair airplanes, leftovers from World War II requiring constant maintenance. After the Navy demobilized, funds were scarce for reserve squadrons and thus our operations were run on a tight-fisted basis. One result was that we pilots could not shift around, checking out in different airplanes. I was an F6F pilot, restricted to that type of airplane.

This annoyed me. The Corsair was considered something of a flying challenge, a fairly unstable plane, quick to stall and difficult to recover from a spin, but none the less a superior gun platform. I longed to master that beast and at the same time possibly improve my gunnery score. One day while I was waiting in the operations office for my airplane assignment, the officer detailing the airplanes piped up: "Hey, I need a Corsair pilot." It happened that at that moment there were none around.

"Put me down," I called. I had been waiting for just such a chance. It never occurred to this officer to ask me if I were checked out in the plane. He neatly printed 'Crossfield' on the blackboard in a space alongside the number of the airplane. In a way, airplanes are like women, that is to say impossible to understand fully, and often ticklish to handle. It takes a little time to get to know them, to find out how and to what they respond. Some must be manipulated by fingertips, with infinite finesse, others must be pushed around like trucks. Some forgive the pilot's sins; some don't. The Corsair was very nearly inscrutable. She was hard to figure, slightly forgiving, and she required a great deal of attention.

I found this out under extraordinary circumstances. Soon after my name appeared on the board, I took off with five other planes. The flight had moved out so quickly I had time only to glance briefly at the airplane handbook in the cockpit. The flight leader was in a frisky mood. When we reached altitude he whipped the formation into the damnedest tail chase I have ever been in. I found myself in that totally strange airplane doing Cuban Eights, loops, barrel rolls, chandelles, and the Lord knows what else. Only a pilot can fully appreciate this situation, I suppose. Locked in that crazy ride, with one plane twenty feet ahead of me and another twenty feet behind, I really sweated. I thought to myself: "You damned fool. How'd you ever get into this?" But I wasn't about to pull out, to admit that I couldn't hack it.

The Crossfield luck rode with me that day. I sinned, but the Corsair was in a forgiving mood. There was no mid-air collision. The whole flight came down alive and landed. From that point on I was a Corsair man and glad of it. My gunnery score improved. Much later someone noticed that my paperwork was not in order for that plane. But it was too late then and the fact was overlooked. The outfit was an action squadron.

Our squadron skipper was Commander William Flateboe, a married man a little older than I, twenty-nine or so. We had served together at Corpus as instructors. When he was an ensign at Corpus, Flateboe was one of the wildest flat-hatters in Texas, a champion windmiller. When we organized the Reserve squadron, he was as conservative in the air as an airline pilot. But as the weeks and months dragged on, both he and I became restless and bored in the air and a second stage of infantile flat-hatting set in. I think I must have logged fifty hours flying below the rim of the Columbia River gorge.

In the midst of this flat-hatting renaissance, the thought struck me that we ought to legalize our flat-hatting. Thus was born the 13th Naval District Stunt Team, which in time became one of the best aerial stunt teams in the country, and we felt, of course, that it was the best. There were four of us on the team: Flateboe, the 'slot' man, Lou Colvin, a wingman, and an ensign named Bill Helsell, my usual wingman; I was the leader. The really remarkable fact about this stunt team was that we performed our precision formations in the supposedly dangerous Corsair.

Helsell was a fabulous aviator, one of the few men I have known whom I completely trusted in the air. He was low on total flying hours, and from a technical standpoint he knew and cared little or nothing about airplanes, but he was a rare natural pilot. I first met him in a University car pool. He was the son of a Seattle lawyer. He studied engineering at Yale, achieving a straight A record; then he switched to law at the University of Washington, graduating cum laude. He was a dour-faced lad, outwardly a cynic and cold as ice. But that was a mask; he displayed many a kindness but feigned annoyance at the necessity.

Formation stunt flying, to my mind, is the quintessence of precision, and beyond any doubt it requires much skill and intense concentration. All four planes, tucked in as tight as we could get them without scraping paint, flew through the air as though locked together by invisible steel bars. As the leader, I guided the team. The other three planes flew 'on me,' adjusting speed in minute increments, always keeping their eyes fixed on my plane. If I looped, they looped in unison. If I rolled, they rolled in unison. If I pulled a Cuban Eight, they pulled Cuban Eights in unison. Had I flown straight into the ground, they would have flown straight in with me in unison.

I set a hard pace. Striving for perfection and developing a flair for showmanship, which is the ultimate goal of most stunt teams, we worked at our drills at altitude. When we flew them cold, we performed right on the deck, a wingspan above the ground. We were soon very much in demand for various events. We felt that even in our aging Corsairs we could show the Regular Navy Blue Angels in their Bearcats a thing or two. The original team did not last long. Flateboe was the first to go. Something had been eating away at him. One weekend evening while working at the base on some papers, he got up and said: "To hell with it." He jumped in an airplane and set a course to rendezvous with one of the squadron flights on a training exercise out over the Strait of Juan de Fuca. Flateboe overhauled the flight at great speed and wound his plane into a gigantic barrel-roll around the formation. That was the last anyone ever saw of him. He evidently dived straight into the water. Later Colvin dropped out, leaving Helsell and me to carry on.

A subtle shift in emphasis then took place. Showmanship became secondary, the spectators unimportant. The stunt team changed into a delightful, though perhaps dangerous, aerial contest between two very competitive pilots. All attempts to make Helsell cry uncle failed. This contest reached its peak one day in Astoria, Oregon. I pulled out of a giant loop not more than twenty feet above the ground, screaming across the airport at 350 miles an hour. A tower, part of an adjoining skeet range, loomed in our path, dead ahead. I bore on, casually lifting my wing to clear the tower in the last second. Locked in beside me, Helsell skillfully followed my maneuver, never once batting an eyelash.

"That ought to scare you," I radioed.

"You'll have to do better than that, Dad," Helsell replied.

There was a professional stunt team, a barnstorming outfit complete with wing-walkers and a delayed-parachute performer, giving a show on the same field that day. After we landed, the leader of this team came up to me and said: "Hey, fellow. Do us a favor, will you? Will you please stay away from the fields where we're working? You'll put us out of business."

I considered that one of the finest compliments ever paid us, but the man had no cause for worry. Helsell and I soon put ourselves out of business. One day during a regatta on Lake Washington, I led Helsell through a low-altitude formation roll over a crowd watching the crew races. Such a maneuver was routine to us then (we had logged five hundred hours of precision-stunt-flying), although by CAA regulations illegal. Probably a hundred amateur movie cameras caught the act. The 13th Naval District received a mass complaint shortly afterwards and restricted us to an altitude minimum of 1,000 feet.

"Hell," I said, "at 1,000 feet it's no fun."

"I know," the Old Man said, "but that's an order." He abruptly ended the conversation. And with that the stunt team folded. Working with that team, working that fine artistry in Corsairs, was one of the most rewarding periods in the air I have ever experienced. Every second of each maneuver was a supreme satisfaction, a delight akin to playing fine music.

With me the bad always comes with the good. The most humiliating experience I had in an airplane occurred during a routine drill with VF-74. The fact that I was a party to this fiasco has stuck like a lance in my side ever since. It seemed impossible that our fine outfit could pull such a blooper. It began one day while we were on two weeks' active duty, flying out of Sand Point.

It seems that the Naval Reserve unit in land-locked Denver, Colorado, was having difficulty in stirring up public interest and getting recruits. Someone conceived a grandiose plan: our whole air group, including VF-74, some twenty-five fighters and fifteen torpedo planes, would fly to Denver en masse and land amid contrived hoopla and press coverage. As a goodwill gesture and public-relations stunt, we would bring along an ice-packed salmon caught that same day in Puget Sound and present it to the mayor of Denver. Afterwards there would be a big official dinner party, more hoopla, and finally a gay time for us on the town, we hoped. We packed our smartest uniforms and took off. Disaster struck the torpedo planes flying in separate formation. Caught in a bad storm, they were forced to land on a field in Helena, Montana, in a stiff ninety-degree crosswind. The long crosswind taxi of these cumbersome birds burned out the down-wind brakes on several of the planes. With no brakes the planes were finished, grounded. The salmon, a key item in the goodwill gesture, was on board one of the torpedo planes. It never left Helena.

The remaining airplanes, our twenty-five fighters, first ran into trouble at Ogden, Utah, when we landed to refuel. Fifteen of us took off without difficulty, but the engine of the sixteenth plane conked out on the narrow taxiway, blocking the remaining nine planes. They could not get into the air until the disabled plane was towed out of the way. The fifteen of us waited at altitude for a quarter of an hour, then radioed that we were pushing on alone. After all, there was a huge reception gathering at the Denver airport and we couldn't be late. No, sir.

We were falling behind schedule now and our leader elected to bypass the ordinary roundabout air routes and steer a direct course for Denver, about four hundred miles away. This course led us directly over the Continental Divide and some of the most desolate, mountainous country in the world, which from 15,000 feet had a remarkable sameness about it. I laid out a course on a chart but, as was customary in fighters, let the flight commander do the navigating. He miscalculated a compass heading and we drove on, aiming considerably south of Denver, all of us thinking he had reasons of his own for this course.

After some time I was convinced that we were steering too far to the south. The same feeling overcame the other thirteen pilots in our formation. Suddenly the radio was alive with chatter and debate. The skipper broke in and said: "If I'm right, then in four and a half minutes we'll pass over Waldron, Colorado." Precisely four and a half minutes later we passed over a town on the fork of a river which resembled the plan of Waldron on the chart. There was an airfield on the opposite bank which seemed to confirm positively the skipper's navigation. However, to make doubly sure, I peeled off and dived into the valley to check the name on any available sign. I missed signs but spotted a large 'W' painted on the mountainside. It was Waldron, all right, I thought. The skipper was correct.

Actually we were over Gunnison, Colorado, considerably to the south of Waldron. Gunnison, too, is located on the fork of a river with an airfield on the opposite bank. The 'W' on the mountainside had nothing to do with Waldron. It was put there by the students of Western State College in Gunnison. Led astray by this strange set of coincidences, we flew on following the skipper, who predicted a second town lying ahead, Fort Collins. Twenty seconds later a town passed beneath our wings.

"We are now forty miles north of Denver," the skipper said. "Close into parade formation."

We pulled our planes together in neat formation, following the highway straight into Denver, or so we thought, then about ten minutes away. We flew and flew and flew. Fifteen minutes passed, but no sign of Denver, no familiar big-city haze, no gradual build-up of traffic on the highway, no increase in housing. On the contrary, the countryside looked, if anything, more desolate. Helsell, who usually had little to say, piped up sourly: "I'm logging a strong Las Vegas, New Mexico, beam." Now we were very concerned. Time was ticking away.

Again there was a confused debate on the radio. In the midst of it we passed over still another small town. I peeled off and buzzed it. The Rotary Club sign on the highway at the city limits read: "Alamosa." Alamosa? No one knew where this could be. It was off our charts. Nine of our planes, low on fuel, pulled out of formation and landed at Alamosa.

I radioed my wingman, Bill Helsell:

"Nuts. I'm going to find Denver. You want to come with me?"

He did, of course, so we cleared with the skipper and took off on our own, fiddling with our radios, trying to pick up a station, any station. Thunderstorms all around us gave little but static. Regretting now that I had not carefully tracked the skipper's navigating, I retraced our course from memory on my plotting board. We had indeed come too far south and Denver lay to the northeast of us. We flew in that direction. Soon we picked up Trinidad radio, which I knew was south of Denver, but still off our charts. We homed eastward on Trinidad and then turned due north, on course to Denver at last. We picked up Pueblo radio beacon as expected. Homing on Pueblo, we flew into a very black thunderhead full of rain and lightning. In that weather we lost the Pueblo radio signal. Minutes later we relocated ourselves by radio. We had passed Pueblo, which was under the storm. We couldn't see the ground.

Long overdue in Denver, the authorities there became concerned about us and sounded a disaster alert. They figured we had exhausted our fuel. The Navy, the Civil Air Patrol, the Air National Guard, and the Lord knows who else, took to the air in search of fifteen Navy planes downed somewhere on the Continental Divide. The nine fighter planes blocked on the runway in Ogden had finally made it, sans fish, to Denver. There was great confusion at the airport over whether to wait for the lost planes or begin the ceremonies with the nine pilots. Helsell and I were doing our damnedest—almost. Used to conserving fuel, another of our private competitions, we were still in the air looking for Denver. Every time we saw a house we zoomed down to see if it held a clue. Convinced that Denver lay to the northeast, I made one more attempt to find it. We flew northeast and came up over a ridge right into the face of another black line of thunderheads. I began to lose heart. It was almost dark, we had only a half-hour's fuel, the radios yielded only static. To plunge into that thunderstorm flying blind, in the Rocky Mountains, with the distance to Denver unknown, could be idiotic.

"What do you think?" I radioed Helsell.

"Do you think we should turn back?" he answered.

"Yes," I said.

"So do I."

And turn back we did, searching for the nearest airfield. At the point of turning we were exactly twenty-three miles southwest of Denver, or about six minutes by Corsair. The thunderstorm line was thin and lying on the last ridge before the mid-western plains. Denver was clear as a bell. If we had pressed on for six more minutes, we would have landed, salvaging part of the day, heroes, pride of the Navy. Instead we were bums. We landed on a mountainside field—elevation 9700 feet—in a small town called Fairplay, Colorado, and joined the skipper and three other pilots who had followed the same course.

When I found how close we had come, I was mortified. The next day when we got to Denver, after the Navy sent a gasoline truck to refuel us, I was even more mortified. Captain Greber flew down from Seattle to chew us out.

"I can understand the torpedo planes grounded in Helena, out of commission," Greber said. "I can understand one plane, or maybe two planes, getting lost. By really stretching my imagination I can conceive of maybe six planes getting lost together. But fifteen airplanes, in largely clear weather on a four-hundred-mile flight! An hour-and-a-half hop. It's beyond belief."

He was right. It was the most incompetent, unprofessional, ridiculous performance I had ever seen in the air, one that I could have tempered if I had held to my convictions and not quit. Worse was the fact that my decision also made Helsell look like a chump.

This brilliant maneuver did little to boost recruiting in Denver, but it brought VF-74 fame of a different sort in Navy circles. For me it was a great personal lesson. Not once since then, either on land or in the air, have I ever turned back from any course that I set upon, no matter how dark the clouds that lay ahead.

12: A Short Man with Santa Claus Eyebrows

During my University years, from 1946 to 1950, the free-thinking, curious, intellectual atmosphere was a pleasure and a delight to me. I ate it up. Most of this time I held firmly on my course, but there were brief interludes when I was buffeted by contrary winds. Once, as I related at the beginning of this account, I was ready to chuck it all to fly the Bell X-1 rocket plane. On the opposite tack briefly, I seriously entertained the idea of remaining at the University as a teacher. For a time, at the University, my mind became overly absorbed in detail of theoretical analysis. A man named Seeger reversed this trend and sent me on my way.

From the outset, my father warned me against becoming an academic bum, an all-too-familiar figure on our college campuses. "Let's be a little careful here," he said. "You don't have the patience to be a pure theoretician. Your inclinations are to see things grow out of ideas and theory; you're interested in things, pieces of hardware, that you can feel with your hands, proofs of theory."

This may have been a calculated taunt; I'm not certain. In any case, the remark stuck in my craw. It was a clear challenge, and it spurred me into a pile-driving effort at the University. Over the gentle protests of my academic adviser, I registered for an extraordinarily heavy load of classes, with the full knowledge that I had mapped out a grueling course of work and study. Since boyhood, long hours and hard work were routine for me. Every course of my free choice was 'engineering,' applications of theory to adapt the things of nature to man-made shape.

Alice and I readjusted to an austere budget. My income dropped drastically from Navy days, and we drew heavily on our savings to bolster the GI Bill income of about $90 a month. We moved into a microscopic apartment in a temporary wartime housing area. Here in this space, decorated with a few sticks of furniture, I studied until one or two every morning while Alice read or listened to the radio through some earphones I had rigged.

The earphones didn't last long. Whenever anything funny was said on the radio, Alice would naturally burst out in laughter. This was a weird experience—to sit in a small room with somebody who laughs periodically for reasons unknown. In time, rather than put up with that, we chucked the earphones and I resorted to natural powers of concentration.

Our wants were quite modest and we purposely avoided the heavy social life of the University campus, but the rising cost of living forced me to seek part-time work. Alice, who found that the tiny apartment left her with time to kill, returned to the telephone company and took a job operating a small switchboard in the evenings while I studied. My first part-time financial venture, a car-repair business, was a flop. I enjoy working with my hands and tinkering with engines. But I made an ill-timed bid to repair a fleet of company cars and lost my shirt. After that I took the job in the University's wind tunnel at fifty cents an hour.

From the outset I was completely fascinated by that job. A wind tunnel is basic and fundamental. Here airplanes are born and grow to perfection. Here the imperfections are discarded—at least, that is the final objective. Here a man's idea in miniature is tested against the great forces and laws of nature. Here the airplane grows to life, amid a thousand calculations and tests.

The wind tunnel was for me a happy combination of study, theory, model airplanes, wonderful machinery, and work. Not surprisingly, we found that a pilot has a natural aptitude for wind-tunnel operations. Several other pilots were on the staff.

Our tunnel team, mostly World War II veterans such as Joe Tymczyszyn, was a conscientious, energetic group. We devised new techniques to increase the efficiency of the tunnel and, as a result, set new records for operational speed and data output. The work was no schoolboy drill. It cost a company about $1,500 a day to use the tunnel. Company engineers were usually on hand when we ran the tests, and for us students this contact with the men in the industry was invaluable. In time I was promoted to Chief Operator of the tunnel and my salary was raised accordingly.

Older and wiser now, I retraced a path through two years of basic college engineering. Then I advanced to my major, aeronautical engineering. In spite of my heavy academic load and the part-time work in the tunnel, I was so much in earnest that I was able to make all A's and B-pluses in my courses, graduating in June, 1949, with a bachelor of science degree. I was elected to Tau Beta Pi and to Sigma Xi, the honorary scholastic societies for science and engineering. My father, a Sigma Xi, was surprised.

Now ready to go on for my master's degree, I was determined not to hang around and be an 'academic bum,' as my father so tersely put it. I'd allow one school year, three quarters, not recommended, but I felt it necessary to set a limit rather than mark time waiting for an end point to appear. This may have been a mistake; my responsibilities were growing. Our oldest daughter, Becky, was a year old. Alice had left her job before Becky was born. After a few months the hard pace began to tell. I was wearing down— but too stubborn to admit it. My father got wind of this and stepped in. After elaborate subterfuge to avoid 'helping' me, he lent me money that made it possible for me to give up all part-time work and concentrate exclusively on my studies. I was very grateful and studied all the harder. The loan meant that I could complete my course in three quarters, as planned.

The University of Washington graduate course in aeronautical engineering is considered one of the best in the country. I found it lacking in one important respect. I felt that too much emphasis was placed on theory and philosophy and not enough emphasis strictly on engineering.

My father was absolutely right in this respect: I am no theoretician. I deal best with application of ideas, not theories. Since, under my concept of it, I was working for a master's degree in engineering, not theory or scientific philosophy, I became impatient with the long hours of theoretical work, the hypothetical cases which required abstract analysis and had no example in nature. I longed to deal with specific problems against which I could apply natural physics and come up with a physical solution. My approach brought me into frequent and sometimes stiff conflict with the graduate-school professors, most of whom were theorists at heart, like my father.

The time came to submit my thesis. Nowadays, regrettably, theses are not required for master's degrees at most schools. According to the concept, I was supposed to make a "new contribution to the art or science of aviation." Most of my fellow students presented theses which contained some elaborate mathematical analysis. I tried something different. My thesis was 'A Semi-Empirical Method of Obtaining Static and Dynamic Aerodynamic Parameters of Swept-Back Wings Analyzed on a Basis of Plan Form.' It was, if you please, a new and simplified method of predicting aerodynamic characteristics. It could be done with a slide-rule in a matter of minutes in place of hundreds of hours of computing-machine time. It was a tool to be used to attain adequate accuracy but replace the laborious rigid mathematical methods which were guesses anyway. It was influenced by my work in the wind tunnel and was, I think, a profitable blending of theory and practical application, the essence of engineering.

This thesis stirred up tremendous consternation among some of the professors. One problem was that it wasn't long enough, or didn't weigh enough, for a master's thesis. My wish was that I could have cut it to one page. Their position was certainly understandable. I hoped that mine was. The paper was accepted, probably by default. The faculty, who were all respected friends, agreed to let me disagree and certainly were not of a nature to flunk me for disagreeing.

I think Alice has a slight touch of claustrophobia. She soon tired of the four walls of our small apartment and set out house-hunting around Seattle. One day she came home bubbling with news of a two-bedroom house in Clyde Hill, a section of Bellevue which almost fit our budget. The house was really charming, set in the middle of a small cherry orchard on a hillside. We splurged and moved in.

The house was owned by an amazing character named Oscar Seeger, who lived on an adjoining tract of land. Seeger, a short man with Santa Claus eyebrows, was one of the most direct and dynamic men I have ever met. One night when he visited us, Alice suggested our house might be improved by installing a counter between the dining ell and the kitchen. Without a moment's delay Seeger found a saw and ripped out an eight-foot section of the wall. The finished job was not thorough, but neither was it unsightly. I was somewhat stunned by his speed and skill.

Seeger was the president of a small electrical contracting company. During World War II he tentatively branched into the manufacture of small aircraft accessories for Boeing—wash basins, seat arms, tables, and the like. When he discovered that Alice and I were scraping bottom financially, he arrived at the house one day with his company's billing lists and asked if I would type and mail them out. (I had learned to hunt and peck on my father's 1910 Corona portable.) For a time this billing was a regular monthly job. It helped Alice and me considerably. Later when Seeger had to submit formal blueprints on some job, I drew them for him on my drafting board set up in the bedroom. And after that we became very close friends.

One day Seeger made me a business proposition. The airlines, he said, were asking for bids on 20,000 aircraft tables. Seeger located some surplus aluminum material which he thought he could get for a low price. If I designed the table, he said, and drew up the specifications, he would take care of the manufacturing.

We would split the profits on a percentage basis which, the way Seeger presented it, was very generous—too appealing to ignore, in fact.

Designing a table is no great feat, but I wanted to do it right for Seeger. I made a federal case of it. I set out to design the perfect aircraft table. I worked for hours, days, weeks. That damned table absorbed me as deeply as my studies at school and the Navy stunt team. Seeger became impatient.

"Look, Scotty," he said. "You've got the wrong idea about life. You can't waste your time trying to design the perfect table. The important thing to do is design a table that will do the job, win the contract, and bring in the money."

"When I do something, I like to do it right," I replied. I thought: Seeger is not an opportunist, but how different he is from my father, the absolute perfectionist.

"We all try to do the best we can, Scotty. But do you realize that you could spend the rest of your life trying to design the perfect table? Did you ever see a table with four legs precisely the same length? The thing to do is give it all you've got for a reasonable time and then move on to something else. Absolute perfection is highly desirable but unattainable."

Reluctantly I hurried the design of that table. At the last minute—just under the wire—we got our bid in to the airlines. To my complete astonishment, we won. Seeger's generous percentage brought in a nice piece of change. But more important, perhaps, was the total, amazing impact of Seeger. He gave me a new perspective on life. I gave up trying to build a table with four legs precisely the same length. From then on, I made the decision that the important thing was to do a job well, to the best of my ability, and move on. Had I not, it is possible that I might still be at the University, seeking perfection in my studies, or in the wind tunnel, or else energetically at work in some shop, striving to build the perfect valve or cotter key. Instead I moved on to Edwards.

13: Barefoot Boy with Cheek

IT WAS A SPARKLY CLEAR SPRING DAY IN THE DESERT, about eight months after I joined NACA at Edwards. When the Air Force B-29 mother plane reached 8,000 feet, its pilot, Captain Pete Sellers, passed that fact over the intercom. It was a signal to me: aft in the bomb-bay compartment, converted to nest the X-1 in the bomber's belly, I climbed on the small elevator—a plank with aluminum-tubing guardrails—hitched up my chute, and waved to the launch operator, Eddie Edwards. The elevator descended slowly through the bomb-bay, and presently I found myself precariously suspended over the wide-open spaces, battered by the slipstream. The vast, desolate desert lay in unobscured view in all directions.

The X-1 'door' was on the side of the airplane. Thus it could not be entered, like the Skyrocket, from the mother plane's bomb-bay compartment. The pilot had to go outside, below the mother plane. The elevator, seemingly a crude way to get to the X-1, was actually considered plush. In the early stages, back in 1947, Chuck Yeager had to climb down a ladder into the whipping slipstream.

I eased into the cramped X-1 cockpit and waved my hand. The elevator ascended and presently came down again, bearing the X-1 door, which had been placed inside the bomb-bay compartment before take-off. I set it in place and dogged the handles shut from the inside. In preparation for my first flight in the X-1, I had practiced this maneuver several times on the ground.

Actually, that day, the fitting of the door in place was much more difficult than I have made it out to be. The reason was that I had three broken ribs. This minor calamity had occurred several days earlier in the hangar while I was skylarking with the mechanics. I had playfully grabbed one by the seat of the pants and thrust him through the stockroom window. As his head disappeared over the sill, his feet came up and accidentally smacked me in the chest, cracking three ribs at once. I had sworn him and the others to secrecy. I knew that if Williams or Vensel found out, I would be grounded for a long period.

There were two additional NACA pilots at Edwards then, Walt Jones and Joe Walker. Walt Jones, about 25, had been hired about the time John Griffith left NACA. A graduate of Purdue, he had served in the Air Force with Griffith. A handsome man, the son of a minister, he was short on flying hours but showed great potential. He later left NACA and was killed test-flying for Northrop. Joe Walker, my age, was an Air Force veteran of World War II, who had worked at NACA's Lewis Lab. A superb foul-weather pilot, Walker specialized in de-icing experiments at Lewis. Walker was a Pennsylvanian, but he talked like a West Virginian, and had a slow easy-going manner and a toothy smile. But Jones and Walker were new to Edwards, and the demands on NACA were increasing. So I had my chest taped and flew anyway.

My flight that day in the X-1, as planned, was nothing sensational; simply a check-out flight. By then, not surprisingly, I had acquired a reputation for encountering an emergency on first flight. I was determined that the X-1 check-flight would go off without a hitch.

After I had dogged the X-1 door in place, there was still a long and monotonous climb to our drop altitude of 30,000 feet. I snapped my lap belt and shoulder harness and settled back, sweeping my eyes across the instrument panel, checking the pressures in the rocket-fuel tanks and other systems. Everything was normal, or as near-normal as it is possible to come in a research airplane.

The X-1 was old then—going on six years—but she was still the fastest and best research airplane at Edwards. The main reason for this was the fact that the plane was a model of simplicity. When Bell had been assigned the job of designing her in 1944, they had ably and swiftly tamed a wide frontier of aerodynamic unknowns. They knew that a .50 caliber bullet had been fired supersonically, so they shaped the X-1 like a bullet. They stuck on a pair of thin, straight, stubby wings and a Navy-sponsored rocket engine, built by Reaction Motors, Inc., a small outfit working out of a garage in New Jersey. From beginning to end, Bell's Chief Engineer Robert Stanley insisted on simplicity. The control system, instrument panel, landing gear, everything about the plane, were deliberately and forcefully held to a minimum of complexity.

Stanley's approach to research airplanes had paid rich dividends a hundred times over. After Yeager had cracked the sonic wall, and Pete Everest had climbed to 73,000 feet in the X-1, a dozen other test pilots had flown the ship during 1948,'49, and '50. Glamorous Glennis was in the Smithsonian, but our X-1 had already logged a total of maybe forty-five flights. They had provided tons of data without a single flight casualty. It would continue to fly off and on over the next few years, providing data in the trans-sonic area and a never-ending challenge for its pilots. In its day, the X-1 was the king of the hot-rods.

Approaching launch altitude, I got set for my first X-1 drop, priming the rocket engine, building up pressures in the fuel system. My chase pilots that day were Air Force Majors Jack Ridley, an old X-1 hand, and Pete Everest. Tucked in close under the tail of the B-29, they watched the puffs of vaporized fuel snaking out prime lines and reported: "Prime looks good."

B-29 pilot Pete Sellers began the countdown. Suddenly I recalled a humorous incident which had happened one time when Bob Champine, the pilot I replaced at NACA, had reached this stage of an X-1 flight. It had been no fault of the plane, just a simple language snafu. An ex-Navy pilot, Bob always spoke in Navy terminology in the air. Seconds before launch, the pressure gauges fell off, and he decided to cancel the flight. From the cockpit of the X-1 he snapped on the radio: "Secure the drop." Dick Payne, in the bomb-bay compartment, was then working loose the pins in the shackles which held the X-1 in its belly nest. Accustomed to working with Air Force pilots, Payne thought "secure the drop" meant "go ahead and complete the drop." Champine had loosened his lap belt and was on the point of crawling out of the X-1 side door to return to the bomb-bay when his plane suddenly fell away from the bomber. Luckily he had time to snap himself down. From then on, "secure the drop" was used to rib all of us ex-Navy types.

To achieve a good launch from the mother plane it is vital that the research plane be in proper trim. This means that the plane's controls should be set for full fuel tanks. A pilot could correct the control trim after launch, but an overly nose-up or nose-down setting at the moment of launch could cause the plane to take off on a wild gyration.

The X-1 stabilizer was always set on 'trim' on the ground before take-off. That morning I had watched the engineer working with a template and inclinometer, attempting to align the stabilizer chord with the wing chord. I had done this many times on models in wind tunnels and knew it was quite easy to make a mistake. I had asked a few questions but the engineer replied, in effect, that he knew what he was doing. I was still feeling my way then with the ground personnel. I let it go. As it turned out, the engineer had made a mistake. The X-1 was launched with a full degree in excess of normal stabilizer trim. The result was spectacular. When I dropped away from the mother plane, the X-1 pitched, stalled, and flipped on its back.

Chase pilots Pete Everest and Jack Bidley, who had been flying beside me, quickly searched the skies, wondering where I disappeared to. When Pete spotted the X-1 below them, upside down, he was dumbstruck. At last, he found his voice and, with the aplomb he could always muster, spoke on the radio: "Well, that's certainly a new way to launch!"

There was no use in blowing my stack, I thought. The launch was hopelessly botched. It was now clear to me that on first flight of any plane I was jinxed, and there was no reason to fight it. The thing to do now, I thought, was to make a respectable recovery from an impossible start. Get the plane right-side up, light off the rockets, and go for broke. I rolled out, cranking the stabilizer back to normal trim, and then I fired all four rocket barrels. When they caught, the X-1 lurched ahead, picking up speed. I held the nose steady and climbed. But there was no chance for high speed on that flight.

During the unorthodox launch and recovery, the X-1 had fallen too far into the thick atmosphere. Drinking fuel at better than a ton a minute, her engine, I knew, would sputter and die in another eighty seconds. I focused all my attention on maintaining a positive gravity (positive G) pull on the airplane. If I porpoised and lost it, including weightlessness (zero G)—that unusual sensation one sometimes experiences in a fast-falling elevator—the fuel flow to the engine would stop, closing it down prematurely. At least I would try to avoid that.

I did. I was hitting about Mach .9 and going through 41,000 feet when the last of the fuel whipped through the engines. The four barrels of the rocket engine blew out almost simultaneously, each one making a noise like a pop-gun. Following that, the X-1 was a tomb of silence. Except for the crackle of static in my earphone, and a gentle scrubbing of air on the fuselage skin, there was no earthly sound. I was now flying a glider—one of the world's heaviest and fastest—which I would have to sail back to Rogers Dry Lake alongside Edwards Base.

If misfortune had dogged my flight thus far, it was nothing compared to what happened next. Quick as a wink, on base leg for landing, the whole windshield was blanketed by a thick coating of ice. I was sealed in—blind as a bat. This time the cause was not attributable to the failure of machinery. The X-1 defogging system was simply too weak. On humid days it was not unusual for considerable moisture to collect inside the X-1 cockpit on the climb to pilot boarding-point while the door was off. At high altitude this moisture turned to ice. It was my first-flight luck to go aloft on a very humid day.

When I reported an iced windshield on the radio, I received little sympathy from my fellow pilots. Jack Ridley laughed over the radio and, in his strange, falsetto voice, cracked: "Funny, isn't it? Same thing happened to me the other day." Both pilots joined me quickly, however, and pulled their fighters close in to my wingtips, standing by to guide me back to the lake-bed landing, if necessary. An old hand with iced windshields by now, I banked around and, with help from Ridley, lined up on the lake.

By Hollywood standards, by now I should have been overwhelmed by fear. Beads of perspiration should have been popping out on my forehead, and my hand should have been trembling on the stick. Alas, such was not the case, nor have I ever known it to be amongst my fellow test pilots.

Pilots are occasionally startled like everyone else. The normal reaction to being startled, like the child's, is to look for the cause. The pilot learns from long experience to determine this cause swiftly and positively. Then, in place of the child's immature laughter, he turns to action. There are set procedures to put matters straight again. If, for example, a fire-warning light suddenly flashes on the instrument panel of a propeller-driven airplane, there are pre-scribed routines. The pilot shuts down the engine, cuts off the fuel lines, dumps a fire-extinguisher foam into the cowling, and feathers the propeller so that it does not cause unnecessary drag on the surviving engines. Then, if necessary, he must look for a field and land. If a pilot is certain of a bad fire in a jet, there is one prescribed procedure: get out fast in the ejection seat.

When startled by an emergency, pilots whose minds dissolve into a frenzy which delays, interferes with, or prohibits corrective steps ought, I believe, to get into some other business. Beads of sweat on the forehead should come only from hard work or too much clothing; a trembling hand on the stick only from a hangover.

Men who climb mountains don't experience fear when faced by some crisis. They take the necessary steps to avoid the crisis. Experienced divers don't melt into a panic when they face an aggressive shark underwater. They take the necessary counter-action. Ship captains don't give up in despair when their craft founder. They launch the lifeboats.

These are cases where the emergency comes swiftly and in an environment that seems to attract the purple-prose experts. But men and women in other walks of life face grave, unheralded emergencies every day of the week. Consider the ponderous emergencies big financiers must slide into as they deal on the stock exchange day by day. Or surgeons who probe the human body, or mothers who must deal promptly with gagging children. We never think of these people as dissolving into fits of fear, yet their responsibility may outweigh the lone pilot in his craft by a factor of a thousand or ten thousand. If something goes wrong, they take the necessary steps to settle it favorably. The incident is rarely noted publicly, as are the pilot's emergencies.

I suppose there are many people who go through all of life beset by a variety of fears. It could be fear of disease, of professional failure; fear of love or of not being loved; fear of the neighbors; fear of government, or their leaders, or fear of fear itself. All these people, in my book, would fare better in this life if they probed the cause of this fear, if they don't know it already. Once the cause were known, they could, or should, take the proper action to right the situation, and rid themselves of it. This could even apply to those people who live in slave nations, under a constant so-called reign of fear of a different order. Witness the birth of this nation.

I have been startled in an airplane many times. This, I may say, is almost routine for the experimental test pilot. But I can honestly say I have never experienced real fear in the air. The reason is that I have never run out of things to do. Someday I might. Conceivably, I might be locked helplessly in the cockpit of a burning airplane in a death spiral, unable to take any further action to save my life. Facing certain death which I was powerless to forestall, I might very well be overcome by fear. But for me this would be a very special kind of fear—a fear of coming face-to-face with a strict God who might look askance on the ways of a test pilot—and not be talked out of it. But so far I have been spared that ultimate confrontation.

What concerned me that afternoon on my first flight in the X-1 was the landing—the possibility I might wind up in the ever-growing 'Nose Wheel Club.' The X-1 had a most peculiar behavior pattern just at the moment of touchdown. In the final flare-out, when the three wheels were reaching for the ground, the plane sometimes bounced skyward without warning. Ordinarily a pilot in a plane that behaved thus would push forward on the stick and bring the nose down. If he did this in the X-1, the nose slammed hard and caved in the nose wheel. That master pilot, Yeager, had discovered by his native skill that if the pilot were to violate all his instincts and pull back on the stick, the plane would recover and grease on with no damage. Only Yeager and a few other pilots had avoided the Nose Wheel Club. It was no disgrace to prang a nose wheel, and to avoid it was a fine point of flying indeed, but I intended, as a matter of pride, to stay out of this club. The iced windshield, however, vastly complicated my first X-1 landing and made my nomination almost certain.

As my altimeter unwound rapidly, I searched the X-1 cock-pit for a rag, a tool, anything I could use to rub off the coat of ice. There was nothing. I had no handkerchief in my flying coveralls. But wait . . .

I loosened my shoulder straps and bent over, pulling at the shoestrings of the low-cut oxford shoe on my right foot, thanking my lucky stars I hadn't worn flying boots. In two seconds I had the shoe off. Then I took off my right sock and replaced my bare foot on the right rudder bar. The metal was frightfully cold. My foot clung to the bar stickily, like one's hand on the bottom of an ice tray just out of the freezer. Using my cotton sock as a scraper, I rubbed hard in one spot on the front wind-shield, just over the instrument panel.

By the time we had descended to 5000 feet—gliding like a brick—I had worn a small hole in the ice, enough to permit me to see the X-1's nose and the long desert lake bed stretching ahead. I squinted one eye and fixed the other on the small hole like a peep-sight, lining up the parallel black lines painted on the dry-lake floor. Ridley was droning off my decreasing altitude, but I didn't need him. I flared out at 135 miles an hour. I brought the stick back slowly; the airspeed got low and the right wing dropped sharply, scraping the desert floor as I touched down. I threw the stick to the left at just about the moment the nose wheel touched. The X-1 rolled out straight and level, rumbling firmly across the hard-packed silt. The nose wheel held.

The usual caravan of vehicles, trailing a huge rooster-tail of dust, tore out across the lake and clustered around the small white bird. When I undogged the X-1 door, a mechanic lowered it to the ground. I climbed out—with my right foot bare as a baby's behind.

Someone shouted: "Where is your right shoe?"

When I held it aloft for all to see, another voice cried: "Barefoot boy with cheek." Then they all broke into laughter. I knew that at Edwards, at least, I had it made.

14: The Need for Speed

The desert spring had fused almost imperceptibly with early summer. The temperature climbed to a routine 105 degrees in the shade. Edwards became a hell of wind and sand. The wind moaned through the cracks in the temporary buildings; the sand and dust heaped in piles on the sills and in the corners. I considered it a minor miracle that the mechanics could keep the jewel-like machinery of the research airplanes operating in such conditions. We pilots retreated, between flights, to the comfort and cleanliness of air-conditioning. One day in late May, 1951, I was killing time in Walt Williams' office, sipping coffee and discussing the future of the research airplane program which had by now become inextricably entwined with my own future.

"Walt, I'm telling you we have got to move in and do something about Bell's X-2. The whole deal is going sour."

My feet were propped up on the edge of Williams' desk. An NACA research airplane pilot at Edwards got to be an old hand fast in those days. I had been there almost a year: I was an old hand. I had accumulated more than half a hundred flights in the X-4, X-1, Skyrocket, and D-558-I. I had flown supersonic. I was becoming wiser in the ways of government and industry politics. One had to at NACA, because the agency was caught in the middle of all the political currents. The X-2 situation was one of those touchy ones.

NACA existed to serve the industry. It received its planes from the military services which, in turn, were customers of the industry. Thus it was dependent on everyone for survival and, as I learned, it was important not to bite the many hands that fed it. The competition among the aircraft companies striving to sell their products to the military was intense, as was the competition among the various military services. Thus there were always a hundred minor controversies going on. We at NACA, to survive, tried to remain aloof from these internecine battles, taking protection behind the cloak of science. The information we garnered was passed out impartially to all of industry and the military services. If the military asked our advice about a certain competitive airplane, we responded in double-talk and purposely contrived, abstruse mathematical formulae. We had to do this. The governing body of NACA itself was a committee composed of the leaders in aviation. Any conclusion NACA reached was instantly known everywhere in the aviation world.

It was like working in a fish bowl.

All of this naturally generated conservatism within NACA. Before we passed judgment or recommended a course of action, we had first to weigh the impact on half a hundred points of contact. Thus, while we flew fast in the air, we moved at a snail's pace on the ground.

The data from my flights were accumulating by the bushel-basketfuls. But all of these were concerned with the subsonic, sonic, and trans-sonic zones, about which we were beginning to know a great deal. In our thoroughness, I felt, we were losing sight of the forest for the trees. The new supersonic Century Series fighters, which could outfly our research airplanes, were almost on the point of factory roll-out. There were a thousand different things we didn't know at Mach 1.5 and above. Two especially grave unknowns loomed before us: high-speed instability and aerodynamic heating. What we needed was much more speed to stay out in front of the combat airplanes. In short, our research airplanes were too slow, and NACA was not, in my opinion, doing enough about it.

After the fabulous success of the X-1, the Air Force had invited Bell to build a second generation of straight-wing, rocket-powered X-1 airplanes. These were to be larger, faster, with longer-burning rocket engines. The planes were to have a 'combat cockpit,' an uninspired idea of someone who thought the craft might be used for brief high-speed reconnaissance bursts over enemy territory. These airplanes were designated the X-1-A, X-1-B, X-1-C, and X-1-D. Some said these planes might fly at Mach 3—three times the speed of sound. At the very least we knew they would nearly double the speed of the original X-1s.

These planes were conceived shortly after Yeager's historic flight in the X-1. By then the ingenious team sparked by Bob Stanley, which had pioneered the X-1, had left Bell. Advanced airplanes are not the product of a company, but the product of men with boldness and imagination. The Air Force blew hot and cold on these advanced X-1s and supplied money, virtually a month-by-month dole. As time passed, inevitably the airplanes grew in complexity and they fell far behind schedule. Even the third model of the original X-1, which was being converted to a low-pressure fuel system, had not yet been delivered to NACA.

The same fate had overtaken the much-heralded X-2, which I was supposed to fly for NACA in due course. The X-2 had been designed years earlier, only a few months after the original X-1s. Two ships were under construction. In concept the X-2 represented a tremendous jump over the X-1. On paper it had over eight times the power—a 15,000-pound-thrust Curtiss-Wright engine—sharply swept wings, and an escape system—a nose that could be separated from the main body of the airplane in emergency. The X-2 was to be built of stainless steel in order to withstand the tremendous frictional heat it was expected to encounter at its maximum speed of nearly Mach 3. Its windshield was to be tinted to resist solar radiation, which might be a menace at the X-2's maximum altitude of 150,000 feet. However, the X-2 was already three years behind schedule.

Altogether, then, Bell had seven rocket airplanes in the plant in various stages of construction. All of them were capable of flying at over twice the speed of sound. All of them were behind schedule, and falling farther behind every day. Meanwhile, at Edwards, no one had yet exceeded Yeager's speed of Mach 1.4, set in the original X-1. The new military fighters were designed to exceed that speed. Even faster military fighters were then in the advance design stage.

"If we don't watch out, Walt," I said, "we're going to be coming up with these data a day late and a dollar short. The gap is closing."

Walt Williams, of course, knew this as well as I. But there was little that NACA could do about it. The situation was an 'Air Force problem.' The Air Force supplied the planes. The Air Force's main attention was focused on producing enough airplanes, right that minute, to fight the Korean War.

"Walt," I said. "We have the technical say-so with these aircraft. We can make recommendations through headquarters in Washington. Why don't we propose that I be assigned to the Bell plant and bird-dog this thing in our behalf?"

"Nobody would buy that, Scotty," Williams said. "We can make technical judgments when invited to do so, but we can't stick a man in the plant full-time."

"Why not?" I asked. "We need these planes in a hurry, don't we?"

"Well," Williams said, "I really don't think you know what you are proposing. Geez. Can you imagine an NACA man in the Bell plant? And you of all people?"

I had developed something of a reputation as a driver and an iconoclast. It was not strictly my doing. Part of it was the fact that I had arrived coincidentally with the outbreak of the Korean War, and the new sense of urgency had come at the same time. It was a fact, however, that I frequently challenged the accepted method. Like many other pilots, I particularly deplored the growing gap between desk designer and pilot. Machinery was being put in illogical places with little thought for pilot efficiency or maintenance ease; the mounting overemphasis on safety had reached the point where engineers were put-ting cotter keys in cotter keys. All of this was slowing us down at a time when we urgently needed to be picking up speed.

As for my proposal to go to Bell to bird-dog the lagging rocket-plane program, on reflection I am certain now that it was the goal of my life trying to peck through its shell prematurely.

I realize now the time was far from propitious. The X-1, X-2 thing was a mess, and in time it would become worse. Had I gone there, I might have helped some. But I might also have fallen far short of my dream. I let the matter drop. Williams had been around NACA far longer than Scott Crossfield. I knew and admired him as a man of action. I was certain that if he could perceive even the faintest glimmer of hope of NACA's bailing out the rocket planes, he would be in favor of positive action, and in spite of the prevailing conservatism within the agency, would press for it.

Obviously, the safest course as far as Bell was concerned was hands off.

"Besides, Scott," Williams said, dangling a diverting sweet, "you have the Skyrocket program."

I couldn't argue that point.

The Skyrocket then was the one bright ray of hope on an otherwise darkly blotched horizon. Douglas Aircraft was a big, bustling corporation with enormous military and commercial business. The company had withstood the postwar aviation famine quite well. In fact, it had thrived on production orders for DC-6 transports, and Navy carrier-launched fighters. At Douglas there had been money and engineering talent enough to sustain a healthy research and development program, which included, of course, the D-558-II Skyrocket. During the fall of 1950 the emphasis had been placed on the conversion of the original jet-only (JATO boosted) Skyrocket to an air-launch, all-rocket vehicle, which conceivably might reach Mach 2 and 100,000 feet. On paper it was easily capable of shattering Yeager's X-1 speed record of Mach 1.4 and Everest's altitude record of 73,000 feet. The Navy and Douglas were anxious.

Bridgeman and the Douglas crew had arrived with the all-rocket Skyrocket in January of 1951. The plane had been parked in the Douglas hangar next door, alongside the older jet-rocket version of the Skyrocket. When the word got around, it caused a sensation. I hurried over to take a look at the ship, which I would fly soon after Bridgeman had established its 'envelope,' and had, incidentally, scratched up some new speed and altitude records for the Navy. The ship was dazzlingly white. Its lines were similar to the old Skyrocket, except that it was cleaner. The jet engine scoops were gone.

When Bridgeman first climbed into the Skyrocket, snugged in the belly of the mother plane, Yeager and Everest flew chase for the Air Force with more than casual interest. However, the first blush paled. The Skyrocket was new and untried. Like all new research airplanes, it was dogged by trouble during the de-bugging stage. During January, February, and March, 1951, Bridgeman had gone aloft six times in the mother plane. Six times the launch had been canceled at the last minute.

On the seventh attempt, in April, a hair-raising event occurred that will never be forgotten at Edwards. When the mother plane bore down over the launch point, all gauges were in the green.

Bridgeman, who through no fault of his own was gaining a reputation for being a Reluctant Dragon, was pressing hard for a launch. At the last second a tank pressure fell off. Grudgingly Bridgeman reported: "No drop. This is an abort."

He prepared to go through abort procedures to return to the base. Then to his horror he heard the mother-plane pilot, George Jansen, ticking off the launch countdown on the radio: "Ten, nine, eight, seven . . ."

"No drop! No drop!" Bridgeman shouted over the radio. Everyone heard him but Jansen, who had keyed his radio mike for the countdown. Nobody, not even the star Bridgeman, could get through to George. Frantically, Bridgeman brought the plane's ailing machinery to life and squared away for an undesired launch.

Falling away from the mother plane, Bridgeman lighted the rocket engines. The Skyrocket roared heavenward, just short of Yeager's record speed of Mach 1.4. Bridgeman growled over the radio:

"Goddammit, George, I told you not to drop me."

"You got keen friends, Bridgeman," said Everest, who was flying chase that day.

After that incident, countdowns were shortened; research airplanes were equipped with a switch on the instrument panel, connected to a light on the mother-plane instrument panel. A green light meant the rocket pilot was ready to launch, and only if it was on would he be launched. And so far as I know, no pilot after that was dropped against his will.

The Douglas test program dragged on through May and June. At NACA we became very anxious to take over the airplane. In fact, in an unprecedented move NACA headquarters wrote Douglas telling them, in effect, to hurry up. We urgently needed the Douglas plane for high-speed flight data. Another reason was that the word had gotten around that Bridgeman was afraid of the airplane. This was unfortunate because Bridgeman, I thought, was one very superlative pilot. He later admitted that flying the Skyrocket unnerved him. But the delay in the Douglas flight program was not his fault. It was the usual work of the gremlins which flock to research planes like seven-year locusts.

Not long after my chat with Walt Williams the slow-starting Douglas Skyrocket program blazed into a stem-winding finish. In the next four powered flights, the last of which took place on August 15, 1951, Bridgeman flew the Skyrocket to a speed of Mach 1.87 and an altitude of 79,000 feet. Both figures were records by a wide margin. Bridgeman assured his place in the Hall of Fame, and demonstrated that the Skyrocket was all that they had hoped. Bill went on to the X-3 and some brilliant airmanship. The Navy, now holding the official records, beamed, and Douglas released a flood of press handouts. With little ceremony NACA took over the plane and mother ship, assigned me as Skyrocket pilot, and I got set to probe the high-speed mysteries the Skyrocket had already brought to light.

These mysteries somehow leaked to the press, which sensationally proclaimed that Bridgeman had discovered a phenomenon known as 'Supersonic Yaw.' Actually we had expected it.

Bridgeman had expected it. It was one of those unknowns about which we urgently needed data. Reduced to simplest terms, 'Supersonic Yaw' meant that airplanes nearly became directionally unstable at high speed in thin air.

The nose turned sideways and the plane skidded obliquely through the air. What we had to do then was to find some means of improving the controls or the design of airplanes to avoid it, or else develop a technique for living with it. This was one reason alone for the need for speed. The same thing could happen to our military planes, causing needless death in peace and war.

Following Bridgeman's footsteps, I made four quick flights in the all-rocket Skyrocket. The first flight was, in a way, a milestone for me. I broke my first-flight jinx, launching and flying with no unusual difficulty. I achieved a speed of Mach 1.6 and an altitude of 60,000 feet. These were not records, but we at NACA were not out to set records. We wanted to find out in actual flight about Supersonic Yaw, among many other things.

On all flights the Skyrocket was loaded with hundreds of pounds of delicate instruments which recorded every significant fact about the flight: speed, altitude, G forces, pressures, air flows. Bridgeman had intuitively conceived a method of taking the plane to its near limits without meeting disaster. Under his skillful coaching, I successfully carried out his idea, and the information we recorded kept the engineers busy for months. After these four flights the plane was laid up for some badly needed repairs which had been deferred during our quick investigation.

One day not long after I had completed the last of these flights, I stopped at the coffee machine to pass the time of day with Hubert Drake and Bob Carmen, NACA's long-range design 'dreamers.' In a friendly way they probed for first-hand information about the Skyrocket.

"How'd it go?" Drake asked.

"It was all right," I said. "You people and Douglas had already sensed what to do and I just did it. No special trick. We got the data, but the problem is that the airplane is already old for its time. The plane is obsolete for those speeds."

"Yes, I know," said Drake.

"Someday I hope we can get ahead of this game," I said. "I would like to see a research airplane built from scratch that can fly like it is supposed to—stable, that is—and far enough ahead of the game to provide some useful data to industry. In another few months they'll be catching up with us."

"You ought to come down and see our stuff," Carmen said.

"What have you got?"

"We think we have an airplane that can perform at Mach 6 and fifty miles," Drake said.

"How do you get that kind of performance?"

"It's simple. First off, the mother plane is a rocket plane. She has five Viking engines. The research airplane, a modified X-2 with a one-rocket engine, rides piggy-back. You take off and launch at Mach 3 and about 70,000 feet. The research airplane goes on up to maybe Mach 6 and maybe 250,000 feet. It's all done with existing hardware."

I had a vision then of trying to make ready and light off the five temperamental rocket engines on the mother plane. The effort would be something like the invasion of Europe. The odds that everything would work, and that the research airplane would launch—and light off—were, conservatively, about a hundred to one. Still, it was an idea. Dreamers should never be discouraged. An engineering analysis of the Columbus voyage had shown it couldn't be done.

"Well, why don't you write it up and send in a report?" I asked. "God knows someone ought to try to get ahead of the game. That would be a big jump forward."

"We did write it up," Drake said, crumpling his paper coffee cup. He aimed carefully but missed the big G.I. can. "What happened?"

"We turned it in to Walt Williams," Drake said. "That was back in November, 1950. He read it and said it was 'premature.' Told us to pigeon-hole it for a while."

The Drake-Carmen report was still in a pigeon-hole, gathering dust. In later years, Walt Williams still felt it was wise to delay that report. Maybe he was right. Had it been brought forward in late 1950, NACA might have been laughed out of school.

No one else was ready.

15: Disaster on the Race Track

The success of the Navy-sponsored Skyrocket caused great consternation in the Air Force camp at Edwards. Suddenly two of Bell's rocket planes were made ready—or almost ready, as it turned out—for flight. One was the long-awaited X-1, model 3 (called 'Queenie'), with a low-pressure fuel system, thus putting its debut years behind those of its sister-ships, Glamorous Glennis and the NACA's X-1. The second Bell plane was the X-1-D, one of the second-generation X-1s with the larger fuel tank and the military cockpit. In the strange way of schedules, the X-1-D was completed before the X-1-A and X-1-B. The planned X-1-C was never built. Its parts and funds were cannibalized to complete the A, B and D models.

The X-1-D was a new animal, a strikingly fast, dangerous research airplane. On paper it could reach Mach 2.5 or maybe Mach 3. Like most of the planes arriving at Edwards in those tumultuous, fast-moving days, its design was already outmoded. We knew that the X-1-D would be unstable at very high Mach numbers. Its new fuel system, nearly identical to that in Queenie, was untried, and full of bugs. Under such circumstances, caution was the better part of valor. But no. At Edwards occasionally the temptation to throw caution to the winds was overwhelming.

As Pete Everest has written in his book, The Fastest Man Alive, mincing no words: "... we had a chance to set another record that would be much harder to beat." Everest goes on: "Bell flew half a dozen tests to prove the new rocket ship's flying characteristics and tested the rocket engine in run-ups on the ground." The historical accounts show that in actual fact two test flights were made, neither of them thorough or conclusive because of pressure of schedule and poverty. On the first, the X-1-D was carried aloft, empty of fuels, cut loose, and steered back to earth, as a glider, by Skip Ziegler. On the second, the X-1-D was fueled for a powered flight with Everest but aborted when the fuel system malfunctioned. The tests had been, to say the least, inconclusive.

Then, as Everest writes, "I was selected to take it up and see what it could do wide open." In short, Everest elected to take over the X-1-D, which had never been flown under power, and never flown at all by Everest, on a maximum-speed run on first powered flight. That he agreed to this at all, I think, demonstrates remarkable courage. That the Air Force would sanction such a first flight has always been a mystery to me. They were smarting badly from Bridgeman's licking.

That day in August, 1951, was a dark one in Edwards' history and a very lucky one for Pete Everest. Al Boyd, then a brigadier general, and still commander of Edwards, elected to fly chase. Jack Ridley was co-pilot of the mother ship, a B-50, a more powerful version of the B-29. At 10,000 feet Everest put on his helmet and crawled from the mother ship's bomb-bay into the X-1-D cockpit. He noticed right off that the rocket plane's gauges were in the red. There was a leak; the tank pressures were sagging.

Everest climbed back into the B-50 bomb-bay compartment for a conference with Jack Ridley. They agreed "reluctantly," Everest reports, that the flight should be canceled. Everest returned to the X-1-D cockpit to jettison fuel. Standing in the seat of the plane, he reached down to pressurize the tanks. As he did, a bone-jarring explosion shook the X-1-D and nearly threw Everest to the floor of the cockpit. A tongue of fire licked into the mother ship's bomb-bay compartment. Everest leaped from the X-1-D cockpit into the B-50 bomber.

Seconds later, Jack Ridley pulled an emergency lever and the burning X-1-D fell away from the bomber, trailed by bits and pieces of the B-50 which were shattered loose by the force of the rocket-ship explosion. The $5 million X-1-D crumpled onto the desert floor, a costly disaster on the race track.

It was lucky for Everest that the X-1-D blew up when it did. In the haste to launch the flight, the plane had only half a load of liquid oxygen. Had Everest launched, the X-1-D would have been so much out of balance that it would have spun in, instantly and uncontrollably. The ship had no ejection seat.

Joe Cannon, a test pilot for Bell, had been chosen to make the initial demonstration flights in the Queenie. With the new low-pressure fuel system and larger fuel tanks, some thought that Queenie might crack Mach 2. This would put her a shade beyond the record Bridgeman made in the Skyrocket. Queenie had 'U.S. Air Force' painted in large letters on the fuselage.

Whether Cannon or some Air Force pilot, such as Yeager or Everest, flew it, the Air Force technically would regain the record. After that, NACA would take charge of the plane for high-speed instability and aerodynamic heating investigations. I was to fly the Queenie for NACA. The new low-pressure fuel system in Queenie gave much trouble. Bell ground engineer Q. C. Harvey, a fox-terrier type with limitless nervous energy, was nearly frantic from the thinly-veiled pressure. The Bell ground crews cut corners. In early November on the second 'heavyweight captive' flight—a trip to launch altitude with fuel tanks loaded for test purposes—Joe Cannon could not jettison the plane's fuel. The B-29 mother plane returned to earth, bearing Queenie fully loaded with volatile fuel.

It was something of a trick to purge the little planes of fuel on the ground. The B-29 moved into the dump area, still mated. Cannon began the ground-jettison routine. Suddenly a tremendous explosion rocked Edwards. Queenie and the mother plane were enveloped by swirling, vaporizing liquid oxygen.

Cannon had removed the side door of the X-1. Through the fog the men saw him come through the opening, feet first. Then they saw his head and heard him yelling: "Get the hell out of here! She's going to go!"

Joe Cannon scrambled down to the ground and ran away from Queenie as fast as his legs could take him. The concrete ramp was flooded with the slippery, dangerous Lox. He fell headlong into a puddle of fuel. The Lox burned through his clothing and froze his skin, putting him out of action for nearly a year.

Queenie and the mother ship went up in a burst of smoke and flames. Fortunately, no one was killed. The loss of the $4 million Queenie was severely felt at NACA. The Navy retained the speed and altitude records. The official investigations into the X-1-D and Queenie explosions went on for months and ultimately delayed the delivery of the X-1-A and X-1-B nearly two years. After the official report came out, all rocket airplanes of this series were extensively modified. At NACA our own X-1, in which I had completed about a dozen flights since last overhaul, was considered 'fatigued' and was withdrawn from active flying. We launched a project to redesign and rebuild our X-1. The plane was redesignated the X-1-E, and years later it got into the air. But it never really produced again. For all practical purposes it was retired that fall.

Along about the same time—that grim fall of 1951—we gave up hope on still another promising airplane. This was the celebrated Douglas X-3, a weird-looking, needle-nose craft with two jet engines and brief straight wings. The X-3 was designed to cruise for long periods at very high speed, hopefully near Mach 2. But she had fallen victim to the cotter-key crowd. No more compli-cated, botched-up, dangerous airplane was ever produced, unless it was the XF-92-A, which I shall deal with in time.

Bridgeman was waiting patiently at Douglas to make the first flights on the long-delayed X-3. I talked to him about the plane occasionally, since like the Skyrocket it was ultimately slated for NACA. It was possible that I might be named X-3 pilot along with my other duties. In time, Bridgeman made twenty flights in the plane. Happy to be rid of it then, he turned it over to Chuck Yeager and Pete Everest, and never again flew an experimental air-plane. Yeager and Everest flew the plane three times each. "It was one of the most difficult airplanes I have ever seen," Everest said.

Apart from its sheer mechanical complexity, the basic trouble with the X-3 was that it was underpowered. The high-thrust engines, which had been planned for it, fell behind schedule and then were canceled because of lack of funds; the interim engines used yielded only about fifty per cent of the desired thrust. Thus it required every trick in the book to get the heavy X-3 into the air and keep it there without falling out. When Yeager and Everest, with few regrets, turned the plane over to NACA, we tried unsuccessfully to fix it. Walker made about twenty flights. The X-3 became a glamorous Hangar Queen, useful mainly for publicity photographs. I never got to fly it.

Thus the Douglas Skyrocket became by default the lone high-speed workhorse at Edwards. I was the lone jockey for a while. As the weeks sped by, the NACA Skyrocket team began to mesh with carrier-deck efficiency. We often flew the Skyrocket every other day—such 'turn-around' time was then considered a near-miracle—probing the dark mysteries high in the sky. No Skyrocket flight was ever routine. But I got to know the ship so well that I could land it dead-stick on the dry lake and coast right up on the NACA parking ramp in front of the hangar door—without brakes! This saved my hard-working ground crew the trouble of going out to the lake with a tow-tractor.

The floor of the Bell plant in Buffalo was immaculately clean. In one corner behind a curtain the shell of the X-2 lay awaiting inspection. In another corner engineers had rigged a simulated cockpit and control system. I was there with Walt Williams and other NACA and Air Force engineers to pass an interim judgment on this much-delayed airplane. I was especially interested because if the X-2 were ever finished I would fly her after Skip Ziegler had made the demonstrations.

I walked up to a mechanic, working near a row of dry-cell batteries. I knew these batteries were to be installed in the X-2 to supply power for the control system. I picked up a battery.

"What's this for?" I said to the mechanic.

"My God!" he yelled. His face was white. "Don't pick that up. It's delicate. It's for the X-2 control system. If you jar it, it might break." It was a new and sophisticated kind of battery.

"You don't mean it?" I said. Then I smashed the battery down on the bench. Sure enough, five plates broke and the battery short-circuited.

Later I learned from a Bell engineer that the delicate batteries had been shipped to Bell from the manufacturer in a nitroglycerine truck. I said to the engineer: "You really expect to put that kind of stuff in an airplane that will be subject to God knows what kind of loads and shocks in the air?"

"Don't ask me, Scotty," he said. "I just work here and we have a thousand bosses in every corner of the government."

While the X-2 control system was a studied attempt to make a tremendous step, there was much we did not like about it. I noticed that when I operated the stick in the simulator cockpit, it whipped. The simulator, for demonstration purposes, was set to operate only at full design loads, which was far from a realistic measure. At my insistence the simulator was rigged to carry low-load conditions. Guessing what force the whipping stick might display, I asked Pete Everest, a member of the Air Force inspection party, to get in the cockpit and try it.

The demonstration was far more dramatic than I could have hoped. When Everest pulled on the stick, the electrical units took hold, the stick whipped violently, and Everest, a small man, was thrown clear out of the cockpit. This highly sophisticated control system, which had already cost $4 million, was symptomatic of the disease that had drained the X-2 program (many programs, in fact) of its vitality. It obviously could not be made suitable for the X-2 in time, and although it meant some further delay on delivery of the airplane, Bell was asked to come up with a reliable and simple control system. Under the revised plan X-2 number 1 was to be hastily equipped with cables, which would not overly delay the glide tests scheduled to take place at Edwards. X-2 number 2 would have a hydraulic-control system. Similar units would be installed in X-2 number 1 after the glide tests.

The X-2 with cable controls arrived at Edwards in June of 1952, hung in the belly of the B-50 mother plane. I should say the shell of the X-2 arrived. The lagging engine (itself overly sophisticated) was still on the test bench at Curtiss-Wright. In its place was concrete ballast. Everybody at Edwards must have turned out to see the X-2. Few of them realized then that the ship was jinxed. They saw only a sleek, swept-wing airplane, looking as though it were moving supersonically while sitting still on the ground.

The X-2 had the conventional nose wheel; and the main landing gear had been made a broad ski which protruded from the fuselage just below the wing center-section. The main purpose of the glide test was to check on the nose-wheel ski concept.

Bets were laid when Ziegler went aloft in the X-2 on his first flight. It was important that the gear work perfectly. A powerless rocket plane landing dead-stick cannot go around for another try.

I watched from the sidelines. The X-2 was heavy, and the B-50 mother plane labored to reach launch altitude of 30,000 feet. Then I saw the X-2, looking like a tiny white toy in the deep blue sky, fall away cleanly. Powerless, silent, Skip guided the plane toward Rogers Dry Lake. His flare-out, at 200 miles an hour, looked good. The skid and nose-wheel popped out. The X-2 touched and the nose wheel failed. When it collapsed, the plane churned around on a wingtip, gouging a hole in the desert runway.

The plane was repaired and the landing-gear unit improved. They also added 'whisker skids'—smaller skis midway under each side of the wing. Skip Ziegler tested the new gear without incident. Then Pete Everest made one hair-raising test—the left whisker ski extended only after the right ski had jarred the earth—and the X-2 was shipped back to the factory for installation of the new hydraulic-control system and the rocket engine.

Months later the plane was ready for 'captive' fuel tests. These were conducted not at Edwards but over Lake Ontario, near the Bell factory, because of Ziegler's dedicated zeal to get the program rolling. On the second captive fuel test in May, 1953, an explosion ripped through the X-2. The blast and flames reached into the mother ship's bomb-bay, killing Skip Ziegler and a Bell crewman, Frank Walko. The X-2 was cut loose and plunged flaming and exploding into Lake Ontario. The B-50, blown skyward and gutted by the explosion, somehow stayed together long enough for Bell pilot Bill Lewshon, with brilliant flying, to get it back on the ground. Then it was junked.

Dr. Hugh Dryden, one of the world's leading aeronautical scientists, was Director of NACA. Technically, Jimmy Doolittle was chairman of the main National Advisory Committee for Aeronautics, which reported directly and only occasionally to the President. But Dryden was Doolittle's chief general. Dryden, an older man who wore thick glasses, ran NACA day by day.

He had a slow, deliberate way of talking. If ever a government agency was the perfect image of its director, it was NACA. In Dryden's face you could see it all: conservatism, scholarship, wisdom, caution. His office in an old building on H Street in Washington was Spartan. It might have been the office of a college professor. I was there on an urgent mission—back on a familiar theme.

"Dr. Dryden," I said. "This X-2 program is in serious trouble. What's lacking is a Bob Stanley or a Skip Ziegler, if you will. The drive has gone out of the X-2 project. If we're not careful, sir, it's going to wind up like the X-3, a great big expensive Hangar Queen. "I know this is an Air Force project, that they're funding it. But I think it is time we stepped in and took a firm hold. That plane's supposed to come to us for serious aerodynamic investigation. There's another investigation going on about the explosion. It may take months. The control system hasn't been checked out. The engine is so far behind schedule you can't say anything good about it."

"Well, you certainly seem quite interested in this program," Dryden said. He weighed each word.

"Yes, sir," I said. "I am supposed to fly the airplane and I would like to do so before I retire."

"What do you propose?"

"I propose that I be assigned to the Bell plant on temporary duty. There I'll help every way I can to spark the program to completion. Then I'll make the demonstration flights for Bell. Then I'll return with the plane to NACA at Edwards and complete the flight-test program. I have talked with Bell people about it and they think the idea has some merit."

Dr. Dryden's answer surprised me, frankly. "Very well," he said. "If Williams approves, you may try it."

I returned to Edwards on Cloud Nine. The X-2 plan, as I had envisioned it, would be immensely valuable experience and background for my future. It would give me time in a rocket-plane factory, flight-test experience in the most advanced airplane man had conceived, and inevitably a little public notice which, I was learning, was a necessary part of moving ahead in my field. The X-2 was not the ideal because it amounted, in effect, to bailing out a sinking boat. But it was a start.

"Damn it, Scotty," Williams said, "we really need you around here. The X-2 can wait. That plane may kill more people yet."

"But Walt," I said. "When you hired me you said I'd get a crack at the X-2. That was three years ago and we haven't got the plane yet."

"Well, maybe it's okay with me if it's okay with Vensel. He's your boss. He has the final say-so. Tell him it's up to him."

Vensel said no. He implied I was urgently needed at Edwards.

16: Bright Light Under a Bush

I EYED THE NEW SHIP SKEPTICALLY. White as a lily, it was the X-5, another product from Bell. The ship was powered by a single jet engine, and from a distance it appeared fairly conventional. What was vastly different about the X-5 was that its wings could be swept to several different angles in flight. Two X-5s had been built. One was turned over to the Air Force; NACA got the other. Joe Walker was project pilot and had gotten our program off the ground. I was to make my first check-out flight.

"What do you want on this flight?" I asked Thomas Finch, an NACA engineer.

"The flight plan calls for aggravated stalls," he said. These would help define the safe low-speed limits of the airplane.

"What do you mean, aggravated stalls?" I said. "How far?"

"Use your own judgment," Finch said. "But if you can take her well into the stall region, that'll be fine."

The wings were to be swept to sixty degrees that flight. I cooled down the runway, followed by an Air Force chase, and climbed rapidly to altitude. I had read the manual on the airplane and all of the early flight reports, which had been prepared by Skip Ziegler before he died over Lake Ontario;

I had also been briefed by Joe Walker. The X-5 handled in the air like a three-wheeled automobile. It was loose and danced crazily. Even so, we thought it would make a fine research tool. With its high sustained speed just under Mach 1, and its variable sweep, NACA could explore a wide variety of unknowns. It was like having a whole stable of swept-wing airplanes in one.

I climbed to 25,000 feet and reported to chase that I would make several aggravated stalls. I pulled back on the throttle and eased back the stick. As the X-5 slowed, she began to buffet; slower and slower, more and more buffet. Suddenly her nose veered sharply to the left. In a split second, the X-5 turned 180 degrees. Then she dropped precipitously into a spin. My first-flight jinx was back.

A kaleidoscope of brown desert, blue sky, and white clouds passed dizzily in review in my windshield as the X-5 wound up steadily toward the desert floor. I pushed the stick hard to forward left and bent on full right rudder—the prescribed spin-recovery-control maneuver—but the X-5 stubbornly refused to conform. Then I tried every trick in the book, pretty thick by now, after those years of flying unstable airplanes at Edwards.

After a drop of over 10,000 feet, the X-5 pulled out. Walker had run into the same thing. This slow-spin-recovery was a dangerous weakness of that airplane. Since the Edwards area was 2500 or more feet above sea level, we made a careful note on the plane's flight handbook never to perform maneuvers which could result in a spin below 20,000 feet.

"Did you get the word on Popson?" Joe Walker asked. Popson was an Air Force pilot assigned to fly the Air Force's X-5.

"No," I said. "What happened?" I had just come in from a trip to the East Coast.

"He was assigned to do aggravated stalls at 12,000 feet. He spun in."

I was sick. We had somehow failed in a basic NACA mission—getting information to the right place in time.

Popson was a well-qualified pilot. If there had been better coordination between Air Force and NACA, he might be alive today; his flight plan was his death warrant, as so often happened. He was dead before he took off, the thirteenth pilot to die at Edwards. Following custom, a street was named in his honor.

Bell's Bob Woods was a tremendous man. He's dead now, so there is no way to check, but I think he weighed at least three hundred pounds. He was the last of the Great Guns of an era at Bell. In spite of the X-1 and X-2 difficulties, Woods carried on in the grand old style. You had to admire his vision and political guts.

Woods had a talent for hypnotizing a crowd—or anyway me, at least. And so it was in the spring of 1952, during a semiannual meeting of the full NACA Aerodynamics Subcommittee at the Ames Laboratory, Woods stood before a blackboard. From my inconspicuous seat in the background, I stared at his girth and the vast outpouring of enthusiasm as he made a case which, to me, was as fascinating as his size.

"As I see it," Woods went on before the large meeting of industry designers, "this would essentially be a research aircraft and come under NACA jurisdiction. The information it returned would be made available to all. The craft would be mounted on top of a vertical booster, in effect a ballistic missile. Launch speed would be 4,000 or 5,000 feet a second. The booster would fall away. The vehicle would continue a climb to about eighty miles. On descent, recovery would be effected by a deployed parachute. The booster vehicle could essentially be a V-2 type missile.

"This vehicle would enable us to probe a number of unexplored areas. Aerodynamic heating at hypersonic speed. Weightlessness for the pilot and research airplane machinery."

As he talked, a lieutenant stood by to flip through a set of expertly drafted drawings demonstrating each point.

"Gentlemen," Woods concluded, "I don't think I have to stress the need for an advanced research vehicle. The best thing we have in the hopper now is the X-2 and we all know the limitations of this aircraft, which has not even flown yet. We must face up to the fact that we are going to do something about this or sit back and let the Russians take the lead."

I listened eagerly while the brass kicked around Woods' proposal. There were many pros and cons from a technical stand-point. As I say, Bob Woods had something of a magnetic personality. After the meeting at Ames, he paid us a visit at Edwards. Then, I suppose, he went on to NACA headquarters in Washington and probably on down to talk to John Stack at NACA's Langley Lab in Virginia. In any case, all at once, all the somnolent parts of NACA were suddenly awake and chirping simultaneously about a new advanced research airplane. One reason was that the timing was good. The other rocket planes were in trouble or dropping far behind schedule. The missile engineers were then beginning to squeeze enormous thrust out of a single rocket barrel, more than twice the power of the V-2 rocket engine developed by the Nazis. The Army's Redstone missile generated 75,000 pounds thrust, about ten times the thrust of the engine in the Douglas Skyrocket. It was clearly time to take advantage of this rapid technological advance.

Walt Williams came alive with enthusiasm. He called in Drake and Carmen and asked them to pull out their advanced report which had been pigeon-holed the year before.

"Damn it," said Williams, "if Woods can get up before a meeting of the Aerodynamics Subcommittee and propose shooting a man eighty miles into space in a missile, I guess we can propose the five-engine monster." The Drake-Carmen report, with Williams' endorsement, was sent on to the Langley Laboratory for serious study. None of this produced any immediate results in terms of hardware. The Drake-Carmen proposal was rejected out of hand. The Woods proposal, because it came from industry, got the full NACA treatment—that is to say, a rejection, complete with technical data attached. Basically, no one at that time was in favor of the 'ballistic' approach, although the U.S., and NACA, specifically, would return to exactly that same approach for Project Mercury some five or six years later. However, all this activity set NACA planning toward a more or less 'conventional' advanced research airplane in the range of Mach 6 and 100-mile altitude. As everyone knows, once the ponderous machinery of a government agency is set in motion toward an objective, it can hardly be stopped.

During the weeks that followed, I paid this paper-study airplane more than casual attention. From exactly this kind of start, I knew, eight years earlier Kotcher, Stack, and Woods had given birth to the X-1 and ushered in a new dimension in aviation. With rocket engines now ten times more powerful, were we on the threshold, were we in the very act of conceiving a new generation that would make the X-1 pale by comparison? Man had yet to fly at Mach 2 and we were talking of Mach 6 and altitudes of 100 and 200 miles. This was Buck Rogers stuff, space flight. This was it!

I knew instinctively that my future lay in that paper airplane. It was then no more than a column of figures together with NACA's resolution to investigate its possibilities. But in my mind it was a thing of steel, or titanium, or whatever material it would be built of—a sleek, perfectly engineered object, a thing of marvelous beauty and near perfection, a boyhood dream in real life.

The X-15 had been born. The name of the game was to get aboard it somehow, and at the right time.

THE MONTHS ROLLED BY AT NACA. I flew sometimes two or three flights a day in the X-4, X-5, and other craft. But my biggest effort was reserved for the Douglas Skyrocket. Lacking other high-speed rocket airplanes for data purposes, I gradually pushed the Skyrocket to Bridgeman's record of Mach 1.8 and beyond. In fact, during the spring of 1953 after I had logged some thirty flights in the bird, I regularly flew to Mach 1.8 and frequently to Mach 1.9 or a little more. Since we had no real technical reasons to exceed it, I kept below Bridgeman's altitude record of 79,000 feet. My speed in the Skyrocket was, of course, a world's record. Typical of NACA we hid this bright light under a bush, and Dr. Dryden ordered me to stay below Mach 2. It mattered only a little to me. I had grown up professionally within NACA and had come to accept urgency in record-making as childish.

The military thought otherwise. That year, 1953, the world was celebrating the fiftieth anniversary of flight, and the publicists were casting around for a sensational drum-beat in memory of the Wright brothers. In short, a new speed or altitude record. That summer the long-awaited Bell X-1-A, a sister-ship of the ill-fated X-1-D, arrived at Edwards. With it came the Air Force's star, Chuck Yeager, temporarily released from another assignment. We knew what he would be shooting for: Mach 2. If he made it, he would go down in history as the first man to fly Mach 1 and then Mach 2. It was a publicity agent's dream, a perfect unveiling for the fiftieth anniversary of flight.

The Navy had not the slightest intention of letting the Air Force pluck this plum without a stiff fight. One day in the summer of 1953 Marine Colonel Marion Carl arrived at NACA. Carl is one of the most fabulous aviators in history. A leading ace in World War II, Carl had set a speed record in the original D-558-I back in 1947. Since that time he had been engaged in other assignments in Washington and was top pilot for the Naval Air Test Center, Patuxent Paver, Maryland, the Navy's counterpart of Edwards. Carl had never flown a rocket airplane. But Walt Williams called all of us into the office to announce that the Navy was 'borrowing' the Skyrocket for a few days. Colonel Carl would try to beat Bridgeman's altitude record of 79,000 feet and set a speed record of Mach 2.

"That will really make Yeager's job tougher," Williams said.

I threw myself into the venture as enthusiastically as if the flight had been planned for me. One reason was that Carl, a big lanky guy, was immensely likable and a superb aviator, in my book. I had to admire his guts. There weren't many pilots in the world who would deliberately jump in the

Skyrocket and go for broke. We stayed up late at night. I told him every detail of the Skyrocket, all her quirks and strong points, what to beware of, just how to balance on that knife-edge high in the thin air, how to avoid the dangerous Supersonic Yaw that had bothered Bridgeman and myself. In many ways this was superfluous: he had done considerable cramming before he came.

Carl had one advantage over most beginning rocket-plane pilots. The NACA Skyrocket team was unbeatable. The plane was by now almost completely debugged. He could count on efficiency and competence up to the moment of launch, and a mechanically near-perfect bird in flight. The rest was up to him.

The first two flights were failures—he never launched. On the first I flew chase. Carl experienced some difficulty in the strange Skyrocket cockpit and I was too far away to help. Thus on the second flight I rode in the mother-ship bomb-bay compartment. I helped Carl suit up and strapped him in the Skyrocket cockpit. Then, up until the moment of launch, I helped Jack Russell operate the mother plane's manual Lox top-off system, pumping Lox into the tanks of the Skyrocket to replace boil-off. Since liquid oxygen (Lox) 'boils away' at altitude, we had equipped the mother plane with a Lox 'top-off system,' which keeps pumping Lox into the research airplane until a few moments before launch. Full Lox tanks also mean a longer rocket flight, always a prime objective. Carl would need every ounce we could squeeze in to break an altitude record.

The second flight ended much like the first. Frankly, I was amazed at the limitless competence of the man in a brand-new and, to him, hostile environment.

On the third flight and first launch Carl made it. After a perfect light-off he stood the Skyrocket on its tail and blazed to 85,000 feet, beating Bridgeman's record by a healthy 6,000 feet. His recovery in that thin air was adroit, and he landed the ship dead-stick on the lake, beaming with pride. Now he was ready to tackle the speed record, to rack up Mach 2 for the Navy.

This would be tough, I knew. My top speed in the Skyrocket, and Carl had to exceed this first, was Mach 1.96. I had achieved that speed only after months of flying in the ship, of learning to tread the knife-edge with extreme care and skill. In that airplane even the slightest over-pressure on the stick would cut the speed back drastically and botch a flight. It would be tougher in summer, when the air was warmer. The Skyrocket performed best when it was cold.

Colonel Carl made two unsuccessful tries for Mach 2. Then, under pressure from some conservative elements in Navy headquarters, he gave up the attempt, after failing to come close. Ever since, I have held Carl in highest regard. In five brief Skyrocket flights he had shattered the world altitude record. His record is usually omitted from most aviation-record summaries. I think that is because he was a Marine. But Carl, in no sense a small man, had never raised the point himself.

Carl's performance made a lasting impact on me. After he left Edwards I began to think hard about records. The names of the famous rocket pilots hummed through my mind: Yeager, Boyd, Ridley, Everest, Bridgeman, Carl. I had seen enough of these men to know that when they spoke they commanded the attention of four-star generals and admirals, even Dr. Dryden. Although only one (Ridley) was an engineer, when they made a suggestion about an airplane it was considered a command, and millions were spent on their intuitive say-so. Their authority had been built not only on a foundation of tens of thousands of data points wrung from research airplanes, but mainly from singular, spectacular bursts—records.

With the right man at the controls I knew the Skyrocket could reach Mach 2, though not easily. Scott Crossfield might be the man, the first man to fly at Mach 2. If so, who knew what the future held?

17: Light in the Open

"WHAT'S THE SITUATION ON THE X-1-A?" Williams asked.

I had just come from an inspection of the ship, which was being readied for flight in the Edwards Air Force hangar.

"There are some technical difficulties in the airplane, some of them critical, I think. I'll give it to you in a report," I said.

"Is Yeager going to go?" Williams asked.

"All out, that's for sure. He was trying to feel me out a little, find out what we were doing with the Skyrocket. I didn't tell him, although I let drop it was a pretty high Mach number. They're going to get this flight in before the Wright Brothers Memorial dinner if it kills them."

"Don't say that."

"I didn't mean it that way, Walt." I said. "But everything indicates that this airplane is going to go directionally unstable at Mach 1.8 and above. I'm sorry to see they have pulled Yeager back especially for this. Something might happen. He is going to Mach 2 or faster if he can."

"How about giving me a written report on the inspection? At least we can show we were trying to make this thing as nearly safe as possible. I've already put in one objection and gotten my ears pinned. Don't get into the flight operations aspects, just confine the report to the systems inspection."

"Okay, Walt." I turned to leave.

"By the way," Williams said, "we're supposed to get some stuff together for this proposed advanced research airplane. I've got a report here prepared by O'Sullivan, Brown, and Zimmerman from Langley."

My heart skipped a beat or two. "What do they recommend?" I asked.

"It's not a recommendation for a specific airplane configuration. They think some more study should be given. They want to run a lot more wind-tunnel studies on shapes. They especially want to investigate aerodynamic heating. They've sent the report to all NACA facilities for general comment, and in some cases for specific engineering studies. Most of the technical work will be done down at Langley—the aerodynamic heating phase. They've rigged up a shotgun-type wind tunnel that will give them a micro-second blast as high as Mach 16. Miniature stuff, but a start."

"What can we do to keep this thing rolling, Walt?" I asked.

"Keep it rolling? You mean get it rolling good and fast, don't you? This thing could die on the vine right quick if the right people don't push it."

"All right, get it rolling."

"What I'd like you to do, Scotty, is prepare a report—take your time, a couple of weeks, if need be—outlining the operational phase of the proposed advanced research airplane. Make this a real positive report. Write it as though the airplane were a definite thing and don't overstress the problems. Show them that for us the flight program of this airplane would be strictly no sweat."

"I can do that because I believe it will be no sweat," I said.

"What kind of guide-lines have they given us on speed and altitude?"

"The numbers they're kicking around now are Mach 6 and 75 miles altitude, close to 400,000 feet."

I got up and walked to a map which covered one part of the wall in Williams' office. I made some mental calculations and spaced off some distances with my thumb and little finger stretched to maximum.

"I think you'll probably have to launch some place over Salt Lake to make a powered flight and land at Edwards," I said.

Williams got up and joined me before the map. "How about this area around Las Vegas?" he said.

We stared at the patches on the map which outlined the many dry lakes. There was a long string of them between Edwards and Salt Lake, forming almost a straight line. Any of the lakes along the route could serve as an emergency strip if something went wrong.

"How far is it from here to Salt Lake?" Williams asked.

"About four hundred miles," I said.

He sat down and doodled on a scratch pad. He slammed open his desk drawer and pulled out a slide-rule. He figured swiftly for several minutes, scratched his closely cropped, stiff hair. I noticed that it was beginning to gray.

"I think that's it," he said. "If the mother plane is fast enough, you can take off from here, fly to Salt Lake in an hour or so and launch. The research plane would be back here on the ground in half an hour more."

"Our first aircraft in space," I said. In NACA's vernacular we called it "extra-atmospheric flight." That afternoon I began my report: "Operational techniques for a research airplane of the type proposed in reference (a) will not present difficult problems if operational people have a strong voice in the philosophy of the design and function of the airplane and its parts ..." I went on to discuss some of the technical details of the mother plane, the launch speed and altitude and recovery phases, recommending the Salt Lake area as a launch point. Then I digressed into a discussion of the pilot safety and escape mechanisms, emphasizing that all could be performed adequately by following known procedures and making use of existing techniques. I expressed doubt that cosmic radiation or zero G weightlessness would prove a problem, although at that time, typically, there were experts in these fields who had made a federal case of each.

I concluded my report: "Directly proportional to operational problems, and hence of vital importance, is the complication of the airplane devices and over-engineering of the systems. From the in-flight point of view, the pilot-protection items lose their value if reliability and airplane performance are sacrificed."

In short, let's not botch up the airplane like the X-2 and X-3. Keep it simple, always realizing that performance means pilot safety and performance comes in this sense from reliability. I completed the report on the following day and forwarded it to Walt Williams. Thus, little by little, and much too slowly for our money, the X-15 was taking shape in people's minds.

They had towed the XF-92-A far down on the lake bed. It was sensitive to cross-wind and the more the take-off run was directly into the wind, the better. Pete Everest was ready to make the last Air Force test flight before turning the plane over to NACA. After the plane was in place, the wind changed slightly. But that was enough to cancel the flight. I was in Williams' office with Everest.

"Well, Scotty," he said, "you're going to fly the plane next week. Why don't you go down to the lake and get it? You can taxi it back and lift it off the lake, just to get the feel of it."

I grabbed my flight gear and drove down to the airplane. The XF-92-A was the worst-flying airplane built in modern times that I know of. It was a delta-wing plane, the first modern delta job manufactured in the country. Originally the plane was designed for a ram-jet engine. When that engine fell by the wayside, the XF-92-A was fitted with first one jet engine and then another. It was a hopeless mess, a patchwork quilt of fixes upon fixes. It was under-powered, under-geared, under-braked, and overweight. It was a nightmare. When it first arrived at Edwards in the early days, Chuck Yeager washed out the gear on take-off. After company demonstration, and Al Boyd's flight, by Air Force order only three Edwards pilots were permitted to fly the plane: Yeager, Everest, and Crossfield. The Air Force was not sorry to turn it over to me.

I climbed into the cockpit, pulled the canopy shut, and got set for a fast taxi, and shallow lift-off, back toward the base area. I gunned the engine, and the plane, heavy with fuel, wobbled into the air. I had read the manual and talked at length with Pete Everest. I knew the plane was weak on brakes. One way to stop the roll was to hold the plane nose-high—very high. With the lake bed running out on me, I horsed back on the stick and brought the nose up. My speed fell off only slightly.

I pulled back hard on the stick and nearly stood the beast on her tail. She plopped down on the lake but continued to roll like a Ferrari. I was in trouble. The lake was all but gone. I was barreling toward a cluster of sand dunes, unable to stop the plane. Well, Crossfield, I thought, the old first-flight jinx is working hard, and this time you're going to wrap this plane up in a ball. It would be a mess, too. The plane was fully fueled, all the tanks around the engine and wheel-wells were brimming. Even under the best of circumstances, she was a fire-trap.

I figured a way to save my own hide. I could see that a small bluff lay ahead directly across my path. I would let the plane roll on until an instant before it smashed into the bluff. At that second I would retract the gear, turn on all the fire-extinguishers, blow off the canopy, and, as the belly skidded onto the bluff, jump out and run. I stop-cocked the engine and shut down all the circuit breakers and pumped what little brake I had, first left then right, to dodge a couple of sand islands in my path.

As the plane raced on toward the bluff, I suddenly noticed a narrow dirt road going off to my left. Could I make that? I jammed on the left brake with all my might. The small brake seized for a split second, then fell off on the lake floor, a molten mass of metal. But the plane had turned slightly toward the rutted dirt road and I turned it still more by sheer will power. When I hit the road, the tires blew and burned. But the plane stayed straight and level. A hundred yards up the road, it finally ground to a halt. I pulled the fire-extinguishers and jumped out.

After that the dirt road was facetiously renamed the Crossfield Pike in my honor. Everest cracked: "You know, Scotty, you're the only pilot still alive at Edwards who has a road named after him."

One of the weakest points of the XF-92-A was the engine installation. During the early phase of the program before I flew it, we burned out an engine on almost every other flight, laying the ship up for repairs for weeks on end. In fact, it took eighteen months to log eighteen flights. We made many changes in the installation and operational procedures, so that by the time I flew it we fortunately never lost another engine. But every time I took off in that plane I held my breath until I reached sufficient altitude to use the ejection seat, if necessary. The pilot never really flew that airplane, he corralled it.

I made twenty-five flights in her during the summer and fall of 1953. On the last one, in October, she collapsed on the lake bed while taxiing after landing. The nose wheel simply got tired and buckled. The plane ground-looped and came to rest, teetering on the nose and one wing-tip. After I was sure that it would not fall over on me, I crawled out.

The plane never flew again after that. It was finished and no one shed any tears. Some mechanics patched it up, and for a while it was used for publicity purposes as a static exhibit at air shows, Rose Bowl parades, and so on. From an engineering standpoint I should not be overly harsh on the XF-92-A. Actually, the combined Air Force-NACA flight program produced a great deal of information which ultimately made the Convair F-102 delta-wing fighter and its newer sister-ship, the F-106, feasible airplanes. The data we accumulated from the XF-92-A enabled the F-102 and F-106 to achieve an acceptable stability in flight, and thus the darned thing had accomplished its purpose.

Not long after the final demise of the XF-92-A, I visited the office of 'Perk' Perkins, the Navy liaison civilian stationed at Edwards. He was the very valuable contact for NACA when we needed something from the Navy. He had been in the thick of the Marion Carl altitude and speed attempts in the Skyrocket. He was a good friend.

"Perk," I said, "I can't be here officially. Dr. Dryden has ordered me not to take the Skyrocket to Mach 2. But this is a Navy-sponsored plane and I thought I would kick around some possibilities with you. Something that the Navy would think beneficial."

Perkins caught on fast. My case made sense. Yeager was going to take the X-1-A to Mach 2, come hell or high water. The X-1-A was a new bird. We knew it would be unstable above Mach 1.8. Yeager had already encountered instability above that speed on a practice run. Knowing Yeager, though, the chances were he would make it. The Wright Brothers dinner was coming up. We could achieve Mach 2 in the Skyrocket because after scores of flights we had learned to live with its instability. I knew the plane well. I could fly it. "U.S. Navy" was stamped all over the project. The Navy would get the credit without risking a failure. If I failed, no one would be the wiser.

"The only thing is," I said, "the pressure for this flight must come from the Navy direct to Dr. Dryden on the highest levels. It's going to be tough because Dryden does not want to challenge the Air Force. He'll be caught in the middle but it ought to be interesting."

I left Perkins' office wondering if I had not slipped a cog. Imagine Crossfield proposing a record attempt. Imagine Dr. Dryden approving it! In the best Navy tradition, Perkins was a resourceful and decisive man. Right off, he found out that the Navy's Chief of the Bureau of Aeronautics, Rear Admiral Apollo Soucek, was visiting on the West Coast. Perkins tracked him down. Soucek had no objections, provided the matter had been cleared through the Chief of Naval Operations in the Pentagon. Perkins got on the wire to the Pentagon and talked with our old friend Marion Carl. Carl knew just how to do it, apparently, because a week later Dryden sent word to Walt Williams to say that the Mach 2 restriction on the Skyrocket had been lifted. Williams was dumbfounded and for some reason suspicious of my role in this caper.

"It's up to you now, Scotty," said Perkins. "The Pentagon says we can have one try at it. If we miss, we have to step aside for Chuck Yeager."

"I won't miss," I said.

The timing was splendid. I was not aware of it then, but a change was taking place within NACA. The cost of operating its laboratories was mounting in direct proportion to the increasing complexity of modern airplanes. NACA urgently required advanced tools to probe new areas of flight. These had to be in place in a hurry if they were to do any good. But money was hard to come by. The administration, in general, had taken a dim view of "research," and NACA's contributions were not easy to explain in lay language. NACA was about to bring its light into the open. The Mach 2 proposal must have fitted very neatly with NACA's new plans.

In fact, a few days later, to my astonishment Dr. Dryden's able assistant, Walter Bonney, arrived at Edwards. Bonney, a good-natured man then a few years my senior, had worked for Bell Aircraft for years as a public-relations man. In 1949 Bonney had joined NACA in Washington, where he soon discovered that his talents as a flack were not so appealing as his talent for writing history. In the prevailing atmosphere Bonney went underground and began preparing the most thorough and objective history of aviation yet conceived. For years, my hobby had been aviation history. During the years Bonney and I had spent many hours together on this subject. I had turned over to him my collection of research.

"Walt!" I said. "What brings you to Edwards? We're not doing anything out here an aviation historian would be interested in."

"Son," Bonney said, tossing me a quizzical smile, "I'm not a historian on this mission." Bonney called everyone younger than he son.

I knew then that Bonney had come out to handle 'press relations' in the event I was successful in reaching Mach 2. What was happening to staid old NACA, anyway?

18: 'Fastest Man on Earth'

November 20, 1953, was a cold, blustery day on the desert. I arrived at the ramp before daybreak, shivering from the frigid wind and weak from a bad dose of influenza. I had slept only a few hours. But it mattered little how I felt. My mind and body would be called upon to perform full-bore for only four critical minutes. I had no doubt that both could be summoned to peak at the proper time. The important thing was how the Skyrocket shaped up.

She was snugged under the belly of the B-29 mother plane, almost lost in a swirl of liquid oxygen fog, which boiled out of a vent. Pipes, wires, and hoses leading from the ground-equipment carts and fuel trucks were plugged into her top and sides. A swarm of mechanics, heavily bundled against the cold, fretted about. In the background was a steady, eerie, high-pitched whistle caused by pressure dumping overboard through a relief valve, signifying to all that the Skyrocket was ready for action. It was a falsetto call to arms.

In truth, the Skyrocket was being called upon to perform a minor miracle. She was not designed for supersonic flight in the first place. In concept she was old, years old, and even at Mach 1.8 we were pressing her far beyond rational limits. One simple fact made her go fast: the 200-second blast of her enormously powerful rocket engine lighted off in mid-air at 35,000 feet, where we could take advantage of the thin air. If the Skyrocket took off from the ground, which she was not designed to do, even with her rocket engine going she would not exceed the speed of sound. Too much time would be lost, too much fuel consumed, leaving the ground and climbing through the thick air that lies between the earth and 35,000 feet. The secret lay in the air-launch. And even with an air-launch, the best any ordinary team could hope for, with luck, was a speed of Mach 1.9. Bridgeman and I had already crowded her limits. This speed was achieved in the thin air above 50,000 feet, where at any instant the Skyrocket, not designed for flight in those regions, could skid slightly and then rumble wildly out of control.

After months of working together, the NACA Skyrocket team had learned many little tricks to save time and gain an edge on the unknown. Take the prime, for example, when we squirted a preliminary shot of Lox through the engine, to chill it down for the big start. The prime exhausted through a tube in the rear of the bird. As soon as the prime flowed smoothly, we launched. If we delayed, we wasted valuable Lox-energy. Jim Newman, an observer in the B-29, had learned to anticipate the prime. He could tell on the first puff if it was going to be good. As another example, I had perfected a rhythmic method of lighting off the four rocket barrels so that each tube gave us every ounce of impulse it was capable of exerting.

All else being equal, in the final analysis the speed we achieved depended directly on how much fuel we could carry. Here, too, we had tried a trick. If we pumped the frigid, unstable, boiling liquid oxygen into the Skyrocket about four or five hours before flight time, giving it time to 'settle down,' we knew we could squeeze in a few more pounds. Storing the freezing liquid in the airplane for so long a period caused the ship to transform into a gigantic deep-freeze. Because of this, we called the procedure 'cold-soaking' the airplane. We also chilled the alcohol fuel for higher density.

The way our orders read, we had only one chance to crack Mach 2. There could be no mistakes and thus we did everything possible to grease the ship, hoping to gain a knot of speed or save an ounce of weight. Everyone scoffed, but I had the crew wax the glistening white wings and fuselage. We placed masking tape over every aperture and crack. We replaced the stainless-steel prime and jettison tubes, used only in an emergency fuel-dump, with lightweight aluminum tubing. We carefully bent these tubes so they curved into the blast of the rocket engine. Once I had lighted off and no longer required them, they would burn away and fall off, shedding another few pounds of drag from the Skyrocket.

"How's everything, Jack?"

Jack Moise, one of the B-29 launch-panel operators, had, along with the whole crew, been awake most of the night nursing the Skyrocket. He was an able mechanic and a cool head in the air at launch time. He often operated the liquid oxygen top-off system in the mother plane, pumping in the last bit of fuel before launch.

"She looks real good, Scotty," Jack said. "We're ready to load hydrogen peroxide." We used peroxide as a fuel for the Skyrocket's fuel and Lox pumps that supplied the rocket engines with the high-pressure propellants at tremendous rates. The peroxide solution—ninety per cent—was so strong that a rag doused in the liquid would spontaneously burst into flames.

"Go ahead," I said. I tightened my jacket against the cold desert wind.

Moise gave the signal and the peroxide flowed from a truck into the Skyrocket. But a calamity was in the making—one of those unfortunate 'accidents' that always seem to haunt the record-breakers at Edwards. The long 'cold-soak' had frozen shut a hydrogen-peroxide vent fitting. The dangerous liquid, pumped in under pressure, sought an escape route. It overflowed into a manifold, rushed through a pipe, and suddenly burst out of an untaped port near the rear of the Skyrocket, showering Jack Moise. He yelled and covered his face with his hands.

A quick-thinking mechanic, Kinkaid, grabbed a fire hose and brutally splashed Moise full in the face with water. Without a second's delay we hurried Moise to the flight-line emergency dispensary. There they carefully rinsed his face and eyes and stripped off his peroxide-soaked clothing. His face was blotched white in a few spots, but fortunately these disappeared within a few days.

Coming out of the doctor's office, I saw Kinkaid sitting on a bench, waiting for a check-up. He was soaking wet.

"You better get out of those wet clothes," I said.

"No, Scotty, it's okay. I'm warm," he said.

I was about to leave when a question flashed into my mind. Why would Kinkaid, wet as he was, be 'warm' on so cold a day? The answer came quickly: he, too, was soaked with peroxide, a thermite bomb, ready to burst into flames. I'm sure Kinkaid thought I had lost my mind. I ran to him and began peeling off his many layers of clothing—two pairs of trousers, long underwear, a jacket, sweater, and shirt. When at last he stood before us completely nude and looking sheepish, I saw that his arms and legs were bleached white. We had saved him from serious injury and possibly a consuming peroxide fire.

This near-disaster delayed our preparations, but not much. Back at the ship another mechanic thawed the peroxide fitting with a hot-air gun, and soon the Skyrocket was loaded, ready to go.

Herman Ankenbruk, the project engineer, had spent many hours working out a flight plan that would give the Skyrocket maximum performance—and then some. Usually after drop I flew the plane on a giant parabolic course, going uphill and then pushing over, achieving maximum speed in a mild dive. Everything was timed to the split second. Too much climb would rob me of rocket-engine burning time on the descent. A sloppy pushover would leave the Skyrocket at too low or too high an altitude at burn-out. The high-speed dive lasted only a few seconds. Plunging earthward, the Skyrocket soon encountered thick air, building up a dragging shock-wave on the nose.

When the drag equaled the thrust of the rockets, they shut off and the Skyrocket slowed like a truck hitting a brick wall.

After a brain-numbing analysis of all previous flight data and endless conferences with me, Herman advised me to climb to 72,000 feet. The winds aloft that day blew from the east. A launch in the western end of the valley, heading east, might add a few miles per hour, we thought. The cold temperature that day suited the Skyrocket fine.

The success of the flight to a large extent depended on the performance of the mother-ship crew. On this day especially, the Lox top-off had to be perfect. Each drop of Lox pumped in at the last moment added precious microseconds to the burning time. I was completely confident. Jim Newman, I knew, would anticipate the prime and call it right. The mother-plane pilot, Stan Butchart, an old friend from the war and the University whom I had recruited for NACA, would drop at precisely the right point at the best speed and altitude. He had done so many times in the past. These men were pros.

At 10,000 feet I crawled into the familiar cockpit of the Skyrocket and the canopy was slammed shut. All the gauges were in the green. Only one thing worried me. When we reached altitude, it was my job to pressurize the cockpit of the Skyrocket by releasing compressed air through a valve. There was no gradual compression. The gas exploded into the cockpit in one burst. The effect on the pilot was similar to that a diver might experience with a split-second change in depth. The sinus tubes sometimes clogged and built up pressure that telegraphed a racking pain through every cavity in the pilot's head.

Long before, from years of flying and pressure-chamber work, I had developed that dreadful occupational affliction of pilots: tortured, mangled sinus channels. On two occasions in the past the pain had been so severe at pressurizing that I had had to cancel. I worried now about how my influenza might have complicated my sinuses. It was possible they might be unbearably painful. Against this possibility I had brought along a piece of insurance, a small cork. Preparing to pressurize, I reached back and plugged the cork in the compressed-air tube outlet. I turned the valve and eased the cork out of the pipe slowly. The pressure in the cockpit built up gradually and caused me no pain whatsoever. When the cabin pressure gauge reached the green, I reported by radio to Butchart:

"Pressurized."

We droned on toward launch point, our path marked by four snowy-white contrails. The air was slightly turbulent and we bounced more than usual. The Skyrocket creaked in its mechanical nest. Too busy to care, I set my stop-watch and began the pre-launch routine. I pressurized the fuel tanks. The gauges, thank God, held steady in the green. Then I turned the switch on the Skyrocket panel which blazed a green 'ready' light on Butchart's panel in the B-29.

"Going to prime," I intoned on the radio.

There was no dramatic nonsense on our radio circuits. Almost before I had completed my sentence, Jim Newman called back:

"Prime looks good."

"Five, four, three, two, one. DROP!" Butchart called the countdown with almost exaggerated calm.

The Skyrocket fell away on its elevator course, and a blinding flash of sunlight hit my eyes. When the ship rolled gently to the right, as usual, I trimmed quickly and hit the rocket-barrel switches, pausing a split second until each caught. The Skyrocket surged ahead. I pulled back on the stick and the horizon disappeared from my windshield. I called Butchart by radio for a steer.

"You're to my right and going uphill, Scotty," Butchart said, placing the Skyrocket in relative position to the mother plane. This was important because in the steep climb I couldn't tell direction.

"All four going good," chase Captain Givens reported.

I soon left them far below and behind. With luck the rocket barrels would burn a total of 200 seconds. These three minutes would spell success or failure. While the Skyrocket bored steadily toward the heavens, I prayed silently to God. "Don't let me goof this one." Meanwhile I kept my eye glued to the needle-ball, airspeed and altitude instruments, an archaic but very effective method. If they charged ahead too much or dropped off suddenly, I would burn fuel needlessly. The way Herman had calculated it, I had to ride an imaginary parabola in the sky, veering no more than a few feet off course. This was the delicate knife-edge.

Coming up on 72,000 feet, I began the push-over. The Skyrocket, engines blazing furiously, arched nicely and began the big downhill run. This was the supreme moment: the Olympic bobsled run, the 80-meter ski-jump, the first and last downhill lunge on my wild rollercoaster. I prayed that the barrels would burn a few more seconds. My eye now alternated from the Mach meter, which was slowly edging toward the magic 2.0 reading, to the needle and ball; if either deviated, precious energy and speed were lost.

I could hear the usual chatter on the radio from chase:

"Do you have him in sight?"

"No. I see the exhaust. But I can't see him. He's lost in the sun some place."

"Well, I'll ease over the base and try to pick him up when he gets back down here."

"Rog."

The Skyrocket was performing like an Olympic champion. She held true on her spectacular dive. The rocket engine burned several seconds longer than usual—207. The 'cold-soak' had paid off. The Mach meter needle edged past 2.0 and hung at 2.04. WE HAD MADE IT! I had become the first man to fly at twice the speed of sound, and this historic milestone had been automatically recorded by the data instruments in the Skyrocket.

The rocket engine cut off with a pop-pop-pop-pop, just about the instant the Skyrocket entered the 'thick' air. The ship slowed abruptly, throwing me forward against the shoulder straps. I drew back on the stick and began the pull-out, still coasting at better than Mach 1.8, taking care to see that the ship did not fall off the knife-edge. Dropping silently back through Mach 1.0, the Skyrocket for a brief instant shook harshly, like a wet dog drying his fur.

Now it was time for the dead-stick lake-bed landing. Coming over the edge of the lake at 15,000 feet, I whipped the ship into a victory roll. As I slowed, the chase planes found me and closed on my wing-tips. I lined up for the let-down.

The Skyrocket's wheels touched down between the two long black lines painted on the dry-lake bed at precisely the point I had picked to land. She rolled to a stop twelve minutes from launch. Walt Williams, followed by

Walter Bonney, ran up to the side of the ship, awaiting my report. I pushed back the canopy and looked at Bonney.

"I don't think you've wasted your time coming out here." He beamed. "Scotty, how did it feel?"

It was a mob scene in a room of the Statler-Hilton Hotel in Los Angeles. In the glare of spotlights, newsreel cameras ground and flash cameras exploded in my face. The reporter who asked the question, one of about fifty jammed in the room, held his notebook in hand, pencil poised. Other reporters were shouting from all corners of the room. The phone was ringing. Everybody wanted an interview. National magazines were on the scent. Walter Bonney was in his element. At last NACA had hit the big time in his business, too.

How did it feel? I turned the question over in my mind slowly, gazing blankly at the reporter. How did you explain how it felt in a word or two, which was all he wanted? Tell them you didn't believe in making records? Tell them it was part of a careful lifetime plan? Reveal the secrets of the proposed advanced research airplane? Tell them you just wanted to show Yeager a thing or two?

"Well, if you want to know the truth," I said, "I didn't feel good yesterday. I had the flu. A real bellyache."

The newsmen scrambled out, leaving Bonney and me to sort through a hundred or more invitations to make speeches, appear at football games in the half-time, and other scientifically significant events, and to fend off still more reporters who wanted to write 'human interest' stories about me and, worse, my family. It was a new and zany world to me. That night when I picked up a Los Angeles newspaper, I stared dazedly at the black headline two inches high and eight columns long:

PILOT FLIES MACH 2 AND GETS BELLYACHE

A few nights later, I was guest of honor at a ceremony in San Diego. Sitting next to me at the head table was movie star and swimming champion, Esther Williams. We all waited patiently while some Air Force general droned through a long, prepared speech about the marvels of science and airplanes in particular. Finally my beautiful dinner companion, dressed in a tight-fitting gold lamé dress, was called upon to speak. Esther Williams approached the mike. Leaning over the lectern until her best features were prominently spotlighted, she spoke slowly: "You know, I've been getting a lot of static all night long about sitting next to the fastest man on earth. But I don't believe it. He hasn't laid a hand on me yet!"

I only wished that the exceedingly eminent Dr. Dryden had been there to see the crowd double up on the floor with glee. NACA had indeed arrived at a turning point. Scott Crossfield, too.

19: "Leaf in a Tempest"

I WAS KING OF THE RACE TRACK FOR THREE WEEKS. Then the old master, Chuck Yeager, did it again. He shattered my record, but he nearly died doing it. I had been expecting the coup de grace at any moment. Chuck had been scheduled to fly the X-1-A on the day after my Mach 2 flight in the Skyrocket. But when I logged Mach 2, the Air Force team pulled back and regrouped, as the military say. Yeager now had his hands full.

Pete Everest describes this Air Force record-breaking in his book: "By this time the old X-1 record had long since been broken by both Bridgeman and Crossfield, so there was no question of keeping ahead of them. Our problem now was trying to catch up."

In early December Chuck flew the X-1-A Mach 2 and caught up. To quote Everest again: "We had matched Bridgeman and Crossfield even money and now we raised the bid."

Yeager would gun the X-1-A all-out.

I watched these warm-ups—between my own press conferences—with more than casual interest. The Wright Brothers Memorial dinner was just a few days away. If Chuck failed, the Navy and Douglas could publicly boast a clean sweep: Carl's 85,000-foot altitude record and my Mach 2 speed record, both set in the Skyrocket.

Yeager flew on December 12. I took up a post that day on the Edwards radio circuit, to listen in on the flight from the ground. Jack Ridley and Major Arthur 'Kit' Murray flew chase. I heard them routinely chatting on the air as the mother plane bore down on the launch point at 32,000 feet. Then like the crack of a starting pistol we heard the mother-plane pilot snap to the co-pilot:

"Drop her, Danny."

In my mind's eye I could see the X-1-A falling rapidly away from the mother plane and Yeager adroitly moving the controls. Now I knew he would be hitting the four rocket-switches at intervals, blasting skyward. In a matter of three minutes he would reach the finish line. The seconds ticked by slowly.

"Got him in sight, Kit?" It was chase Ridley speaking to chase Murray.

"No," Murray replied. "He's going out of sight. Too small."

That was a good sign—for Yeager. The radio circuit was silent. There was no word from Yeager. I dragged on a cigarette thinking: It's just like him to keep everybody on the hook. Then suddenly all hell broke loose. Something was wrong. I became aware of it when I heard Murray and Ridley shouting over the radio to Yeager.

"Chuck! Chuck! Yeager! Where are you . . ."

Then Yeager came on the air, his voice hoarse and rasping, and barely audible:

"I'm ... I'm down ... I'm down to 25,000 feet ... over Tehachapi. Don't know ... whether I can ... get back base or not ..."

"At 25,000 feet?" Ridley asked incredulously.

"I'm ... I'm ... Christ!"

"What say, Chuck?" Ridley called. "Chuck!"

"I say ... don't know ... if I tore ... anything or not ... but, Christ!"

Yeager was obviously in serious trouble. The word flashed across the base. Emergency trucks screamed toward the flight line. Helicopters lifted off, heading for Tehachapi. We leaned over the radio speaker, hanging on each word. Race-track competition was one thing, but now a pilot's life—a great pilot's life—was in jeopardy. I felt helpless—almost sick.

"Chuck from Murray," the radio crackled. "If you can give me altitude and heading, I'll try to check from outside." The chase pilots were trying desperately to find Yeager's tiny craft, to guide him back to base, to tell him if his wings were still in place.

"Be down at 18,000 feet. I'm about ... be over the base at 15,000 feet in a minute," Yeager reported.

On the ground we cheered the master on. His last radio report indicated he would make it. His voice had new confidence.

"Yes, sir," Murray snapped on the radio. We heard the routine as Chuck jettisoned and vented fuel tanks. He sounded much better. The chase closed in.

"Does everything look okay on the airplane?" Yeager called, lining up for the lake-bed landing.

There was still time to bail out if the ship was busted. But he got little help. In his eagerness Murray had lined up on the wrong airplane, a T-33 jet trainer. Quickly Murray shifted targets and gunned his engine to close on Yeager's craft, but it was too late. Yeager was already letting down, committed.

"I don't have you, Chuck," Murray called.

"I'm on base leg," Chuck reported. His voice sounded firm and strong. "I'll be landing ... in a minute."

We heard some additional chatter and then Yeager said:

"Going to land long. I would appreciate it if you'd get out there and get ... this thing ... this pressure suit. I'm hurting ... I think I busted the canopy with my head."

He landed like the pro he is. Yeager's had been the fastest and wildest airplane ride in history. The grim details of it spread through Edwards, hurriedly passed along by tongues stammering in disbelief and admiration.

After drop, Yeager had lighted off the four X-1-A rocket barrels one by one to achieve maximum speed. He pointed the X-1-A's nose toward the deep blue and at 75,000 feet he pushed over. The X-1-A, in level flight, roared to Mach 2.42, or about 1600 miles an hour, faster by a wide margin than man had ever flown before. Then in that rarefied air, at a speed the X-1-A was not designed to fly, the plane 'uncorked.' The X-1-A tumbled wildly like a "leaf in a tempest, a cork in a flooding stream," as Everest puts it.

The X-1-A spun uncontrollably, dropping 51,000 feet in fifty-one seconds, smashing Yeager about in the cockpit. As Yeager later recalled the experience: "The voices have no reality in this lost moment of your life. You're taking a beating now and you're badly mauled. You can see stars. Your mind is half blank, your body suddenly useless as the X-1-A begins to tumble through the sky. There is something terrible about the helplessness with which you fall. There's nothing to hold to and you have no strength. There is only your weight knocked one way and the other as the plane drops tumbling through the air. The whole inner lining of its pressurized cockpit is shattered as you're knocked around, and its skin where you touch it is still scorching hot. Then as the airplane rolls, yaws, and pitches through a ten-mile fall, you suddenly lose consciousness. You don't know what hit you or where."

Probably no other pilot could have come through that experience alive. Much later I asked Yeager, as a matter of professional interest, exactly how he regained control of the ship.

He was vague in his reply, but he said he thought that after he reached the thick atmosphere, he had deliberately put the ship into a spin.

"A spin is something I know how to get out of," he said.

"That other business—the tumble—there is no way to figure that out."

The Air Force squeezed in by the skin of its teeth. Yeager's new record was triumphantly announced at the Wright Brothers Memorial dinner in Washington. Yeager received many accolades. I didn't begrudge him one of them. If ever a pilot deserved praise for a job well done, it was Yeager. After that X-1-A episode, he never flew a rocket airplane again. While it still retained control of the X-1-A, the Air Force itched to make a try for an altitude record. As Everest says: "While we waited for the engineers to tell us why Chuck got into trouble, we began an alternate program to set a new altitude record . . ."

By then Everest must have come to believe his own Air Force press releases. He says: "Bill Bridgeman's record of 79,000 feet in the Douglas Skyrocket was the mark ... to beat." In reality the "mark to beat" was Marion Carl's 85,000-foot record established in the Skyrocket. But, as I said, Carl's record was seldom included in the aviation-record summaries.

Major Kit Murray, who had flown chase for Chuck Yeager on the ill-fated X-1-A flight, was picked as pilot for the Air Force altitude attempt. His boss, Pete Everest, was reserving his strength and skill for the X-2 flight program, if and when the airplane became ready. Murray had flown chase on the X-1-A many times, but he had never flown a rocket plane. Even so, as Everest puts it, Murray was "well qualified" for this all-out attempt in the unstable X-1-A. After long months of study, and conferences with Yeager, he was thoroughly familiar with the airplane. However, as Everest reports: "... we approached his flights with extreme caution."

Inevitably there were delays. Murray's "gravy flight," as the Air Force termed the record tries, did not arrive until June of 1954. After drop and light-off Murray duplicated Yeager's flight plan up to 65,000 feet. Then in place of Yeager's high-speed run, Murray raised the nose of the ship sharply and zoomed toward the sky. At 90,000 feet Murray pushed over in a gentle parabola, his speed just under Mach 2. Says Everest: "Had he kept the nose up he could have gone higher ... We wanted to play this one safe and use proper techniques and not take chances."

Then, Everest goes on, in spite of these "precautions," the X-1-A flipped out of control, virtually duplicating the final phase of Yeager's last X-1-A flight. As Everest explains it: "In thin air of the upper atmosphere the plummeting rocket ship uncorked and fell forty thousand feet before Kit was able to get control again. Because he was going considerably slower than Yeager when he tumbled, fortunately he did not take as bad a beating. After regaining control he returned safely to base and landed, having flown higher than any other human being."

Murray had topped Carl's record by 5,000 feet. Following these demonstrations the X-1-A and its sister-ship, the X-1-B, which had undergone several check flights by Everest and Murray, were turned over to NACA for aeronautical research and investigation. In his pilot report Pete Everest recommended that both planes, "by using a cautious approach," could probably be flown to a maximum theoretical speed of Mach 2.5, or just a shade faster than Yeager flew the X-1-A on his record-breaking flight. Neither airplane was ever flown again to such speeds and altitudes.

By then the need for an advanced research airplane of stable design was urgently felt throughout the entire aviation industry. At NACA, Edwards, we then had four rocket planes in our hangar. These included the X-1-A and the X-1-B, our rebuilt X-1, renamed the X-1-E, and the trusty Skyrocket. All these airplanes were obviously unstable above Mach 2; the Skyrocket could just barely squeak through to that speed. The swept-wing X-2, by then almost ten years old from a design standpoint, was at Edwards, in Everest's able hands, but the engine was still not ready for flight test. On a powerless glide test, with ballast, the X-2 nose wheel had again skewered, causing the plane to ground-loop at high speed, badly shaking Everest. This convinced us—if we needed convincing—that the X-2 was really jinxed.

It was vital for the research airplanes to reach far ahead of the military combat airplanes. Already the first of the Century Series supersonic fighters had arrived at Edwards, and Air Force pilots were flying at impressive speeds, encountering dangerous instability and high-altitude engine malfunctions.

One of these military planes, a Lockheed F-104 straight-wing, light-weight day-fighter, with the pilot's pilot, Tony Le Vier, at the helm, cracked Mach 2 only a few months after my Mach 2 flight in the Skyrocket. However, it was plain that if we had learned more from the research airplanes in time, the F-104 and the military planes that came with it—the F-100, F-101, and F-105—good as they were, would have been immeasurably better craft. At that time, moreover, the advance designers were laying plans for a new generation of Mach 3 military airplanes.

We had yet to achieve Mach 2.5 in research airplanes. So the requirement for data was even more pressing. It is possible to tell a great deal from wind-tunnel data, of course, but wind-tunnel data are always corrected with assumptions, which inevitably contain errors. Airplanes must be flown full-scale to find out the true story. In reaching to Mach 6, the NACA's paper-study advanced research airplane would provide a long-overdue and much-desired quantum leap.

The plane was slowly making its way into the world. In April of 1954 NACA completed its engineering studies, proposing a design that looks very much like the X-15 of today. After the usual headquarters shake-down, NACA forwarded this report to all of the senior members of the main NACA committee and to the chairman, Jimmy Doolittle. A few weeks later, in July of 1954, NACA brass met with the Pentagon brass to hammer out the final details of the airplane. During this meeting the Navy revealed that Douglas had prepared a paper study of an 'advanced Skyrocket,' with essentially the same performance of the NACA-conceived craft. This report was received with great interest, and some of its suggestions were later absorbed into the X-15 program. But it was clear from the outset that the X-15 would be primarily an Air Force show, with the Navy playing a supporting role. There was not enough money in the kitty to build both Navy and Air Force versions of a Mach 6 research airplane.

"About all this airplane will do is prove the bravery of the pilot."

The speaker was the chief designer of a large aircraft manufacturer, addressing a very influential body, NACA's Aerodynamics Subcommittee. The Subcommittee was composed of the chief design engineers of the major aircraft companies of the United States. They were meeting at NACA's Edwards facility for a final rehash of the X-15. At that pronouncement my heart skipped a beat. I was sitting on the sidelines, a very interested bystander.

From conception the X-15 had proved controversial, just like most matters in the highly competitive, uncertain aviation industry. Some engineers believed NACA should reach for higher speed in measured increments, that is to say, Mach 3, Mach 4, Mach 5, with separate vehicles. Experts in the new and growing field of aero-space medicine believed that zero G weightlessness and cosmic radiation would render flight in the fringe of space, or in space itself, impossible. Structural experts worried about the 're-entry' heating of the

X-15. It was known that the plane would glow red, like a blacksmith's forge, when it plunged back into the thick atmosphere. What known metal could withstand so hot a blast and retain its integrity? Still others were concerned about the very low L-over-D of the X-15. Designed for stable, high-speed flight in rarefied air—or no air at all—on landing, the ship would come in fast, dropping like a brick.

These were technical details. Even more significant was an ominous philosophy underlying this historic meeting. By then—October, 1954—the U.S. had embarked on a massive, semi-crash program to build a family of long- and medium-range ballistic missiles, to include the Thor, Jupiter, Atlas, and Titan. In anticipation of these weapons, missile-test vehicles had already achieved speeds—Mach 10 and up—that made our manned aircraft efforts seem puny, indeed, in some people's eyes. These test vehicles were accumulating a vast storehouse of limited-flight data within and beyond the atmosphere on high-speed control, structure and aerodynamic heating. It was not precisely airplane-type information, but it was very closely related. Thus some of the engineers questioned the very need for a high-speed manned research aircraft. Detractors suggested that an automatic missile-type guidance system replace the pilot in the X-15.

Without quite realizing it, these engineers, who must always look five to eight years down the road in their business, were, in a way, debating the future of the manned airplane, as we think of it. Not one of them would then have come right out and said that the manned aircraft was diminishing in importance. On the contrary, they would have protested it to the heavens. But the impact of the guided missile was beginning to be felt, even though none of the proposed missile weapons had been test-fired. In a subtle way, the missile was creeping into all considerations of future projects. The fact that the need for the X-15 and a pilot to fly it was questioned at all was clear proof.

Despite strong objections the NACA Aerodynamics Subcommittee at this meeting put the final stamp of recommendation on the X-15, in effect ratifying Dr. Dryden's course of action in Washington. Like other research airplanes in the past, the X-15 would be an 'open secret,' that is, everything learned in its construction and flight operations would be made available, through NACA and contractor reports, to all of industry. The airplane would be thrown open to all industry for bids. The Air Force would supply ninety per cent of the funds, the Navy about ten per cent. When completed, it would be flown at Edwards in accordance with the scheme I had developed earlier and presented to Walt Williams. Just who would fly the plane was left open for further consideration. The whole project was to be carried out with high priority as a "matter of national urgency."

A few weeks later the Air Force called for bids. Subsequently NACA displayed unusual boldness in dealing with the Department of Defense over the proposed technical flight program of the X-15. NACA demanded and received sole authority to determine who should fly the airplane, and to what speed and altitude it should be flown on each flight. Deference would be shown the Air Force, of course, since that agency was footing most of the bills for the plane, but NACA made it clear that aeronautical research would take precedence over record-breaking. The X-15 would shatter existing records, all in the line of business.

There was much that worried me after the aeronautical design titans had departed Edwards. As I saw it, there was danger that the X-15 would wind up with too many cooks. Almost any member of the many interested agencies had the authority to impose his ideas on the airplane. Each was a specialist in one field or another; each an advocate of this or that controversial, and often unproven, concept. The overall shape and power requirements of the plane had been fixed by physical law, but everything else was subject to change: the instruments, the control surfaces, the control mechanism, the landing gear, the escape system, and a lot of things yet to be invented. The X-15, subjected to many individual influences, might wind up not the ultimate, but a 'bucket of worms' (all too familiar) as the inevitable result, and far too late.

One thing worried me more. This was the growing influence of the unmanned missile that had been so evident at the meetings. This same influence had permeated the staff at our Edwards outpost. One day during a bull session with the pilots, one of them said to me:

"You know, this X-15 might very well be the ship that closes a grand era in aviation. The last of the great manned airplanes."

"The hell you say!" Anger flushed my face. "The X-15 won't close anything. On the contrary, the X-15 will open a whole new era in aviation: the second phase, the second fifty years. Centuries from now historians dealing with space flight will look back to the X-15 as a starting point. They will compare its flights to the great voyages of discovery, to the exploratory probes of Prince Henry the Navigator's captains down the coast of Africa, preceding the voyage of Columbus. This is the beginning, not the end."

"Say, Scotty," one of the pilots said, "you feel pretty strong about that airplane, don't you?"

"You're damned right I do."

And that was a fact. I did.

20: "Please Come to a Complete Stop"

OVER THE SWIFTLY PASSING YEARS THE FACE OF THE Edwards base had dramatically changed. The Air Force, NACA, and civilian contractors had erected modern, air-conditioned offices, engineering spaces, and massive hangars. A new concrete runway, miles long and as much as two feet thick, crossed the flatlands. Installations for fueling and testing experimental airplanes and rocket engines were now formal, restricted areas.

Pancho's Happy Bottom Riding Club was gone, gobbled up by the Air Force, which pushed the boundaries of the base in all directions, including up. The sleek, modern Edwards tower occupied the space that once held the complete, historic town of Muroc. The old tarpaper 'Kerosene Flats' living area had been replaced by comfortable housing. Edwards was big and busy, encumbered with red tape and a new formality.

The people had changed, too. General Al Boyd's one-man show, the jet-age flying circus, had passed into history. The new Edwards commander was a no-nonsense general, Stanley Holtoner. Holtoner endeared himself to no one by deliberately snubbing Pancho Barnes, but he reorganized the expanding base on a businesslike basis. The Air Force pilots who had reigned in my early days at Edwards—Ridley, Wolfe, Sellers, Bryce, Hoover, Lathrop, Gregorious, Popson—were gone, almost all to their graves. Yeager had moved on to other assignments. Only Pete Everest hung on, playing a tight-fisted waiting game with the lagging X-2.

The shift to the elaborate new NACA 'laboratory' had considerably changed the atmosphere in our outfit. More distant now from the mechanics, and the smell of grease and fuel, we discarded our sport shirts for business suits and ties, and played the scientist role to the hilt. This was inevitable. NACA's record at Edwards had far exceeded all expectations. Our prolonged tour on the frontier of flight had not only developed millions of data points, but new theory as well. We had challenged many old and accepted wind-tunnel methods. We had raised warning flags on trouble to come and desperately tried to head it off.

In truth, the High-Speed Flight Station was no longer a gypsy caravan camped on the fringes of Edwards, but a solid, permanent NACA installation, an important new source of aeronautical think-how and know-how. Occasionally I longed for the old racing-pit days, the time of sweating all night long side-by-side with a bunch of mechanics over a balky valve, but I knew this deprivation was the price of progress.

The emphasis in the air had changed as well. The rocket airplanes were still far and away the most spectacular craft on the base. But the big push was now placed on the new production airplanes, which were afflicted with the aches and pains of faster and faster speed. These airplanes had to be made safe—or as safe as humanly possible—for the green Air Force second lieutenant just out of flight school.

The aches and pains had been anticipated years earlier. Flying near the speed of sound, an airplane creates a resisting field in its path. The air immediately ahead of the plane, in effect, is transformed into a rugged area of angry sound waves which criss-cross, backwash, tumble, speed up, and slow down, behaving somewhat like the foaming water in an ocean wave when it tumbles against a rock-bound coast. In the beginning at Edwards the job was to design and fly a plane to the edge of this coast. The bullet-shaped X-1, deliberately built to withstand tremendous stress, had blazed right through to the smooth beach beyond. But military airplanes, which could not be so heavy and brutal, had a tough time of it. As they felt their way along, they were battered and smashed about in the surf. And when they finally reached the beach, they still had trouble.

The most common afflictions the airplane experienced in piercing the turbulent trans-sonic air were two abrupt, divergent motions which we called pitch and yaw. These were terms adopted, appropriately enough, from the seamen. Pitch describes the movement of the airplane if the nose suddenly and unexpectedly jerks up or down, like the bow of a ship in a heavy sea. Yaw describes the movement of the airplane if the nose cocks sharply to left or right, somewhat like the clumsy wallow of a vessel in a following sea. When or if both abrupt movements occur simultaneously—a dreadful and often fatal sequence—it is called 'coupling.'

The impact of pitch and yaw on the airplane varies with altitude and speed. In the thick air of low altitudes a fast-moving airplane pitching or yawing severely is subjected to intense strain, so much that it is not uncommon for the ship to disintegrate in mid-air. At higher altitudes where the air is much thinner, a fast-flying airplane can 'take' a greater divergent motion. If it yaws, pitches, or couples, the airplane simply skids through the air in whatever awkward or ungainly position it assumes. However, an airplane in such altitudes must be slowed before it reaches the thicker air; otherwise, it will enter this blanket beyond stress-design and disintegrate. At any altitude, if a plane flips out of control, the pilot must respond with care and skill. Over-controlling, or pumping on the wrong controls, compounds the problem.

There was no known way to avoid completely such divergent motions in supersonic airplanes built especially for combat and near-routine take-off and landing on ordinary airfields. Thus, from the beginning we had focused attention on 'damping' the motions, striving for minimum instability by various wing and tail designs, angles of sweep, and mechanical devices on the wing called fences and slats. Control systems were devised with a built-in 'damping' system which, in theory, automatically sensed a divergence and automatically moved the controls just enough to compensate. These were called SAS, short for Stability Augmentation System.

After production airplanes were delivered to Edwards, the experimentation continued unabated. New vertical tails and fancy devices were tacked on the airplanes. The horizontal stabilizers were moved to new positions on the fuselage. During 1954, like other pilots at Edwards, I was swept up in the new race to bring the fast new jets within safe flying limits. I made twenty-five additional flights in the Skyrocket in support of these experiments. In between, I went aloft many times in early-model production aircraft such as the F-84-F, an advanced version of the Republic Thunderjet; the F-102, a direct outgrowth of the horrible delta-wing XF-92-A; and the 'hard-wing' F-86, so-called because its automatic slats were removed, which had been hastily engineered especially to destroy MIGs in Korea. The F-86 Sabrejet particularly held my interest from an aeronautical-engineering point of view. The plane had already earned its niche in history, and hundreds were flying from Air Force bases, but its complete range of dangers had yet to be defined in any report. The thought that some second lieutenant might be killed because we at Edwards had fallen down on the job haunted me. I resolved to do something about that particular airplane.

Customarily we began investigations which would push an airplane to the limit at high altitudes, where the air was thin and the ship would stay in one piece if it uncorked. Joe Walker, Stan Butchart, Jack McKay, a promising new pilot at NACA, and I divided the hard-wing F-86 work, starting at 40,000 feet and working down slowly. As we edged down into the thick air at lower altitudes, the F-86 pitch-up became more violent and dangerous. Our boss, Joe Vensel, drew the line. He ruled that we could not deliberately uncork the airplane below 30,000 feet.

"But the most important area," I said to Walt Williams, protesting, "is down around 25,000 feet. That's where the military pilot can get in serious trouble, chasing a target sleeve or something. If this plane has a serious divergence at that altitude they ought to know about it."

"Look, Scotty," Walt said, "we're in the middle. We can't come up with a negative opinion of some company's airplane like that. All we can do is fly the thing and collect data and present the data objectively in an NACA report."

"Okay, fine," I said. "Then let's keep on going. Let's do the 30,000-foot data and then drop down to 25,000 feet."

"That's up to Vensel," Williams said. "He's your boss."

"Vensel says no."

"Then the answer," Williams said, "is no."

For the first time in my life I deliberately violated my boss's orders. Without rechecking with Vensel, I recorded the hard-wing F-86 maneuvers at 25,000 feet. As we all expected, the pitch-up was severe. The airplane held together—North American traditionally built rugged planes—but the stress, or

G force, caused me to black out. A pilot bent on a mission other than paying strict attention to the unique maneuver could get in serious trouble. When I turned over the data, Vensel was understandably incensed. After the data were released—to save the lives, I hope, of some pilots—Vensel pouted and claimed I had conducted the test at 25,000 feet to prove that the other pilots were 'chicken.' Walt Williams called me to his plush new office, decorated with new space-charts, and gave me unshirted hell. I guess I tossed it back as fast as he dished it out.

Another of these advanced planes with supersonic aches was the North American F-100. It had been flying experimentally, off and on, about one year, when we received the twenty-third production model at NACA in September, 1954. She was a powerful, wonderful beast, capable of reaching Mach 1.3 in level flight. At that stage in her test-flight program, mechanics spent fifteen hours working on her for every one hour she spent in the air. She had a reputation for being mean, if mishandled. She had uncorked and disintegrated, killing North American's top test pilot, George Welch. There was a big debate raging among the pilots at Edwards about whether or not the F-100 could be landed dead-stick. North American had not yet demonstrated it. It fell to me to find out on my first F-100 flight.

We were down for an 0800 take-off, but the unbeatable NACA mechanics were ready ten minutes before, so I went aloft ahead of schedule, before the radars and tracking stations were warmed up to zero in on me. There had already been built at North American new, bigger vertical tails for the F-100. We needed some specific data points. Our F-100 was packed full of NACA instruments. The ship was not a research airplane. I had declined a chase plane.

Poised on the end of the new three-mile concrete runway, I fire-walled the throttle. The F-100 rolled, picked up speed, and then stood on her tail, afterburner blazing, climbing almost vertically into the desert sky. I was quite impressed. The F-100 was no toy but it handled well. By then, North American had built thousands of F-86 jets in all models and it was obvious they knew what they were doing.

When I reached 35,000 feet, I leveled the ship. At that very instant a blaze of red flashed on my instrument panel. Fire in the compressor section! My old first-flight luck was stalking me again. (It had never left me, really. Some time before this, during a first flight in a new F-84-F, I had run into serious trouble and made an emergency landing on the lake.) There were two fire-warning lights in the F-100. One covered the aft end of the engine, the other covered the forward end, or compressor section. A fire, or heating up, in the aft end was not uncommon in a jet with afterburner. If the pilot throttled back or otherwise varied the running conditions of the engine, it usually disappeared and the light went off.

But a fire warning in the compressor section, crowded with fuel lines, gear boxes, and other vital parts, was serious indeed. Usually a compressor-section fire did not last long; it raced through the intake into the compressor and the plane disappeared in a puff of smoke and flame. There was an old and tired axiom about it at Edwards: "If you see a compressor fire-warning light and you haven't blown up, well, you're going to in just a second."

A small notice riveted to the panel next to the compressor fire-warning light informed me:

COMPRESSOR SECTION FIRE WARNING LIGHT ON:
STOP-COCK ENGINE. IF LIGHT REMAINS ON BAIL OUT.

A hell of a sign to put in a cockpit, I thought. It inhibits one's thinking.

I got busy fast. I throttled back on the engine. As I did, the fire-warning light flickered and dimmed. Then it flashed back on again full-strength. Following the instructions on the panel, I stop-cocked the engine completely, turning off all fuel valves. The engine unwound and settled down to a slow wind-milling. The fire-warning light flickered but remained on. When the powerless F-100 slowed to glide speed, the leading edge slats, which provide lift and stability in slow flight, cracked and extended automatically.

This produced a steady rumbling noise which I assumed to be the fire blazing in the engine air-intake directly beneath my feet. (At that time few pilots had remained in an F-100 with a wind-milling engine long enough to hear that slat noise.)

I called NACA radar and asked them to take a look through their field-glasses and see if I was trailing smoke. Since I hadn't blown up yet there was a possibility that the fire might blow itself out. As a matter of professional pride, I was reluctant to abandon a new airplane that was still in one piece. Somehow, NACA radar failed to find me. After several garbled radio exchanges with them, I snapped impatiently: "Never mind."

The fire-warning light blazed steadily. However, I saw no other signs of real fire, so I concluded that it was a false warning. I would bring the ship down dead-stick. To my knowledge at that time, only one man, North American test pilot Bob Hoover, had ever dead-sticked an F-100. On that one occasion the struts had been pushed up through the wing, demolishing the plane. As a matter of fact, North American test pilots were then flipping coins to see who would deliberately bring an F-100 in dead-stick to fulfill a requirement of the Air Force acceptance tests. I was not concerned. Dead-stick landings in low L-over-D airplanes were my specialty. Every test pilot develops a strong point. I was certain that my talent lay in dead-stick landings.

With the engine then idling and generating no energy to the plane's systems, I was running out of hydraulic pressure to operate the controls. Following the handbook instructions, I pulled a lever which extended a miniature 'windmill' into the slipstream. This 'windmill' churned, building up pressure in the hydraulic lines. Unknown to me, there was a major leak in the line. The windmill was not helping, but hurting me. It was pumping hydraulic fluid overboard as fast as it could turn.

I called Edwards tower and declared an emergency. All airborne planes in the vicinity of the base were warned away from the lake area. I held the ailing F-100 on course, dropping swiftly, lining up for a dead-stick lake landing, following the same glide path that I used for the dead-stick Skyrocket. I flared out and touched down smoothly. It was one of the best landings I have ever made, in fact. Seconds later, while the F-100 was rolling out, the remaining bit of hydraulic pressure in the control lines drained out and the controls froze.

I then proceeded to violate a cardinal rule of aviation: never try tricks with a compromised airplane. The F-100 was still rolling at a fast clip, coming up fast on the NACA ramp, when I made my poor decision. I had already achieved the exceptional, now I would end it with a flourish, a spectacular wind-up. I would snake the stricken F-100 right up the ramp and bring it to a stop immediately in front of the NACA hangar. This trick, which I had performed so often in the Skyrocket, was a fine touch. After the first successful dead-stick landing in an F-100, it would be fitting.

According to the F-100 handbook, the hydraulic brake system—a separate hydraulic system from the controls—was good for three 'cycles,' engine out. This means three pumps on the brake, and that proved exactly right. The F-100 was moving at about fifteen miles an hour when I turned up the ramp. I hit the brakes once, twice, three times. The plane slowed, but not quite enough. It was still inching ahead ponderously, like a diesel locomotive. I hit the brakes a fourth time—and my foot went clear to the floorboards. The hydraulic fluid was exhausted.

The F-100 rolled on, straight between the yawning hangar doors! The good Lord was watching over me—partially anyhow. The NACA hangar was then crowded with expensive research tools —the Skyrocket, all the X-1 series, the X-3, X-4, and X-5. Yet somehow, my plane, refusing to halt, squeezed by them all and bored steadily on toward the side wall of the hangar. The nose of the F-100 crunched through the corrugated aluminum, punching out an eight-inch steel I-beam. I was lucky. Had the nose bopped three feet to the left or right, the results could have been catastrophic. Hitting to the right, I would have set off the hangar fire-deluge system, flooding the hangar with 50,000 barrels of water and ruining all the expensive airplanes.

Hitting to the left, I would have dislodged a 25-ton hangar-door counterweight, bringing it down on the F-100 cockpit, and doubtless ruining Crossfield. Chuck Yeager never let me forget that incident. He drew many laughs at congregations of pilots by opening his talk: "Well, the sonic wall was mine. The hangar wall was Crossfield's." That's the way it was at Edwards.

Hero one minute, bum the next. The fact that I was the first pilot to land an F-100 dead-stick successfully, and memorized elaborate and complete instrument data on the engine failure besides, was soon forgotten.

The F-100 is a tough bird. Within a month NACA's plane was flying again, with Crossfield back at the helm. In the next few weeks I flew forty-five grueling flights in the airplane, pushing it to the limits, precisely defining the roll coupling. (On one flight the coupling was so severe that it cracked a vertebra in my neck.) These data confirmed, in actual flight, the need for a new F-100 tail, which North American was planning to install on later models of the airplane.

Every night after landing, I taxied the F-100 slowly to the NACA ramp. At the bottom, placed there on orders of Walt Williams, there was a large new sign, symbolic of the new atmosphere at Edwards. It said:

PLEASE COME TO A COMPLETE STOP BEFORE TAXIING UP RAMP

21: END OF THE LINE

DURING MY FIRST FIVE YEARS AT EDWARDS, NACA achieved a remarkable safety record. No NACA pilot had bought the farm; no airplane had been lost through accident. This was due partly to luck, partly to excellent maintenance and a thoughtful approach to flight test. But our luck was bound to run out. It did, finally, in August, 1955.

I was sitting at my desk in the pilots' room, roughing out a report on a Skyrocket flight—the old ship was still going strong—when the emergency broke. Somewhere high over the base, Stan Butchart, the B-29 mother-plane pilot, was about to air-launch Joe Walker in the X-1-A. I was absently following the progress of the flight over the radio loudspeaker as mother-plane pilot, chase pilot, and Joe Walker, strapped in the cockpit of the rocket plane, talked back and forth, getting set for the drop.

"We have a fire." The words crackled from the loudspeaker.

I snapped to attention.

"Fire?" Butchart repeated.

"Yes. There's been an explosion."

I raced upstairs to the NACA control tower. Soon it was jammed with NACA engineers and mechanics, crowding the loudspeaker, shouting conflicting accounts of the accident, and helpful and unhelpful suggestions.

By that time NACA had had possession of the flashy X-1-A, in which Yeager and Murray set their speed and altitude records, and her sister-ship, the X-1-B, for a little over one year.

We had not logged much flight time on the ships. NACA had shipped them back to the Bell factory for ejection-seat installation, and then filled both planes with data instruments. All this took time and delayed the flight program. The installation of the ejection seats caused considerable controversy. I was in favor of proceeding without them because of the urgency of the program and because Yeager, Murray, and Everest had demonstrated that the airplanes could be recovered from unstable flight. As senior pilot my views were carefully weighed, but the majority at NACA favored the escape device.

The fire that broke out in the X-1-A was later traced to a similar source as that which destroyed the X-1-D, Queenie, and the first X-2 over Lake Ontario. After those accidents the airplanes were modified to reduce the possibility of a single catastrophic explosion. In theory, a fire from that source might be 'controlled,' or held down to a smoldering effect. This was all theory, however. In my view, a fire in any airplane was dangerous. A fire in a rocket plane, loaded with tons of Lox and alcohol, brought to mind the picture of a bomb with a lighted fuse. In my opinion, there was only one thing to do: get rid of it, and fast.

Each rocket-plane pilot had worked out, in conjunction with the pilot of the mother ship, a procedure to follow if an emergency developed in either plane. Jack McKay, who had developed into a very able test pilot, and I had agreed with Butchart that if something went wrong after either of us had entered the cockpit of the Skyrocket and had closed the canopy, he would immediately jettison the rocket plane, leaving the rocket-plane pilot to look after his own hide. As a matter of fact, McKay and Butchart later ran into such an emergency. One day something went haywire in a propeller on the B-29 mother plane.

As agreed, Butchart instantly cut loose the Skyrocket. A split second later the B-29 prop tore loose and cartwheeled through the space the Skyrocket had just vacated. McKay landed without difficulty; but had Butchart not cut the parasite plane loose, the prop would have ripped into its fuel tanks, causing an explosion that would have killed everyone, including McKay.

"What's the situation up there?" Vensel yelled into the control-tower mike.

"Well, we've got a fire in the X-1-A," Butchart replied coolly.

"We got Joe Walker out of the cockpit. He's standing by in the bomb-bay compartment now. The fire's pretty bad. I figure we ought to drop this thing pretty quick."

"Now let's not take any chances," Vensel said. "Don't try to save the airplane if there's any danger."

I fought down an urge to grab the mike and tell Butchart to pull the jettison lever then without another second's delay. But he was already getting enough advice from the ground, and I couldn't get near the mike, anyway. The Air Force chase plane was piloted by Major Kit Murray. He had been tucked up close to the X-1-A when the explosion occurred. The X-1-A wheel doors had blown off and smashed into Murray's plane.

Above the chatter in the control room I heard Murray report: "I might have a little damage here. I'll try to stick around . . . Butch, you're getting a lot of smoke out of the back end. The Lox and hydrogen peroxide are dumping overboard ..."

Murray, with a plane damaged to an extent no one thought to investigate, was still hanging on, relaying an account of the scene from the outside. But how long could he remain on station with a damaged plane? Was he needlessly risking his own life?

I ran to the nearest telephone and put through a call to Air Force Fighter Ops. Pete Everest answered.

"Pete," I said, "Murray's up there. His plane's been hit. How soon can you get a relief chase-plane up?"

"We'll be up there in five minutes," Everest said, ringing off hurriedly. I think he jumped into an airplane and flew up to relieve Murray. In any case, Murray soon landed without further difficulty.

Now a big debate was raging in the NACA control room about what to do: keep the rocket plane attached to the mother plane and try to save it, or throw it away? No one asked me my opinion, but I gave it anyway: "Throw that damned thing away as fast as you can."

The experts thronging the control room soon swung to this conclusion. Then a second debate arose over where to drop the airplane. There was concern that the X-1-A might fall on a house or an automobile. Vensel called the Air Force and requested they assign a remote bombing area into which the stricken rocket plane might be jettisoned. While this discussion took place, the fire in the X-1-A raged about the plane.

A new thought flashed to my mind. If the Lox had drained out of the rocket plane and the alcohol remained in its tank, the plane would be dangerously tail-heavy. When it fell away from the mother plane, it might pitch up sharply, perhaps fatally ramming the mother plane. Had the fact that the Lox drained away reached Butchart amidst all the bureaucratic chatter about where to drop the X-1-A?

I ran downstairs and found a radio mike in a secluded room. "Butch," I called, breaking in on the radio circuit. "This is Scotty." I kept my voice low, trying to restore some semblance of order in the chaos on the radio circuit.

"Go ahead, Scotty," Butchart replied.

"The Lox is drained, Butch. Be sure to pull some G's when you drop her. Otherwise, she'll pitch up and might climb right into the bomb bay."

"Okay, Scotty, already thought of it, thanks anyway. I'm going to cut her now. I'm pulling G's. I'm in a hard left bank. I think it will go okay."

Butchart pulled the lever and the smoking X-1-A disengaged from the mother plane. As we feared, the tail-heavy plane pitched up. In fact, it climbed right by the B-29 and almost looped before dipping and spinning crazily into the desert floor. Butchart received further instructions from the ground. Among other things, he was advised to land the mother plane as quickly as possible. I knew Butchart's good judgment would prevail. He would check his ship thoroughly, with landing gear down and locked, before descending. Butchart had brought many damaged airplanes back to base in the Pacific during World War II.

This accident reduced our stable of rocket airplanes to three: the X-1-B, the X-1-E (still being slowly rebuilt by hand), and the Skyrocket—and set off another prolonged investigation which grounded the Bell airplanes. It also influenced the future of the Bell X-2. That jinxed ship had finally arrived back at Edwards and was then being feverishly prepared for its first powered flight by Pete Everest and the Bell crew. Following the loss of the X-1-A, the Air Force passed the word that if the X-2 had not flown by December 31 of that year, the project would be completely abandoned. The plane would be consigned to the Smithsonian.

Facing this harsh deadline, Everest finally got off a shaky powered flight. It took place on November 18, 1955, less than six weeks before the expiration date set for the X-2 program. It was almost ten years to the day since the X-2 had been conceived, and about three years and five months after Skip Ziegler had made the first X-2 powerless glide-flight at Edwards. Everest held the X-2's speed subsonic and landed hastily after a fire broke out in the tail of the plane. This flight gained the program a reprieve—an extension. In spite of this Pyrrhic victory, it seemed dead certain at the time that the X-2 would never provide the U.S. with useful aeronautical research data in time. The other rocket planes in our stable were almost obsolete.

By comparison, NACA's advanced research airplane, then officially dubbed the X-15 (the experimental vehicles from the X-6 to X-14 were mostly unmanned missiles), was showing strong promise. Six months after the Air Force asked for bids, or by June, 1955, all returns were in. Four companies—North American, Bell, Douglas, and Republic—submitted proposals.

The lack of interest among the other aircraft companies is explainable. Research airplanes, as their stormy history clearly indicates, are unprofitable projects from a management standpoint. In the beginning they require superlative and expensive design and engineering talent. They do not result in big production orders, which are the bread and butter of the industry. Since the X-15 was an NACA project, all information and new theory and ideas developed with the plane would be made available without charge to all of industry. Many companies reasoned: why assign our most talented people to develop ideas which our competition can exploit?

The bids were meticulously analyzed. The Republic proposal was extraordinarily good, but it showed clearly that the company lacked experience in the research-airplane field. The Douglas airplane was essentially a redesigned version of the 'advanced Skyrocket,' which its engineers hoped to sell to the Navy. The Bell airplane looked very good and demonstrated the company's long experience in rocket airplanes. But because of many political factors, Bell's wonderful flair for exotic inventions, and the recent performance of the X-1-A and X-2 planes, the Bell bid was not approved. In retrospect, it seems to me that from the beginning the contract was almost pre-ordained for the fourth company, North American.

Ironically, many at North American, for many of the reasons just cited, were not seriously interested in building the X-15. Its designers, like those of other companies, had huddled with NACA engineers to find out what was wanted. Afterward the North American advanced-design group came up with a scheme superior in detail to, but in general outline quite like, the other proposals. Actually, the North American proposal was carried through only as a 'design exercise' for the company engineers, a not uncommon practice in the industry. One man, however, Harrison ('Stormy') Storms, Chief Engineer of the Los Angeles Division, with a long-range look ahead, had sparked a growing interest in the endeavor within the high levels of the company.

There were several reasons why the Air Force found North American the ideal company to build the X-15. For one thing, North American was an old friend of the Air Force and primarily an Air Force contractor, with an outstanding history going back to World War II, when it produced P-51s and B-25s by the thousands. At that time North American had built more jet airplanes—F-86s and F-1000s—than any other company, and its relationships with the Air Force were close and very simpatico. North American's engineers were conversant with high speeds and the problems of aerodynamic heating and instability.

The company had great depth, in terms of engineering talent and money, on which it could draw in case of trouble. Its Rocketdyne division was producing the most powerful and reliable rocket engines in the U.S.—the power plants for the missiles Thor, Jupiter, and Atlas. North American engineers were then in the advance-design stages of a Mach 3 fighter, the F-108, which would benefit directly from the X-15 experience. Finally, North American, a Los Angeles corporation, was convenient to the Edwards test base.

"Walt, I want to make a proposal to you."

"What is it, Scotty?" Williams said. He bounced out of his chair and paced about his office. I followed him with my eyes, but I didn't move from my chair.

"Do you remember my proposal in 1953 to Dr. Dryden to go to Bell and ride herd on the X-2?"

"Sure. Certainly."

"You see where the X-2 is now," I said. "That would have been a pretty good idea if we had followed it through. Right?"

"Maybe," Williams said. "Then again, maybe not. It may be that no one could have salvaged the X-2. Why?"

"I've been thinking about this X-15," I said.

"Well, now, that's a surprise. You wouldn't kid me, would you? Have you been thinking about anything else?"

"It's a little difficult to spend time thinking about it, what with having to do most of your thinking besides."

At that, Williams chuckled and tossed his pencil at me, missing by yards.

"Okay, Scotty. I can see you're being real serious," he said. "What do you have in mind?"

"I want to do with the X-15 what I proposed for the X-2. I want to be assigned to the North American plant full-time on the X-15 project, carry out the company demonstration flights, and then return with the airplane to NACA, Edwards, and make the maximum-performance flights. I want to get in on the project from the beginning and stay with it right on through to completion."

Williams sat down heavily in the chair behind his desk. He doodled on his scratch pad, rubbed his head, turned and peered out the window, staring fixedly into the desolate wastes of tumbleweed, and said nothing for fully three minutes. I could imagine in detail every single political thought running through his mind. (The stars had long since gone from my eyes.) I could see him mentally arranging the complicated chessboard, putting NACA men, North American men, Air Force men, and other industry men in their proper starting order and mentally playing the game through. I had done it many times myself.

Apart from the strictly personal relationships, there were larger questions to resolve in this game: how would it affect NACA's relationship with the Air Force, with North American? How would it affect the operation at Edwards? What about the Air Force pilots—Pete Everest, Chuck Yeager, Kit Murray, and the other experienced hands? There were a thousand moves that might leave the King—in this case, Williams—or the X-15 Program—vulnerable.

"Why does this thing mean so much to you?" Williams asked me.

"I've told you before, Walt. We must do something to get one of these research airplanes built in time to do some good," I said.

"But what will North American say?" Williams said. "That's a huge company. A good company. They've got about five thousand engineers on the payroll down there. You know how they'll react if we come butting in."

The answer from Williams was already coming through loud and clear. It was 'no.' His reasons for arriving at that conclusion were perfectly sound, but the answer ill-suited my ambition. The time had come, I knew, to part company with NACA. It would not be easy to walk away dry-eyed. I had cut my teeth there, and formed many deep and lasting friendships, including that with Walt Williams. My future, however, lay not with NACA but with the product of its total genius, the X-15.

"Walt, this is the end of the line," I said.

"Scotty. You want to think this one over carefully. You're not a young pilot any more—you're thirty-four. If past history is any example, that plane won't be flying for a long, long time. You might be forty years old by then, and they might be looking for a younger pilot. A hundred things could go wrong."

"But you don't understand. It's not just the flying. I do want to fly the plane. But I want to help build it, too. I want to be a part of that airplane," I said.

"We've still got a lot of airplanes around here you can be part of," Williams said. "You practically built the X-1-E yourself. And if they ever finish the X-15 you can fly that, too—if you live that long."

"I'm sorry, Walt. I may never be able to explain this properly to anyone. But I am going with that airplane."

22: END OF AN ERA

I DROVE SLOWLY, GAPING AT THE PALE GREEN hangar-sized North American production buildings strung along the south edge of Los Angeles International Airport like some titanic freight train. Hundreds upon hundreds of automobiles were parked bumper to bumper in lots adjoining the buildings. Inside those buildings, I knew, tens of thousands of skilled workmen were riveting away on the last few hundred of the six thousand Sabrejets the Air Force had ordered, and tooling up for mass production of the supersonic F-100. Having taken the measure of its size from close quarters, I then understood how North American had ground out 43,000 airplanes in World War II. It was a tremendous operation—five hundred times the size of NACA, Edwards—a company that had built more airplanes than any other firm in the world. Its bid for the X-15 alone—about $50 million—almost equaled the yearly budget for all of NACA.

"How do you do, Mr. Crossfield." North American's president, Lee Atwood, a thin, soft-spoken man with deep-set green eyes, held out his hand. In stark contrast to the California environment, he was meticulously dressed, conservative style. An aeronautical engineer, in 1948 he had taken over day-by-day operation of North American from the dynamic Dutch Kindelberger, the famous airplane-builder who gave North American its great fame and reputation. Dutch had moved up to be chairman of the board of directors. Atwood offered me a seat and then returned to sit behind his broad desk. The office was mahogany-paneled and decorated with deep-green potted plants.

As I wound up for my pitch, it occurred to me that I was then about to address one of the most important men in the aviation industry. That I was in his office at all, I believe, was due solely to the fact that I was the first man to fly at twice the speed of sound. In the two years since I had made the record, this flight, technically insignificant though it was, had opened many doors. Like Yeager, Everest, and Bridgeman, I came to know four-star generals and other big shots in aviation on a first-name basis. For example, I had met Atwood the previous year in New York when at a gathering of aeronautical engineers he presented me the Lawrence Sperry award for my high-speed flight work. It was a farce, in a way, but for a man on a mission it made the job a lot easier.

I was not really up to the interview that day. I was suffering from influenza, the same malady that weakened me on the day of the flight which paved my way to Atwood's door. My nose was draining and every few minutes I had to take out my handkerchief and blow. It was annoying. I probably impressed Atwood as the least likely physical specimen to fly the X-15 he ever saw.

"Mr. Atwood, I want to come to work for North American on the X-15 project." I paused to let this sink in, and to see if it might bring an immediate 'no.' Mine was something of a bold and unorthodox move, to put it mildly. North American already employed a team of perhaps thirty test pilots, bossed by Bob Baker and Jack Bryan, both of whom had been with North American for many years. No doubt many of these pilots had their eyes on the X-15 and were fully capable of test-flying it. I had long since learned that big corporations like North American did not usually draw from the outside. They used their own talent for special jobs.

"Rocket planes are my business," I said, blowing again. "I've been flying them for five years at Edwards, as senior pilot for NACA. I not only flew them, I laid out flight-test programs, recorded the data, drew up the reports, and presented NACA conclusions. I also oversaw maintenance and participated in the re-building of the X-1-E to the extent of laying out the new propulsion system—a combination of the best features of the Skyrocket and the X-1—and other hardware."

Atwood interrupted me briefly to receive an important telephone call. I blew my nose and cursed my flu. When he hung up, I rolled on.

"I know you have a very experienced organization down here with plenty of able talent. But if you have never tackled a rocket plane, there are some special problem areas. There'll be a lot of problems on this particular ship. It's revolutionary. We've had a bad history in research airplanes, as you know. Delays. Explosions. Investigations. Instability. I think I can contribute. And I'd like to have the privilege of working on this airplane. I want to help make it as nearly perfect as possible and get it to Edwards in time to do some good."

"What do you want to do specifically?" Atwood asked. It was clear from the telephone call I had overheard that he was a man of a few well-chosen words.

"I'd like to start from the beginning. Work on the plane as an engineer, helping with the systems, in a sort of advisory capacity. In that way, when it came time to fly the airplane, I'd be thoroughly familiar with all of it, down to the smallest bolt. During the construction I could interject my experience with other rocket airplanes. At the same time, as an ex-NACA hand, I'd be useful as a liaison with that agency during all phases of construction and flight test."

I talked on, stressing my strong points—my master's degree in aeronautical engineering, my background in the wind tunnel at the University of Washington, my brief experience at the Boeing plant in Seattle during the early days of World War II, my Navy tour as a flight instructor, my experience in manufacturing aircraft accessories, my flight and engineering record at Edwards. Whether it was all this combined, or the simple magic of Mach 2, I don't know, but in spite of my influenza and runny nose, Atwood, as is his nature, gave me the benefit of the doubt.

As president of North American, Atwood bossed six separate divisions of the company. Only one of these, the Los Angeles division, would build the X-15. A president of a company of that size delegates total authority to chiefs. He doesn't hire men off the streets and thrust them upon his lieutenants. He operates by suggestion.

"Would you like to go down and talk to Ray Rice about this? The proposal is a kind of unusual arrangement for us. His division will build the airplane and he knows what kind of people he needs."

"Certainly," I said.

"When can you get by to see him?"

"Right now, if it's convenient."

Ray Rice, Chief Engineer of the Los Angeles Division, bought my proposal, I have often thought since, with some reservations. At that time the X-15 project was still so new in the company and I was so new to the company that there was no specific job slot available to me. Thus I was hired, more or less, as a consultant, and didn't really learn who my boss was for a long time.

Coincidental with my move to North American, in December of 1955, the great and glorious era at Edwards was in the twilight of its life. The Skyrocket, after a total of about 130 flights, was slated for moth-balls. The X-1-E, so long in the rebuilding, flew shortly after my departure but never lived up to our expectations. Soon it was grounded for good, when NACA learned that the pilot's boot-tips might strike the instrument panel in the event of an emergency ejection. The X-1-B made a few more flights, some to collect advanced information for the control system of the X-15, but this airplane was old before its time and it, too, was ultimately grounded. The X-2, the plane I was supposed to fly in the spring of 1951 for NACA, was still slowly winding her tragic course into history, six years or more behind schedule.

A few weeks after I departed Edwards, Pete Everest took the X-2 on her second powered flight, firing only one of the two rocket barrels. In the weeks following, in a startling burst of activity, he clicked off six additional powered runs, achieving on his eighth and final flight a speed of about Mach 2.9, or 1900 miles an hour. When Everest landed, as he wrote in his book, he telephoned his wife and said, "Honey, you are talking to the fastest man in the world." She was—and his 1900-mile-an-hour flight in that unstable airplane was, in my opinion, remarkable. As Everest himself said, "Control was marginal and if the pilot over-controlled or maneuvered the airplane too violently, anything could happen."

Walt Williams was anxious to take over the X-2 for NACA in order to press ahead with a series of aerodynamic-heating studies at extreme speeds. But after its years of frustrating toil and heartbreak, the Air Force understandably was not about to turn the plane over until some additional records had been chalked up. On the verge of his departure for other duties, Pete Everest assigned two new, young Air Force pilots to make these flights. Iven

Kincheloe, a handsome blond captain, a graduate of the Empire Test Pilot School, and a Korean ace, would make the altitude attempt. Captain Milburn ('Mel') Apt, a balding veteran of Edwards, would make the speed attempt. NACA dutifully protested these flights, pointing to the dangers involved. The Air Force compromised, setting a deadline of November 1, 1956, for turning the plane over to NACA, whether or not Kincheloe and Apt were successful.

Kincheloe came up to bat first. He made one check-flight in the X-2, under Everest's direction. Then after Everest left, Kincheloe reared back to hit a home-run. He opened the engine wide when the X-2 was dropped, and pointed the tapered nose skyward, the stick hauled full back in his lap. On the first two flights the X-2 reached high, but not high enough. On the third try, Kincheloe's fourth flight in the X-2, he succeeded. The X-2 hurtled to 126,000 feet. In that rarefied air, when it ran out of momentum, the X-2 fell back toward earth. When the plane reached the thicker atmosphere, Kincheloe, in a remarkable piece of piloting, recovered, slowed, circled, and landed. He never again flew a rocket airplane. On the strength of these four flights and his inexhaustible enthusiasm for the business, the Sunday newspaper supplements labeled him 'Mr. Space.'

With the NACA deadline coming up fast, Captain Mel Apt, who had not yet had a check flight in the X-2, made hurried preparations for a final effort to break Everest's speed record. Four days before his time expired, he launched in the X-2 for the ship's thirteenth powered flight. There was evidently no time for a preliminary flight at low speed. In any case, the Air Force did not specifically limit Apt on his first flight. He dropped, flicked on the rocket barrels, and flew a near-perfect parabolic flight plan. The X-2's rocket burned six seconds longer than it ever had before. Mel Apt drove the X-2 to the amazing speed of about Mach 3.1, or 2,094 miles an hour, beating Everest by a wide margin.

The thirteenth flight proved to be the unlucky one. At the end of the speed run the X-2 behaved as many had predicted. It cartwheeled out of control, subjecting the X-2 and Apt to tremendous G forces. He could not recover. As the plane whipped into a deadly inverted spin, he tried to abandon ship.

He blew the nose capsule and it separated from the main fuselage, but before he could dive out and open his parachute, the capsule struck the desert floor with terrible impact. Apt was killed, the X-2 destroyed. Around Edwards, Pete Everest's title was changed from 'Fastest Man in the World' to 'Fastest Man Alive.' A new street at the base was named in Apt's honor.

That was the final, dreadful end of the X-2. In eleven years from start to finish, the program had cost the U.S. millions of dollars. It robbed two excellent pilots and one crewman of their lives and destroyed, altogether, three airplanes. In its total of thirteen flights the X-2 had provided the U.S. a speed and altitude record, but precious little else. The X-2 yielded hardly a scrap of aerodynamic-hearing data, the purpose for which it was intended. The premature loss of the ship left the U.S. without a research airplane to probe the Mach 3 zone and created, in a sense, a larger and more urgent mission for the X-15.

The way I see it, that last flight of the X-2 drew the curtain on the grand era at Edwards. It closed out what might be called the first phase of the history of the experimental research airplane in the United States. The big NACA installation went on, of course, piling up data points by the tens of thousands, which proved useful. But all the old race-track excitement was gone completely. There was no plane to probe exciting new areas.

Edwards became a place of hard work and routine. NACA pilots wrung the last drop from the group of tired planes. The Air Force pilots concentrated on the newest production-model jets—Republic's F-105 fighter-bomber; North American's experimental F-107; Convair's F-106, a faster, larger version of the delta-wing F-102; and Convair's delta-wing, medium-range bomber, the B-58. The Navy pilots were busy de-bugging a stable of comparable carrier-deck fighters and bombers, and a pilotless missile, the Regulus.

I don't mean to imply that the test work was not dangerous. On the contrary, it was hair-raising at times and many pilots lost their lives. Missing from the busy, formal scene, however, was the echoing boom of a rocket engine exploding to life at 35,000 feet, the long snaky trail of white rocket-exhaust across the sky, the satisfaction of the free drink at Pancho's, another milestone on man's inexorable journey toward the stars reached or passed. In the period following the loss of the last X-2, almost everybody who cared to flew Mach 2 regularly in production-line airplanes. But no faster. It is only human to be nostalgic, and to view one's own life from a special point of view. So I draw some satisfaction from the thought that my work on the frontier of flight contributed considerably to the story of the grand era at Edwards. True, I came on the scene late, three years behind Yeager's epic Mach 1 flight; and I left early, about nine months before Mel Apt's epic Mach 3 flight. But I had come when the experimental plane program was picking up, as the new ships came from the factories, and I left just before the whole show ran out of steam.

In those five years I logged only six hundred hours in the air, but what hours they were! When I flip back through my own flight book, I am astonished. Where did I find the time? Eighty-nine flights in the Skyrocket; eleven flights in the X-1; a grand total of one hundred rocket flights. For what it's worth, that total is about equal to all the rocket flights of Yeager, Everest, Marion Carl, Bridgeman, Murray, Kincheloe, and Apt put together. No less interesting were the twenty-five flights in the XF-92-A, thirty-two flights in the X-4, twelve flights in the X-5, sixty-five flights in the F-100, seventeen flights in the D-558-I, three flights each in the F-102 and F-84-F, one flight in a B-47 which I had studied years earlier in the University of Washington wind tunnel, thirteen flights in an F-S6, one flight in a Navy F9F, sixty-four flights in the YF-

84, and scores upon scores of routine flights in the wide variety of propeller-driven airplanes in NACA's stable. I had even flown, briefly, a Hiller helicopter.

In sum, I believe it is fair to say that I was good for NACA and NACA was good for me. My six hundred hours of flight time, plus countless hours of preparation and analysis on the ground, helped lay bare many secrets in the transsonic area. It was a small contribution, admittedly, but when taken together with all the aeronautical research and experimentation in the United States, I believe it helped to advance the state of the art. At the same time, the education provided me by NACA in engineering, flying, industry and government politics, and a thousand other things, was invaluable. At NACA, Edwards, I graduated in my field. Most important, I found the means of bringing my life full circle, to the X-15, the airplane that would begin a new era at Edwards, the second phase in the turbulent history of the research airplane, the second fifty years of aviation history.

23: Secrets in the Cafeteria

Building number 20, a relic of World War II, stood across the street from the main North American engineering offices, almost lost in a towering cluster of manufacturing buildings adjoining the Los Angeles International Airport. Building 20 housed the cafeteria for North American employees. During the first half of 1956 a cramped space alongside the cafeteria, which we called the 'garret,' served as home for the X-15. The space was restricted. A North American guard stood watch at the doorway, which bore the sign: SECRET, UNAUTHORIZED PERSONNEL PROHIBITED. Visitors cleared to enter our workroom had first to sign a log book and be vouched for by an escort known to the guard on duty. It was all very hush-hush.

Under ordinary circumstances, North American builds airplanes like Detroit builds automobiles—on a razzle-dazzle production-line basis. The plant people are divided into teams which specialize—excel, I should say—in various fields of aeronautical engineering, design, and manufacturing. One group, the Advanced Design Section, conceives the new airplanes, inventing and laying out drawings of concepts. This group then takes these plans and, working closely with the Washington office of North American, submits proposals to the government or, in the rare instance of a commercial airplane, to airline executives.

If the government buys a North American design, or awards a production contract, the remaining teams of the plant, amounting to some 16,000 people, move in to transform the layout drawings and specifications of the Advanced Design Section to working hardware.

This is an immensely complicated task, much too involved to describe in detail here. In brief, North American project engineers, working hand-in-glove with demanding 'customer' project engineers, rough out a working concept of the airplane after first settling on the engine, or engines, usually furnished separately by the customer. In the initial stages the toughest problems are the weight and balance analyses, crucial to the final performance of the airplane. This delicate work goes on for months, turning hair gray and keeping many engineers preoccupied with wind-tunnel models of varying shapes and designs. The goal is to squeeze maximum performance out of the total package, taking into account infinite variables such as engine power and fuel consumption. Few people realize it, but in these days the fuel of an airplane, which, of course, constantly diminishes during flight and can change the center of gravity of the ship, sometimes accounts for sixty per cent of the total weight of the airplane at take-off.

When the general scheme is finally agreed upon, and the equipment to go into the airplane, such as armament, navigational and safety devices, has been fixed, North American project engineers then call upon all sections of the plant for help. Hundreds of engineers in the structures, aerodynamic, thermo-dynamic, manufacturing, and sub-systems design departments, go to work, designing specific pieces for the airplane—instrument panels, for example, and landing-gear shock absorbers, dive brakes, windshields, and fuel tankage. At the same time, still another team builds a full-scale 'mock-up' or dummy model of the airplane, complete with instrument panel and moveable con-trols, which the design engineers use to insure that all of the tens of thousands of pieces of the puzzle fit properly before they order production.

The entire process from that point on is an endless, nerve-shattering bat-tle to design parts that will perform the required task for the least weight. Every pound of payload (that is, armament, fuel, passengers) in an airplane can add more than seven pounds of weight to the total structure which the engine, with a fixed thrust, must force through the air. The drive to save weight is restrained only by safety considerations. Even these are pared to the bone. The safety factor of a big, lumbering merchant ship is about ten to one; that of a modern jet airplane, about one and a half to one, at best. The rea-son is simple. On a ship an engineer can design a motor to run, say, an electric fan, with little concern for total weight. Thus he builds it big and tough. It works fine, but it weighs twenty pounds. On an airplane engineers design a fan to perform the same job, but stay within a weight limit of, say, one pound. The result is a thin, sophisticated product—usually new and untried—with a minimum margin of safety.

The North American Project Engineer rides herd on the entire plant force assigned to his airplane, watching schedules and doling out weight restrictions to engineers like so many gold doubloons. Each piece that goes into the air-plane is tested for strength and reliability a hundred times over, under the amazing variety of temperature ranges which the modern airplane encoun-ters in flight. A sample is fitted in the mock-up.

When all the parts are in place, the customer conducts a formal inspec-tion of the dummy plane, probing for weaknesses, suggesting improvements, and usually adding items, again driving the engineers into weight-trimming frenzies. Many additional customer checks follow the mock-up inspection as the work progresses.

When, at last, the customer is satisfied, or as nearly satisfied as possible, he gives a green light and the North American Project Chief 'freezes' the de-sign. At that point detailed engineering drawings are released to the Manufacturing Division or to various subcontractors—'vendors,' as we call them in the trade. Manufacturing brings all of the tens of thousands of parts together at the right time and place on the assembly line, and soon thereafter the near-miracle is done. Finished airplanes roll out the door for a final paint-ing or polishing in the California sunshine. Following several shake-down flight tests by North American pilots, the new planes are then delivered either to

Edwards for customer tests, or, if the airplane is a proven concept, to operational units specified by the customer.

The experimental X-15 did not fit this general production scheme. It began like other North American projects in the Advanced Design Section. But because it was something special and only three models would be built, North American conceived an unusual method to see the X-15 to completion.

Management formed a special team under direction of Advanced Design, but divorced from the other departments of the plant, each man a specialist in one phase of aircraft design or manufacturing. To boss this group, management selected Charles Feltz, a 39-year-old mechanical engineer, who was pulled off the F-86 project. Lacking other quarters for this new team, management temporarily assigned it to the cafeteria building.

Charlie Feltz was truly astonished by the assignment. Until he was named to head it, he had never heard of the X-15 project. It may seem surprising, but in a huge, decentralized company such as North American, project engineers are busy with their own problems and rarely have time to rub elbows with advanced design engineers, and vice versa. Moreover, from its inception the X-15 was a closely guarded secret. Thus Feltz was stunned by it all when I joined the X-15 group—consisting of eleven North American engineers besides Feltz—in the garret adjoining the cafeteria.

"Morning, Charlie," I said, sticking out my hand.

Feltz was sitting at a cluttered desk pushed into one corner of the X-15 home. He was a short man with rumpled, graying hair and deep green eyes. He was a native of Texas, a graduate of Texas Tech and, as I soon learned, he affected a country-boy air. He dressed informally and butchered the King's English.

Behind Charlie's relaxed exterior, however, lay a steel-trap mind and an unyielding ambition to build good airplanes. He had joined North American in 1940, on the eve of the industry's gigantic expansion. He had not only survived the production ordeal of World War II but had also risen to the top of the best company in one of the most competitive professions in the world. In many ways Charlie Feltz reminded me of Chuck Yeager. In appearance and ability he was to the design of an airplane what Yeager was to the flight of an airplane.

" 'lo, Scotty," Feltz said, eying me casually. "Welcome aboard. Maybe you can give us some idea what this darned thing is all about." He raised up a sheaf of about twenty drawings which had been passed on to him from the Advanced Design Section.

Appropriately enough, I noted, these drawings had been prepared by two engineers named Owl and Canary. Having won the competition, these engineers had moved on to other projects and were no longer concerned directly with the X-15.

It is true that in the beginning North American management, completely absorbed with profit-making production-line airplanes such as the F-86, F-100, and other series, paid the X-15 scant attention. At first the X-15 was an annoyance to be tolerated. To be perfectly frank, only a few of us on the small X-15 team really grasped the fierceness of the tiger we had by the tail.

Feltz, however, happened to be one who knew. It was characteristic of him to play ignorant about it. As I learned, that was his way of finding out even more, or of sizing up new men assigned to him.

If the X-15 ill-fitted North American's usual method of producing an airplane, I certainly ill-fitted the X-15 team concept. I was something of a mystery at first, a kind of fifth wheel. I did not work directly for Feltz. I was hired by someone else and my paycheck came from another source. For all Feltz knew, I might have been some vice president's son-in-law. The arrangement for both of us, accustomed to a more or less rigid bureaucratic structure, was awkward and uncomfortable. In contrast, say, to those of a structural engineer or an aerodynamic heating engineer, my duties were undefined. Lacking a specific slot on the team, Feltz entered me on the rolls as a 'Design Specialist,' which seemed broad enough to cover my general role as a high-level adviser or consultant to the project.

On that first day, after Feltz had introduced me to the small X-15 team, we returned to his desk and talked a long time about the ship. Although the precise limits or mission of the airplane had not yet been established, the general outlines were known and the design had more or less been set by NACA engineers together with Hugh Elkin's Advanced Design group. There was enough on paper to indicate that Feltz faced the most challenging assignment of all aeronautical engineers in the fifty years of aviation history. After our talk I went back to my desk, lost in wondrous thought.

What was this big tiger we had by the tail? I studied the sheaf of drawings Charlie Feltz had turned over to me. I was familiar, of course, with the various bits and pieces, but this was my first opportunity to think of the project in terms of hardware. It was enough to excite any pilot or engineer.

In her three-dimensional profile, as conceived then, the X-15 shape appeared fairly conventional. In the side view she looked something like a high-performance jet fighter, poised in a level position, resting on nose wheel and center skids. (The X-2 skid concept had been carried on to the X-15 primarily as a weight-saving measure.) She had a tall, sweeping, vertical tail, elongated nose, and a smoothly fared-in, V-shaped cockpit canopy. Her wings were stubby and straight, like those on the X-3; they were mounted far aft on the exceptionally long, trim fuselage, almost butting against the horizontal stabilizer.

According to the drawings and concept in those early days, the X-15 would be carried aloft in the belly of a B-36 mother plane. The B-36 was an enormous ten-engine bomber, built by the Air Force in quantity to deliver the nation's largest nuclear bombs. In time, on this peaceful mission, the B-36 would depart Edwards with its fifteen-ton load and head to the launch point near Salt Lake, Utah, four hundred miles to the north.

The mother plane would drop the X-15 at a launch speed of Mach .7 and at an altitude of about 35,000 feet, fast enough to insure stability at launch and high enough to avoid the fuel-wasting contact with the 'thick' atmosphere. On its own then, the X-15 would fly south toward Edwards over the route we at NACA had conceived several years before. The rocket engine would burn for 88 furious seconds, consuming eight tons of fuel. After burn-out the X-15 would coast silently on course for Edwards and land dead-stick but hot on Rogers Dry Lake in the desert.

The one fact that made the X-15 far from conventional was the powerplant. It was not shown in detail on the drawings, but the entry on the specification sheet told all: "ENGINE, REACTION MOTORS, INC. XLR-99. THRUST 57,000 POUNDS AT 40,000 FEET ALTITUDE." Like the engine in the X-2, this engine was to be throttleable; it had nine times the power of the Reaction Motors engine in the X-1 or Skyrocket. It would generate nearly one million horsepower, or as much power as seven Navy cruisers.

On a shallow, ballistic-flight profile, it would hurtle the X-15 to a maximum speed of 7200 feet per second, which is over a mile and a quarter a second, 75 miles a minute, and better than 4500 miles an hour, or about Mach 7.0, twice as fast as man had ever flown. On a 'zoom,' or steep ballistic-flight profile, the powerful engine could boost the X-15 to an altitude above 250,000 feet, twice as high as man had ever flown. In between those extremes, the X-15 could explore more unknown areas than all of the research airplanes in history, and then some.

To meet these dramatic dimensions of flight and to perform her role as a research tool, the X-15 had some new and startling wrinkles which were detailed in the specifications. For example, in addition to the conventional control system for flight in the relatively thick air girdling the earth, the X-15 was to be equipped with a set of 'ballistic' controls to steer the ship in the virtually airless space above 200,000 feet. These were small rocket motors on the nose and wingtip through which the pilot could squirt a jet of hydrogen-peroxide steam to tilt the wing or raise or lower the nose. This system had never been tried.

But NACA was already busy with an experimental set of ballistic controls it had installed in the Bell X-1-B rocket plane. Jack McKay later tested the system at an altitude of 70,000 feet. When the X-15 plunged from its extreme altitude back into the thick coating of earth-atmosphere, it would be subjected to intense frictional heat like a meteorite, or the nose cone of a ballistic missile. To withstand this tremendous heat, estimated to be dozens of times greater than any airplane had ever before experienced, the fuselage nose and wing leading edges were to be built of an ablating material which would absorb the brunt of the heat and then erode and melt away, leaving the major portion of the fuselage and wing-structure intact. The remaining skin of the airplane was to be made of a new metal known as Inconel X, a nickel alloy capable of withstanding heat up to 1200 degrees Fahrenheit without losing its structural integrity. This metal would also serve as a conductor to soak up heat throughout the plane. One of the principal purposes of the X-15 was to see what effect extreme temperatures would have on the airplane structure and equipment, not to say the pilot.

Such, then, in briefest outline, was the grand and simple concept. It was truly revolutionary to me. For fifty years we had struggled to learn to fly within the earth's atmosphere. It had been fifty years of sheer technical agony. Now we had designed an airplane that would not only fly double the speed man had ever flown in this coating, but also zoom beyond it—to the fringes of space. The ship would soar a few moments in this dark weightless void. Then it would make a controlled descent into the atmosphere and finally land on an airfield like an ordinary airplane. It occurred to me that the X-15 was more than simply an airplane or research tool. It was the prototype of man's first space ship. In time, it was clear, all useful, piloted space craft would follow in the trail blazed by the X-15.

How could I best help Feltz in this fabulous project? Sitting silently at my desk I thought about it for many hours. I could see the mock-up inspections that lay ahead, the inevitable delays, breakdowns, and requests from the customer for added equipment. The X-15, if permitted, could become the perfect pigeon for every new invention, half-baked or otherwise, of every engineer in the country. Each new device would add more and more weight to the total and, since the engine thrust was fixed, cut the performance. It would also add to the complexity and inevitably delay the day I first flew her. This past pattern of research-airplane growth simply could not be allowed to happen with the X-15 and cause her demise like a few of her predecessors. Someone had to resist it, if possible, before it began.

Most of these additions, I knew, were likely to occur in the cockpit, or 'pilot's office,' my special province, the command post of the X-15. With my background in rocket planes and as the X-15's designated pilot, I concluded, I was probably least vulnerable politically and thus best equipped to say 'no.'

Thus, that day, my specific role in the X-15 project was defined to my satisfaction. I would be the X-15's chief son-of-a-bitch. Anyone who wanted Charlie Feltz or North American to capriciously change anything or add anything in the cockpit, or in the whole X-15, for that matter, would first have to fight Crossfield and hence, I hoped, would at least think twice before proposing grand inventions. This negative approach was not a role I particularly treasured. It was quite foreign to my nature, which is basically positive, I think. But I was willing to play any role that would best serve our ends and contribute to the prestige of the nation by seeing the X-15 completed and flying on schedule.

24: Ullage and Capsules

We gathered close around Charlie Feltz's desk in the garret. In two months our team had grown, seriously crowding our temporary quarters. Feltz now had two assistant project engineers, Bud Benner, a 33-year-old Pennsylvanian, capable, ambitious and relatively new to the company, and Raun Robinson, an old hand who had been around North American since the beginning of World War II. L. Robert Carmen had finally broken his 'dreamer' partnership with NACA's Hubert Drake.

Now Carmen, who had helped Drake conceive the five-engine rocket-mother plane idea in 1950, was a member of the X-15 team. He was way out most of the time, too far into space for us, but destined to make one crucial suggestion that would pull us out of a deep hole.

We were all still new to the project and new to each other, feeling our way carefully, sizing up the talents and weaknesses of the individual players. It is not easy to start from scratch and organize a major-league team. In the field of rocket airplanes there were no minor leagues to draw upon. The major teams at Bell and Douglas which had preceded us in history had long ago drifted apart. Except for Carmen and myself, no one on the X-15 team had any experience whatsoever with rocket airplanes.

What we lacked in experience we made up in spirit. Although we still had not yet been completely 'recognized' by North American—the dark secrecy surrounding our project hurt us from this standpoint—each of us knew, or was beginning to wake up to the fact, that we were working on something very special and important. In no sense was the approach routine. Feltz set the pace. He worked twelve to fifteen hours a day seven days a week; the rest of us fell into step without complaint.

Although overtime was normally paid for extra working hours, no man on the X-15 team got it.

"All right," Feltz said to the group around his desk. "Here is the bad news. In two months we have jumped from a 28,000-pound airplane to a 31,000-pound airplane. That's three thousand pounds added weight."

Someone let loose a long, low whistle. All of us knew the plane had been getting heavier, but this was the first time Feltz had totaled it up.

"To make matters worse," Feltz added, "the specific impulse of the XLR-99 engine has dropped, according to Reaction Motors. It's down from 278 to 269." Specific impulse was our technical way of stating the efficiency of the engine, hence airplane performance.

"What does that mean in velocity altogether, Charlie?"

"Maximum velocity has slipped from 7200 feet per second to 5700. That's about twenty per cent loss in speed, a little over a complete Mach number," Feltz replied.

When Feltz was glum, he could be glummer than any man I ever met. He reached his nadir that morning. The engine under discussion, the XLR-99, was a customer-furnished item over which we had no control. If it failed to live up, it was not the fault of North American or our team.

At that point North American's Rocketdyne Division had built more rocket engines than any other firm in the free world. In one of its original X-15 proposals, North American had suggested an NAA-built Army Redstone rocket engine as a power-plant for the X-15. In that year, 1955, NAA tested the Redstone engine perhaps 5,000 times with singular success. But the Air Force picked Reaction Motors to supply our engine. There were good reasons for this decision. RMI had long experience in building rocket airplane motors, reaching back to the early days of the X-1. Furthermore, North American's Rocketdyne Division was very busy designing and building new engines for the Air Force ballistic missiles Atlas and Thor. The Air Force was reluctant to dilute the division with still another complex engineering project.

It was no easy task the Air Force assigned RMI. In many ways the RMI engine project for the X-15 was as revolutionary as the X-15 itself. The customer hoped to wipe out all past weaknesses of rocket-airplane engines. The goal was to come up with a 'dream' engine many times as powerful as any in the past, and throttleable as well. The demands placed on RMI from the standpoint of reliability and precision were unprecedented.

In our eagerness and search for perfection, we frequently became impatient with RMI. The fact that RMI was a small company facing a tremendously complex job on a fairly modest budget, with a thin line of engineering talent, rarely entered into our sharp discussions. Lying a full continent's distance away and completely beyond our jurisdiction, RMI naturally became a favorite whipping boy in our camp. We blamed them unfairly in some instances. Later they were absorbed by Thiokol, a large company specializing in design and production of solid-propellant rocket engines for ballistic missiles.

"I think we can get some of this back," Feltz said, referring to the lost velocity.

We leaned over a drawing which Feltz had spread across his desk. For background Feltz began to explain the external shape of the X-15, changed from NACA's original views.

"On the X-1 and X-2 they mounted the maintenance tunnels on top and bottom," Feltz said.

Maintenance tunnels were housings or large pipes through which wiring, control cables, and plumbing were routed. Like missiles, the main body of a rocket airplane consists of a series of fuel and oxidizer tanks, as large in diameter as the fuselage. The wiring and plumbing cannot run through the sealed tanks; it must go around. Thus the tunnel concept was born years before.

"We found out in the wind tunnel that if we shift these tunnels from the top and the bottom to the side," Feltz continued, "we can fair them out like a wing stub, running the length of the fuselage. This surface will add to the lift and give us more efficiency. Besides that, the tunnels being at eye-level will make for easier maintenance. We tried running them all the way out to the nose, but we got a severe pitch-up in the wind-tunnel tests. So we just cut them off here, right behind the cockpit."

The new X-15 tunnel concept, the idea of George Owl, was absolutely ingenious. There is no other way to describe it.

"Now, back to the weight," Feltz went on. "We have still another problem. NACA is demanding a three per cent fuel ullage. Three per cent of eight tons of fuel is a lot of weight. It's damned near five hundred pounds."

"Ullage? What the hell is that?" one of the younger engineers asked.

"Ullage is the allowance to be made for the fact that no tank can be completely filled," Feltz explained. "In other words, we get five hundred pounds shaved off the total fuel supply. That means two or more seconds less burning time on the engine."

We were all mentally calculating the performance penalty.

"Now, the big weight increase on the airplane itself comes from the customer. The ablating leading edges and nose are out. They believe these might make the plane unstable. At least, the wind-tunnel tests seem to indicate that. So from here on, the leading edges will be solid Inconel X. That will add considerable to the airframe. In addition, there's some more instruments to go in, and more dampers for the control system.

"To get the performance back, we're going to add six inches to the diameter of the fuselage and lengthen the tanks within the airplane. That will give us 2500 pounds more fuel capacity. But that's as far as we can go with it. If we get any bigger, the weight of the tankage and fuel already begins to offset the gain of the added fuel. It's a point of diminishing return. With the bigger fuselage and some ideas I have to save weight in the landing gear, I figure we can get the velocity back up to 6600 feet a second. That's a net loss of only half a Mach number at maximum speed—down to Mach 6.5.

"But I want to tell you right now," Feltz went on seriously, "I don't intend to add another ounce to this airplane. It weighs 31,000 pounds now. It will weigh that when we roll her out. That means all you people have to trim every doggone thing out we can."

"Say, Charlie," an engineer said. "You know we got a space between frame 210 and 220 that you can see through. If you don't watch out, someone's going to stick something in there."

"How big is that space?" Feltz asked.

"About ten cubic inches, I'd say."

"Well, now," Feltz said, "I just might cut a few inches off the length of this danged airplane. That'll get rid of the space. No one can put something there if the space is gone."

The meeting broke up in gales of laughter. But the engineers were soon glum again, busy at their desks figuring new ways to save weight. I hung behind. Feltz had indicated he wanted to talk to me.

"Scotty," he said, propping his feet on a corner of his desk, "we got more problems. This one could really bust us for good. Take a look at this."

He handed me a letter addressed to North American from a high-ranking Air Force general. I scanned through it hurriedly, stunned by the contents. The letter said that under new Air Force policy all Air Force aircraft would be equipped with 'escape capsules' rather than ordinary ejection seats. An escape capsule could assume many forms. Basically it was a 'can,' as we called it, in which the pilot could enclose himself before ejecting from a disabled airplane. In theory the capsule would protect the pilot from wind-blast, heat, and high G forces associated with modern high-speed escape. The Air Force policy change had been prompted by experiences such as that of North American test pilot George Smith who had bailed out from an F-100 at supersonic speed. The blast tore the skin from his face. It was a miracle that he lived, really.

"Does this mean us, too?" I asked.

"It says all new Air Force planes. The Air Force is paying for this one."

"How much will this cost us?" We referred to weight like money.

"Twelve hundred pounds at least, to start," Feltz said.

"That'll ruin us." I mentally estimated the total added weight to the plane—over eight thousand pounds. It would cost us at least a Mach number in performance, maybe more, and I knew it would take years to develop the capsule. I could see in my mind the new problems the capsule would generate. Set within the cockpit, all the wires, controls, and plumbing would have to pass through it. It would have to be big or heavy enough to withstand the impact with the earth to avoid breaking the spine of an escaping pilot. It would require automatic ejection and automatic separation devices, and a parachute that would deploy automatically. In short, the capsule meant not only added weight, but greatly increased complexity, a dozen more things that might go wrong. "This capsule thing," I said. "It looks good on the surface, I know. But has anybody ever really engineered this thing out? We had a capsule nose on the Skyrocket but knew from the wind-tunnel data that if you separated the nose from the fuselage, the G force would be so great it could kill you. I made up my mind I would never use the Skyrocket capsule. I would ride the ship down and bail out. The X-2 has a capsule nose. It will probably kill the pilot, too."

"You don't have to convince me, Scotty. The way I look at it, if something goes wrong, the cockpit of the X-15 is the safest place to be, at least for a while. It's going to be pressurized with non-inflammable nitrogen gas. You can't have a fire. You can't have a fire in space, anyway, because there's no oxygen to feed it. The cockpit is stressed for plenty of G forces. If you are moving at maximum speed, that in itself means nothing is wrong. If something goes wrong, it means inevitably that the plane will slow down fast. So what's wrong with just staying in the cockpit until you get down low enough and slow enough to eject?"

"I agree," I said. "What can we do about it?"

"Well, we're not going to get exception to an Air Force policy ruling with a phone call. The way I see it, we've got to engineer this thing out with a fine-tooth comb. Since this falls into the pilot's realm, I think it would be a good one for you to take on. Call on anyone in the plant that you need for help. We've got to shoot this down or we're dead."

I turned to with a vengeance. I asked a half-dozen engineers to set to making studies on the big electronic brain in the main plant. Meanwhile I searched all the technical literature, pulling any and all engineering studies of escape systems. In the end, our team put in a total of 7000 engineering man-hours on this study. When it was completed, I was more convinced than ever that a capsule escape system was no good for the X-15. It might be suitable for combat-type airplanes. But for the X-15 it was superfluous.

In Santa Barbara, California, a few weeks later I presented the complete study to a gathering of Air Force and industry big shots. The presentation, probably the most thorough ever assembled on this subject, critically analyzed all escape capsule concepts as applied to the X-15. In every case, as I showed in chart upon chart, they were found wanting. Capsule development would increase the weight of the X-15 from 31,000 to about 40,000 pounds and delay the completion date perhaps years.

The cost in terms of money would be enormous and unless a more powerful engine were used—at a cost of more millions—the X-15 would never be more than a Hangar Queen. And finally, I concluded after two hours at the lectern, the pilot would be no better off than he would be in the X-15's special ejection seat. The audience, I hoped, was impressed.

A few weeks after that, in July, 1956, our customers came to North American for the first formal cockpit inspection. By then we had finished the cockpit mock-up, complete with instruments and a control system. The X-15 cockpit had no capsule escape system. It was rigged with the original X-15 ejection seat, a specially-designed affair with a new type of pilot-restraint harness and small stabilizers to 'weather-vane' it into the wind blast and prevent fatal tumbling or oscillation. A small solid rocket, developing the thrust of the engine in the F-86, would blast the seat up and behind the X-15. The seat, without a formal reversal of Air Force policy, passed the inspection with flying colors. There was no alternative, really. Tied to the XLR-99 engine as we were, if the customer had insisted on a capsule for the X-15, it would have killed the ship right then.

After the customers departed, Feltz said to me: "Scotty, you really earned your pay on that one."

"Somebody's got to be stubborn and hold the line," I said. "It might as well be me."

25: Girdles, Brassieres, and Shattered Sinuses

At sea level, where most of us live, man breathes a mixture of twenty per cent oxygen and eighty per cent nitrogen. As man moves up higher into the thinning air, the percentage of oxygen and nitrogen remains the same, but the amount in each breath diminishes and breathing becomes more difficult. Most of us have experienced this sensation at high-altitude mountain resorts or retreats, where the breath becomes 'short' and camp-fires or cigarettes which thrive on oxygen are difficult to keep going. Nowadays man carries his own oxygen to high places.

Mountain climbers, seeking new and more dangerous heights, pack lightweight oxygen flasks so that they can continue climbing at near-normal rates. Pilots flying above about 15,000 feet must, by regulation, wear rubber 'oxygen masks' to keep themselves constantly supplied with pure oxygen from a tank in the airplane. These masks are fitted to the jet pilot's crash helmet, or 'hard-hat,' which he wears to protect his skull against a rough landing.

In high-flying passenger airliners designed specifically for transporting large numbers of people it is impractical to supply each person with an oxygen mask. Instead, the whole cabin is 'pressurized,' meaning that the thin air through which the plane flies is scooped up, compressed, and fed into the cabin under pressure. In this way the airplane cabin moves through its hostile environment like a submarine hull through the ocean, and like submariners airline passengers may walk about the cabin freely and unrestrained, just as at low levels. At higher altitudes where the jets fly economically, cabin pressurization for commercial airliners is complicated by the fact that the cabin must be tougher and the compressed air demands are high.

This introduces new weight and structure problems which must be balanced against payload and safety factors. The 'mysterious' crashes of the first British Comet jet-airliner series were caused when the cabin structure failed under pressure. The Comets, of course, have been beefed up since then. In light of the Comet experience, our own jet airliners were subjected to exhaustive structural analysis and test before they were put into service. Today they are a much safer means of travel than the automobile.

In the unlikely event of cabin-pressure failure on a commercial jet airliner there is little cause for concern. Individual oxygen masks, stowed in the service compartment over each passenger seat, would pop down virtually into the laps of the passengers. The passengers would breathe through these devices until the pilot brought the plane down to an altitude of, say, 7000 feet, where no artificial breathing devices are required.

At altitudes above 45,000 feet the human body requires more than a supplementary supply of oxygen. In an unprotected environment the water and blood of the human body, held back only by human skin and accustomed to sea-level pressure, seek to 'boil' or 'explode' into the thinner air outside the body. The skin is not strong enough to contain this force. At present there is no reason for a commercial airliner to exceed an altitude of about 40,000 feet, so for ordinary passengers this factor is no problem. But for the military pilot or test pilot who flies above 45,000 feet some additional means of protection must be provided in case the cabin pressurization of the airplane fails. And, incidentally, the chances of a cabin-pressure failure in a single-engine combat or test airplane are much greater than those in a multi-engine airliner or bomber.

For want of a better name the emergency devices supplied to pilots who fly at extreme altitudes are called 'pressure suits,' simply because they exert a restraining pressure on the skin and chest, which helps keep the blood and breathing in a normal state. Even under the best of circumstances the best of pressure suits is uncomfortable and restricting—clumsy, like a deep-sea diver's outfit. The pilot must go aloft with his suit completely rigged, ready to operate the instant it automatically senses a cabin-pressure failure. This is somewhat comparable to a diver who must sit inside a submarine hull in full deep-sea rig.

Pressure suits are infinitely complex. Not only must they be made sensitive to pressure, they must also be cooled at all times; otherwise, the pilot would faint from the heat generated by his sealed-in body. The windshield on the sealed pressure-suit crash helmet must be designed so that it does not fog or frost over when the pilot exhales against it. The suit must contain an independent oxygen supply, a parachute, and floatation capability, in case the pilot has to bail out at high altitude, possibly over water. Since the pilot wears the suit during the complete flight, it must support his radio earphones and mike. And it must have rubber bladders—anti-G devices—which automatically inflate when G's are pulled on the airplane, to keep the pilot's blood from draining from his head and causing a blackout. To complete the pilot's protection, the suit must be worn with special gloves, boots, and insulating layers against heat and cold.

Indeed, as I think about it, the pressure suit is far more complex than the deep-sea diving rig. And for the high-flying pilot it is as important and necessary as the diver's suit. Without it he cannot go aloft. The history of the pressure suit in this country is long and tortuous, paralleling the history of the modern airplane. For the benefit of posterity it should be the subject of an exhaustive study. All spacemen will wear some type of pressure suit, and they might want to know its origin. Meanwhile, my knowledge of early work on the suits is hazy. The first pressure suit I know of was built for aviator Wiley Post before World War II by Goodrich Tire and Rubber Company. It was a monstrous thing of rubber, closely resembling the analogous deep-sea diving rig. I don't think it was ever used more than once or twice in flight.

During World War II the armed services, absorbed with more vital matters, advanced the pressure suit not a whit. But after the war, when it was obvious that airplanes would someday fly routinely above man's tolerable limits, the Air Force and Navy both embarked on low-key, back-burner types of pressure-suit research and development programs, funded on shoestring budgets.

The Air Force and Navy experts differed sharply then on the approach to the pressure suit. Eager for quick results, the Air Force contingent at Wright Field, sparked by Dr. James P. Henry, believed the best solution was a partial-pressure suit, that is, a cloth-rubber suit which would cover not the full body but critical portions of it—originally only enough to enable the pilot to get back down in a hurry if the plane's cabin pressure failed.

The Navy, eying future space travel and capability to stay on target for hours, chose to go to a full-pressure suit, one that would support a human being on the face of the moon. In 1947 a young lieutenant named Paul Durrup, at the Naval Aircraft Factory in Philadelphia, drew up the Navy specifications which served as the basic full-pressure suit guide-lines for a decade.

In spite of the shortage of money, the Air Force's partial-pressure suit program inched ahead significantly. By 1949, when Pete Everest was ready to try for an altitude record in the X-1, Wright Field had produced a partial-pressure suit which, amazingly enough, worked. This suit, in fact, saved Pete Everest's life. On one flight above 60,000 feet the X-1 cockpit canopy cracked and the cabin-pressure gas escaped. The laced partial-pressure suit automatically came into play, squeezing Everest along the torso, arms, and legs, supporting his skin. He landed, uncomfortable but unhurt. When Bill Bridgeman later flew the Skyrocket to 79,000 feet, he wore a similar suit with an improved helmet.

Just prior to my NACA assignment to the all-rocket Skyrocket in late 1951, I naturally developed more than a casual interest in pressure suits. The Air Force issued me a partial-pressure suit, which I used in the NACA airplanes. Eventually I wore out two Air Force partial-pressure suits during my many Skyrocket and X-1 flights. The Air Force had done the best job possible, considering its budget, but as a pilot who anticipated close association with pressure suits during prolonged high-altitude flight in the X-1-A and X-2 series, I was looking for something a little better.

This search took me to the Navy's pressure-suit lab in Philadelphia in 1951 and shortly thereafter into the strange and wonderful world of a brassiere and girdle manufacturer.

"I'm Scott Crossfield," I said, extending a hand to the Navy group at Philadelphia. The laboratory was a small loft crowded with manikins, sewing machines, plaster of Paris molds, regulators, airbanks, and all the novel tools of this arcane trade. Lieutenant Commander Harry Weldon, who had inherited the project from Lieutenant Durrup, introduced me around.

"I'm going to be doing some high-altitude work at Edwards and I want to check around and see what you fellows have for me to wear," I said. "I have an Air Force partial-pressure suit. But there are some things I don't like about it. I understand you fellows are working on full-pressure suits which would better suit our plans."

"That's right. But our approach is a long-range one here, looking toward the future. We still have a long way to go with this program. We don't get much money from the Bureau. They say: 'Who the hell wants to walk around on the face of the moon?'"

"We might be walking around on the moon before you know it," I said.

"That's what we believe. Here, have you seen this suit? This is a David Clark suit, model number 7. It's the most advanced thing we have. It was designed for me."

Commander Weldon proudly displayed Clark's latest creation. I noticed in the rear of the building an altitude chamber, a heavy tank from which air could be drawn to simulate the vacuum of high altitude.

"Mind if I try this thing in the chamber?" I asked.

Weldon hesitated. Then after glancing at his co-workers he said, "Why not?"

I put on the suit. It was made of rubberized nylon over which was stretched a layer of flexible white cloth. When the suit expanded, the cloth would hold the rubber in place close about the body, something like the principle of the inner tube and tire on an automobile. The helmet was attached to the suit the same way. I climbed into the chamber and closed the heavy steel door. The mechanics drew air out of the tank until I had reached an 'altitude' of 90,000 feet. The suit worked well. I thought it far superior to the uncomfortable partial-pressure suit, and with improvements I thought it could be better.

After the chamber was 'lowered' to earth-atmospheric level, I climbed out and removed the suit, rattling off comments. I learned much later that my stint in the altitude chamber was the first time the suit had ever been tested under extreme conditions. I was surprised. I had simply assumed that the suit had been wrung out, perhaps hundreds of times. In later years Weldon and I often laughed about my being his "guinea pig."

I went directly from the Navy laboratory to the factory of the suit manufacturer, the David Clark Company in Worcester, Mass. David Clark, the owner and president of the company, turned out to be one of the most interesting men I have ever met in the aviation world. He was a stocky man of about fifty-five, with bushy eyebrows and delicate hands which, like his mind, seemed to be always in high-speed motion. He was a chain-smoker, shifting from cigarettes to cigars without missing a beat. He was proud and stubborn, but gentle by nature, the patron and father confessor of the David Clark

Company family of employees, who were as loyal and hard-working a group as I have ever seen.

Clark had begun his career in New England as a young man in the garment trade. Right off, he invented a knitting machine that would automatically make a seamless, one-piece, two-way-stretch girdle which, for its time, was considered fantastic. (The structural loads imposed on a girdle, as we all know, can be tremendous, and a machine that can build a good one automatically is an amazing engineering accomplishment, believe me.) With his ingenious machine Clark had all but cornered the important, expanding girdle market. Braving new frontiers, Clark moved into manufacture of brassieres, which, considering those structural loads, was even more awesome.

During the war Clark became interested in the military field, inventing and making boots, shoes, helmets, goggles, anti-G suits, ear-muffs to protect crewmen from engine noise, and other specialty items. Since 1941 almost every piece of pilot 'soft goods' has been pioneered by Dave Clark. The brassieres and girdles were his bread-and-butter business, but he was a compulsive gadgeteer and thus found himself in the pressure-suit line, not because there was money in it but because it was a new challenge to his inventive mind.

I returned to Edwards immensely impressed with the David Clark operation. In late 1951 I wrote a letter to NACA headquarters, recommending that we encourage the Navy-Clark pressure-suit effort. This letter was forwarded routinely to the Navy. The Navy lab in Philadelphia was encouraged by this show of interest and immediately set to work on a 'crash basis.'

Clark, investing his own money in the project (there was little official contract money behind the work), built several suits by hand. He sent some men to NACA, Edwards; I worked with them, welding and gluing various pieces of the complicated suit into place. This work went on for months and it gave me solid groundwork in pressure suits that later paid handsome dividends.

It also led indirectly to one of the most agonizing physical experiences of my life. We had no chamber at Edwards for tests, and I decided to use an airplane if I could get high enough. So, wearing the tried and true partial-pressure suit, I took off one day in a war-weary P-51, one of NACA's miscellaneous test planes, and climbed as high as it would go. When I reached 43,000 feet, the suit automatically pressurized. Then for the next twenty minutes or so I tried to go higher, nursing the complaining airplane to 44,000 and then 44,500 feet, finally to 45,000 feet, reporting by radio to the ground.

The flight seemed to go perfectly, but the next day I had an awful headache. The pain was indescribable. It forced me to bed, where I remained for twenty-two days, my first illness since childhood. No amount of drugs, not even morphine, would ease the pain. Then, thank God, it went away. The doctors were baffled. No one could ever explain it. Some said it was the suit; some said I had contracted the 'bends' -- they later said 'sinus.' The mystery remains unsolved to this day.

Little by little, we brought the Clark full-pressure suit to a state of near-perfection. We switched regulators, experimented with new cooling systems, and a dozen different helmet-defogging devices. When Marion Carl came out briefly to borrow the Skyrocket for his altitude record, he wore the new Clark full-pressure suit. We stayed up half the night before his flight working out last-minute adjustments to the suit and making parts on a lathe. In my view, the fact that he wore this untried, jerry-rigged suit to 85,000 feet on his third flight made his record all the more remarkable. (When Kit Murray broke Carl's altitude record about a year later, he wore an Air Force partial-pressure suit.)

A ludicrous piece of journalism temporarily derailed our efforts to bring the Clark suit to operational perfection. The new money allotted the Navy lab at Philadelphia had naturally generated public interest in the pressure suit. A national magazine, now defunct, sent a writer to Philadelphia who composed a story describing the Clark suit in glowing terms. This pleased Commander Weldon, the Navy, and the Clark Company. But when the magazine photographer arrived in Philadelphia to take pictures, he was not impressed by the dirty khaki-colored Clark suit. It didn't seem glamorous enough to be a 'space suit.'

To satisfy the photographer's demands the Navy people pulled out a big, bulbous, experimental pressure-suit that was years, if not decades, old, and dead from a development standpoint. But it was photogenic. The photographer was satisfied; his editor selected the picture of the hopelessly obsolete concept for the cover of the issue containing the article.

This misguided publicity unintentionally touched off a minor but bitter pressure-suit battle between the Navy and the Air Force or, rather, brought the long-standing feud over the approach to the suit into the open. The ins and outs of this flap are much too complicated to relate here. The upshot of it all was that the pressure-suit people—both partial and full—got new and unprecedented appropriations. The Navy's Philadelphia lab, for example, received what in that poverty-ridden field was considered a small fortune, $250,000. As the battle rolled on, alas, not the David Clark Company, but the firm whose suit had been on the magazine cover, received the contract to build the Navy's full-pressure suit. All the money David Clark had spent out of his own pocket availed naught. The knowledge we had gained in years of pressure-suit work was turned over to a competitor.

Such are the breaks of the aviation trade. Typically, Clark never complained. He is a true patriot and sporting competitor. The Clark suit was too good to die. When the Navy lost interest, the Air Force at Wright Field began to eye it with considerable excitement. A foresighted Wright Field technician, Ernie Martin, awarded Clark a small but encouraging contract to continue work on the suit, even though it was competitive with other Air Force projects. Clark kept on, spending large sums of his own money. Feeling somewhat responsible for his deep and profitless plunge into the pressure-suit field, and convinced that his suit was the ultimate answer for the Air Force and specifically the X-15, which I would fly, I urged Clark on and helped him with experimental work as best I could. I believe that during my five years at Edwards I logged more time in pressure suits than most of the pilots put together. This time the intense pressure completed the destruction of my sinus cavities. When I left Edwards they were shattered.

In 1953 and 1954 during the preliminary studies on the X-15 at NACA, I had urged the incorporation of a full-pressure suit in the ejection-seat concept. The helmet and full suit would provide additional blast-protection for the pilot in the event of bail-out, an argument I effectively used against the capsule.

The suit I proposed had all the best features of the Clark suit. The North American X-15 did included the Clark-type suit, listed as a contractor-furnished item. Because of my long background in pressure-suit work in general, and past association with the David Clark Company in particular, the X-15 pressure suit naturally became one of my special projects at North American. In time, the Air Force's Wright Field lab took over the development work on the suit and supervised the altitude-chamber tests. But the final product was a direct outgrowth of the old NACA-Navy-Clark suit which I first saw at Philadelphia.

Knowing much of the discouraging history of pressure suits, I tackled my new responsibility with grim determination. But I was unaware then that during those early days of the X-15 Dave Clark had a whopping surprise up his sleeve. It was a new 'break-through' (and here I mean that overworked word in its literal sense) that would revolutionize the full-pressure suit business. In time the Clark-X-15-Air Force suit would become the standard full-pressure suit for the Air Force. A copy would be worn by the Mercury Astronauts, the seven men scheduled to orbit the earth in a capsule. It would serve as a prototype for suits to be worn by the first U.S. spacemen to land on the moon.

26: THE AGRICULTURAL APPROACH

"AND THAT, GENTLEMEN, IS THE STORY OF THE X-15 TO DATE."

My assistant switched on the lights in the briefing room. The group I was addressing—the fifth that month—was part of an Air Force headquarters inspection team. In aviation circles word of the X-15 was beginning to spread. We were besieged by official delegations from NACA, the Pentagon, and Congress, who wanted to know what it was all about. Charlie Feltz abhorred briefings—they seriously interfered with his work, for one thing—and had dumped this 'public relations' chore on me. Through growing experience I developed an hour-long 'road show,' complete with slides of charts and artists' conceptions of the ship, and I thought it was pretty good. I could spout the speech in my sleep and, I think, frequently did.

"Are there any questions?" I concluded.

"I have a question about the seat," a captain spoke up. "As I understand it, the pilot may spend long hours in the cockpit on the ground before take-off and during flight to launch-point. Have you given any thought to a seat cushion, an air-inflatable or foam-rubber base, to add to the pilot's comfort? Seems to me it's asking quite a lot for the pilot to sit on cold, hard steel for all that time."

"Captain, as I believe I pointed out earlier, our overriding consideration in this airplane is saving weight. There are, of course, foam-rubber seat pads and inflatable air cushions under development. There is even an undulating air cushion which gently massages the behind during prolonged flight ..."

"Yes," the captain said. "I have read reports on these projects ..."

"Well, any one of these seat pads could weigh as much as a pound, maybe two pounds. In the final analysis this is pure luxury payload. To take it into the air, we must add seven or maybe fourteen pounds to the overall weight of the airplane. Besides, these pads might slip around during ... ah ... shall we say ... the rough portions of the flight profile.

"Now, I'll tell you what we did about this. We sat down and said to ourselves: 'Who in this country has had the most experience in keeping someone in a seat under rough conditions over prolonged periods?' The answer, we found soon enough, was the International Harvester Company, manufacturers of tractors and farm equipment. We learned they had investigated the natural frequency of a man's spine and how long a spring you should sit him on, and what's the best shape of the seat, so that he gets the best opportunity to stay on a piece of farm equipment bouncing over rough ground, bearing in mind that a farmer might ride that seat twelve to sixteen hours a day."

"Is that a fact?" the captain asked in wonderment.

"That's a fact," I said. "So you will see that the seat in the X-15 is an exact duplicate of a tractor seat, with apologies to International Harvester. It's of minimum weight and maximum comfort and will keep the pilot solidly in place in event of rough flight.

"Around here, we call this type of engineering the agricultural approach, getting right down to fundamentals, as basic as land and seed, and figuring the thing out. It's typical of our thinking on this airplane."

27: A Tornado Named Stormy

HARRISON ('STORMY') STORMS, CHIEF ENGINEER OF THE Los Angeles Division, who had sparked the initial management-level interest in the X-15 project, remained aloof from the day-to-day work on the airplane. But as Chief Engineer (he had replaced Ray Rice, who moved up to a Vice President's slot), the technical responsibility for the ship was his. When we ran into trouble, he was first to answer the alarm and bring his high-level prestige and authority to bear. At no time was he ever more than a few minutes away.

As time passed and all of us began to see the full dimensions of our tiger, Stormy came around more often. By then, the fall of 1956, we had moved to larger quarters on the second floor of the main engineering building. Our team had grown to about sixty-five men, and every day we leaned more heavily on the various departments of the plant for aerodynamic, heating, structural data, and other help.

Stormy was short and wiry, 41 years old, a native of Chicago. As a young boy he had developed an obsession for aircraft through contact with model planes. He took a master's degree in Mechanical Engineering at Northwestern University and later made advanced studies in aeronautical engineering at Cal Tech.

When the Japanese attacked Pearl Harbor, Stormy joined North American. A tough, uncompromising, technical man, and an articulate one as well, Stormy had fought his way to the top of North American. Although for years he had lived in the nation's outdoor playground, Southern California, Stormy ignored the comforts and luxuries of life. Every waking moment he devoted exclusively to thinking of new and better ways to make airplanes.

Stormy naturally became one of the ideal men to lay new proposals before the military. Thus when the Preliminary Design Section came up with a new concept, Stormy took it to Washington and pounded the halls of the Pentagon. He became a master at handling a presentation because, for one thing, he hated to lose a competition. He was scrappy, cocky, and confident.

Under his direction the Los Angeles Division all but cornered the market of the future flying Air Force. Stormy had won the competition for the Air Force's advanced fighter, the Mach 3 F-108, and the advanced bomber, the Mach 3 B-70, both of which would benefit from the X-15's flight experience. There were no other advanced combat aircraft in the Air Force inventory.

In the fall of 1956 the X-15 ran into serious trouble, both from political and technical standpoints. Air Force Captain Mel Apt had just died in the crash of the final X-2 airplane. The basic cause was high-speed instability, a weakness in the airplane that was predicted years before. The loss of the X-2 denied the X-15 program badly needed flight experience and data in the

Mach 3 zone and raised many new questions about acceptance of high-speed instability. The loss, in effect, vastly broadened the area which the X-15 would have to explore. From a political standpoint, it put North American and the government on the spot. If the X-15 also turned out to be unstable and crashed as a result of this instability, it might jeopardize not only all future research airplanes but also the entire future of manned aircraft. Thus in a twinkling the X-15 became an enormously important project at North American—indeed throughout the government and aviation industry—bringing to a climax a problem that had bothered us for some months.

According to the preliminary design studies and wind-tunnel tests, the X-15, with its high-swept vertical tail, would be unstable during certain brief periods of the flight profile. It is impossible to build an airplane that can fly at six times the speed of sound and land like a conventional airplane without a compromise somewhere along the line. We had compromised in the tail. Its shape was not ideal. After the X-2 crash Stormy moved in like a tornado.

The top members of the X-15 team gathered in his office. Stormy was emphatic and wasted no words.

"This airplane is going to be directionally stable. One week from now I want all of you back here with every tail-study you have made on this configuration. I want the weight analysis, flutter studies, drag studies, the dive-brake studies, the whole works from A to Z. Bill Johnston says we have got to add some more tail below the fuselage, so be thinking about that."

We were back one week later with the paperwork in hand. Our engineers had collected data from wind tunnels and other sources on every conceivable tail shape. Ideally for our purposes, the best was one that looked like the tail of a ballistic missile, with fins protruding full length above and below the fuselage. But a fin below the fuselage conflicted with the rear landing-gear arrangement, the two skids which we had moved all the way aft to save weight. The lower fin would stick down below the skids and dig into the ground and become the world's fastest plow, as we jokingly called it.

The discussion in Stormy's office was deeply technical and no joke, though. We pored over the paper studies, matching weight and drag against performance, proposing, rejecting, theorizing. The problem was complicated by a variety of factors. For example, the dive brakes were attached to the upper tail. According to our design scheme, to gain the biggest bite in the air the upper tail would move as a complete unit. Then there was the nagging question of the shape, or airfoil, of the upper and lower tail sections. Seen from above in cross-section, a diamond-shaped tail was best because the air 'clung' to it better at low speeds. But at high speeds a diamond-shaped tail, thick at the middle of the diamond, would add little but weight to the X-15. Our goal was to conceive a new tail shape without adding an excess pound.

We were in the midst of discussing a truncated lower tail, one that would not scrape the ground on landing, when Stormy suddenly exploded:

"Why the hell can't we simply drop the lower tail in flight, just before landing? We don't need it then. It's during the high-speed, high-altitude phase that we need it."

"Drop it? Drop the ventral?" someone asked, startled. "It's never been done. How would you drop it?"

"Blow it off with a ballistic charge," Stormy shot back. "Who cares if it's never been done? No one ever built an X-15, did they? This ventral could have a small parachute to lower it to the ground after it's jettisoned. It would cost us only a few pounds."

We thought that over for a while. It was indeed a startling idea. But, as we finally concluded, why not?

Next we tackled the airfoil of the tail, batting around the diamond shape versus other, more conventional shapes. As related, the diamond was the best approach for the X-15's low-speed flight, and it would still have some high-speed advantage. The one problem was that it was marginally adequate and much too heavy.

"What would happen," Stormy asked, "if we cut that diamond shape off in the middle? Slice it right in two. Once the air passes the hump of the diamond, it has finished its work. It separates from the surface. The air won't know it if the rear of the diamond isn't there. That might cut the weight of the tail in half."

He was right. Wind-tunnel studies showed that the air behaved properly with only half a diamond, as seen in cross-section. We chopped the diamond in half, with the result that the X-15 in final form has a tremendous, wedge-shaped upper and lower vertical stabilizer, about which much ill-informed speculation has been spread around. It was no more and no less than a new attempt to get the most tail for the least weight. With this innovation, plus the droppable lower ventral (also wedge-shaped), the X-15 was supplied a tail that would make it completely stable in all speed ranges. Thanks to Stormy's ingenious mind and courage, it was done despite the strong objections.

In November of 1956 the design of the X-15 was frozen, and a special team started work on the mock-up of the airplane. The dummy mock-up was completed in a frenzy the night before our formal customer inspection in December, 1956. As I recall it, the painters were up half the night putting finishing touches on the wood and soft-metal fuselage. When we saw the "complete airplane" the following day, squatting behind a walled-off area marked "SECRET," we were amazed and proud. All the parts fitted, and to the untrained eye the airplane in its final shape appeared ready to take off. We had reached this point, from conceptional design to mock-up inspection, in twelve months flat. Considering the product we were building, I believe this must be a record of some kind.

About a hundred customers, including both NACA and Air Force personnel, came to the North American plant to gawk at and criticize our tiger.

Among these was my old friend and boss, Walt Williams, who was still running NACA's High Speed Flight Station. Now that the X-2 had gone by the boards, I could see the eagerness in his face. He was literally panting to get his hands on the X-15. I might add that we at North American were equally eager to deliver it to his test facility.

I escorted Williams about the dummy airplane. His mind was churning with questions. He, of course, knew about the new tail concept—we reported all changes or modifications on the X-15 to our customers immediately, and NACA passed them on to the industry—but when he saw the rear of the full-scale model for the first time he eyed it skeptically. I put his mind at rest with a technical dissertation, flavored with a smattering of North American sales pitch. Williams poked his head inside the cockpit, shot-gunning questions.

No detail, however small, was overlooked in this inspection. For example, one Air Force officer, after a careful survey of the instrument panel, said to me: "Scotty, I don't see a landing-gear-position-indicator light on the panel. How will you know for sure if your gear is down?"

"The wiring and gauges for gear-indicator lights, we figured, would weigh about five pounds. Now when you get right down to it, they really aren't necessary. Figure this. You're coming in dead-stick at 200 miles an hour ready for touch-down. To maintain your air-speed and prevent a high rate of sink near the ground, it's best not to put the gear down until the last few seconds. Otherwise, the drag would be too great. So you pull the gear handle. If the gear doesn't come down, you've had it. You have no engine power. You can't take off and go around again for a second landing. So what good does a gear-position indicator light do you?"

All in all, our customers gave us a hearty pat on the back. The X-15 passed its inspection with flying colors and Charlie Feltz released the engineering drawings. To be sure, there were many minor requests for changes. I believe they totaled about ninety-five, half of which we had anticipated. At the time of the inspection, in fact, our engineers were busy modifying these items. The only really big proposal that emerged from the inspection was an idea of Walt Williams' that the X-15 engine be designed so that it could 'idle' while the plane was still mated to the mother ship. Williams wanted this to avoid the prospect of an engine failure after drop. But that was a problem for RMI, not North American. The engine was a customer-furnished item.

The one cloud gathering on the X-15 horizon at that point in history was the rocket engine. Facing unprecedented problems, the thin line of technicians at RMI had wavered and fallen back. By mock-up time the XLR-99 engine was six to eight months behind the overall X-15 schedule and, we guessed, destined to drop even further behind schedule. For all of us on the X-15 team, this turn of events, inevitable in an advanced technological jump of that order, caused great concern and loud cries of anguish. We knew that in the end such a delay would reflect on our own efforts at perfection.

Once again Stormy took the reins. After several prolonged meetings with our propulsion engineers, we wrote a letter to the Air Force which loudly rang the alarm. North American again offered to supply the engine from its Rocketdyne Division. But it was too late. By then the Air Force was heavily committed to the RMI effort. Contracts had been let; many millions had been invested in the small company. North American's Rocketdyne was still busy supplying engines for Atlas and Thor, and designing even more powerful rocket engines, and the Air Force was still opposed to calling upon the division for technical assistance for the X-15. We would have to sweat it out.

I was considerably put out about the engine delays. The engine was obviously crucial to the entire project. If it failed, we all failed, and I in particular failed in the goal of my life. The situation reached the point where I was no longer invited to attend the rocket propulsion meetings. On that one subject I had turned into an outspoken zealot, and the others soon tired of my needling.

28: Wilting Straws in Plaster of Paris

The impasse in the perfection of the full-pressure suit was primarily in the restraining material or 'tire' which holds the inflatable rubber 'inner tube' against the pilot's skin. Many materials were tested to keep the ballooning inner tube in place against the skin, but each was so heavy and rigid that when the suit was in operation, the pilot was trapped in a bulbous vise, unable to move his arms, legs, or head. The suit engineers tried to offset this by hinging the elbow, neck, wrist, and knee joints with bellows and bearings. But the end result was a complicated, mechanical monster, obviously unsatisfactory for a pilot working within the tight confines of an airplane cockpit, and quite marginal if escape from the aircraft became necessary.

David Clark's suit number seven, which I had first tested in the altitude chamber in Philadelphia in 1951, was an attempt to get away from the 'stiff' suit concept. It was a step in the right direction but a long way from an operationally sound item. But if enough time and effort are devoted to any technical problem, the solution will come eventually. Obsessed with this new challenge, David Clark kept plugging away, with Air Force support, and in time came up with the answer.

He revealed it to me one day in his factory, not long after we completed the X-15 mock-up inspection. After a tour of his fascinating plant we went to his private office. I could tell that he was bursting with pride.

"Scotty," he said, "did you ever see one of those 'Chinese fingers' made of straw? You know, those things you put your index finger in? You try to pull your finger out and the straw grips it even tighter?"

"Yeah, sure," I said. "I used to play with those when I was a kid."

"Well, take a look at this. I made this on an airplane when I was going up to Alaska last month to see my daughter." He passed me a sample of hand-woven material which looked not like a Chinese finger but something like an Anchor Fence, except that it was made of nylon thread. I gave it a good pull and right off I saw what he was driving at.

"We call this 'link net' material in the trade," Clark said. "I think it's the answer to the pressure-suit restraining cloth. It will work just like the Chinese finger. If you bend your arm, the material on top will contract and the material on the bottom will stretch. It also twists easily from side to side under stress. At all times you will have an even pressure on the rubber bladders. It's as flexible as cotton cloth, strong as steel, and weighs little or nothing. I think that with this material and the new regulators and other improvements we can give you a complete full-pressure suit with a total weight of thirty-five pounds."

"What?" I was astonished. At best, present equipment for the job added up to as much as 110 pounds, give or take a few.

"Yes, thirty-five. Now it's going to take a little time because we have to make this stuff by hand. But maybe we can come up with a machine to weave it."

Our long-standing faith in David Clark had paid off. The link-net material proved to be the great 'break-through' in the full-pressure suit game. It relegated all the stiff suits to the junk-heap. The restraining material was as flexible as a suit of long-johns and almost as comfortable. It eliminated the need for bellows-joints at the knees and elbows and for bearings at the shoulders and wrists.

As I was leaving the factory we passed through the Research Department. Amid the great humming looms and rattling sewing machines, I spotted a piece of shiny cloth lying on a long table. The material looked somewhat like silver lamé. I went over and picked it up.

"What is this?" I asked Clark.

"That's a piece of nylon with a vacuum-blasted aluminum coating. Just something one of the boys was trying out."

"Pretty glamorous looking."

Then a light went on in the back of my mind. "Say, Dave, why don't you make the outer cover of the pressure suit out of this material, in place of that awful-looking khaki coverall?"

"Whatever for?"

"You remember that time down at Philadelphia when they took that picture for the magazine cover? We don't want to make that mistake again. A coverall of this material would look real good, like a space suit should—photogenic. To justify it technically we can tell them this silver material is specially designed to radiate heat or something."

"A marvelous idea, Scotty. I'll make the boots and gloves out of black material for contrast."

"Great touch," I said. Ever since then all pressure suits have been silver.

I made my way to New York City. To save his fitters expensive, time-consuming cross-country trips each time they modified or improved the new suit, Clark suggested that we mold a 'statue' of me just as I would sit in the cockpit of the X-15. I bought the idea without a second thought. How I lived to regret it! Believe me, no one can claim to have lived the full life until he has been cast in plaster of Paris.

The appointment Dave Clark arranged in New York took me to a ratty building on 42nd Street just off Broadway. John Flagg, now a vice president of the Clark Company, met me, and together we took a squeaky elevator to the studio of a theatrical sculptor. He specialized in devices for stage sets, armor suits, horribly distorted masks, and the like. The proprietor, a tall, balding man with a walrus mustache, was a 'mad artist,' a Romanian whose name I have forgotten. He had an assistant, just off the boat and unable to speak English. The studio turned out to be a cluttered, unheated attic. It was mid-winter.

"Very well," the artist said, rubbing his hands from the cold, or the unexpected windfall, or the artistic challenge standing before him, I'm not sure which. "We'll make a plaster of Paris mold in two parts, the body and the head. Later we will cast the statue in this mold. Now first you must strip down completely and shave all the hair off your body except your head."

"All the hair off my body?" I asked incredulously.

"Yes," the artist replied. "All of it. Otherwise, it will stick in the plaster of Paris."

"I don't have a razor," I said feebly, eyeing the nearest exit.

"Never mind, Scotty, I'll go get one," John Flagg said, chuckling. He ran down the stairway and in a few minutes was back with a small electric razor, the size used by ladies.

"I don't know how in hell I'll ever explain this on my expense account," he said, "but here it is."

I stripped, put on an athletic supporter, and shaved the exposed portions of my body. After applying a thick coating of Vaseline to my skin, I sat down on a rickety chair, feeling like a half-frozen Greek god. The mad artist prepared the plaster of Paris mixture, screaming in Romanian and gesticulating wildly at his assistant, pausing at his work only to stand back to size up his victim. I noted with dismay the ripples on my stomach in a sitting position. I would be cast forever with a row of rubber tires on my waist!

The artists erected a mold about my body and then, without warning, began slapping on the frigid plaster of Paris. At the beginning it felt like being immersed in ice water, but as time passed my sealed-off body heat began to build up, and for the first time since I entered the attic I was warm. But soon I was too hot, sweating and breathing heavily under the increasing load of plaster.

The artists erected a cage of steel within the plaster to hold it together. Then they turned me upside down in the chair and did the other side. I waited in stolid agony for the plaster to harden, afraid to move a muscle lest the mold be ruined and the process repeated.

"Now we must do the head," the artist said. "This is the most difficult part. You're not subject to claustrophobia, are you? Do you prefer to breathe through your nose or mouth?"

"Mouth," I said. "No, I don't have claustrophobia."

The creation of the head mold was slightly different but no less taxing. First they covered me with a kind of rubbery moulage, and after putting two paper straws in my mouth so I could breathe, they then applied the plaster. After a few minutes the straws wilted and I could barely suck in enough air for survival. I couldn't swallow because the movement of my Adam's apple would destroy their work. With my head rigidly set in the heavy mold, I listened as the artists babbled.

Their voices seemed to come from far away, from some deep cave. They watched me closely. With their heads so encased, some people become overwhelmed by claustrophobia and come up fighting—ripping at the mask.

John Flagg was doubled up on the floor with laughter.

Before applying the plaster over the rubbery moulage, the two artists had laid a string across my head from shoulder to shoulder. The idea was that when the mold hardened it could be cut in two and thus removed by pulling the string, something like opening a package of chewing gum or cigarettes.

Now a great debate arose between the two artists about when to pull the string. Actually, this is a matter for careful consideration because the string must be pulled at exactly the right time. If it is pulled too soon, before the plaster has hardened enough, the whole thing crumbles, or the seam rejoins.

If it is pulled too late, after the plaster becomes hard and brittle, the mask must be chiseled off and the process begun all over again.

In the midst of the debate, the head artist remembered he had to make an urgent telephone call. He disappeared from the room, leaving his assistant to watch over the victim. It was clear from muffled conversation that the assistant was very concerned. He touched the plaster repeatedly, testing its hardness, shook his head glumly and paced the floor, obviously as torn by indecision as Hamlet. Finally, he could stand it no longer. He rushed over and pulled the string.

A few moments later the chief artist returned and smilingly said: "Well, now, it is time to pull the string."

Then with a look of horror he saw that he had been beaten to the punch. He exploded and turned on the assistant in fury, babbling in Romanian, English, and, I think, six other languages.

"I'll fire you—you don't know anything about this work—I'll have your visa revoked—you'll go home on the next boat—" And so on.

The mold held together, after all. It was finally removed and I could breathe again. I tried to wash the Vaseline coating from my body with cold water, and then I got out of there as fast as I could.

As it turned out, the crazy artist made a fairly creditable statue from the mold and my rubber tires were immortally preserved. Clark used the statue to make number one and number two X-15 pressure suits. As far as the fit was concerned, they were perfect as long as I didn't gain a pound.

After that I spent the equivalent of years of flying in the Air Force's altitude and test chambers at Wright Field testing the Clark pressure suits. The Air Force people—notably the Command Flight Surgeon of the Air Research and Development Command, Brigadier General Don Flickinger—displayed keen interest in the work and their support was unlimited. We wrung out the suits, not only in repeated 'trips' to 150,000 feet altitude, but also in ovens and refrigerators, to make sure they, to say nothing of the pilot, could stand up under extremes of temperature.

These prolonged tests became somewhat of a minor physical challenge for me. The aero-medical officers at Wright Field submitted, half-jokingly, that considering my age (I was then 36) my body would never take the beating. When they matched my performance against the data accumulated on human guinea pigs over several years, my record defied their statistics.

"You're a physical freak," someone remarked. "No one can take that kind of punishment. How do you do it?"

It seemed superfluous to point out that for centuries man has been out-performing and outliving the statistics of the physicians, and that, as I have said before, if the spirit is willing the flesh can exceed all probable limits. History is full of such accounts. Teddy Roosevelt is a good example.

The sled track at Edwards was the brain-child of Air Force Colonel John Paul Stapp, an aero-medical officer who specialized in the physiological effects of high-speed and high-altitude bail-out and severe G forces. The track was a mile long. The sled was powered by a cluster of solid-propellant rockets. When touched off, the sled accelerated with great speed. It roared down the track for a few seconds and then splashed into a pool of water. The water stopped the sled, subjecting it to tremendous G. On the front of the sled we mounted a dummy nose of the X-15, complete with cockpit canopy, ejection seat, and a plastic anthropomorphic form in the seat dressed in a Clark pressure suit.

We gathered behind a concrete shield listening as the countdown was intoned on the loudspeaker: "5 ... 4 ... 3 ... 2 ... 1 ... Zero!"

The powerful rockets on the rear of the sled exploded to life. Within a few seconds the big sled was hurtling down the track at 1000 miles an hour, almost faster than the eye could follow. Cameras, mounted in a half-dozen positions, recorded the motion of the sled and the X-15 nose. Sensitive instruments on the seat and inside the plastic dummy telemetered back a constant stream of data. These data would tell us the total effect of wind-blast and heat on the dummy and pressure suit. It would settle once and for all the controversy of the X-15 ejection-seat principle.

At the peak of acceleration of the sled—1000 miles an hour—the X-15 seat fired automatically. The V-shaped canopy blew off. The seat, with the dummy firmly restrained, rose from the sled and zoomed skyward. Over one hundred feet in the air the dummy separated from the seat and a parachute automatically deployed, lowering the pressure-suit-clad dummy to the desert floor. The parachute was a lightweight model with a twenty-four-foot canopy, built and tested especially for the X-15.

The test was successful. To make certain we were right, we ran the sled several more times. All the data indicated the X-15 pilot, protected by a Clark full-pressure suit, could eject under the most severe conditions we could anticipate without bodily injury beyond the usual bruises associated with an escape from a disabled airplane.

"Charlie," I said, pulling a chair alongside Feltz's desk. "Here is the final word on the suit as we see it." I laid out a series of reports and schematic drawings. "The basic deal is this: the first layer is winter underwear, the second a ventilation garment to cool the pilot. The third layer is the rubberized air-tight pressure garment with the anti-G bladders. The fourth layer is this new link-net material for strength. The outer layer is this silver lamé material, mainly for photo appeal.

"We have run the suit through heat and cold tests. It will withstand anything we can expect to meet. The suit itself, during X-15 flight, will be cooled by nitrogen gas from the same tank we use to pressurize the X-15 cockpit; you'll hardly be able to measure the quantity. Here's the way we have the oxygen regulators and supply set up. During ride to launch point the pilot in the suit breathes oxygen from a supply from the mother plane. When he's ready to launch, he can turn a valve and get oxygen from a supply in the X-15. This will save us some oxygen weight. The suit itself contains a bottle of oxygen, enough to get him down on the ground, which automatically pressurizes the suit and helmet in case of ejection. Incidentally, we've got a rubber seal in the helmet just above the pilot's mouth and nose to prevent fogging the helmet lens. No electrical heating required.

"We worked it so that the parachute harness also serves as the seat-restraint straps. No need for extra shoulder straps and a lap belt. This will save us a few pounds. The sled tests show that the manacles will hold the pilot's feet in place, and that the blast on ejection is far from fatal. The seat weather-vanes, as expected. The pilot will pull some G's going out, but not enough to black him out. Now, to top it all off, I'm giving you the whole pressure suit for thirty-nine pounds. You could walk around in it on the moon."

"Dad-gummed," Feltz said. "This sounds too good to be true. Where's the hooker?"

"The only problem is this. We're still ironing out some improvements. We can't go much faster than we're going. I'm afraid that's the way it's going to wind up. We will be flight-testing the new pressure suit and the X-15 all at the same time."

"You won't be able to flight-test the suit before then?"

"No," I said. "We'll have a lot of chamber time, but no realistic in-flight operations."

"Well, that's the breaks," Feltz said. "Just make darned sure the thing works."

29: Eyes Toward Space

In mid-1957, two severe hurricanes struck the X-15 project within a matter of weeks. As they roared through our working space, we launched a series of crisis meetings beneath battened hatches. Again Stormy leaped in, bringing his authority to bear.

The airplane was well along by then. Manufacturing had begun the difficult experimental welding of the Inconel X skin metal; other engineers, after prolonged agonizing, brain-numbing conferences, had finally set the design for the complex fuel tanks for the rocket engine. At that stage in X-15 history the slightest change in one part of the airplane ricocheted throughout the entire structure.

The first storm was a request from the customer to add additional instrumentation devices to record the effects of wind, temperature, and G load on the airplane. Charlie Feltz announced this new request one morning at a meeting.

"What they want among other things will double the instrumentation load, from 800 to more than 1500 pounds," he said.

We sat silently, each mentally calculating the loss in X-15 performance. The news fell over us like a death sentence. Charlie Feltz later told me he was ready to quit. "What do they want?" someone asked.

"Well," Feltz said heavily, "they want some more stuff in the instrument bay, and they want us to put in hundreds of pressure pick-ups, strain gauges, and thermocouples, and six manometers of archaic vintage. They want this stuff not only in the wing but also in the horizontal and vertical tail."

"Why didn't they say so before now?" one of the engineers said.

I closed my eyes and visualized the new request as it would finally show on the airplane. The thin wing would be pitted with tiny holes. Clusters of steel tubing, pencil size, would run from these holes and crowd through the wing root to the data-collecting manometers in the instrument and engine bays. As the X-15 whipped through the air, each of these tiny holes would have a story to tell, to relay through the tubing to the recording manometers. To install these pick-ups, and to route the tubing to the proper place through the thin wing was a terribly tough and delicate engineering job, comparable to engraving the Lord's Prayer on the head of a pin. In the aft end of the ship the pick-up tubes would have to be arranged in some kind of infinitely complex universal joint because the horizontal elevator rotated.

"Ah, to hell with them," an engineer said. "Let's don't do it."

Although Feltz was deep in the dumps, this comment, which to him bordered on treason, brought him to his feet. As always, he spoke slowly and calmly.

"I guess we have to remember this isn't our airplane. We're building it for the customer. He knows all the facts. He isn't dumb. If he wants these pick-ups, then there must be a good reason. I'll try to talk them out of putting them in the horizontal tail, but we'll probably have to settle for the others. He knows what the extra weight will cost him. But let's remember it is his decision, not ours. We have to do what they want."

Charlie was correct in making that point and his timing was good, as well. All of us had become so intensely wrapped up in the project that we frequently tended to think of the airplane as our own personal property. We resented any new suggestions and intrusions, the same way a parent becomes irate when somebody else corrects his child. We sometimes lost sight of the fact that the X-15 was a nation-wide project, conceived for the good of the entire industry, and that the customer had certain prerogatives which were denied us.

"God only knows," Feltz went on, "where we can cut out some weight, but we have to do it. The engine weight is up again, and this hurts us even more."

He began to detail some weight-saving ideas he and the structural engineers had recently conceived. One was a new arrangement for the fuel tank-plumbing that would save a hundred pounds without seriously affecting the overall center of gravity of the airplane. The second was a plan to install the nose wheel telescoped on the plane, saving considerable space and weight.

The nose-wheel concept—Feltz's own baby—was new and appealing. It greatly reduced the nose-wheel storage space and saved us half a hundred pounds or more. Few people realize it but the landing-gear apparatus alone on some airplanes can account for as much as eight per cent of the total weight. With our lightweight rear skids and new nose wheel, the gear on the X-15 made up only about one per cent of the entire weight of the airplane, or a total of 300 pounds.

The second storm struck a few days later. It was more severe in force, but as I think back on it now it helped the project tremendously. But when it first came we thought it might delay us fatally. Again the news was passed out at a meeting in Feltz's office.

"Now, you won't believe this," he started out, "but the customer wants to change the mother plane."

A chorus of groans echoed through the office.

"The customer says the B-36 is being phased out of the Air Force inventory. Spare parts will be hard to come by, maintenance on the B-36 is staggering, and so on. They want us to use a B-52."

The B-52, a monstrous eight-jet bomber, then being manufactured in quantity by Boeing, was designed to replace the B-36. The substitution of this new mother plane immediately raised grave new problems, which we batted about in the meeting.

"You can't put the X-15 in the B-52 belly," an engineer said.

"The landing gear is in the way."

"I know," Feltz said. "We'll have to hang the X-15 externally, out on the wing."

This concept in itself was extremely controversial. For some years the Air Force had been conducting experiments with external stores—the Rascal missile, for example—on high-performance jet airplanes. The appendage completely modified the overall configuration of the aerodynamic shape, and added drastic new problems to the already tough job of piloting a jet in the trans-sonic zone. The planes vibrated and the stores shook loose, or else produced so much drag that the original anticipated performance of the airplane was never reached. We were now asked to hang the largest external store ever conceived on a B-52—with a man in it.

The wing-mounted X-15 and the use of the B-52 as a mother plane presented great new operational troubles. The pilot would have to board the X-15 before the mother plane took off, for example. The Lox top-off system would have to be not only remote but automatic, as well, because no mechanic could crawl out on the B-52 wing to adjust it. The B-52 flaps, which provide extra lift, could not be used on take-off because the X-15 tail would be in the way. Some means would have to be devised for a visual check on the X-15 in flight. There were no side windows in the B-52. We would have to put a switch in the X-15 so the pilot could launch himself if anything went wrong.

This was not all. As conceived, the X-15 would be suspended from a pylon on the right wing, between the B-52 fuselage and the first, or inboard, engine pod. The 'flutter and noise engineers,' especially a lady engineer at North American named Rose Lunn, who had a habit of being right, challenged this method, pointing out that the noise from the B-52 engine pod might seriously damage the X-15. Feltz set in motion detailed studies to determine the full extent of the vibration effect. The engineers strapped a dummy model of the X-15 on a B-52 wing and ran the B-52 engines for ten hours. Concrete ballast representing the weight of the X-15 was hung on the B-52 wing and dropped to see what effect it would have on the bomber. There was much juggling back and forth. In the end we beefed up the X-15 tail. The X-15 nose was mounted ahead of the B-52 wing leading edge, so the X-15 pilot could eject if necessary.

It was not easy to locate a couple of spare B-52 bombers for this mission. Air Force General Curtis LeMay, then boss of the Strategic Air Command, needed every airplane he had either for training or for the active deterrent force. But at last the Air Force located a couple of ancient B-52s, the third and eighth planes built, which were not rigged for combat. North American converted them, installing the X-15 mating pylon, automatic Lox top-off system, and remote TV sets, mounted to give the launch-panel operators in the B-52 a full picture of what was going on out on the wing.

Air Force Captains Gahl and Charles Bock were designated mother-plane pilots. They perfected a system of horsing the giant airplane into the air carrying the X-15 load without flaps. When Gahl was killed in another airplane, Captain Jack Allavie, a test pilot at Edwards, moved in to take his place. Both Allavie and Bock were superb aviators.

After this work was well along, Charlie Feltz said: "You know, Scotty, I think we might come out ahead on this mother-plane switch. Luckily we can save a loss in the schedule. With the B-52 we can launch a little higher and a little faster, and in the long run, this will give back some X-15 performance. I think we will also get back some of what we lost on the added instrumentation."

I had to agree. Although the shift caused great technical pain, it paid off. The new mother-plane launching scheme came at an interesting and provocative time in U.S. aviation history and set us to thinking in terms of even more exotic X-15 launching vehicles.

Far-seeing engineers in the industry were beginning to turn their eyes toward space. The power of rocket engines had increased enormously. The Atlas missile, plus boosters, had a thrust of 450,000 pounds. The U.S. had already announced a plan to put a basketball-size satellite into orbit to gather data for the International Geophysical Year. Russian scientific publications hinted that the USSR might orbit an object even sooner. Engineers were beginning to talk seriously among themselves about putting a combat vehicle into orbit. Primarily as an aero-medical experiment, Air Force General Don Flickinger asked industry to look into an orbiting capsule which could support a chimpanzee and, perhaps later, a man. This project was labeled MIS, for Man In Space. The North American Advanced Design Section was busy drawing up plans.

Good-natured but intense debates on the proper course to follow in space exploration broke out among the engineers. Some engineers and scientists claimed space travel was nonsense.

Others, especially the Army's Redstone group in Huntsville, Alabama, urged that it was necessary to retain our freedom.

The majority of us knew that man would go into space simply because space was there. At that time few could anticipate the psychological impact of space triumphs on the world.

Charlie Feltz, Stormy, and I spent many hours after work at the plant discussing the coming space age. I think we agreed on all aspects of space exploration (Stormy eager, Charlie thoughtful, and me ready). The first step, we surmised, would be the launching of unmanned, highly-instrumented space devices to gather information on gravitational forces, radiation patterns, meteorites, communications, and unusual environmental conditions expected in space.

Following these probes, man himself would go there, no matter what the cost in terms of money and scientific effort.

"If the Russians get to the moon first," Feltz said, "it will be a heck of a note. And who knows what's up there? The moon might be solid gold. Think what that could do to the economy. Think what you might find out if you set up an astronomy lab in that clear atmosphere. We might change our entire concept of the origin and nature of the universe."

"I think the military phase of it will be important," Stormy said. "You don't know what you will run into until you go there. We might turn up some whole new concept which will make our present defenses inadequate."

Talking in these heady realms naturally led into a discussion of the hardware that would take man into space.

"The moon thing is a long way off," Stormy said. "You'd have to build a space station to orbit the earth first, and take off from there. Within the state of the art of power-plants, the thrust to offset gravity of the earth alone would make a non-stop earth-moon trip unfeasible."

"You'll need some kind of space ship to commute back and forth between the orbiting space station and the earth," I said. "Something you can control in space, shift orbits with, so you can pull alongside the space station and all that. And you'll have to be able to re-enter the earth's atmosphere and land, like an airplane. Personally, I can't see this coming out of orbit with a parachute on a capsule. I'd want to fly in and out. Makes a lot more sense to me."

"I feel pretty certain the first experimental steps will be something like Flickinger's MIS project. A brief orbit flight in a capsule, then a slowing down, and re-entry automatic, with a parachute."

"Yeah," I said. "But you're liable to land in the ocean, or any place. Pretty undignified way to come down, I'd say."

"True, Scotty," Stormy said. "But, as I said, that is the logical starting point to see how man reacts to the new environment. Later on, we would get into your commuter space ships. Something like an X-15, perhaps. As a matter of fact, why not the X-15? We've got the capability to go into space, the systems, rocket engine, and full-pressure suit. What would happen if you put the X-15 on top of a big rocket booster like the Atlas? Or, say, the Navaho?"

The Navaho was an intercontinental-range, air-breathing missile, which had been conceived by the Missile Division of North American. The Navaho was mounted piggy-back on an enormous three-engine rocket booster which developed about 415,000 pounds of thrust. The building of this booster had pioneered North American's way into the rocket-engine field and ultimately provided the U.S. with a reliable rocket engine for Redstone, Jupiter, Thor, and Atlas. It had also led to the development of a very reliable automatic inertial-guidance system, which was later used by the Nautilus on the submarine's first submerged voyage under the North Pole. But the Navaho vehicle itself had been overtaken by technology—by the superior ballistic missiles.

"You'd have some terrific aerodynamic heating problems," Feltz replied. "The X-15 as it now stands doesn't have the capability of anything much above Mach 7. You're talking now about Mach 20 and above."

"But the basic vehicle is there," Stormy insisted. "The power-plant, the shape, the internal systems, the communications, the instruments, the landing gear, pressure suit, escape system, and all the rest. What you're talking about is simply a beefing-up of the skin to resist heat, aren't you?"

"Yeah, heck, I guess I am," Feltz said. But I could tell what he was thinking. The skin would add weight, the higher heating loads would call for greater air conditioning for the instruments, and back we would be again in the maddening battle of weight versus thrust.

"It would take a new airplane," Feltz said. "The shape would be the same, but a new airplane, I think. Of course, we're organized to handle it. We have the only rocket-airplane team in the country in being. We know this thing backwards and forwards. And like you say, it's just a question of beefing it up. Yes. We could do it. I don't think it would take long."

"How long?" Stormy pressed.

"Two years," Feltz said. "Two years from right now."

Stormy added figures in his head, then he scribbled on a piece of paper. Soon we were all scribbling on pieces of paper—envelopes, I think they were. Stormy said: "With a Navaho booster system and X-15 second stage, we could reach Mach 12 two years from now, or 1959, say early 1960 at latest, right?"

"Right." We confirmed his figures. My mind was spinning, trying to visualize an X-15 perched atop a Navaho booster on a launching pad, then blazing skyward at twelve times the speed of sound. At that speed it could zoom deep into space and cover a distance over the earth of perhaps nine thousand miles.

Such a vehicle would have the capability of flying from a U.S. base to Russia and beyond. It could be a combat weapon, I thought.

"It'd take a lot more to get into orbit," Feltz said. "A new booster concept and a new X-15 altogether. Same shape but different materials. You've got a Mach 25 re-entry problem to contend with."

"We can get to that later," Stormy said. "But if we've got to have a commuting space ship, why not get started on the initial step-by-step program now? We've got the team to do it. We've got half a dozen Navaho boosters lying around gathering dust in the attic."

"Stormy, you can't go proposing that to Washington. Hell, we haven't even flown this airplane yet. Mel Apt flew Mach 3 and died doing it. Now you're talking about leaping to Mach 12. They'd just laugh at us."

"I won't make a formal proposal, Charlie," Stormy said. "I'll just feel them out about it. If we can get the speed, we ought to be after it. The concept has military potential, a weapons system, something like the German boost-glide bomber idea of World War II. It's a logical course to my mind. I'll maybe put the thing through as a change-order."

"A change-order?" Feltz laughed. "A $90 million change-order?"

Stormy talked it up in Washington informally, but the customers, while intrigued by the idea, were reluctant to move into an advanced X-15 project before the ship had proven itself in flight. Stormy argued that the flight experience itself was a logical stepping-stone toward an advanced X-15. While the X-15 was being debugged in flight test, the more advanced model could be coming along. By the time the latter was ready to fly, the original X-15 and its machinery would be a proven, reliable concept, as safe as an ordinary jet fighter plane. But in those days before Sputnik, money was scarce and most space, or semi-space, projects, taboo by order of Secretary of Defense Charles E. Wilson.

30: Muting the Cassandras

A CENTRIFUGE IS A LARGE WORD TO DESCRIBE WHAT IS ESSENTIALLY a simple piece of machinery. A centrifuge is a seat, cockpit, capsule, or gondola mounted on an arm which whirls around at high speed. I have often seen a low-grade centrifuge in an amusement park, mounted in a vertical position. The people whip around in circles right-side up and upside down, amid screams of delight and fear.

The armed forces have used horizontally mounted centrifuges for many years to impose G loads on pilots for experimental purposes. When the gondola whirls in its circle like a bucket of water on the end of a rope, the pilot in the gondola goes through a series of tests under severe G. Lights flick on which he is supposed to turn off, and so on. In this way, the theory goes, the aeromedical officers can determine man's reactions and limitations under severe flight conditions.

The largest and newest centrifuge in the United States, built by the Navy, is located in Johnsville, Pennsylvania. The gondola is mounted on a fifty-foot arm. The powerful engine which rotates the arm from the centrifuge hub can accelerate from zero speed to 250 feet a second in a few seconds. The gondola can be tilted to almost any angle (for additional tests), and by using cams in the position control of the gondola, the gondola can be rocked gently or severely, slowly or rapidly, simulating the motions of an aircraft in distress, while pulling very high G.

From the beginning, we had been anxious to test the X-15 sidearm control system under strong G loads. The sidearm control had much merit (there is no real point in locating the airplane control stick in the center of the cockpit; it was simply put there in the early days of aviation and nobody bothered to change it), but I was eager to see what happened, if anything, when it was operated by wrist motion under the severe conditions for which it was designed. Thus I proposed that we put a wrist control in the Johnsville centrifuge and run some tests.

It was a decision I lived to regret.

The Navy's Aero-Medical Acceleration Laboratory at Johnsville, having received little attention since inception, was overwhelmed by our show of interest in their machine. They seized on the X-15 tests like eager young starlets, and the first thing we knew we had a real and, at times, disconcerting, show on our hands. After the engineers rigged a complete X-15 cockpit in the gondola, I spent many hours whirling around in that crazy machine. Later, the Navy engineers ingeniously hooked the centrifuge to an electronic computer, which fed back instrument readings to the panel in the gondola, somewhat like our North American cockpit simulator. It then became possible to 'fly' the ship on various missions, not only with actual instrument presentation, but also with theoretical G loads imposed on the pilot, a fantastically sophisticated tool.

Most of these tests centered on that critical phase of the X-15 flight profile when the ship re-entered the 'thick' earth atmosphere to which we added several emergencies. This was the point, in theory, when the G loads would be most severe and the temperature the highest and flying the most difficult.

There were many ways to approach this atmospheric layer in the X-15. The pilot could enter lightly and slowly, decelerating in the process, or he could dive straight into it like a swimmer plunging directly into a pool. We favored a 'shallow' penetration, a gradual straightforward descent, such as a commercial airplane might make on approaching an airport for a landing.

It was important that the X-15 pilot be 'lined up' almost perfectly for this approach on the atmosphere. If he came in skidding sideways—yawing—or nose high—pitching—the re-entry could be sloppy and subject the X-15 to unnecessary strain and motion; it would cause high temperatures on areas of the ship not specifically designed to withstand them. The X-15 nose contains a special 'ball' sensor to relay yaw and pitch attitude to the instrument panel. If the pilot is not lined up properly, he can realign the ship with the peroxide-rocket ballistic controls on the wing and nose.

At Johnsville we conducted hundreds of re-entry tests, in most of which the X-15 was made to approach the atmosphere under the worst possible conditions—an extreme emergency. We brought her in cocked sideways, with severe yaw and pitch angles—almost every way except upside down and backward, and with failed damping devices. Obviously under such circumstances, when the G loads approached the maximum the airplane could stand, we had some interesting results in the gondola cockpit. Pulling as high as nine or ten G's, I was squashed into one corner of the seat. I blacked out and my head fell to one side. My eyes rolled up and the skin on my face was grotesquely distorted, but the sidearm control worked beyond our best hopes, even in these extreme conditions. All of these test runs were recorded by a remote movie camera mounted in the gondola.

In their eagerness to call attention to their role in the development of the X-15, the authorities at Johnsville took this movie film, selected the worst possible frames, and patched them together as a full-length documentary of their operation. They claimed to have greatly influenced the X-15; yet we had changed nothing as a result of the tests. The next thing we knew, the Johnsville people were showing this film at various aero-medical symposiums and conventions. Then the word began to spread that the X-15 pilot couldn't stand the re-entry loads. The fact that almost all the movie scenes represented the X-15 in emergency, just short of the point of total destruction, was not emphasized.

This kind of thing is inevitable, I guess. Specialists in their own fields, not looking at the over-all picture have cropped up all during history. These people claimed that the steamship, the airplane, the automobile, the atomic submarine, and who knows what else—perhaps even the wheel—would fail. They are proved wrong time after time, yet they reappear to frustrate dedicated people who are trying to get things done. You may think the engine in your automobile is a fine piece of machinery capable of operating for months without repair. Yet I'll bet I can find a specialist who has run extreme tests on pistons who can convince you that your engine, under certain circumstances, would disintegrate. So what?

Inevitably, as the X-15 neared completion, the effects of this movie and other dire predictions, as well, began to take hold. The specialists came after us in full fury. To offset this nonsense I hit the road with charts, movies, and slides which laid out an honest picture of the X-15 and its flight mission. In the months that followed I attended no less than a hundred meetings, conventions, symposiums, and other gatherings of so-called 'experts' in various fields. This 'public relations' activity, an attempt at muting the Cassandras, became a vital factor in the life of the X-15, not to mention my own. Without it, it is possible that the ship might have been talked out of existence.

One such problem that developed in the very early days was the matter of radiation. It is well known that the layer of atmosphere surrounding the earth provides a kind of umbrella for earthbound folk against various energy emissions from the sun and space. Long ago a group of experts began to predict that when man went higher, beyond the protection of this umbrella, and came into direct contact with these strong emissions, disastrous things would happen. The tiny, invisible particles would bombard his body, causing his hair to fall out, and ultimately bringing premature death from radiation disease. The predicted altitudes at which these dire consequences would limit flying moved higher as we flew airplanes and balloons higher and higher. The meteorite scare followed the same pattern. Ultra-violet and X rays caused some concern.

"Scotty," Charlie Feltz said to me one day, "somebody here wants us to tint the windshield of the X-15. You know anything about this?"

"Well, they tinted the X-2 windshield," I said. "Tinting might keep some of the glare out and maybe protect the eyeballs a little against sunburn, but I don't think it will make much difference as far as any other radiation is concerned. I'll look into it."

We conducted experiments to tint the X-15 windshield. But they were complicated by the fact that the X-15 windshield consists of two layers of glass with a space between for defogging nitrogen gas. The best we could get out of it was a piece of smeared glass full of reflection and distortion. To be honest, we really didn't put much effort into the scheme.

By then, considerable high-altitude flight experience had been accumulated by various people. Air Force Major David Simons had soared to 100,000 feet in a balloon, and several Navy and civilian types nearly as high, after first sending aloft a dozen-odd mice. Dave didn't seem to be suffering unduly, and his reports and data did much to debunk the radiation myth. By that time, too, the U.S. had logged considerable experience with the U-2 'high-altitude research airplane,' designed to overfly the Soviet Union on photo-reconnaissance intelligence missions.

None of the U-2 pilots were losing their hair—at least not from radiation. Much later, of course, one of our satellites discovered the Van Allen radiation belt deep in space. But this layer of cosmic particles is too far out for the X-15 or earth-orbiting capsules. Deep-space travelers en route to the moon may have to thread through the belt, like a submarine through a mine-field, but it is a long-range problem, and definitely not an insoluble one.

"Charlie," I reported, "this radiation is a lot of bunk. To hell with trying to tint the windshield."

"If you say so, Scotty," Feltz replied.

"Just make damned sure those windshields don't ice up," I joked. "This airplane is not designed to be flown blind."

Zero G, or weightlessness, which a pilot will experience in flights beyond the appreciable pull of the earth's gravity, first came up with force in early 1950 during a meeting of 'space' experts. Some serious scientific questions were raised. For example, would the fluid in the inner ears 'float' and cause critical disorientation? How could a man drink water? With no pull of gravity to take it to his stomach, might he not drown?

And so on.

Weightlessness is the one condition we cannot simulate on a machine, such as the centrifuge, located on the face of the earth. The nearest we can get at present is to fly an airplane on a parabolic curve, during which time the airplane, for a variety of complicated reasons, very briefly becomes apparently disengaged from the pull of gravity. Chuck Yeager was one of the first pilots in the country to try this experiment. As early as 1950 he flew weightless trajectories in a jet airplane for periods of about thirty seconds. He reported slight disorientation and slight nausea.

I was curious about this because I was then preparing for the Skyrocket flights which would take me on a parabolic flight-path at, or close to, weightlessness for a brief period. I took an NACA F-84 jet and flew about fifty weightless trajectories. I suspended a pencil on a string in the cockpit to check that I was really weightless. When the pencil floated and the string slackened, I knew I had achieved the desired result. Not once during these fifty flights did I experience any undesirable effects or dangerous disorientation. As a matter of fact, I rather enjoyed the sensation. It was fun, like riding a roller-coaster. Occasionally during the weightless portion of the flight, my weightless arm would overreach. But soon I adjusted to this and piloted the airplane without mishap or discomfort.

Sometimes I flew the trajectory upside down. On three occasions during the recovery from this maneuver, when the airplane was rotating about three axes, and building from zero to a high G level, I felt weird, as though I were going into a loop, quite similar to the common experience of an accelerating or decelerating centrifuge. But this was due, I knew, solely to the recovery maneuver, not the zero G condition. I wrote a report downplaying the effect of zero G.

Unfortunately, my notes from these flights actually served for years as a rallying point for the zero G doom-criers. Some experts seized on the three inverted-recovery disorientations and trumpeted them throughout aeromedical circles. I tried my best to curb these charges, but the truth never caught up. It still hadn't caught up when I joined the X-15 project. It was well known that the X-15 pilot would experience about three to five minutes of weightlessness on the altitude trajectories. These experts predicted alarming consequences.

To me this was nonsense, if not downright scientific dishonesty. And it really irritated me to realize my own flight notes were being used to foster this untruth. I believe people are affected by weightlessness somewhat as they are by motion sickness. Some people become air-sick and disoriented; others don't. Any pilot, especially a test pilot, will be able to adjust to short durations of weightlessness in the X-15 or any other sub-orbital space craft.

A prolonged period of weightless flight may be another story altogether. I don't know what will happen to spacemen orbiting the earth for a matter of days. New ways of 'forced' eating will have to be developed. In fact, the Air Force has already come up with a toothpaste-tube method of injecting water into a weightless body, and other innovations. Just what effect prolonged weightlessness will have on the heart, urinal tract, and other vital organs of the body where moving fluids are located, is a mystery. Thus I quite agreed with Air Force General Don Flickinger's MIS aero-medical proposal to orbit man for progressively greater durations. But I strenuously fought off any suggestion that the X-15 might be compromised because of short periods of weightlessness. And I stubbornly resisted the flight surgeons who proposed 'instrumentating' the X-15 pilot's body, so that they could listen in on his heart, respiratory system, and so on. The line must be drawn somewhere.

"Here we go again," Charlie Feltz moaned one day.

"What is it now?" I asked.

"The low L over D on landing again," Feltz said. "They're worried about it."

The L over D, or sink rate, of the X-15, as I have related, was a controversial matter from the outset. We all knew the ship would come in for its landing hot, and falling like a brick.

The landing would be tricky, with little margin for error. But we had concluded long before that it was well within the capability of a qualified pilot. It was astonishing to have this matter come up again so late in the game. The L over D ratio of the X-15 was about two or three to one. In other words, for every two or three feet it moved ahead in the glide, it would drop one foot. During my days at NACA, Edwards, I had made many low L over D landings. For example, we had made tests in the X-4 with speed brakes open, calculating the L over D to be less than three to one. The L over D of the horrible XF-92-A on a dead-stick landing was about three to one. The L over D of the Skyrocket, which I flew almost routinely, was about five or six to one. To lay this matter at rest once and for all, I organized a special flight-test program to simulate the X-15 sink rate. I found that if I landed an F-100 with engine idling, dive brakes and gear extended, and a drogue chute deployed, I could come close to approximating the X-15 landing glide-path. At Edwards I made hundreds of such landings. Later I came closer to the real thing by shifting to an F-104. With the engine idling, the dive brakes extended, and the gear out with landing flaps down, the F-104 bad an L over D of less than three to one. I demonstrated this simulated X-15 landing scores of times at Edwards.

Even so, some Cassandras remained, bleating in the wings. These demonstrations to prove that any experienced pilot could land the X-15 were important for a number of reasons, the biggest of which we were not then free to discuss. The safe so that they could listen in on his heart, respiratory system, and so on. The line must be drawn somewhere.

"Here we go again," Charlie Feltz moaned one day.

"What is it now?" I asked.

"The low L over D on landing again," Feltz said. "They're worried about it."

The L over D, or sink rate, of the X-15, as I have related, was a controversial matter from the outset. We all knew the ship would come in for its landing hot, and falling like a brick.

The landing would be tricky, with little margin for error. But we had concluded long before that it was well within the capability of a qualified pilot. It was astonishing to have this matter come up again so late in the game. The L over D ratio of the X-15 was about two or three to one. In other words, for every two or three feet it moved ahead in the glide, it would drop one foot. During my days at NACA, Edwards, I had made many low L over D landings. For example, we had made tests in the X-4 with speed brakes open, calculating the L over D to be less than three to one. The L over D of the horrible XF-92-A on a dead-stick landing was about three to one. The L over D of the Skyrocket, which I flew almost routinely, was about five or six to one.

To lay this matter at rest once and for all, I organized a special flight-test program to simulate the X-15 sink rate. I found that if I landed an F-100 with engine idling, dive brakes and gear extended, and a drogue chute deployed, I could come close to approximating the X-15 landing glide-path. At Edwards I made hundreds of such landings. Later I came closer to the real thing by shifting to an F-104. With the engine idling, the dive brakes extended, and the gear out with landing flaps down, the F-104 bad an L over D of less than three to one. I demonstrated this simulated X-15 landing scores of times at Edwards.

Even so, some Cassandras remained, bleating in the wings. These demonstrations to prove that any experienced pilot could land the X-15 were important for a number of reasons, the biggest of which we were not then free to discuss. The safe landing was a vital plank in our case for the advanced X-15. By the fall of 1957 we had progressed far with this dream—to the point of making drawings and adding up figures. As a matter of fact, our preliminary design section had conceived an advanced X-15 which, with powerful boosters, such as a cluster of Navahos, could be put into orbit. We called this dream craft the X-15B, but we were under orders not to discuss it beyond the confines of our secret workshop. Stormy was afraid that if we did the men in white coats would come after us.

31: Working in a Fish Bowl

WE, AMONG OTHERS, HAD ANTICIPATED SPUTNIK but utterly failed to predict its profound impact on the minds of all men. When it came, on October 4, 1957, we were astonished by the reaction. As the sense of public shame spread throughout the country, we—engineers on the most advanced 'space' project in the United States—were overwhelmed by special misgivings. Maybe we should have pushed the X-15B, the orbiting vehicle, harder. We debated. Had we been right to lie low, virtually keeping it to ourselves? Perhaps a concerted, intelligent presentation in Washington would have sold our case, even in those days before Sputnik when space was taboo.

This painful speculation did not go on for long. No sooner did we feel the impact of Sputnik than a second rocket crashed into our camp. This one had North American insignia. It was Stormy, urging us to put together a completely detailed proposal for an orbiting X-15B right now. Fortunately, the preliminary design section had worked out most of the details. Ours was mainly a job of assembling various loose pieces of paper and bringing the report up to date. Within a few days it was ready and Stormy hurried off to Washington.

The X-15B concept was awe-inspiring even to those of us who had thought about it for many months. In the plan Stormy took to Washington it was a three-stage monster, tall as a seven-story building. The basic booster system, or first two stages, developed the staggering total of 1.3 million pounds of thrust. The first stage consisted of two giant Navahos, bound together and calculated to generate about 830,000 total pounds thrust. The second stage was a single Navaho, capable of 415,000 pounds thrust.

The third and final stage, perched atop the cluster of boosters like some massive arrowhead, was the X-15B itself, with a slightly more powerful engine than the RMI XLR-99. As a matter of fact, the engine we had in mind for the X-15B, a proven, reliable chamber, was the North American-built Atlas 'sustainer' engine, which develops about 75,000 pounds thrust.

The X-15B was a far more sophisticated ship than the craft we were then building. It was larger, capable of carrying not one pilot, but two. The skin was tougher, to withstand the higher post-orbit re-entry heating. The fuel tanks were rearranged and larger, to gain added third-stage thrust. But as for the basic shape and the systems—controls, both conventional and ballistic, pressure suit, instruments, and so on—the two airplanes were fundamentally the same. Years of development on the X-15 would save much time in perfecting the X-15B.

According to our proposed flight plan, the X-15B would be fired from a launching pad in Cape Canaveral, Florida. The huge double-Navaho first stage would lift the massive structure toward the sky. After about eighty seconds the first stage would fall away. Then the second stage would light off and boost the shrinking structure higher and faster. When the second stage burned out, it too would fall away, leaving the X-15B alone in the sky. At that point the X-15B pilot would light off the rocket engine and the 30,000-pound ship would soar into orbit, 75 miles above the earth and at a speed of 18,000 miles an hour.

After three orbits around the earth, the X-15B pilot would prepare to return. First he would fire 'retro-rockets' to slow down the craft and bring it back out of orbit. When the ship neared the thick atmosphere the pilot or pilots would align the ship with the ballistic controls and then make a similar approach to that planned for the X-15, a shallow, gradual descent into the atmosphere. When the ship had fully re-entered and slowed to more or less conventional X-15 speed, the pilot would set up for a conventional landing on one of the dry lakes near Edwards. This was, in essence, my 'commuter' space ship.

We were proud of that proposal and damned happy that we were in shape, that we had created a team and the think-how to carry it through to completion within a matter of four years, the terminal date we set in the proposal. But as we were soon to learn, other airframe companies had not been idle. When the space taboo was forced aside by Sputnik, hundreds of engineers descended on Washington with literally hundreds of proposals for every conceivable type of space craft. Stormy returned to the plant in a dark mood.

"When I left Washington," he said, "there were exactly 421 new proposals before the Pentagon and NACA. There's talk of creating a new 'space agency,' and I'm afraid some time is going to elapse before they get organized and sort through all those proposals. Furthermore, the President has stated publicly that he is opposed to having the Air Force and the Navy engage in big space projects unless they have some clear military application. We'll have to take that heavy instrumentation load out of the X-15B proposal and substitute a weapons system, a bomb, reconnaissance cameras, or something like that."

"Well, that's certainly no problem," Feltz said.

"The other thing is, I encountered a lot of resistance to an advanced X-15. They still want to see how a plain X-15 will do on landing and so on, before they move to any more advanced projects. Also, they don't like the Navaho booster system and I'll have to admit they have a point. The Navaho is proven, but the staging is complicated and big. I have a feeling, as far as orbiting man is concerned, they will probably want to start with something smaller and a little less complex. My guess is that whoever is given responsibility for putting man in space will probably begin with Don Flickinger's MIS program."

Stormy, as usual, had shrewdly sized up the Washington scene. A few months after his informal report to us, Congress did, in fact, create a new space agency—the National Aeronautics and Space Administration (NASA). NACA formed the nucleus for the new agency. Dr. T. Keith Glennan moved in as NASA Administrator, and NACA's former boss, Dr. Hugh L. Dryden, remained as Glennan's deputy. The President gave NASA responsibility for almost all non-military space projects. And as Stormy had predicted, NASA selected Flickinger's MIS program as a start for putting man in space. MIS became Project Mercury. (Late in 1959 Walt Williams moved from Edwards to NASA's Langley Laboratory to help push the Mercury program.) NASA awarded the contract to build the orbiting, manned Mercury capsule to McDonnell Aircraft Company in St. Louis, Missouri. Then NASA selected seven members of the armed forces, all of them test pilots, to serve as our first spacemen. NASA labeled these seven men Mercury Astronauts.

Although both the X-15 and Project Mercury came under NASA jurisdiction, they were separate, distinct programs. The X-15 has frequently been confused with Project Mercury, and I have often been mistaken for one of the seven Astronauts, but there is no connection between the two projects other than a friendly rivalry and a complete exchange of information. Sputnik hit us hard in more ways than one. The press, inquisitive by nature and eagerly seeking an answer to Soviet space triumphs, turned klieg lights on the X-15 project. Reporters, radio and television commentators, and a variety of other media descended on us in droves, seriously complicating our already difficult task. These endless news reports, stories, and feature articles generally exaggerated the X-15 mission. The X-15 was confused with the X-15B proposal, which had been published in a trade journal, or else it was deliberately misrepresented. Quite soon our research airplane had the title of "the U.S.'s first space ship."

We were astonished and baffled by this activity, and especially concerned when the government removed the secrecy from all but the most obscure technical details of the X-15. For the first time in history an aircraft company found itself building a research airplane completely in the open. All details, failures as well as successes, were available almost day by day to the nation. It was like working in a fish bowl. It made us uncomfortable, not to say edgy. It is disconcerting to build an airplane as revolutionary as the X-15 with a reporter leaning over one's shoulder.

Believe me, under such circumstances the multifarious demands of the modern communications media can be overwhelming. I should know. As the X-15's first test pilot, I was naturally singled out for special press treatment. Invitations to interviews, to make speeches, to appear on television shows, came by the hundreds. There were so many that I could have stopped all work on the X-15 itself then and there and devoted full time to fulfilling these requests. In some special cases—those I thought would particularly benefit the project—I did make time for them. But although I rejected about ninety per cent of these invitations and ducked the press whenever possible, I was soon glamorously and erroneously tagged "Our First Man in Outer Space."

It is not easy to deal with the press. It is a time-consuming and delicate operation. If you grant one man an interview and refuse another, the latter becomes angry. In the press, as in the aircraft industry and elsewhere, there are many good men but there are also many small-minded and bigoted prima donnas.

For months upon months I walked this tightrope, desperately hoping that I would not offend someone who would take out his anger on the X-15 project itself, or on Charlie Feltz or Stormy. I tried, actually, to steer the reporters to Charlie and Stormy, the two men who deserve the real credit for building the X-15. But the press was not too interested. They kept returning to me, the pilot, kept on giving me undue credit. This constant publicity, unsought but unavoidable, considerably strained my day-to-day working relationship with the fine X-15 project team at North American and with our customers, the Air Force, the Navy, and NASA.

To all of the press there was one line I refused to cross: the threshold of my home. Each newsman, naturally, wanted to interview Alice and our tribe of children, five of them by that time. Since my Mach 2 flight in the Skyrocket, I had conscientiously shielded my family from the press. There were many reasons for this. First and foremost, this attention embarrassed Alice and made the children uncomfortable. I was willing to give my all for the X-15 and the nation, but I saw no compelling reason to involve the members of my family against their wishes.

Another reason was my uncertainty about what effect the publicity might have on the children. There was always the chance that, seeing their pictures in a newspaper or magazine, their young heads might be turned early in life. I wanted to avoid this at all costs. My adamant policy in this regard made many of the newsmen, especially the photographers, furious. Some of these men suspected that I had some mysterious ulterior motive. Perish the thought! Behind the scenes, ironically, my role in the flight test of the X-15 was being cast in almost inverse ratio to my press clippings.

From the outset NACA or, as we now call it, NASA, had deliberately seized a firm technical grip on the X-15 flight-test program. Unlike most previous rocket-research airplanes, the X-15 would not go first to the Air Force for shakedown flights and then later to NASA. After contractor demonstration flights the ship would go direct from contractor to NASA. The complete flight-test program would be laid out by NASA. The Air Force, Navy, and NASA would contribute one pilot plus a 'back-up' pilot for the airplane. But these men would fly under strict NASA supervision.

As contractor test pilot I would fly the airplane first. We would demonstrate many points, such as engine reliability, flight stability under negative G and positive G, Lox top-off and launch capability, and safe landings. These flights would be short-legged, conducted over or near the Edwards base. I had been specifically told that I would have speed and altitude restrictions which would keep me well within established records.

NASA did not want a long delay in contractor demonstrations just seeking new records. We protested this at first, not because North American was interested in establishing records, but because some of the restrictions made the demonstration points more difficult and dangerous. For example, at high speed and altitude we could demonstrate high-speed controllability without fear of disaster, but at lower speed and altitude it was far more ticklish and less fruitful. Nevertheless, NASA had the final say-so, and very early in the game they set North American flight limits on the airplane of Mach 2.0 and 100,000 feet.

Iven Kincheloe, who had earned the name 'Mr. Space' in four flights of the X-2 before Apt crashed, was selected as the Air Force X-15 pilot. A handsome, eager young blond, with wavy hair and deep blue eyes, he was the press agent's dream of a test pilot. But Kinch, as we called him, was much more than that. He was an engineering test pilot, an educated man, dedicated, fearless, and able. During the building of the X-15, he was constantly in the plant going over the plans and discussing the technical details of the ship. Kinch was obviously a winner and we were glad to have him on the X-15 team. His back-up on the Air Force team was Major Robert White, a graduate of the Edwards test-pilot school and a very able pilot.

White had never flown a rocket plane—by the time he came along they were all either retired or crashed—but he had plenty of experience with all of the Air Force's supersonic fighters and bombers.

NASA selected its most senior pilot, Joe Walker, to fly the X-15. I knew Walker well. He had worked with me for years at NACA, Edwards. He learned to fly rocket planes and the other weird vehicles in NACA's stable, including the X-4, X-5, and the underpowered X-3. In his tour of duty at NACA, Edwards, Walker had accumulated thirty-one rocket-powered flights in the X-1-A (in which he narrowly escaped death when it exploded in the mother-plane belly), X-1-B, and the X-1-E. He was well qualified for the X-15 assignment. Since the Navy had contributed a small percentage of the X-15 cost, it, too, was entitled to assign a pilot to the flight-test program. Lt. Comdr. Forrest ('Pete') Petersen, a pilot from the Navy's Patuxent River Test Station, was selected. Petersen had helped wring out most of the new Navy carrier-based fighters, such as the F-11-F, F-8-U, and F-4-H. A quiet-spoken man who liked to stay out of the limelight—and did—Petersen impressed me as a 'sleeper,' a man of Colonel Marion Carl's caliber. I was certain that, given the opportunity, Petersen would perform very well for the Navy.

In due time the government considered the X-15B proposal which we had submitted in the wake of Sputnik and, as Stormy had predicted, rejected it. Convinced that our approach was a sound follow-on, or parallel program, with NASA's Project Mercury, we kept trying to sell it as a laboratory or weapons system. We greatly simplified the booster system, switching from Navaho to Martin's newer and more powerful Titan ballistic missile. But NASA had its hands full with Mercury.

The President was not yet convinced that the Air Force could mount a weapons system in space. Communications and early-warning satellites were obviously valuable, but there was considerable controversy about the efficiency and practicability of launching a bomb from space. Pending the President's final decision, the Air Force awarded a long-range study contract to Boeing and Martin for an orbital, or sub-orbital, vehicle known as DYNA-SOAR.

Meanwhile, our X-15, which was then beginning to take shape in the manufacturing division, was regarded with new and increasing respect, not only throughout the nation and aircraft industry, but also at North American. Our baffling step-child had suddenly ballooned into the nation's front-running vehicle to put man into space. Our project group increased in size from 65 to over 250 people. Every division of the plant was eager to help us with our problems. Beaming proudly, North American erected with pride a huge neon sign over the main production buildings proclaiming:

HOME OF THE X-15

From the very beginning of the X-15 project we worked with a sense of urgency. Our goal was to build a research aircraft to provide data for military combat airplanes in time. Now, having seen the psychological impact of Sputnik, we realized that a safe flight of the X-15 to the fringes of space would not only provide these data but also, as a by-product, bring the nation great prestige, especially if we got our man there—and back—before the Russians. Frankly, considering the size and advanced state of development of the Soviet booster rockets, we believed our chances of getting there first were slim indeed. Nevertheless, following Sputnik, we of the X-15 group felt we were engaged in a kind of private race with the Russian scientists, and we ran to win despite the odds.

32: Time for Extraordinary Action

By January of 1958 the X-15 team had moved into high gear. North American's F-100 contract was running out. The production space was absorbed by the jigs and dies for our three 'space craft.' We had subcontracted about two hundred items on the airplane to vendors, but most of the ship was manufactured right on the premises.

By then all the engineering drawings—some six thousand altogether, and one of them fifty feet long—had been released. The never-ending battle to get the most from a part for the least weight was reaching a climax. Charlie Feltz had detailed every man on our team to keep track of the weight, to make certain the total did not climb above our final estimate of 31,000 pounds. Since there were more than 10,000 parts on the X-15 weighing a pound or more, our weight-watchers were firm and exacting.

Everything about the fabrication of the X-15 was new and challenging and therefore, from a technological standpoint, exciting. Every day at his command post on the second floor of the engineering building, Charlie Feltz faced a hundred new problems, each one of them a minor crisis. As I look back on those long days and nights, I wonder how he kept his sanity.

We hear much about pressure on Madison Avenue and in the city rooms of newspapers at press time, but no one can persuade me that it is any greater than that we experienced on the X-15 project. Night after night I returned to my home late—punchy, almost shell-shocked. Month by month I watched Feltz aging, long before his time. But no matter how intense the work, or how baffling and seemingly insoluble the crisis, he seldom lost his country-boy composure. I believe this fact, more than any other, held the team together amicably under the great strain and enabled us to achieve our goal.

Most of the technical details of the fabrication of the X-15 are, sad to say, too involved to relate here. Thus I fear this marvelous technological story will never be told in full. But there is one understandable detail which I would like to describe. This is our pioneering metallurgy with the skin of the X-15, Inconel X. In the sense that it was new and untried, it was fairly typical of most of the fabulous shop-work on the X-15. Inconel X, as I have said, is a tough nickel alloy, capable of withstanding high temperatures without losing its structural integrity. When we launched the X-15 project, Inconel X had been proven in a laboratory. But no one had ever built a machine of it. There were no handbooks to tell us how to work it. For example, only a few people in the nation had ever tried to weld Inconel X. The skin of the X-15 had to be welded because traditional rivets were not strong and resilient enough to stand the temperature beating without leaking. Besides, we figured we could save a thousand pounds of weight by eliminating rivets.

Consider half of the X-15 wing as typical of the metallurgy problem we licked. From fuselage to wingtip, the wing is only six feet long. At its peak cross-section the wing is only eight inches thick. There are seventeen spars in the wing. At the root near the fuselage joint the spar caps are 3/16 of an inch thick. At the tip they are a mere 30/1000 thick.

When the X-15 re-entered the heavy atmosphere of the earth, we had calculated, the leading edges would be subjected to 1200 degrees Fahrenheit. They would glow red from the heat. A few inches aft on the wing, however, the temperature would be much lower. Where the temperature is higher, the metal must be thicker and heavier to carry the load. But at the same time it is foolish to waste weight by overloading at points where the temperature is low. Thus we viewed the wing skin in hundreds of sections, each capable of withstanding a certain maximum temperature, plus a safety margin, and each of different thick-ness to save weight and still carry its share of load.

Inconel X came to us from the manufacturer, International Nickel, in sheets 36 inches wide and 140 inches long, rolled and milled to normal aircraft specifications. We figured that if the total skin of the X-15 were as much as 1/1000 of an inch too thick, it would cost us a critical 100 pounds in weight. Thus when we received the sheets, we re-milled them in grinders down to incredibly low tolerances. Since each different piece of the wing-skin varied in design thickness from the others, each had to be ground separately to those tolerances. (The same was true of the fuselage and tail-skin.) It was like making a Stradivarius, if not even more delicate. Once these pieces were completed and the spars set in massive jigs, the technicians then set about welding the many parts into one solid piece. Ordinary welding is difficult enough: extreme care must be taken to see that no 'bubbles' form to weaken the joints. Welding Inconel X almost drove our men to distraction.

They worked like artists, experimenting with new strokes and mixtures until they were able to produce a true masterpiece of craftsmanship. Each of the thousands of joints was X-rayed to make certain no bubbles had formed. The pieces, after welding, were heat-treated like fine steel knife-blades. Let me explain that further. When you weld two pieces of metal together, each is subject to varying temperatures from the welding torch. As the torch moves along, the new area heats up while the one just passed cools. Thus there are stresses and strains in the molecular structure of the metal undetectable to the naked eye. By placing the entire structure in an oven after welding and raising the temperature to 1900 degrees we were able to cool it uniformly, ironing out the strains. After this stress-relieving process each piece remained in the oven for twenty-four hours at high temperature to heat-treat or 'age' the metal. Then the joint and the parent metal were stronger than originally.

After a fine polishing, the hundreds of welds were impossible to locate with the human eye. The wing looked like one solid piece of smooth metal.

Our metallurgists didn't learn this new craft overnight; it took years. They started out experimentally by building three mock fuselages of the X-15 to serve as ground test beds for the rocket engines. One of these was installed at Edwards, the other two at the RMI engine factory in New Jersey. This experience brought our welders to the artist level, but when it came to building the three airplanes, Feltz was even more demanding.

In fact, as I recall, about seven different wing-skins were built for the first airplane before he gave his approval. In the end, I think, the experience and knowledge we gained on this new frontier alone were worth the entire cost of the X-15 program.

It was one big reason we believed our case for the advanced X-15 was sound. All future space projects will benefit directly or indirectly from our work with Inconel X. The RMI XLR-99 rocket engine was steadily falling behind schedule. This fact was no secret. It was well known in the Air Force, NASA, and throughout the entire aircraft industry. There were many technical locusts plaguing the RMI engineers. One of the biggest was the fact that during tests, while burning the X-15's exotic fuel mixture of Lox and ammonia, the rocket-engine chamber had a habit of exploding. By February, 1958, the XLR-99 engine was exactly one year behind schedule and considerably heavier than originally planned.

I believe that under ordinary circumstances our customer would simply have ordered us to wait for, or 'sweat out' the engine. But the X-15 was not being put together under ordinary circumstances. She loomed on the horizon as a national symbol of our ability, or lack of it, to make good in space. Because of this and other factors, insofar as the engine was concerned, it was time for extraordinary action. But complex rocket engines don't grow on trees. What to do?

Charlie Feltz called for help. Stormy, who was then also busy laying out plans for the Air Force F-108 fighter and the B-70 bomber among other things, took over the X-15 engine crisis at full throttle, bringing his authority to bear. He got on the telephone to North American's Rocketdyne Division. Could they run some Lox-ammonia tests on a Redstone chamber and see what happened? Rocketdyne converted a Redstone chamber and successfully conducted the tests. (Rocketdyne engineers even made the Redstone chamber throttleable.) We were impressed, because these tests were run off in a matter of weeks without interfering with Rocketdyne's major ballistic-missile projects, and at no cost to the government.

After the tests Stormy again asked the Air Force to allow us to equip the X-15 with a working engine. Again the proposal was turned down, for most of the aforementioned reasons. But the Rocketdyne demonstrations had a dramatic impact at RMI. RMI engineers, beaten at their own complex game by the great depth of North American engineering talent, turned to on the XLR-99 engine with new and vigorous enthusiasm. But we knew that no matter how hard they worked they couldn't make up much of the lost time. What was the answer?

We debated that question during countless meetings with Stormy and Charlie Feltz in the following weeks. Then one day our 'dreamer,' Bob Carmen, spoke up.

"I've been doing a little figuring here. Suppose that instead of waiting for the XLR-99 engine we substitute, pending its arrival, two X-1-type engines. They could be built in a few months, at most."

I flew out of my chair.

"Boy," I said, "if you really want to kill off a project, this is one way to do it. Start yielding. Start making inferior substitutions. Make the airplane more complex. Sure. That's what happened to the X-3, the X-1-A series and the X-2. If we allow that to happen to the X-15, we're going to wind up with nothing again."

"Now, hold on a minute, Scotty," Feltz said. "We're really up a tree here. We can't use a Rocketdyne engine. We have to wait for the XLR-99. Maybe Carmen has got a point here. Pending the arrival of the big engine, we could be checking out the other systems in the airplane."

"Damn it, Charlie," I snapped. "I think we'd be making a big mistake."

"Let's take a look at the performance we might get out of the two X-1 engines," Feltz said, obviously warming to the idea.

"Can we use the same fuel-tank system?" an engineer asked.

"Yes," Carmen said. "Nothing about the fuel tanks would have to be changed. You just change the engine, substituting the eight small chambers for the one large one. I think we could fix it so that when it arrives the big engine could be installed with hardly any delay."

"What's the fuel for the X-1 engine?"

"Lox and alcohol. We just put the alcohol in the ammonia tanks. No sweat."

"There's another advantage, too," someone else put in. "Those engines have a lot of time on them. They ought to be reliable. The X-1 engines are not throttleable. But each engine has four barrels. That's a total of eight barrels, all of which can be lighted off separately. Thus you can attain just about any speed range you want within the limits of the airplane. I mean, it would be almost the same as being throttleable."

"I figure the extreme performance with these two engines at about Mach 3.5 and 150,000 feet," one engineer said. Each X-1 engine would have a thrust of about 8,000 pounds or a total in both chambers of about 16,000 pounds—compared to 57,000 pounds for the XLR-99. The two X-1 engines together weighed more than the single XLR-99 engine.

"Mach 3.5 and 150,000 feet," Feltz repeated. "That would give us enough performance to make a good many demonstrations on the airplane. In fact, we could make all the structural demonstrations, as well as re-entry, ballistic controls, Lox top-off, and so forth. Let's see what the customer says."

The substitution of the two smaller X-1-type engines was the obvious solution to our dilemma. Actually, the customers had already considered exactly the same idea. They approved it at once, and Edwards got busy building up a dozen 'proven' X-1 engines from old parts. We planned to put two each in the first two X-15S, holding the third X-15 in the factory for the first XLR-99 engine and other improvements which flight test would generate. The remaining X-1 engines would be used for ground tests in the X-15 engine test beds at Edwards and RMI.

A few nights after this decision was firmed up, Stormy, Feltz, and I met after work in Charlie's office at the North American plant. I was still grumbling about 'interim measures.' I let off steam.

"As far as I'm concerned, we've botched the whole deal," I growled. "You watch. We're never going to get that big engine. The X-15 is going to die on the vine. I've seen it happen before."

"You're wrong there, Scotty," Feltz said. "We'll get the big engine sometime. Meanwhile, we'll get a lot of Mach 3 data which will really help the F-108 and the B-70. We'll prove out the X-15 systems and by the time the big engine comes the ship itself will be as reliable as an F-100."

We debated this point for a long while. Stormy was also in favor of substituting the smaller engines. "I want to get this thing in the air as fast as possible," he said. "I think that as soon as we start flying the X-15 and prove our systems and landing and the rest, Washington will be impressed and may look with more favor on an advanced X-15 or the X-15B."

That remark was typical of Stormy. He was always looking far down the pike. He had cornered the Air Force combat aircraft market with the F-108 and the B-70, but he was stung when we lost out on the X-15B. He had not given up—and never would.

Frankly, Scotty," Charlie Feltz broke in, "this engine thing may be a blessing in disguise. I'll tell you honestly that all along I've been a little concerned about busting into space all at once with a brand-new airplane and a brand-new, untried engine. They did it with the X-1, it's true, and it was a real good show. But this is a new dimension we're getting into. They were just trying to crack Mach 1. We're trying to crack space, with a new pressure suit, re-entry, new metal, landing—everything at once. I've got a real good buddy who's going to be flying that airplane for the first time, and I'd just as soon have him around for a while."

Put that way, on a personal basis, there was nothing I could say in reply. From that point on, I resigned myself to the engine substitution, even though, in a sense, it marred my dream to help build and then fly the perfect airplane.

In fact, after some weeks, I came to believe that even from a pilot's point of view the engine substitution was wise. We could learn to crawl before we entered the Olympic hundred-yard dash. I was confident that in time and with God's help we would eventually succeed with the big engine.

There was too much at stake to allow it to fall by the wayside.

33: Circus Day

By the fall of 1958, Edwards Air Force Base had matured to the world's foremost flight-test laboratory. It was busy and business-like. Skilled, schooled Air Force test pilots, flying under rigid regulations, took off or landed every ten or fifteen minutes or so, creating the impression of a modern, tightly-run commercial airport. Brigadier General Stanley Holtoner had been replaced by another spit-and-polish Air Force commander, Brigadier General Marcus Cooper, and he, in turn, by Brigadier General John Carpenter. A new crop of Air Force planes came along to replace the original Century series. Now the Air Force men were in the advance stages of wringing out Republic's F-105, Convair's F-106, North American's F-107, and Convair's B-58 bomber. Private industry, operating from modern, well-furnished office buildings and hangars, was testing the new family of commercial jet airplanes, Boeing's 707, Douglas's DC-8, and Convair's 880.

NASA's big 400-man plant was idling, preparing for the arrival of the X-15. Here, more than any place else, one could feel the tremendous impact of the X-15. It was no longer just another research airplane. It was a revolutionary jump, a craft that would make all other airplanes at Edwards, or all that had ever seen Edwards, seem insignificant by comparison.

Paul Bikle, who would replace Walt Williams as NASA's director at Edwards, regarded the coming flights of the X-15 as one might look upon the voyages of Columbus or Magellan. Throughout the station there was a feeling that history was in the making. Every micro-second of that coming voyage would be recorded in almost incredible detail. From the maximum launch point near Salt Lake to Edwards, the Air Force and NASA at a cost of over $3 million laid out a series of radar and telemetering stations along the X-15's proposed flight-path. These stations would 'track' the X-15 and electronically quiz the craft's instrumentation. The X-15 would respond at the rate of several thousand data points every second. A battery of electronic machines and magnetic tape recorders was installed in a room adjoining the NASA tower at Edwards to absorb and correlate these data as they were collected. By these new methods one flight of the X-15 would provide more data than thirty flights of the old X-1 or Skyrocket. If something went wrong and the plane failed to return, the recorders would follow the plane to the last second of its life. The pilot who followed in the next X-15 would then have a broader base of flight knowledge. With the X-15 nothing was being left to chance. Seat-of-the-pants flight test was buried deep in Edwards' past.

But before these spectacular long-range flights North American would first demonstrate the airplane. Until this was accomplished, the responsibility for the airplane and the flight-test program lay on our shoulders. Our own preparations for these first critical flights in the strange bird were not inconsiderable.

Like the other aircraft companies North American manned a large and well-organized flight-test establishment at Edwards.

Our office and hangar space by this time was about twice the size of the original NACA High Speed Flight Station which Williams had created on the desert. The North American installation at Edwards was bossed by Ed Cokely, who had been supervising the initial flights of North American airplanes at Edwards since before the days of the jets. There were about one hundred flight-test engineers and maintenance men working under Cokely. During 1958 they were de-bugging and flying North American's F-107 fighter and North American's prototype T-39, a small two-engine commercial type jet transport-trainer, which we hoped to sell to the Air Force or the Navy as a trainer, or to private enterprise as an efficient company airplane.

Ed Cokely picked 35-year-old Q. C. Harvey to organize and boss our X-15 flight-test group at Edwards. Q.C., a short, energetic man with graying crew-cut hair, was an experienced hand.

He had come to the desert ten years earlier with the McDonnell XF-85. Later he worked in flight tests on McDonnell's F2H Banshee and a more advanced version, the F3H. Skip Ziegler had recruited Q.C. for the Bell rocket-test flight team in 1951. Q.C. had cut his teeth on the Queenie, which blew up and nearly killed Joe Cannon, and the X-1-A, in which Yeager and Murray made their speed and altitude records. He joined North American in 1953 to work in the flight-test group on the last model of the F-86, and later the F-100 and the F-107.

Q.C. was a live-wire type who knew better than most the importance of the X-15 to North American and to the nation. Early in the fall of 1958 he began a series of planning meetings with the Air Force and NASA to lay out the North American phase of the X-15 flight program. From that point on I divided my time between the North American plant in Los Angeles and the North American flight-test facility at Edwards. I commuted between two desks in my private red, white, and blue single-engine Bonanza which the Air Force very kindly permitted me to land on the Edwards base. I did not actually consider the Bonanza a luxury. Without it I could never have met my ever-growing responsibilities in the X-15 project.

The table in the conference room at the Edwards North American flight-test facility was twelve feet long. At each place there was a pad and pencil for jotting down notes. Q.C. sat at the head of the table. The rest of us, Air Force and NASA flight-test supervisors, the designated X-15 pilots, the B-52 mother-plane pilots, the 'chase' plane pilots, North American's Sam Richter, who would man a communications van out on the lake bed, and Bill Berkowitz, who would operate the X-15 launch panel in the B-52, took places around the table. Another dozen-odd men, including the pilot of the emergency helicopter, a representative of the security division of Edwards, a medical officer, and the leading X-15 mechanics, sat in chairs along the wall. There was a blackboard against the far wall behind Q.C.'s chair, on which someone had chalked a crude map of the Edwards area.

Each of the men in the room was the leader in his particular field. Each represented a separate organization with special responsibilities during an X-15 flight. Thus for every man in the room there were another fifty or one hundred men behind the scenes, not counting the radar and optical trackers, the camera-men, telemeter operators, and the Lord knows who else. The Edwards flight-test operation had become a vast pyramid of people supporting one man at the apex, the pilot. Everything was planned down to a gnat's eyelash.

The general outline of North American's initial X-15 flights had long been established. Every detail of it was designed to save time, to cut our schedule to the bare bone. We would begin with X-15 number one. We would mate her to the B-52, take her aloft and check out all ship's machinery under actual 'captive' conditions. We would make certain the cabin pressurization, pressure suit, instrumentation, radios, shackles, communications, oxygen and Lox top-off connections with the B-52, and the X-15's multifarious electrical systems, worked. When we were satisfied, then we would take X-15 number one aloft, devoid of fuel, and drop it on a powerless glide flight, simulating the beginning and conclusion of an actual rocket-test flight. Meanwhile, we would keep X-15 number two on the ground to check out the fuel tanks and rocket-propulsion system.

The theory was that any weaknesses which showed up either in the air on these captive flights, or on the ground during the engine checks, could be quickly remedied simultaneously on both airplanes, and on the third X-15 which was still in the factory awaiting the XLR-99 engine.

"All the North American flights will be conducted locally," Q.C. said, addressing the room. We were reviewing the whole plan for the benefit of some new people and some others who had no reason to be concerned until then. "Following the captive flights and initial glide flight, each launch will be made over a predesignated dry lake. The object is to land each time on Rogers Dry Lake, alongside the base here."

Q.C. used a pointer on the blackboard.

"We will have to have emergency vehicles—an ambulance and fire trucks—in readiness at B-52 take-off time. These will line up on the Edwards runway during B-52 take-off. Afterwards they will shift and take up position on the lake bed along the anticipated glide-path and touch-down point of the X-15. Sam—" Q.C. looked at Richter—"your van will go to the lake at B-52 take-off time. Now, the helicopter will hover at the edge of the lake bed on the X-15 approach end. In event of landing emergency, it should be able to reach the X-15 within sixty seconds or less."

North American's flight surgeon, Toby Freedman, and Air Force flight surgeons would be in the helicopter.

"The personnel in the helicopter should become familiar now with emergency procedures for removing the X-15 cockpit canopy in case the pilot is unable to open it from the inside. The helicopter pilot should, of course, radio immediately a visual report on the landing. Sam, you'll be able to see the landing from the van. You report, too. The chase plane missions will be fairly routine. We'll use F-104s. Two airplanes will be assigned to close chase by the X-15 at drop and rocket light-off. The third chase, an F-100F, will serve as photographic chase and get what pictures he can without interfering with the close chase. The only problem I see here is that the F-104s will have some trouble hanging in the air at launch altitude, slowed to B-52 speed at launch."

He went on, describing action to be taken in a score of various emergencies, including everything from a B-52 engine failure on take-off to an outright mid-air explosion of the X-15 at light-off. Then he distributed a mimeographed 'check-off' list thirty pages long, which all of us would carry during the flight.

On each flight we would work our way through that long list, moving on to an item only after the previous item had been completed. This list represented the combined thinking and checking of a hundred people. If we followed it, the danger would be reduced to a minimum, or as near minimum as it is possible to come with a rocket airplane, and we would learn the most for every minute in the air.

"I will take up station in the North American tower," Q.C. went on. "I will have, sitting at a table near my mike, a specialist on each system of the X-15. If anything goes wrong on the ship prior to launch, I will designate the appropriate engineer to get on the mike and talk to Scotty. That way we might be able to fix it and avoid an abort. Incidentally, if we do have to abort a flight, we will always go right through launch countdown, right down to the point of drop, without dropping. This will give us more detailed experience and an opportunity to check out systems. We will not follow this procedure if the abort is the result of an emergency. In that case, we will follow emergency procedures for getting the B-52 and the X-15 back on the ground.

"At Scotty's request we are deliberately restricting the number of men authorized to talk on the radio circuit to hold down confusion. I will be on the circuit continuously. Sam Richter is authorized to come on the air, if necessary. The only others are Scotty in the X-15, the B-52 pilot, and of course the chase pilots. As far as the ground is concerned, I want everything to be funneled through me. In the air Scotty will have the final say-so. Any questions?"

There were many questions and this meeting, and a hundred others like it, churned on for long hours. As a result never in the history of Edwards was there finer co-operation between government agency and contractor. October 15, 1958—one year and eleven days after Sputnik— was circus day at the

Los Angeles Division of North American. X-15 number one was officially 'rolled out' of the plant ready, or almost ready, to fly. All activity in the plant slowed for this festive occasion. The chips were swept from the floor. All the grandees of North American were on hand. A plane-load of aviation reporters flew in from the East to herald the event in headlines the nation over. Senators and Congressmen and other VTFs crowded a special grandstand facing the X-15 to hear Vice President Richard Nixon, who came to California especially for the event, proclaim that the X-15 had "recaptured the U.S. lead in space." There were special exhibits of the pressure suit and other parts of the X-15. VIP's tried their hands in the X-15 cockpit simulator in the assembly building. Then all attended a gala luncheon during which all praised one another and the subcontractors. For the X-15 team it was a moving occasion.

During the ceremonies, Vice President Nixon said to me: "You certainly have a dangerous job."

I couldn't repress the reply that popped to mind: "My job is not nearly so risky as yours, sir."

Six years from inception, four years from final approval by the old NACA Aerodynamics Subcommittee, three years almost to the day the contract was let, and thus right on schedule, the X-15 was at last a reality. What's more, her airframe, thanks to Charlie Feltz, was 325 pounds under our design specification.

Even with the two heavier X-1 rocket chambers and the additional load of instrumentation, the airplane was only a hundred pounds overweight, a fantastic, unprecedented achievement in the aircraft industry. But the cost was great. The X-15 represented over 10,000,000 engineering man-hours. In time each of the three airplanes cost the government $40 million. In terms of weight, each would be worth three times as much as solid gold.

While I was posing for photographers alongside the X-15 that day, a reporter asked:

"Mr. Crossfield, why is the ship painted black? Most of the research airplanes were painted white like ice-boxes, weren't they? I thought white reflected heat and that was what you were trying to do—get away from the heat."

"Well," I said, "this is a kind of complicated thing. It's true that white does reflect heat, solar heat, for instance. But up where this ship will be, the sun will be only a tiny, intense beam of heat in a vast zero-cold universe. Our main problem is not solar heat, but frictional heat, the heat we will run into flying through the air—from bumping into molecules of air. The way it works out, this black paint will throw away that heat faster than white paint. In other words, it radiates the heat from friction at a faster rate. Is that clear?"

I'm afraid it wasn't clear. Our beast, from paint job to final mission, was simply too complicated to explain in a word. This was frustrating, in a way, because we were proud of what she was. But in the press she had been labeled a 'space ship,' and a space ship she would remain in the public eye, although in actuality she was a research tool, deliberately designed to search out trouble. In time, I was confident, the X-15's real mission would be grasped.

No matter what she was called, she was a beautiful thing, a masterpiece, if you will, and I remained long after the photographers departed to drink her in and contemplate the trying days I knew lay ahead at Edwards. Not long after the VIFs moved on, the circus folded and the men towed the X-15 to a flat-bed truck. Then they wrapped her in a tarpaulin and drove her to Edwards. Two weeks later X-15 number two followed.

On the eve of our flight-test operations, sad to say, we lost one member of the X-15 pilot team. Iven Kincheloe was killed while flying an F-104. Just after take-off his engine flamed out. The F-104 has a downward ejection seat. Too close to the ground for escape in that direction, Kinch rolled the F-104 on its back, so that he could eject upwards, away from the ground. He got out and his chute opened, but it was too late. His loss was mourned not only throughout the Air Force, but also at North American. Although I, as first pilot, had received from the press most of the X-15 'spaceman' build-up, we believed that Kinch would be the one to make the maximum-performance X-15 missions.

When Kinch died, his 'back-up,' Air Force Major Bob White, moved up to take his place. White is a handsome pilot, swarthy, with deep, piercing blue eyes. He has a fine wife and children. If he lacked rocket-airplane experience, he soon made it up. He studied the X-15 intently and checked out in a Clark pressure suit.

Following Kinch's death many people asked me if I were not disappointed that I had not been 'selected' to make the maximum flights of the X-15. Some reporters indignantly complained to NASA that it was completely 'unjust' to restrict me, considering my long experience in rocket airplanes, as against, say, Bob White, who had never flown a rocket plane. I would like to say here once and for all, and with a fervent hope that this will end the matter, yes, I was disappointed. No man with my background could have felt anything but disappointment.

For many reasons I believed I was best qualified to make these maximum flights. I would have accepted the assignment eagerly.

But in fairness to NASA, let me say that I went into the X-15 program with my eyes wide open. From the outset I knew the government pilots would be top dog. Walt Williams had predicted before I left NACA that I might never fly the X-15.

When the contract was let, it specifically stated that North American demonstrations would be limited in speed and altitude. Only a few weeks after I joined the program, as I have said, these restrictions were set at Mach 2 and 100,000 feet. That I would be 'the first man in outer space,' that is to say, that I would make the maximum demonstration flights of the X-15, was an invention of the press. I repeatedly stressed that this was not the case, but the press refused, or couldn't bring itself, to believe me. The Air Force and NASA pilots were ticketed for that role, and I simply accepted that fact of life.

To repeat: I knew from the beginning that in all probability I would never make the maximum flights of the X-15. But I was promised, unequivocally, the first flights of the craft. As I suspected, and as it turned out, these flights would provide danger and challenge enough. When Kinch died, I hoped these restrictions might be lifted. When they were not, I didn't pout like Achilles in his tent, as some reporters have implied. A maximum flight, a new speed or altitude was not my point. The point which concerned me, and one I have never been able to get across, is that I would participate in both the building and test flying of the airplane. That was the goal I sought—the closing of the circle of my life.

34: A Carnival at Dawn

My mental alarm clock, a handy, precise instrument which seldom failed, woke me at exactly 0500 on the morning of March 10, 1959. Charlie Feltz was snoring loudly, deep in sleep on the other twin bed in our room at the Edwards Bachelor Officers Quarters. I prodded Charlie gently and then went into the bathroom and drank a glass of water. I drank sparingly: soon I would be tightly laced in the X-15 full-pressure suit, which has no provisions for answering the call of nature.

At long last the day had come to take the X-15 into the air, snugged beneath the right wing of the B-52 mother plane, for her first realistic test. The purpose of this preliminary 'captive' flight was to check out the X-15's many systems under near-flight conditions and to make sure the B-52 could support her external store at launch speed of Mach .8 or 530 miles an hour. We would go through all the motions of an actual flight—I would operate her control systems and flaps, and lower the landing gear—but we would not drop the X-15. Our plan was to spend a couple of hours circling the Edwards base at 40,000 feet and, if all went well, land again with the X-15 still hung on the B-52 wing.

"Come on, Charlie," I said, "let's go find out if we built an airplane."

We dressed in business suits and ties, like anybody preparing for a day's work at the office, and drove to the flight line in one of North American's green station wagons. Take-off was scheduled for 0700. Based on my previous experience at Edwards with experimental airplanes, I calculated we would be lucky to make it by noon or 1400.

We could see the tail of the B-52, five stories tall, from half a mile away. The sun, just beginning to rise in the east, cast heavy shadows into the Edwards basin. The runway lights were still on. Two jet fighters, returning from a pre-dawn flight, taxied in the distance, their dazzling landing lights ablaze.

Maintenance and fuel trucks, painted a garish yellow, sped by. It was freezing cold and we kept the windows in the station wagon shut, the heater turned up full. We drove past row on row of jet airplanes parked and silent.

"You'd think that with all this activity," I said, "they'd have a place open around here for a cup of coffee."

Feltz didn't reply. His mind was fixed on the scene which paraded across the windshield as I turned into a parking place in the 'mating area.' There were half a hundred cars parked two-deep in a neat row. A team of North American guards directed traffic and checked badges.

Most of us, I suppose, have visited fair grounds at dawn to watch the carnival pack up and leave town, to stare in awe as the tents are torn down and the stakes pulled up, as the trucks back and churn in low gear and the carnival hands scurry here and there, sleepy but determined. This is what the scene in the mating area reminded me of that morning. It was a kind of organized pandemonium moving with a sense of urgency. The big bomber dominated the concrete mating area. It towered over everything like some colossal creation on a Cecil B. DeMille set, a monster with drooping wings 185 feet long and a bulky body over one-half the length of a football field. Mechanics swarmed over the B-52, preparing it for flight. I saw a man on the wing silhouetted against the dull early morning sun, a tiny speck on a massive expanse of aluminum. Far up in the cockpit the lights shone through the small windows and I could see the bobbing heads of the ground crewmen, working through the long pre-flight check list. The story of how a B-52 is made ready for flight is a book in itself.

Beneath and around the bomber there were not less than twenty-five trucks and carts, and probably a hundred men. A few were working on the huge ship. But most were clustered around the strange, shark-like store mounted beneath an inverted, stream-lined pylon on the right wing—the X-15. Just forward of the B-52 wing leading edge, the X-15 cockpit canopy was cocked up and open. Had it been closed, the X-15 might have been some over-sized missile, to the untrained eye. Despite the cold and their heavy clothing, the men worked feverishly, like mechanics in the pits a half hour before the Memorial Day race in Indianapolis.

They had been working at that pace in the North American hangar three shifts around the clock for four months. I wondered how any mechanical device could generate so much enthusiasm and dedication.

One truck stood apart from all the rest. This was Sam Richter's communications van, which resembled a beat-up, miniature school bus, though it was painted the company green. The rear of this van was fitted with radio transmitters and receivers, a tape recorder, and devices to transcribe data from the battery of weird-looking weather instruments and antennae which protruded, like a forest of prehistoric trees, from the top of the van. During the pre-flight operations in the mating area, Sam's well-heated van served as a kind of headquarters for the engineers and crew foremen. Crowded in among the radio gear were a swivel chair and seats which had long ago been salvaged from some office.

Feltz and I opened the door on the rear of the van and pushed our way inside. Mel Beach, overall ground boss of the X-15 crew, was there, as well as Q. C. Harvey, flight-test director, and Si Fohl, the chief foreman. They were urgently leafing through a clipboard thick with forms.

"Will we be ready for an on-time take-off?" I asked.

Si answered by rattling off a list of items yet to be fixed which spelled at least an hour's delay. No modern airplane ever takes to the air with all its machinery in perfect working order. On a B-52, for example, an average of ten per cent of the equipment is usually out of commission. On the X-15, more complex than ten B-52s put together, the ground crewmen were doing their best to shrink the first-flight 'carry-over' list to acceptable limits. The out-of-commission, or carry-over, items were compiled on the clipboard, on pages of special forms. It would be up to me in the end to review the list and either 'buy' the carry-over items or cancel the flight.

I leafed through the forms, noting the many anticipated, minor items not working: a valve, a leak, a piece of complicated NASA instrumentation not essential for the X-15 flight performance. I signed my name at the bottom of the sheets, indicating a 'buy' on the part of the pilot. After all, the captain of the S.S. United States would not refuse to get his vessel under way on a scheduled transatlantic voyage because the coffee pot was out of order or a water faucet wasn't working.

I climbed out of the van, slammed the door, and made my way into the confusion of crewmen and supervisors crawling about the X-15. The ground service carts, linked to the little craft by a snarl of heavy cables and hoses, were pushed up close. The vast array of dials and gauges on these carts told a complete story of what was going on inside: helium-source pressures okay, both hydraulic systems okay, number one electrical system okay, liquid nitrogen tank-pressure okay.

Squeezed up against the cockpit was a steel-tubing work platform. I went up the steps to talk to the three men standing there probing into a section just behind the cockpit area. Here in this bay lay the most sensitive, and up to then the most frustrating, piece of the X-15's machinery, the Auxiliary Power Unit (APU). A series of failures of this equipment had kept the X-15 grounded for three months in a row. If it was not working properly today, I would have to cancel.

"How's it going?" I said, addressing 'Robby' Robinson, a General Electric technical representative. Several G.E. engineers had come to Edwards over two months ago, when Stormy rang the bell after the trouble developed.

"I think we've really got it made this time, Scotty," Robby said. "I think we have it licked." We were a long way from completely licking the problem, we knew, but Robby had caught the X-15 team spirit. Like the rest of us now, he was a determined, indefatigable optimist.

The two APUs in the X-15 are separate turbine engines that run on concentrated hydrogen peroxide to drive generators and pumps which give electrical and hydraulic power for the instrumentation and flight controls. There are two separate systems, in case one fails. Jets and prop airplanes get their auxiliary power from their engines, but since in the X-15 the rocket engine runs only a short time, separate powerful sources of energy are necessary for the unpowered glide.

This was not a problem unique to the X-15. All the rocket airplanes preceding it had some form of auxiliary ship's power. The first craft, the X-1, was equipped with batteries which supplied enough juice to operate the simple instruments and other electrical devices for about twenty minutes of flight. The 'muscle' for the controls came from the pilot. But as rocket planes became more complex, and the instrumentation load for obtaining aeronautical data in flight became heavier, the batteries, which are basically heavy and bulky, could not keep pace.

Thus the engineers shifted to small, immensely powerful turbines which, independent of the main rocket-propulsion system, whirled electrical generators that in turn supplied the electrical power. The same turbine also powered hydraulic pumps to supply control 'muscles.' The turbines burn hydrogen peroxide, a chemical that yields a vast amount of energy and doesn't need air to burn, as does gasoline, for instance. Many ballistic missiles have APUs.

The demands for the X-15 APU were far and away the most severe ever placed on any manufacturer. What we asked was that each unit supply 8,000 watts of continuous electrical power—more than enough to supply a modern house with many electrical appliances—at all times during the flight and more than 30 horse-power each for hydraulic controls. To save precious fuel, we asked that the hydrogen-peroxide-powered turbine run very efficiently and yet be able to assume large changes in load without slowing down as demands were put on it. The unit had to operate at any altitude under extreme temperature conditions; in effect, it had to be capable of operating on the surface of the moon. We imposed a weight limit of less than two hundred pounds, including turbine, pumps, generator, and full fuel load for thirty minutes of flight.

The subcontract for the APU had been let to General Electric in 1956 before the first cockpit mock-up. The giant company, with decades of experience in building all kinds of engines and odd-ball electrical devices, put its top talent on the project. All told, hundreds of thousands of engineering man-hours were devoted to this one piece of machinery for the X-15. I am certain that before the contract was concluded, G.E. must have spent millions to make good its promises. The APU design was ingenious and delicate, and it met our requirements. This unit, or one like it, will pioneer the way for APUs on true space craft. North American and its vendors furnished all the maze of plumbing, valves, regulators, and tanks for the system. Like the APUs, everything worked well in the laboratory tests but, as is ever the case, when in the airplane both G.E.'s system and ours gave us untold trouble.

Ground 'APU runs' during December, 1958, and January and February, 1959, followed a grim pattern. After the specialists were certain they were ready, I would climb into the X-15 cockpit at the test stand and run through an 'APU start,' testing number one APU and number two APU in turn. The two small units would come to life, gulping down the potent peroxide. As the turbine wheel spun at 50,000 rpm (five feet from my head), the generator and pump would begin to pump the vital electricity and hydraulics into the X-15's system. Then something would happen. Bearings would overheat and the turbine would seize, or even more, valves and regulators would fail, leak, or not regulate. Then the mechanics would remove the offending part and rebuild it, preparing for another test.

It was absolutely mandatory that these units be made reliable. A total APU failure in the air would leave the pilot without instruments and hydraulic control power. He would have to bail out.

These were sleepless weeks of sheer agony. The APUs and their fuel systems were, in effect, pieces of jewelry. Each of their hundreds of parts was as carefully and delicately balanced as a watch. A piece of lint or some dust would clog microscopic apertures and cause the unit to turn sour. Even low-key vibration came into play. We noted after much experience that when one APU failed with vibration the other unit almost invariably broke down a minute or so later, seemingly without cause. Then we learned the reason. Both APUs were mounted on the same bulkhead. The slight vibration in a failing or seizing APU was enough to send a fatal tremor through the bulkhead to the other APU. We fixed this by mounting the units on separate bulkheads.

When we were deep in APU trouble with no solution in sight, Stormy moved in and brought his prestige to bear. One conference with General Electrics top engineers followed another. The APU systems were analyzed and re-analyzed, down to every single nut and bolt. It was then that the special G.E. team joined us in the North American hangar at Edwards and worked day and night to bring this pioneering device up to snuff. Finally this sensitive, temperamental race-horse was broken to the bit. Prior to our first scheduled captive flight, both APU units had been run without failure almost every day for two weeks. But a question remained unanswered: were they ready for the sweepstakes? Blake Staub, our systems engineer, had practically ruined his health to assure it.

I stared down at the APU in the X-15 bay and listened as Staub and Robinson assured me again that the units were ready. Well, I thought, who can really tell, but we're not going to launch, so what the hell? I'll buy it.

I climbed down from the work stand and walked over to one of the trucks parked near the B-52. This one was as large as a moving van, with colorful Air Force insignia painted on its side and above them the words "16th PHYSIOLOGICAL TRAINING FLIGHT." This was the 'home' for the X-15 full-pressure suit. As I opened the rear door, I could see that it was crowded inside.

There along the wall were oxygen manifolds and pegs on which the various layers of my pressure suit were hung out, like a diver's rig. Several X-15 suit-helmets were fitted into other racks.

Air Force Captain Ralph Richardson was in charge of the van. His assistant was Sergeant Crow. The van was a restricted area; supposedly, I was the only one allowed in besides Richardson and his men and Pete Barker, North American personal equipment specialist.

"Hi, Scotty," Richardson said as I closed and dogged the rear door. "Have a cup of coffee?"

Sergeant Crow handed me a steaming cup which, after my tour in the frigid mating area, was welcome.

"You boys really know how to live," I said, sipping the coffee.

"This van is like a home. You could drive it anywhere, park and live like a king. How about a martini?"

"Well, we try to make our customers comfortable," Richardson said. "But you have to fly first."

"Are you joking?"

"No, we have all the ingredients right here," Richardson said, sweeping his long arm toward the front of the well-lighted van.

"A great idea," I said. "Like the old days in England after a raid. A shot of whiskey for the de-briefing."

"Exactly."

"I'll buy it."

Time was ticking away rapidly. Charlie Bock and Jack Allavie, the B-52 pilots, had arrived on the scene and reported the mother plane ready for flight. Bill Berkowitz, the North American launch-panel operator in the B-52, had been up the entire night preparing his 'office'—from the moment the rocket craft was rolled to the mating area and lifted on hydraulic jacks into its nest on the B-52 pylon. On the Edwards base a hundred other people were moving to stations, in accordance with the plans laid during the final flight-briefing the day before. At Air Force Fighter Ops the three chase airplanes were being groomed for take-off. One precautionary delay or another had already pushed our take-off time back an hour and a half.

With Pete Barker's help I began to put on the full-pressure suit, starting with the first layer, the set of long Johns. Twenty-five minutes later Pete zipped up the silvery, photogenic outside layer. We 'plugged' the suit into a special manifold and ran several tests to make certain the delicate valves were operating properly. The suit pressurized as designed, although like the X-15 it was new and untried, and months would elapse before it could be considered a standard issue item. By the time I left the van, helmet in hand, I was uncomfortably hot and remained that way until I got inside the X-15 cockpit and plugged in the nitrogen gas source which ventilated the suit.

The area around the B-52 was not so cluttered now. The carnival was pulling out. The ground service carts were pushed to one side, the cables and hoses were pulled from the X-15. All the access panels on the side of the rocket ship were back in place and she looked sleek and clean. Now finished with their work, the ground crewmen clustered in knots here and there beneath the B-52 wing, rubbing their hands to keep warm.

The X-15 instrument panel was alive and humming with electrical power from the B-52. All the gauges were in the green. Oscar Freeman, North

American X-15 Crew Chief, and Pete Barker remained on the steel working platform, heads poked inside the X-15 cockpit, cinching up my restraint harness and offering words of advice. It seemed impossible that we were almost ready. But we were. The time had come.

Barker picked up my helmet and lowered it gently over my head, clamping it in place. On the left side of the X-15 cockpit there was a valve marked: OXYGEN. B-52 SUPPLY. X-15 SUPPLY. I turned the valve to 'B-52 SUPPLY' and breathed in deeply. A special seal prevented the nitrogen ventilation gas from the body of the suit from seeping into the helmet. I waved my black-gloved hand sharply, and Barker slammed the canopy shut. The inside of the canopy roof pressed against the top of my helmet. My vision was now restricted by the narrow, V-shaped, left-and-right X-15 windshields.

Fully settled in my tiny flight office, I could speak by radio to the B-52 pilot, Charlie Bock, who was about thirty feet away in the nose of the mother plane, out of sight.

"Okay, Charlie," I said. "I'm ready when you are." I had a small portable tape recorder rigged in the X-15 cockpit, to take notes in flight.

I watched from my perch forward of the wing, as the B-52 ground chief, wearing a radio headset, waved his arm in a circle. Bock wound up the eight jet engines one by one. When he started numbers five and six, the two engines on the pod nearest the X-15, I felt a gentle shaking inside the cockpit and was conscious of the muffled noise. Then Bock rammed on power, and the massive bomber began the long five-mile taxi to the main Edwards runway.

As we rumbled down the taxiway, the B-52 wings flexed up and down. The X-15 flexed with the wings but the sensation was not unpleasant. In fact, as I noted on the tape, it was much more comfortable than being inside the bomber itself. A long line of emergency trucks sped to pre-plotted positions along the runway. Sam Richter's comic van, trailed by a snake of North American ground-maintenance vehicles, struggled to keep up.

From his command post in the North American tower, Q. C. Harvey, surrounded by his team of X-15 experts, came on the air. Charlie Feltz and Stormy were riding in Sam's van. The Edwards and NASA towers reported in. Then chase planes briefly checked radios. The emergency helicopter took to the air. Police on the base at Edwards closed off certain roads. At the end of the main runway Bock turned the ship and lined up for take-off. Sitting ten feet from the concrete surface, I noted the many black skid-marks left behind by the tires of countless experimental planes which had preceded us, blazing the long and turbulent history of aviation. Now, God willing, we would begin a new and fabulous chapter in that history.

35: Smoke in the Cockpit

Until now, I like to think, the story of the X-15 was in essence an array of engineering problems without equal or magnitude in the history of aviation. I have deliberately tried to tell the highlights of that story in coldly objective terms, the way every engineering problem should be approached. I have introduced only those elements pertinent to a full understanding of the flight accounts which follow, and for the purpose of setting the X-15 in true historical perspective. Except where it bore directly on the history of the project, and therefore in some manner influenced our technical judgment significantly, I have restrained a natural—I should say at times nearly overwhelming—tendency to inject personal attitudes and opinions. Some have seeped in, I know, but like the visible portion of an iceberg, they only hint at what hangs beneath.

Perhaps it would be well if this account of the X-15 could be continued in an unimpassioned vein. But this would be dishonest. An objective, well-engineered airplane such as the X-15 is one thing. But now it is being joined for the ultimate tests with a human being. The final outcome, then, is the sum product of both, each in one way or in several ways heavily dependent on the other. To be sure, mechanical failure could spell spectacular failure; but equally important is human failure.

And thus, I am sure, all that came before in my life, and everything that was a part of my life during those months at Edwards—my thoughts, reactions, goals—becomes important and, for the first time, a vital part of the X-15 story.

From the human standpoint alone there were many incalculable forces at work, and I have had some difficulty sorting them out in my mind and attaching the proper weight to each. To begin with, from the pilot's view the first flights of the X-15 turned out to be a fierce challenge. The plane is no toy.

After it is launched from the B-52, every second of flight involves a severe physical and mental exercise wherein one is completely oblivious of all earthly influence except the job at hand. Added to this flying challenge is another challenge accruing through the flow of circumstances. The X-15 has become an important symbol of our national scientific ability—or lack of it. A simple mistake could severely tarnish the national image and grant the Soviets a tangible gain in the cold war. Because the X-15 had attained this prominence, North American's prestige as an aircraft company was laid squarely on the block.

Having developed a deep respect and admiration for the people of that company, I assumed a special responsibility. Moreover, the success or failure of the X-15 would directly influence the decision for or against our much-hoped-for advanced X-15B, the vehicle to which we believed man should turn next on his path to the stars. Finally, to a great extent the flights of the X-15, we knew, would have a decisive impact on the future of all manned combat airplanes, which were then beginning to be viewed in high councils as less practical as a deterrent than the ballistic missile, much to our disagreement.

From a strictly personal side, there is still another factor involved, one which may be more important than all the rest. Unfortunately, though we try to make it do so, the human mind does not move from point to point on well-traveled, fairly straight tracks like a commuter train on schedule. So I cannot, in all honesty, round out this story as an orderly progression of personal reaction to our many successes and several near-disasters—to form a neat closing of the circle. It wasn't that way at all. As it turned out, a fresh and vital personal analysis was born in the cockpit of the X-15. Maybe it was the closing circle focused here which brought it to the fore. Maybe, as some people are moved to deep thoughts when near the sea, so I was moved as I stared into space.

As is often the case in life, where nothing is black and white and thus relatively simple like a mechanical problem, I discovered, like many before me in dramatic circumstances, that to close one circle is only to invite another, even larger and more challenging. Or as Ralph Waldo Emerson put it: "Our life is an apprenticeship to the truth, that around every circle another can be drawn; that there is no end in nature, but every end is a beginning; that there is always another dawn risen on mid-noon, and under every deep a lower deep opens."

Ironically, the demanding flying of the X-15, which I had so desperately sought and worked so hard for nine years to achieve, came as an anticlimax, in a sense. The curve of a new circle was beginning to form. After thirty-eight years, most of them dedicated to a single purpose, one I had thought ambitious enough, my thoughts dissolved into a tumultuous whirlpool of probings and questions. The X-15 was not enough. But what was the new circle? The search for the answer to that question paralleled my flights in the X-15 and seemed, at times, even more demanding.

My daily life was necessarily crowded to the limit with preparations for flight, or post-flight de-briefings, endless conferences at North American, or NASA, press interviews, symposiums and technical gatherings, urgent telephone calls, and what else I cannot remember now. It seems strange, indeed, but the only place I could find time for reflection and appraisal—time to probe the meaning of the new circle—was the X-15 cockpit, during the long, lonely hours I sat there, strapped in that tiny plane slung beneath the wing of the B-52. Until then, I had neither time nor inclination to dwell on my past life. But now I knew it was important to understand it in order that I could intelligently chart my future.

There was not much time for reflection on the first flight. Everything was too new and strange. We moved from one semi-crisis to the next, it seemed.

As we sat, waiting at the end of the long runway while the chase planes took off and circled, the clock on the instrument panel of the X-15 showed 0955. I made a note on the tape recorder: the clock's second hand was not working. On signal, B-52 pilot Charlie Bock cobbed the eight jet engines, standing hard on the brake pedal. As the engines wound up to full military power, the X-15 trembled and the noise was tremendous.

Through my radio earphones I heard Bock call a countdown for the benefit of the official movie cameramen who would record every inch of the take-off: "Five ... four ... three ... two ... one. BRAKE RELEASE." One hundred and thirty tons of aluminum, fuel, Inconel X, five men, and the hope of a nation began rolling down the long runway. Success or failure of this first take-off was now entirely up to Charlie Bock. I was simply a first-class passenger, occupying a private compartment out on the wing.

Without flaps to give added lift to the B-52, the take-off roll would be unusually long, the lift-off a ticklish maneuver requiring a delicate pivotal movement on the rear landing-gear truck of the B-52, a sudden and severe raising of the nose.

The greatest point of concern was the predicted, possibly destructive vibration the X-15 external store might impose on the B-52. A hundred times in the past, Bock and I had reviewed corrective procedures to follow if this should happen. We knew it would take 190 knots to get the B-52 and its load into the air.

We agreed that if severe vibration developed during the take-off roll before he reached 170 knots, he would chop the B-52 throttles and abort the take-off. But if no vibration set in up to 170 knots, he would continue the take-off, climbing out. If during the climb at 260 knots the vibration rose to a degree that seriously endangered the bomber, we agreed that the X-15 must be jettisoned without delay. I would have a few seconds warning—time enough to start the APUs and shift from B-52 electrical power to X-15 power. Then I would attempt to glide the X-15 in dead-stick. We plotted the take-off so that I would have a fairly good shot at the lake bed in this event, but we both knew that our scheme was pretty marginal—impossible, in fact —below 15,000 feet. In other words, if cut loose below that altitude, it was most unlikely that I could reach the lake bed. I would try. If I failed, I could always bail out at the last second.

The important thing was to separate the X-15 from the mother ship. There were four men aboard that airplane. There was one in the X-15. As we rolled, the huge runway distance markers flashed by, clocking our path: 14,000 ... 13,000 ... 12,000 ... 8,000. When the X-15 air-speed indicator reached 170 knots, I noted only a minor vibration. We would continue the take-off. 6,000 ... 5,000 ... 4,000, and we broke ground. It was smooth and gentle, like the take-off of an airliner. The air-speed indicator needle crept up to 260 knots. The parched brown desert fell away rapidly. The vibration did not increase.

My eyes were fixed now on a small but ominous trickle of water slowly filming between the two layers of windshield glass in the X-15. It was water which had accumulated in the insulation out in the open during the long weeks of ground tests on the APUs. Who could have guessed this would happen on the dry desert? The nitrogen de-fogging gas flowing between the layers was designed to keep it clear under ordinary flight conditions. But I knew it would not be sufficient to check the vapor accumulation of three months of exposure to the rain and night dampness. Already a faint haze, the first sign of ice, was forming on the right panel. Charlie Bock spoke on the radio: "We're at three thousand feet now. I'm going to throttle back on number five and six engines." Slowing these two engines on the pod nearest me would reduce the noise and some of the vibration on the X-15. Even with two engines idling, the giant jet bomber gained altitude rapidly, circling Rogers Dry Lake.

By the time we reached 15,000 feet both windshields of the X-15 were solidly iced over, recalling those early days at Edwards when I faced an iced windshield in the X-1 and the Skyrocket.

An emergency launch was feasible. But an emergency dead-stick landing with iced windshields would be tough, to say the least. I might make it, I thought, if I blew the canopy. I made a mental note never to go aloft again in the X-15 without a plastic windshield scraper. (Later this item was installed on the X-15's instrument panel.)

The three chase planes tucked in close, and our $60 million space task force bore skyward. There was not much noise beyond a steady hum and some static on the radio circuit. We were all—the men in the B-52, I in the X-15, Q. C. Harvey and the others on the ground, and the chase pilots nearby—leafing our way simultaneously through the thirty-page flight-check list.

Occasionally Q. C. spoke: "Going to item 39-A." Or I would say: "Item 43 completed, going to item 44." Charlie Bock put the B-52 through several stiff banks and turns to check vibration and X-15 mating. I followed these maneuvers on my instrument panel. Everything was going better than any of us had dared expect.

Then, as on every subsequent flight of the X-15, we prepared for a dress rehearsal of an actual air-launch. Since there were no rocket propellants aboard on this first trip, we would eliminate an engine prime. Except for this one step, it would be a realistic 'dry run,' which would give us much-needed practice for the real thing and an opportunity to test the systems as well.

Especially the temperamental APUs. Like the X-15, the Clark full-pressure suit, designed to protect the pilot in the event the cockpit pressurization failed, was also undergoing its first realistic test. Thus we planned each flight to give the suit a chance to show what it could do. The cockpit of the X-15 was designed to be pressurized 'down' to 35,000 feet. The suit was designed to go into operation if it sensed that the pressure in the cockpit rose 'above' 35,000 feet.

Thus if we left open a connection between the outside air and the cockpit and flew above 35,000 feet, the cockpit would fail to pressurize and the suit would automatically go into action at slightly above 35,000 feet. This connection between the cockpit and the outside air was called the 'ram-air door.' We simply left it open on the climb to altitude and during the full-pressure suit experiment.

When we passed 30,000 feet both windshields were thick with ice. However, I could still see the instrument panel: it was brilliantly lighted by two strong thunderstorm flood lamps beamed over my shoulders. Every five minutes I turned a switch which automatically recorded all the gauge readings within the cockpit and at certain key positions throughout the airplane, and I reported on the radio circuit: "Data burst." In addition, I kept a running log of gauge readings on my portable tape recorder, along with some private, personal observations.

At 35,000 feet, with the ram-air door open, I felt the Clark suit pressurize. The link-net material seized me on all parts of my body. From that point on my movements were slightly constrained and slightly awkward, although not nearly so awkward as a deep-sea diver's.

Satisfied with the test, I strained forward at 38,000 feet to grab a lever between my legs, the hardest piece of equipment in the cockpit to reach. The lever operated the ram-air door. Grunting and puffing, trying to get a good grip on the lever with my glove, I finally pulled it shut. As soon as the outside air was closed off, the nitrogen gas began to build up inside the cockpit, pressurizing it back 'down' to 35,000 feet. When the cockpit altitude stabilized at 35,000 feet, the pressure suit relaxed its grip and once again I could move my arms and legs with ease.

Now still at 38,000 feet we began final preparations for the mock launch. Assuming everything else is going well, that is to say that the fuel-tank gauges (which we were not concerned with on that flight) are in the green, the big step is to make the X-15 independent of the B-52 with its own electrical and control power. It was a crucial moment: the first airborne test of the X-15's heart, the electrical and hydraulic power source, the APUs. I flicked a switch to start these units, keeping a close eye on various gauges that would tell me if all was well in this department.

When the APU turbines turned up, I could hear a faint whirring noise inside the X-15 cockpit. So far, so good. The turbine bearing temperatures, a critical factor and frequent cause of breakdown, were within normal range. Then I turned a switch which should have put number one generator on the line. It failed. I tried to bring number two generator to life.

Again no luck. I re-cycled both, trying to shift from B-52 to X-15 power source. Hopeless. The APU turbines were turning up, but the generators for each were out of commission. With iced windshields, if Bock had to cut me loose, I would have to bail out. The X-15 would have hydraulic control power essential to flight, but no electrical power for instruments essential to 'blind' flight.

I cursed to myself, and then on the radio called: "Q.C., I can't get the generators on the line."

"Okay, Scotty. Let's move on to the next item," Q.C. replied.

This was a visual check of the X-15 controls—rudder, aileron, elevators—and flaps. I horsed on the stick and kicked the rudder pedals, following detailed instructions on the check list. The chase-plane pilots reported control response. Good. Just about then I noticed a thin wisp of smoke curling up between my legs. Impossible! I thought. We couldn't have a fire in the cockpit; it was completely sealed off, pressurized with inert nitrogen. No fire could possibly burn in that space. The only answer was that some wire must have overheated, smoldering the insulation. The smoke thickened.

"Q.C," I reported. "I've got a little smoke in the cockpit. Nothing serious. Must be a hot wire some place."

"Okay, Scotty," Q.C. responded quietly.

These, I learned later, were anxious moments at Edwards. But I was not overly concerned. Except for the APU hydrogen peroxide, the X-15 was empty of its usual load of volatile fuels, and the chances of a serious fire or catastrophic explosion were negligible. Besides, what could I do about it? If it came, it came. I had no generators, no vision. If a bad fire developed, we'd have to cut loose and I'd bail out. In any case, the plane would be lost.

When the smoke in the cockpit became so dense that I could no longer see the instrument panel nor observe any test intelligently, I spoke quietly to Charlie Bock: "Let's go home."

Q.C. broke in: "On the descent make a test of the X-15 gear."

"Okay, Q.C."

At 15,000 feet the chase planes moved in close. I pulled the gear handle. The telescoped nose wheel, extended by a ballistic charge, snapped into position with a jolt that felt like a swift kick in the behind. When the two rear skids popped down satisfactorily, chase reported gear okay. Since the gear cannot be retracted again, we left it in place as the B-52 lined up on final.

Automatic movie cameras mounted on the side of the B-52 and hand-held cameras in the chase planes recorded all these drills. The smoke in the cockpit was pretty thick, and I noticed a new and heavy vibration somewhere in the rear of the X-15. What was that? It was too late to find out; we were committed. Landing the B-52 with its external store and no flaps was no cinch. But I could see that Bock and Allavie were already practiced artists. They brought the giant plane in very nose-high and greased in on the rear gear-truck, one hour and ten minutes after take-off. Then the nose fell forward heavily and we began the roll-out, long, easy, with the X-15 rear skids almost touching the runway. If something happened on landing—such as a crash and fire—I was in the safest possible place. Sealed inside a cockpit designed to withstand 1200 degrees Fahrenheit, I would just wait until the men put out the fire and then open my canopy. If the heat became unbearable, I could always eject right on the ground.

When the B-52 stopped rolling, I opened the X-15 canopy. Dense smoke billowed forth, greatly and unnecessarily exciting the firemen. They rushed in with trucks and sprayed the rear of the X-15 with water. But there was no fire, as such, to put out. The smoke was caused when one of the APU generators seized in flight and burned up. As we discovered later, the generator was a mass of ashes. The fact that the smoke had seeped into the cockpit turned out to be a blessing in disguise.

It revealed that under certain circumstances the protection of the cockpit was compromised. This was quickly corrected. Bock taxied the B-52 back to the mating area. The ground men skillfully directed the parking so that the X-15 hung directly over her hydraulic lifting jacks used to lower the ship from the pylon. They shoved the steel work platform against the nose and Mel Beach climbed up and removed my helmet. I wriggled out of the cockpit and chatted with Stormy and Charlie Feltz for a few moments, trying to puzzle out the smoke in the cockpit, and then I walked somewhat wearily over to the 16th Physiological Training Flight van.

Inside, to cool off, I quickly removed the top layer of my pressure suit, and then washed the perspiration from my face and hands. When I turned for a towel, Captain Richardson was standing there. He handed me a martini—a real martini, with an olive. It was the perfect touch. I wished that our first flight in the X-15 had been as perfect.

36: The Reluctant Dragon

At 0730 on April 1, I climbed into the X-15 cockpit, ready for a second 'captive' flight. Although we had learned a great deal on the first, none of us felt the ship was quite ready for a free glide to earth. First, we would make another dry run, to be sure. In the intervening two weeks we had made many improvements on the X-15. The temperamental APUs had been pulled out, rebuilt, and tested in repeated 'runs' on the ground. We had removed the canopy and baked it in a hot oven for hours to purge it of the water trapped in the insulation, and then water-proofed it. As a further precaution against windshield icing, the nitrogen de-fogging gas was routinely turned on three hours prior to take-off. By Stormy's edict, we had installed a radio intercom between the X-15 and B-52, which would, in theory, keep a line of communication open to me, if the single X-15 radio transmitter conked out at a crucial moment.

As usual, there were some pre-take-off delays. The men swarmed about the fuselage of the X-15, pulling wires and making last-minute repairs which were checked and rechecked by the ground service cart operators. The X-15 panel was alive. I sat staring at the lights and gauges looking for signs of trouble. By that time I had spent at least three hundred hours in that cock-pit and I could sense a fault or impending crisis almost subconsciously.

At 0812 Oscar Freeman and Pete Barker slammed the X-15 canopy shut. Charlie Bock and Jack Allavie wheeled the giant mother plane to the take-off runway and cobbed the engines. At 0844 the wheels left the ground and we were airborne for the second time. I tested the new intercom (unsatisfactory) and droned off the gauge readings, making a 'data burst' every five minutes. At 25,000 feet altitude the X-15 radio transmitter and receiver, perhaps because of the intercom modification, faded drastically. But the windshield remained clear. The chase moved in close and we droned skyward for a launch rehearsal.

At 25,000 feet altitude, I could faintly hear Q. C. Harvey come on the radio circuit: "I guess we'll have to abort. I can't hear Scotty. His radio is out."

I already had the transmitter on, but the amplifiers were not putting out. Breaking a long-standing personal rule, I shouted as loud as I could over the radio mike: "No, Q.C. No. No. Don't abort. No abort."

"Okay, Scotty," Q.C. replied. "I can just barely hear you, very faint and intermittent."

Determined that a simple radio malfunction would not stop the test, I shouted myself hoarse. Then Q.C. came up with an ingenious, spur-of-the-moment solution to our radio difficulty.

"I can hear your mike loud and clear when you key it, Scotty. But I can't hear your voice. We'll follow a system here. You key your mike in response to my questions. One click means yes. Two clicks mean no. Okay?"

I keyed the mike one click. Following this system, we worked through the thirty-page flight-check list with Q.C. in command on the ground. "Okay, Scott," he would say. "We have completed item 10. Are you ready to go to item 11? Repeat, are you ready to go to item 11?" If I was satisfied, I responded with one click of the mike. If I did not think the ship was ready for the next item, I transmitted two clicks. Slowly we accumulated the necessary data, which included various severe maneuvers of the B-52, a carefully monitored speed run to check the X-15's air-speed indicator, and finally the big item, the launch rehearsal. The APUs came on the line and held steady, purring like kittens.

Taking advantage of our good luck, we circled Edwards for well over an hour and a half. When I noted the coolant for the APU bearings was getting dangerously low, I waved my hand at the B-52, suggesting we return to base and land. Bill Berkowitz, the launch-panel operator, watching the X-15 through a closed-circuit television installation, caught the signal and relayed my request by radio to the ground. Q.C. came on the line:

"You want to land, Scott. Correct?"

I keyed the mike one click, and Charlie Bock banked toward the Edwards runway. We dropped the X-15 gear for a routine test, and shortly thereafter Bock greased on, one hour and forty-four minutes after take-off.

Except for the simple radio failure, the X-15 had performed well on this flight. But the full-pressure suit had not. The seals were leaking, and the valves failing. In fact, in the post-flight report, I noted thirteen discrepancies in the suit and asked that the Clark company send a team to Edwards without delay to make the necessary modifications and adjustments. With all our tests on the ground and in the air, we were wearing the suit out. On one of the hundreds of ground tests I nearly killed myself.

It happened right in the X-15 cockpit while the canopy was open. Decked out in the suit and helmet, I was running a test which involved innumerable selections of oxygen supply, on, off, on B-52, on X-15, etc. I made an error and got out of sequence. I proceeded with the test, breathing not X-15 oxygen as I supposed, but the nitrogen gas suit coolant which was leaking into the helmet through a crack in a rubber seal. There were several ground crewmen working about the X-15, and Pete Barker was bending down in the cockpit helping me with the test. Nobody was aware of the developing crisis.

Nitrogen gas is an insidious suffocant. Man cannot long survive breathing only nitrogen. Quite soon I began to feel its effect. The instrument panel facing me seemed to be floating away. I gazed in wonder at this phenomenon for several seconds, too stupefied to realize my predicament, then I drifted off into unconsciousness.

Barker, working with me on the test, still had no inkling of the danger. By the grace of God I suddenly snapped back into momentary consciousness. Bewildered, I sought to escape from my slow suffocation. Not knowing what caused the blackout and dizziness, and unable to think clearly, I was desperate. I clawed helplessly at the fittings of my helmet, and then cast up my arms in one final protest and, as I recall it dimly, probably yelled.

Luckily for me, Barker saw me raise my hands and sensed trouble. He jerked off the helmet in the nick of time. I feel I owe my life to his quick response.

On the evening before an X-15 flight was scheduled, Stormy always came up to the desert for a last-minute look-see. He checked in at the North American hangar, talked to the X-15 mechanics, and toured the mating area, where the men were working to attach the X-15 to the mother plane and to check out the systems. When Stormy was satisfied, the two of us slipped away and drove far down the desert to a remote roadside restaurant, where we could lay plans during dinner without interruption. On April 13, the eve of the third flight, Stormy was restless and quietly angry. He was involved in a tight poker game with high stakes.

Like all the rest of us, he wanted to see the X-15 fly—and the sooner the better. But we knew that if we pushed too hard and fast and something catastrophic happened, the country would suffer a black eye and we and the company would be severely criticized. At the same time, if we didn't show more promise, we would be chided for dragging our feet. Thus Stormy—all of us in fact—was seeking to strike a balance between fast action and sound technical advance. Ridiculously petty items were sabotaging us: APU regulators, radio intercom wiring, two-dollar valves—horseshoe nails that could conceivably lose us a kingdom.

Each time we aborted a flight we lost two weeks, the time it took to 'turn around' the X-15 or prepare it for a new trip into the air.

Stormy is one of the few men I have met in my life whom I sincerely admire. I like his approach to building airplanes. He is not only enthusiastic and eloquent in presenting his case for this or that airplane, but also he is more technically honest than any engineer I have ever known. If something doesn't work, it doesn't work, and it is discarded. He doesn't prolong it, building an empire of paper-pushers. He knows how to take on a job and do it right. And once he begins, he is completely objective and ruthless about it.

"We'll play it like this," Stormy said. "Tomorrow we'll go through rehearsal. If the APUs look okay, go through another rehearsal. If everything seems to be going well, then we'll drop. But wait for the word from me. The final decision to drop, of course, is yours."

Just after dawn the following morning I climbed in the X-15 cockpit and droned the gauge readings into my portable tape recorder: "Liquid nitrogen source 3700. Number one hydraulic temperature 18 degrees. Number two hydraulic temperature 5 degrees. Number one APU source pressure 3500. Number two APU source pressure 3500 ..." As far as the X-15 was concerned, everything was near-normal. Except for a radio line in the helmet, which was snagging on the neck seal, the Clark suit was working well. It had been completely overhauled in the past ten days by Clark's experts.

After reading the gauges I stared at the instrument panel, waiting for the ground crews to seal up. Stormy, wearing a gabardine topcoat, was huddled with Q. C. Harvey and Sam Bichter next to the communications van. At 0823 Charlie Bock released the B-52 brakes and we rolled down the runway to begin the third X-15 flight. When the B-52's wheels lifted off, the three circling chase planes squeezed in close and climbed out toward what I hoped would be, by Stormy's decision, our first launch. I was anxious and eager. By then we had been grooming the airplane for five months. To gain added X-15 performance, the launch altitude was raised from 38,000 to 45,000 feet. It took almost an hour to reach peak altitude.

After the usual checks of the pressure suit, the X-15 cabin pressurization, and some special B-52 speed-tests and maneuvers to feel out the 'mating' at that extreme height, we proceeded to the first launch rehearsal. Everything worked perfectly—almost.

Radio communications were good, and the APUs came on the line with no trouble, although we expected trouble at higher altitude where the temperature is colder. I deliberately opened the ram-air door to try to fog the windshield. It remained clear. We simulated a drop and closed down. Then Bock wheeled the B-52 through a gigantic ten-mile turn high in the sky to repeat the rehearsal. The chase planes, hanging in the thin air at reduced speed, struggled to keep position. Our path through the sky was marked by seven white contrails.

For the second time on that flight we moved in to a launch rehearsal. I started the APUs again, anxiously awaiting the key words from Stormy on the ground. But Stormy, who was watching and listening at Sam Richter's truck out on the lake bed, didn't say a word on the radio. His intuition told him the time was not ripe.

With no positive word from him we continued the launch rehearsal and at one minute before drop time aborted the flight. I was quite disappointed. As a matter of routine, after launch rehearsal on the descent to Edwards, I kept the APUs on, so that the X-15 would have power in the unlikely event that an emergency arose and Charlie Bock had to cut me loose in a hurry. The APUs were still running as we descended through 42,000 feet. At 41,000 feet both APU generators suddenly dropped off the line. I recycled number one and got it back on, but number two refused to connect. I reported this by radio.

A few seconds later I became aware of an ominous, heavy vibration somewhere in the after end of the X-15. Something was quite wrong. My eyes automatically swept across the gauges; my ears tuned to the growing rumbling. Number two APU had failed. I was not aware of the full extent of the malfunction then, but I knew it was serious. Later we discovered that the unit had seized and shaken completely off the mounts. This severe wrench also disturbed the second APU. I shut both units off, thankful then that Stormy's intuition was working. A minute later I noted a wisp of smoke in the cockpit.

This time there was no connection between the APU failure and the smoke. A wire in one of the cabin blowers simply overheated and caused the insulation to smolder. I was tempted to ignore the smoke because nothing strikes fear in the hearts of the ground people quite so rapidly and decisively as smoke or fire in a rocket airplane. But one of my duties as test pilot was to report every routine and non-routine event in the X-15 cockpit. Reluctantly I passed the word on the radio circuit and, as expected, there was quite a bit of excitement on the ground. But the smoke diminished and by the time we reached the ground, an hour and nineteen minutes after take-off, it had disappeared altogether.

When we parked in the mating area, the ground mechanics opened the doors on the APU access compartment almost immediately. Charlie Feltz, Stormy, and I peered in at the shambles of metal that had once been two highly refined, critical pieces of X-15 machinery. The APUs at that point had been under laboratory and field test for a whole year, yet they were still obviously a long way from being reliable. Sick with disappointment, Stormy hurried off to Los Angeles to set in motion words and action that soon solved the X-15 APU problem. I don't know how much money and time were spent in the extensive APU rebuilding and testing that followed in the next few weeks, but I do know that with one exception in the year that followed we had no more APU trouble.

These APU problems, which I probably have dwelt upon at too great length, were not confined exclusively to the X-15 rocket airplane. Other companies were having much the same kind of trouble in ballistic missiles. At Cape Canaveral scores of multimillion-dollar birds blew up on the pads or in flight because of APU failure. This is one part of the price of progress, of probing into the unknown. The big advantage in the X-15 was that we did not lose our bird. With a pilot at the controls we were able to detect and avert fatal trouble, and save the ship for another flight.

We could bring the broken APUs back to earth in one piece—or sometimes in one piece—for engineering analysis. The fixes we made, I hope, were passed on to the missiles at Cape Canaveral.

Thus in one sense the X-15 was already beginning to pay its way as a research tool.

After the flight Captain Richardson was waiting in the 16th Physiological Training Unit van with the usual martini. It tasted weak. I commented on this while squirming out of the pressure suit.

"It's watered down," Richardson said.

"What?"

"That's right. If you can't pull off a full-blown flight, you don't get a full-blown martini."

Ribbing of this kind was directed toward us from many official sources. Our tiger was gaining a reputation for being a Reluctant Dragon. This hurt in more ways than I can remember.

21 MAY, 1959. THIRTY-ONE WEEKS HAD FLOWN BY since we trucked X-15 number one to the Edwards test base. Seventy-two days since our first shaky captive flight in the airplane. Forty-one days since captive flight number three. NASA and the Air Force were becoming increasingly anxious and no longer hiding it. Our saga of troubles had stung the X-15 flight-test team badly. Every man felt a personal responsibility. Each worked with an intensity and devotion that no amount of money could buy, and at last we were ready to go into the air once again. This time there was no talk of a drop. Our sole objective was to stage a completely successful captive test, to prove that all the machinery of the X-15 would perform as designed under flight conditions.

On this climactic day, when they placed their mechanical stethoscopes to 'listen' for signs of trouble in the X-15, the ground crews were more meticulous than ever before. They checked every system three times over, and then once again. Although I knew we couldn't possibly take off before 0900, I climbed into the X-15 cockpit, fully rigged in the pressure suit, about 0700. I did this mainly for morale-building purposes. I wanted the ground crews to know that I had confidence in the airplane and that I was ready —eager—to get into the air. It was an uncomfortably long wait, yet a necessary one, I believed.

It was 0922 by the time Bock and Allavie lifted the B-52 off the runway. We were late but the X-15 was tuned to a fine pitch. A few minor items cropped up, as usual—a screeching in my radio receiver, an insufficient flow of nitrogen coolant in the lower half of the pressure suit—but during the familiar launch rehearsal the X-15 ran like a jeweled watch. We circled Edwards for an hour and fifteen minutes, starting and stopping the APUs with no difficulty. The APU bearings, cooled by nitrogen gas, held to a normal temperature range: about 115 degrees Fahrenheit.

It was clear now that we were over the big hurdle. We would have stayed aloft longer that day, but the supply of APU nitrogen gas coolant, designed to last only for a normal X-15 flight of about half an hour, was dwindling rapidly, and as I have said before we preferred to land with APUs operating in case Bock had to cut me loose in emergency.

During the gradual descent the APU bearing temperatures began to climb. Number one reached 245 degrees; number two moved up to 200 degrees. I was not unduly concerned. The bearings, G.E. had calculated, could reach 400 degrees without seizing. Certainly we could keep below that figure. To decrease the drain on the single nitrogen gas supply, I turned off the windshield defogging and pressure-suit ventilation. But the diminishing supply of nitrogen gas to the APUs was not sufficient. Number one crept up to 295 degrees. I watched the gauge closely. If it got much hotter, I intended to shut it down and make the descent on one APU.

At 15,000 feet number one APU had inched ahead to 350 degrees. Since it was approaching a danger point, I reported the fact by radio to Q. C. Harvey. After consulting his panel of X-15 experts, gathered near his mike in the NASA tower, Q.C. responded:

"Scotty. Q.C. We suggest you shut down number one APU if the bearing temperature reaches 395 degrees."

"Okay, Q.C," I replied. "That's what I was going to do. Number one bearing temperature is now 376 degrees."

My eyes were glued on the number one APU bearing gauge. It moved steadily ahead: 376 ... 380 ... 390 ... 395. I reached for a switch on the instrument panel and turned it, reporting by radio:

"Number one APU 395 degrees. Shut down."

My eyes remained on the gauge. I expected it to 'coast' still higher for a moment or so and then drop off rapidly. The gauge swung to 400 ... 416 ... 430. Number two APU, which was then getting all the nitrogen gas coolant, leveled out at about 200 degrees, as expected.

I snapped into my mike: "Q.C., this damned number one is up to 450."

"You can expect it to peak a little bit and then fall off, Scotty," Q.C. replied.

"Yeah," I said. "I know. But it isn't falling off. It's now up to 460 and climbing. Number two is okay, steady at 200 degrees."

When the temperature of number one APU reached 475 degrees, I heard a familiar rumbling in the rear of the X-15. The unit had seized and vibrated to a stop. But why? Then in a flash I realized I had made a dreadful error. I had not shut down number one APU at all. Instead, I had shut down number two.

"Holy smoke," I muttered on the radio circuit.

My spontaneous comment touched off a tremendous flurry of excitement on the ground. Sam Richter came on the radio instantly.

"Scotty. Did you say smoke? Repeat. Do you have smoke in the cockpit?" (I later learned that Charlie Feltz, who was in Sam's van, and whose ear was not then attuned to airplane radio circuits, leaped from his chair and said: "Wha'd he say? Wha'd he say?" And thereafter "Wha'd he say?" became a very big joke on the X-15 team.)

"No. No. Sorry," I replied. "No smoke in the cockpit. I just goofed. I shut down number two APU by mistake. Number one was running all the time. It blew."

It took only the thinnest imagination to conjure up the disbelieving expressions which spread over the faces of the people on the ground. After six agonizing months of APU difficulties, we had finally made a successful airborne demonstration. Then at its climax I had stupidly blown an APU because I turned the wrong switch. Short of losing the airplane altogether, no mistake I might have made in the air that day could have stung our team deeper.

They could not have been more depressed. I felt like a fool, and of course I assumed full responsibility for the blooper.

The APU failure was properly judged pilot error. Since everything, including APUs, was considered satisfactory, all hands agreed the ship was fit for her next great test, the first glide flight to earth.

37: Engulfed in Disappointment

"Three minutes to drop," Charlie Bock intoned on the radio circuit.

We were turning over Rosamond Dry Lake at 38,000 feet for a final run to the launch point, within sight of the Edwards base and Rogers Dry Lake, where if all went well we would launch and I would dead-stick the X-15. It was June 8, eighteen days since our last successful captive flight. We had been airborne thirty-five minutes.

I reached up and set the sweep second-hand on the X-15 dashboard clock. Then I checked all the gauges. With one exception they couldn't have looked better. The APUs, which had been running eight minutes, were holding. APU bearing temperatures were a mere 116 degrees, well within safe limits. The nitrogen gas coolant supply was ample for both APUs, defogging, suit ventilation, and cockpit pressure. I rechecked the altimeter setting and listened when Edwards tower called the winds on the lake bed: 10 to 12 knots from 240 degrees.

A yellow light near my knee beaconed the single malfunction in the X-15's machinery. It was an indicator on the X-15 Stability Augmentation System (SAS), the automatic control damping device, which in flight would sense an impending violent maneuver and take action to forestall it. Most of the new supersonic fighters we had tested at Edwards, such as the F-100, were equipped with SAS to minimize the possibility of unwanted yaw, pitch, or coupling divergence. The X-15 was the first experimental airplane to have such a system, and, like most of the gear, it was more sophisticated than ordinary versions.

The 'pitch mode' of the SAS, which would sense an abrupt rising or falling of the nose and automatically move the controls to correct for it, was out of commission. On the climb to launch altitude, I had quietly reported this fact to Q. C. Harvey. He in turn had consulted with the SAS expert, Blake Staub. We tried a dozen different tricks, switching electrical circuits, to correct it.

But the yellow malfunction light remained on steadily. The decision to 'go' or 'no go' was entirely up to me. I had elected to 'go.' For our first low-speed glide test the pitch damper was not vital. I had had much experience in dead-sticking airplanes without the help of such a device. We simply could not cancel another flight. More than a thousand eyes on the Edwards base were trained skyward for this milestone in aviation history.

There were one hundred reporters, photographers, and TV cameramen camped along the edge of the lake bed. If we failed again, the press would not be so patient and generous this time. In brief, we were on the spot. But this was just another time when the skill and training of a test pilot could overcome the deficiency of a piece of machinery.

I was busy turning switches. I shut off the B-52 power source. The X-15 was now operating on its own power generated by the APUs. I shifted the oxygen supply to my helmet from B-52 to X-15. I armed the ballistic charge in the lower ventral fin, which I would jettison close to the ground just before touchdown. I started the data instrumentation and cameras, which would operate throughout the glide to earth. Finally I flashed a green light in Charlie Bock's cockpit, indicating I was ready to launch. I confirmed this fact orally: "Ready when you are, buddy."

"One minute to launch," Bock replied calmly.

My right hand moved to the sidearm control handle, which I had elected to use on this flight in place of the center stick, to show there was no question in my mind that it was an improvement. I cranked in one degree of nose-up-trim to make certain that when Bock cut me loose, the X-15 would not dive too steeply.

If I launched at higher trim, it was possible the X-15 might hang momentarily beneath the wing, bumping against the mating pylon or the B-52 engine pods. Chase pilot Bob White, flying just off my wing-tip, confirmed the trim change by radio.

I waited, my eyes alternating between the gauges and the handle of the clock. In the last few seconds, I prayed. My extremely sensitive tape-recorder picked up the movement of my vocal chords, but not the words. I said: "God. Please help me make this a good one. Please don't let me let these people down."

Bock called a brief countdown, unkeying his mike between each number in case I wanted to break in and say "no drop."

"Three" .. . "Two" . . . "One" ...

"DROP."

Inside the streamlined pylon, a hydraulic ram disengaged the three heavy shackles from the upper fuselage of the X-15. They were so arranged that all released simultaneously, and if one failed they all failed. The impact of the release was clearly audible in the X-15 cockpit. I heard a loud 'ker-chunk.'

The X-15 hung in its familiar place beneath the pylon for a split second. Then the nose dipped sharply down and to the right more rapidly than I anticipated. The B-52, so long my constant companion, was gone. The X-15 and I were alone in the air and flying at 500 miles an hour. In less than five minutes I would be on the ground.

My flight plan called for me to make a huge 'S' turn in the sky, spiraling down toward Rogers Dry Lake. It was designed to provide me with a wide margin for error. Should the glide calculations be wrong, I could vary the S turn to correct the error and land where I wanted to on the lake. The glide-path was laid out over an uninhabited area, so the airplane was no hazard to the lives of people on the ground.

There was much to do in the first hundred seconds of flight. First I had to get the 'feel' of the airplane, to make certain it was trimmed out for the landing just as any pilot trims an airplane after take-off or in flight as passengers move about or when dwindling fuel shifts the center of gravity. Then I had to pull the nose up, with and without flaps, to feel out the stall characteristics, so that I would know how she might behave at touchdown speeds. Her characteristics had been calculated on machines, and of course I had 'flown' the simulator a thousand times or more, both at North American and in the Navy's Johnsville centrifuge. I had also made many low L over D landings in the F-100 and F-104, with engine idling, wheels down, and dive brakes extended. But these amounted, all in all, only to an approximation of the real thing.

The real thing, as it developed immediately, wasn't such a challenge. Our engineering was sound. The X-15 is not the easiest airplane in the world to fly, but she responded as we expected. Sensitive in roll because of her shape, sensitive in pitch because of the damper failure, but even as a heavy glider spirited to the touch of control, responsive, and high-strung. Not designed to mush around at low speeds, she still handled like a champion. Falling down and to the right, I moved the sidearm control gently to bring the X-15 to level flight. The response was remarkable. The plane porpoised through a huge oscillation, hanging on its side. I again moved the control arm gently. At 36,000 feet, after a drop of 1,400 feet, the tiger leveled out and the nose held steady.

I put the plane in a shallow dive. Having lost the momentum of the launch, it slowed from 500 to 400 to 300 miles an hour. When I pulled the nose up, the speed dropped even lower. I performed these maneuvers with extreme care, tentatively, so as not to offend her lest she bite back as so many others have and become unmanageable. The three chase planes were having no difficulty in keeping up at my ever-decreasing speed and altitude, and they hung in close. The radio circuit was dead silent. Except for the roar of the ventilation blowers, there was a tomb-like silence in the cockpit.

Now at about 30,000 feet and three minutes from touchdown, I simulated a landing. I pushed the nose down sharply until my speed had picked up to 300 miles an hour. I lowered the flaps.

The nose rose slightly, but the ship did not buffet as it did when we lowered the flaps while mated to the B-52. Satisfied, I raised the flaps and put the ship into a steep descending turn, aiming for the broad lake bed. My altimeter unwound dizzily: from 24,000 to 13,000 feet in less than forty seconds.

I knew that the men on the ground—Stormy, Feltz, Q.C., Sam, and the others—were holding their breath, waiting in nearly indescribable anguish for some word. My mind was too busy trying to learn about this ship, planning for the touchdown, now less than a hundred seconds away, to think of some way to put them at ease, tell them we had a winner, and still not stick my now proud and cocky neck out. What came out was this: "I'd like to try a roll," the words Yeager had uttered on his first X-1 flight.

Passing over the Edwards skeet range at about 6,000 feet, I touched off the ballistic charge which blew off the ventral fin. It fell away as predicted, and a small parachute deployed, lowering it gently to the ground. Chase pilot White reported: "Ventral away." The desert was coming up fast. At 600 feet altitude I flared out. I lined up for my approach, sighting along the three black strips painted on the desert dry lake. Then, for the first time, I noticed a peculiar distortion caused by the fact that I was looking through three panes of glass: the helmet visor and the double-layer X-15 windshield. I knew the black lines on the lake bed were parallel. From my position in the cockpit they now seemed to spread out in a large V. It was not a serious matter, but one I had to adjust to quickly. The distortion might affect my depth perception and cause a rough touchdown.

In the next second without warning the nose of the X-15 pitched up sharply. It was a maneuver that had not been predicted by the computers, an uncharted area which the X-15 was designed to explore. I was frankly caught off guard. Quickly I applied corrective elevator control.

The nose came down sharply. But instead of leveling out, it tucked down. I applied reverse control. The nose came up but much too far. Now the nose was rising and falling like the bow of a skiff in a heavy sea. Although I was putting in maximum control I could not subdue the motions. The X-15 was porpoising wildly, sinking toward the desert at 200 miles an hour. I would have to land at the bottom of an oscillation, timed perfectly; otherwise, I knew, I would break the bird. I lowered the flaps and gear.

My mind was almost completely absorbed in the tremendous task of saving the X-15, of getting it on the ground in one piece. But I could not push back a terrible thought that was forming. Something was dreadfully wrong. We had pulled a tremendous goof. The X-15 in spite of all our sweat and study, our attempt at perfection, had become completely unstable. Somewhere along the line we or one of our machines had made an unbelievable miscalculation. Four years of work, ten million engineering man-hours, 120 million dollars, and our machine from a stability standpoint was less satisfactory than the man-killing X-2.

My speed dropped below 200 miles an hour. In the middle of a wild oscillation I tried to grind the two rear skids into the lake bed. But apparently the windshield confused me. I missed the ground by a good four feet, pumping in more control as the nose started to rise again. For minimum strain on the tail skids and nose wheel we had calculated ideal X-15 landing speed to be 210 miles an hour. I was already down to 170 miles an hour. The X-15 would soon not fly at all and would fall toward the ground like a brick. In my mind's eye I could see the final picture: a big ball of Inconel X.

Now I was half a mile beyond my intended touchdown point and drifting off to the right toward a rough spot on the lake. Instinctively I pumped in a little left rudder control to get back on the marked landing strip. With the next dip I had one last chance and flared again to ease the descent. At that moment the rear skids caught on the desert floor and the nose slammed over, cushioned by the nose wheel. The X-15 skidded 5,000 feet across the lake, throwing up an enormous rooster-tail of dust. The emergency helicopter swooshed down and landed alongside the ship. A long caravan of emergency trucks roared out from the sidelines. I sat in the cockpit, canopy still closed, engulfed in disappointment.

"Stormy," I said, "something is radically wrong." Stormy had driven out to the airplane and snatched me away before the press arrived. We were tearing across the lake at seventy miles an hour in a company car headed for Captain Richardson's van. I had given Stormy a quick run-down on the landing.

"That airplane can't be unstable," Stormy said.

He was right, of course. I had jumped to the wrong conclusion. Others did too, blaming the instability on the sidearm control. But these critics were wrong. In the days following we carefully analyzed the recorded data and found out what really happened.

The control system in the X-15 is quite similar to the power steering in a car. The pilot makes a control motion, but hydraulic pressure supplies the 'muscle,' does the work, and moves the control surface, just as the power boost in the car turns the wheels. This hydraulic pressure operates the flight controls and the flaps. Given limitless space and weight, it is no problem to design a hydraulic system which can perform almost any job on the airplane, and if necessary, all jobs simultaneously. However, the hydraulic pump in the X-15, like all the other equipment, was a carefully calculated compromise from the weight standpoint. It was not limitless in power. It could not do everything at once; nor did it do one assigned task fast enough.

One result was that when the pilot pumped in a motion on the stick, the control surfaces were slow in responding. Years earlier I had run up a warning flag in this area; in fact, I had demanded a faster control response. However, since it is pretty hard before flight test for a pilot to support his opinions against simulators and calculations, and because my demands meant more weight, we had settled on low-control response, thinking we could live with it. This had almost done us in.

When the X-15 nose pitched on landing, I had instantly applied corrective control. The hydraulic 'muscle,' then also working to lower the flaps, fell behind and then overshot trying to catch up.

As a result, the controls were doing one thing and I another. In an effort to regain control of the porpoising airplane, I pumped in full up-and-down control, in effect chasing back and forth from one extreme to the other, and by great luck or possibly intuition, struck some kind of crude balance, bringing the ship safely to earth. Had our bird been an unmanned missile, I'm certain it would have been destroyed. But for future operations we knew the pilot couldn't live with that slow control response: the X-15 landing was difficult enough. The pilot had to have absolute and positive control of the airplane.

By the simple expedient of adjusting a valve, to borrow power, in effect, from other places in the ship, we increased the control rate upward to more like my original request. Thereafter, we never again experienced the porpoising motion, either in the air or at touchdown, with center and sidearm control.

X-15 number one, which had been used on these five pioneering flights, was pulled out of action so that the engineers could make many minor fixes that were long overdue. We then turned to X-15 number two, the airplane designated for the first rocket-powered flights.

38: "She Blew Sky High"

X-15 NUMBER TWO, IDENTICAL IN APPEARANCE with X-15 number one, was anchored to the concrete ramp in the engine-test area.

Her fuel tanks were brimming. In the big forward tank there were four tons of liquid oxygen, so cold that a thick coating of ice had formed on the outside fuselage and all the machinery in the vicinity of the tank had chilled. In the after tank there were five tons of a mixture of water and alcohol or, as we called it, "Wale," a very volatile liquid. Altogether, then, nine tons of liquid energy, the fantastic stuff that would propel the X-15 through the air faster than man had ever flown.

Wearing street clothes, I climbed into the cockpit to begin the practice engine test, a simulated launch and engine run just as it would take place in the air. The men who had fueled the X-15 moved back their big tank trucks. The specialists on the propulsion system grouped at a distance and talked to me by radio from Sam's van. Q. C. Harvey manned his post in the North American tower two miles away.

I quickly ran through the familiar pre-launch routine: APU start, shift to X-15 power, and so on. Now for the first time I added to this routine the in-volved rocket-engine start procedure. First I turned a switch which touched off a flow of nitrogen gas through all the fuel lines. This was a safety measure to purge fuel which might ignite prematurely in the lines and cause an explosion. Next I pressurized the big Lox and Wale tanks with helium gas to force the fuel through the lines aft to the rocket engine pumps.

The helium is stored in a cylindrical tank surrounded by the Lox tank. We purposely put it there to keep it as cold as possible. By cooling the helium we can store almost three times as much in the same size cylinder, or cut down on the size of the cylinder and save weight. The regulator valve which adjusts the gas flow from helium tank to the fuel and Lox tanks is a fantastically sensitive device which operates at a temperature of minus 300 degrees Fahrenheit. The pressure inside the helium tank is 3,600 pounds per square inch; the regu-lator reduces this to a mere fifty pounds per square inch, which is all we need to get the fuel moving aft. The regulator had already caused a lot of trouble.

It would cause much more in the future. The X-15 is designed to land empty of fuel. If something goes wrong—if the engine should fail to start—it is absolutely necessary to get rid of the nine tons of fuel weight. Like other rocket airplanes, the X-15 is equipped with a fuel jettison system. This is care-fully arranged so that both tanks exhaust fuel at about the same rate. If one tank emptied too far ahead of the other, it would throw the X-15 out of bal-ance and possibly into a flight attitude from which the pilot could not recover.

There is a control mounted in the cockpit to adjust the flow-rate for each tank.

Before the launch, before lighting off the engine, we always check the jettison system to make sure it is not clogged or frozen shut. (Every time I jettisoned the Wale, I could not help feeling a twinge. I was throwing away 6,000 fifths of pure vodka that some unimaginative temperate had contaminated to prevent useful consumption other than in rocket engines.) At launch altitude of 38,000 feet, where the air temperature is about minus 60 degrees Fahrenheit, the rocket engine and pumps are very cold just prior to launch. If we ignite the engine cold there is danger of erratic and rough starts or malfunction.

Thus just prior to launch, the pilot must turn a switch which allows a trickle of hydrogen peroxide to flow through the engine pump gas generator, warming it up or, as we say, 'pre-heating.' Thirty seconds or so before launch the pilot 'primes' the engine with a burst of Lox and fuel. The prime is dumped overboard so it can be checked visually by the chase pilots. The purpose of the prime is to make certain the fuel and Lox lines are full—right up to the rocket-engine fuel pump which sucks the fuel from the tanks and forces it into the burning chamber at a tremendous rate.

Now on the ground as I went through these procedures, the outside observers reported: "Prime looks good." Simulating a drop from the mother plane, I then ran my hand across eight toggle switches on the left side of the X-15 cockpit, igniting each of the eight barrels of the rocket engine. They roared to life with a noise that could be heard for twenty miles across the desert.

A long blast of rocket exhaust—flame, fire, and smoke—spewed from the rear of the X-15. The little ship strained against its ground moorings. One barrel of the engine ignited improperly and, as designed, automatically shut down. The other seven blazed on, gulping the fuel at the rate of two and a half tons a minute. Then after 250 seconds, fuel exhausted, the seven barrels "blew out" or stopped, making a "pop-pop-pop-pop-pop" sound. The ground crew moved in to check the results. The ground tests on the X-15 rocket engines, supposedly reliable X-1 types with a great backlog of experience, revealed many surprising weaknesses and faults. It might have been a case of familiarity breeding contempt. Or perhaps the experts who had originally designed and wrung out these engines had moved on to other fields, leaving behind personnel lacking their genius.

There were many difficulties too in the X-15's infinitely complicated tankage and fuel plumbing system.

The regulator valve on the Lox tank is one good example. That extremely sensitive piece of equipment was tested in the laboratory at least ten thousand times. Yet when we put it in the air-plane, it failed again and again. Each time it failed, the ground crews had to tear into the airplane to get inside and replace it. The tale of woe with this single valve would make a book in itself. Charlie Feltz, Bud Benner, and John Gibb, his assistant, stayed up around the clock many nights, almost hand-building and testing new regulators. Then, like some priceless set of jewels, these were carried to Edwards by hand and installed in the airplane—only to fail again at the crucial moment. Before long, Stormy entered the picture. He and the engineers re-designed the valve a dozen times. I don't think any valve in the history of the world received so much high-level probing, so much laboratory testing, so much money and engineering man-hours. This single item had to be perfect. A failure could cause a catastrophe in the air and wash out the whole X-15 program.

Slowly—all too slowly for my money—our complex bird was gaining in reliability, inching ahead toward the pay-off point. Her story was accumulating in tens of thousands of pieces of paper—reports, work change-orders, engineering analyses, written by hundreds of people. Our ground crews, feeling their way with this strange tiger and her dangerous fluids, grew in maturity and experience. Where once they resembled a platoon of raw recruits, they now worked with carrier-deck efficiency and enthusiasm.

But men are fallible. They can't think of everything. Somewhere an obscure mistake was made, and the consequences were nearly disastrous. After a ground engine run one day, I hurried to my Bonanza and flew back to the plant in Los Angeles. When I landed, one of the company guards came up to me and said: "Is it a total loss?"

"Is what a total loss?" I asked.

"The X-15. Didn't you hear? She blew sky high."

I raced for a telephone and put through a call to Q. C. Harvey, my mind spinning with anxiety and apprehension. Q.C. got on the phone and rattled off the awful story.

After I had left, the ground crew began grooming the X-15 for her next test. Part of this routine called for purging the hydrogen-peroxide lines of all residual liquid. This was usually accomplished by connecting a nitrogen-gas hose to a fitting on the outside of the X-15 and blowing gas through the plumbing.

Despite careful procedures and great caution the hose used for this had a residue of oil, doubtless left there a long time back when it was tested in some remote factory. When the mechanic applied gas pressure to the hose, the film of oil was forced into the X-15 hydrogen-peroxide lines. When these two hostile chemicals met, a violent explosion was set off. Fire raced through the engine bay of the airplane.

The firemen at Edwards rushed to the X-15. By then the ship was an inferno of flame and white smoke, reminiscent of the Queenie explosion. They put out the fire, but not before it inflicted severe damage in the engine bay. The fire gutted the rear end of the airplane. When the peroxide blew, one of the X-15 crewmen was badly burned. If he had been standing two feet closer, he would probably have been killed. It took weeks to repair the airplane.

24 July, 1959. Forty-six days since my first glide flight in the X-15. The fire damage in X-15 number two had been repaired. The rocket engine had been tested on the ground several more times. The Lox tank helium regulator had been redesigned and replaced almost daily. Now we were nearing the second big milestone: a powered flight.

But before this could take place there were many more pieces to fit into our technological puzzle. X-15 number two had not yet been aloft. No X-15 had yet been aloft with fuel on board.

Uppermost on the list of items to check was the B-52 Lox top-off system. As previously related, unstable Lox 'boils' away at a fast rate at high altitude. As much as 600 pounds an hour of the X-15's four tons of Lox evaporates through the tank vents. This loss could throw the ship seriously out of balance at launch time. A Lox loss also reduces the rocket-engine running time.

The B-52 Lox top-off system is a highly sophisticated piece of machinery, far advanced over anything installed previously in mother planes at Edwards. A complicated pressure system moves the Lox from two huge storage tanks in the B-52 belly, through pipes in the B-52 wing, down into the X-15 mating pylon, and then into the X-15 Lox tank itself. A probe in the X-15 Lox tank 'senses' when the Lox supply drops and automatically relays this 'word' to the B-52 storage tank pumping system. Then the B-52 Lox valves go into action, refilling the X-15 Lox tank.

In theory, this system is supposed to keep the X-15 brimming with Lox all during the climb and the flight to launch point. The system had been checked on the ground and in flight many times, although never with an X-15 mounted on the B-52 pylon in flight.

I boarded the X-15 at 0830. The ship with its load of Lox was like some massive deep-freeze. I noticed, for example, that the temperature of the hydraulic oil in the control system was minus 80 degrees Fahrenheit. We had anticipated that. We would have to watch this carefully. If it completely froze in flight, it would be impossible to operate the X-15 control system.

I droned off the gauge readings into my tape recorder. Then I received news from the ground crew that there would be a two-hour "hold" in take-off. Some seal, sensitive to the intense cold, had failed at the last minute.

The take-off delay seemed interminable. When at last the ground crews finished repairing the faulty piece of X-15 equipment, a baffling new problem arose. In the repair process the mechanics had removed an access door on the ship, a piece of the fuselage skin. The X-15, influenced by its freezing load of Lox, had shrunk considerably in size. The access door, lying in the hot desert sun, had expanded to its normal size. Now it wouldn't fit back in its original place. We couldn't go up without it. What to do? Five hundred people wondered.

It was one of the X-15 crewmen, Joe Jingle, who provided an ingenious solution. He hurriedly soaked the access door in a bucket of liquid nitrogen until it shrank enough to fit back in place. As I watched this operation from the cockpit—Joe's gloves were too thin for the intense cold and I knew he was suffering—I was filled with admiration. Our team was becoming truly professional.

Charlie Bock poised the B-52 and its precious load at the end of the runway. We were now much heavier. The Lox in the B-52 storage tanks and the fuel and Lox in the X-15 had upped the B-52 gross take-off weight by almost twenty tons, including the extra B-52 jet fuel required to operate the heavier airplane. The X-15 alone weighed 32,215 pounds, or about the same as a heavily loaded DC-3. Bock cobbed the engines. It was a long run. We broke ground at 11,500 feet.

The X-15 and its jewel-like machinery underwent an amazing kaleidoscope of temperature ranges. On the ground the little ship was intensely cold. Now as we flew through the hot desert air, it began to warm up. The hydraulic temperature zoomed from minus 80 degrees to plus two degrees Fahrenheit. Then as we climbed in the thinner, colder air, the temperatures fell again to well below zero. I kept an almost continuous log of these temperatures. It was important to know just how the X-15 responded. If we overlooked the possibility of a frozen valve, it could result in serious trouble and more delay.

Bill Berkowitz in the B-52 reported by radio: "The Lox top-off system is erratic." Bill was watching a panel of gauges and lights in the B-52 which continuously kept tab on the stream of Lox flowing from the B-52 to the X-15 tank. The lights had signaled a malfunction. Bill shifted from one B-52 Lox storage tank to the other. But it was no use.

"I have no indications here of a top-off," I reported.

Something had gone haywire in that sophisticated, vital piece of machinery. I would have to stay on guard. The X-15 Lox was boiling away rapidly, imbalancing the airplane. If we had an emergency launch—always a possibility—I would have my hands full. The system was intensely cold, it was mechanical, it was electrical, it was new, Murphy's Law prevailed: "If it can fail, it will." (Murphy's Law, the enigma of designers, is to engineering lore akin to the natural laws referred to by Robert Louis Stevenson when he speaks of a piece of dropped toast which always falls buttered side down, and of assuring sun-shine by wearing a raincoat.) We never really got used to this tarnish on our most hopeful engineering.

There followed a half hour of diligent test and search for the trouble. The top-off system was clearly on the blink. Berkowitz tried to prove top-off by looking through the closed-circuit television set beamed on the X-15. But we were not in a TV studio. The expensive set was not discriminating enough to tell him what was happening at the overboard spill on top of the X-15 fuselage. We later got around the inadequacy of the TV circuit by installing a hemispherical window in the side of the B-52 so Bill could look with his own eyes.

Following this, we turned to other drills in the sky. As usual, we proceeded to a launch rehearsal, this time including the rocket-engine pre-start routine. I pressurized the X-15 fuel and Lox tanks and for once—or so it seemed—the helium regulator performed as designed, or as re-designed. At one minute before 'Launch' I shut down the propulsion system. Then to see how long it would take to get rid of the X-15 propellants at altitude, I jettisoned the six hundred pounds of hydrogen peroxide, four tons of Lox, and five tons of Wale. The peroxide streamed away in 140 seconds. The Lox and Wale tanks, jettisoned simultaneously, ran dry in 110 seconds, leaving a long white contrail across the deep blue sky. The jettison times were exactly right. If the X-15 pilot encountered trouble after launch he would be mighty busy, but we knew he could dispose of nine tons of fuel before the ship touched down dead-stick on the lake.

With the exception of the B-52 Lox top-off failure, we considered the flight a whopping success. The X-15 had weathered its temperature extremes without difficulty. The pressure-suit, the APUs, operated for the first time in this airplane at altitude, the engine-start rehearsal and other checks were entirely satisfactory. The fact that the helium tank regulator worked was a reward for Gibb's sleepless nights. In short, once the Lox top-off system had been debugged, the bird was ready for powered flight.

In spite of these setbacks, inevitable in a craft so advanced as the X-15, we were on schedule. Four years before this—in the early fall of 1955—North American promised delivery of a debugged X-15 airplane to NASA by August of 1959. Even including a thousand or more changes from the original concept, including a major shift of mother ship, and a switch to the interim engine, we believed then that we would meet this schedule. We would get off one powered flight to make some of our demonstrations and then turn an X-15 over to NASA.

The agency was eager, although it seemed to me that the line of volunteer X-15 pilots was beginning to thin out considerably. Bob White and Joe Walker and their 'back-ups' were still in there pitching, flying chase on most of our flights. However, we noted there was no great rush of new applicants. We failed to meet our four-year-old X-15 schedule. August, 1959, came and went without a successful powered-flight demonstration and we were not able to deliver an airplane to NASA.

It took much time to repair the balky B-52 Lox top-off system and to install an emergency by-pass in case it failed again. The little ship itself suddenly developed a hundred minor leaks and pains, each requiring thousands of agonizing man-hours to rectify. The weeks ticked by at an alarming rate. Finally on September 4 the X-15 was mated, fueled, and ready. If all went well on the flight I would drop and fire off the rocket engine.

Because our tight schedule had 'slipped' by a week, we prepared for this climactic flight with a growing sense of urgency. All hands worked and talked as though they were Marines on the verge of invading a beach-head. On the night before the flight I stayed up late in the BOQ memorizing the flight plan.

We wanted to collect data readings at about forty different combinations of speed, altitude, and angle of attack during the flight. After I fell away from the B-52, there wouldn't be time to consult the flight plan.

I arrived at Captain Richardson's van at 0540, put on the pressure-suit, and checked its systems. By 0625 I was strapped in the X-15 cockpit. At 0717 the B-52 took off, climbing slowly to launch altitude. I kept a sharp eye on the gauges, although I was blinded somewhat by the early morning sun, and droned the numbers into my portable tape-recorder. The B-52 Lox top-off system performed adequately. As we approached this dramatic moment in X-15 history, we joshed on the radio.

"Say," Charlie Bock called out, "looks like they have a heavy overcast down in Los Angeles. Scotty, you want to make an instrument approach in the bird into Los Angeles International Airport?"

"I don't have a glide-path indicator in here," I said.

"You might create something of a new noise problem with that engine. Everybody would move away from the airport," Bock said.

We climbed to launch point.

"Seven minutes to drop," Charlie Bock said. We had reached 38,000 feet, heading southwest, to make a final turn over Randsburg. Then we would aim for Mojave, swing over Lancaster, and if all went well launch over Rosamond Dry Lake. I was busy flicking switches in the X-15 cockpit. I made a note on the tape-recorder: "The black gloves may look fine with the silver suit, but they have to go. They soak up the bright high-altitude sunlight and they're uncomfortably warm."

Q. C. Harvey wanted to make certain the Lox top-off was complete. He broke in from the ground: "Hold at seven minutes."

We waited, boring holes in the sky, while Bill Berkowitz checked to see if the top-off was successful. When he reported it was, Q.C. 'released' us and we proceeded toward the final countdown.

"Five minutes," Bock announced.

"I'm going to pressurize the Wale and Lox tanks NOW," I said. I emphasized 'now' so that we could get the precise time of the operation. When I spoke the word I moved the lever that set in motion the worrisome Lox tank regulator. Helium gas rushed into the large X-15 tanks. I watched the gauges as they swept from zero to 50 pounds per square inch in ten seconds. The Lox tank pressure continued up. Then I heard a strange, loud clank in the rear of the X-15.

"Oops," I said on the radio. "What was that?"

The clank came from a safety relief valve on the Lox tank. Too much helium gas had rushed into the tank, the pressure was too high, and it tripped. The helium regulator had failed again. I swept my eyes back to the gauges. The Lox tank read 65 pounds per square inch.

I double-checked with the chase pilots: "Is the Lox venting overboard?" There was clearly no possibility of a powered flight that day, but I wanted to make certain the safety vent was operating properly. If not, the mounting helium pressure could cause the thin X-15 fuel tanks to burst. At 38,000 feet, that could be a real mess.

"Affirmative," chase reported. "Safety vent operating."

By then I was sure it was operating properly. The vent, in fact, was flapping rhythmically, in time with the gauges, which fluctuated as the gas pressure built up in the tanks to limits, tripped the safety vent, and then fell off again.

"I'm dead," I reported on the radio. "Regulator is running away. Relief vent cycling. Letting out the over-pressure."

"Abort," Q.C. responded. I could imagine his disappointment. I know because I felt it too. We would have to try again.

We jettisoned the unused fuel—its cost, about $1,000, was a mere drop in the bucket—and returned to base. That night, as I recall it, we spent several very uncomfortable hours in Stormy's office. For the next three nights Charlie Feltz, Bud Benner, and John Gibb slept not at all. They spread their time between the Manufacturing Division and the Testing Laboratory, hand-carrying the hand built helium regulators.

There was a new and urgent reason for reaching X-15 flight perfection at the earliest possible date. Almost casually the U.S. had drifted to a major turning point in its history of aviation and national defense. Guided missiles were pushing the manned combat aircraft to the side. The missile zealots in their eagerness to obtain funds had convinced the powers that be in Washington that the manned aircraft was an obsolete concept. Anti-aircraft missiles, such as the Nike and Bomarc, could do the job of the manned fighter in defending the nation against air attack, they claimed. Surface-to-surface ballistic missiles, such as Atlas, Titan, and Polaris, could replace the manned combat aircraft for the retaliatory mission.

All of us, of course, believed in missiles. Few could deny that they would ultimately become a dominant weapon in the deterrent force. But we believed this day was still a long way off and, moreover, that there would always be a place for the manned combat aircraft. Manned airplanes are flexible. They can be moved about or dispersed quite simply, or shifted in flight from one target to the next, or assigned to several targets. If there is an alert, they can be launched and, more important, recalled, if it should all turn out to be a mistake. Airplanes can approach the enemy's borders from a wide range of points on the compass at a variety of altitudes, vastly confusing the enemy radar warning and interception system. The simple fact of having manned combat airplanes in our inventory forces the enemy to take tremendously expensive countermeasures to prepare a defense against them. Manned aircraft are fundamentally more reliable mechanically than missiles, and they can be repaired without total loss if something goes wrong. (This we had demonstrated again and again in the X-15.) By building military airplanes we keep the art of aviation alive in this country and enable the nation to compete and prepare for the fantastic future already being revealed on the technical horizon.

In the industry we had noticed the drift a long time ago. I first picked it up in 1954 during the meeting of the old NACA Aero-dynamics Subcommittee when the X-15 was under discussion. Since then, the number of Air Force planes on order and types under development shrank rapidly. As I have related, by the time we began the X-15 flight-test program there were only two advanced combat Air Force airplanes on the drawing boards: the F-108 fighter and the B-70 bomber, both North American designs. In the summer of 1959 as we approached the climax of the X-15 flight program, we received the stunning news that one of these planes, the F-108, had been canceled outright.

In the field of Air Force manned combat airplanes for the future this left only the B-70, and from what we could ascertain it too was in jeopardy.

These fateful decisions were made—over the protests of the Air Force and NASA—by men temporarily on loan to the government from fields other than aviation. The decisions were made in comfortable Washington offices far removed from the reality of Cape Canaveral and Edwards and failing helium-regulator valves. That fall we hoped that a successful flight of the X-15 might dramatize the validity of the manned-aircraft concept and bring about a reconsideration of these decisions.

All my life I had staked my all to foster and further the concept of manned airplanes. Now, with the X-15, we had our last chance to make intelligence prevail and I intended to help, even if it killed me.

39: The Old Pro

On the morning of September 17, the weather at Edwards was as blustery as it usually is in the rainy season in December. There was a heavy cloud layer hovering near the edge of the base. The winds on the lake bed were gusting to twenty and twenty-five miles an hour. But as I have said, landings are my strong point. Crosswinds have never kept me on the ground. On that day I don't think anything could have kept me on the ground. "Let's go," I said to Stormy and Charlie Feltz.

And we did.

Bock lifted the B-52 off the runway at precisely 0730. Major Bob White, Joe Walker, and Al White, the North American X-15 back-up pilot, flew chase. Of the forty critical gauges on the X-15 panel, only one was out of line. The nitrogen gas supply for the equipment that cooled the electronics gear was sagging. When I called the gauge readings to Q.C., I deliberately skipped this one. After four years I knew intimately the requirements of each system. I had three limiting figures in mind: the specification figure, which was conservative; our agreed-upon 'no go' realistic figure, less conservative, and one which Harvey must cancel on; and then I had my own absolute minimum that I knew would not endanger the X-15 (after all, the final decision is the pilot's).

Today we were going to fly.

At 0756 Bill Berkowitz switched on the Lox top-off. This time it did not fail. We moved into a launch rehearsal.

Q. C. Harvey spoke from the ground: "Okay—let's go ahead."

"We're in good shape," I said. We were—all but the coolant nitrogen. Charlie Bock called the ten-minute warning. Q.C. reported the cloud front holding stationary. The lake bed was clear. Watching the creeping rate on the nitrogen pressure, I made up my mind we could be committed without hazard. I made last-minute preparations to fly, zipping through the lengthy check-list fixed to my knee-pad. At six minutes to launch I started the APUs. At five minutes to launch I released the pressure to the main tanks. The helium regulator worked beautifully. At four minutes to launch I checked the jettison system. I started the fuel-line purge and opened the main fuel shut-off valves. The pre-heat lights came on green.

Suddenly I heard a familiar—and ominous—clanking. The Lox tank safety vent had popped. I thought, here we go again. I sang out on the radio: "Hold the phone." Too much pressure had built up in the Lox tank. I held my breath momentarily, watching the Lox tank-pressure gauge. It dropped off slowly and the vent reset properly. The Lox tank regulator had a slow leak. I timed the pressure cycles and decided it was acceptable.

"Okay," I said. Bock resumed the countdown.

At the one-minute warning we shut off power and oxygen from the B-52 and the X-15 was in effect 'on its own.' I turned on the rocket-engine master switch and started the prime of fuel and Lox through the engines. Then I rolled the automatic photo-recorders, which would keep a concise record of all events in the X-15. Finally I flashed the green launch-light for the second time on Bock's panel.

"Ready to go," I said.

Bock called the brief countdown: "Three . . . Two . . . One . . . DROP!"

For the second time in eight flights I fell away from the B-52 pylon into open sky. My left hand felt the toggle switches which would light two barrels of the lower motor. I flicked them as soon as I heard the 'kerchunk' of the shackles releasing the X-15. In less than five seconds my hand moved to the other six toggles, and before I had dropped 2,000 feet I was able to report: "Got eight of 'em going."

On the earlier rocket planes we felt a push, like a gentle kick in the rump when we lit the rockets. We would feel a much greater push when the 57,000-pound thrust XLR-99 engine was installed. With the smaller X-1-type engines, the heavy X-15 responded rather slowly. The effect is somewhat like opening the throttle on a jet airplane.

I fell to about 33,000 feet before the rocket took hold and began pushing the X-15. I reported: "Going uphill at 33,000." I added: "Looks good across the board." It was good—even the helium pressure, which was still within my absolute limit. Since the X-15 has no compass and I cannot see the horizon during the steep climb, I had to rely on Bock during the first few seconds for a steer. He reported I was to his right. The F-104 chase planes were now flying wide open. I soon left them in a cloud of vaporish white rocket exhaust.

Pushed by the eight flaming barrels the X-15 suddenly became a tiny thing of immense power and speed darting across the deep blue desert sky. Had it not been for my exhaust trail the observers on the ground could not have followed my course except by radar. More at ease now after a successful light-off, I directed my attention to these questions: Did we have a stable airplane? Was it dangerous or difficult to fly? Were the controls now adequate?

It was apparent almost instantly that we had built a beautiful airplane. Her nose held straight and firm without the yaw and pitch common to most high-performance planes. As I blasted toward the heavens I alternated between side-arm control and the center stick, pumping in tentative control motions to feel her out. She remained sound and stable. Because she is long and slim and has stubby wings, she was extremely sensitive when I rolled her. But this we had anticipated and it was no surprise. The plane eased through the speed of sound imperceptibly with little or none of the usual buffet-and-control disturbance.

As I was nearing 50,000 feet I was startled to hear a loud buzzing. What could it be? My first thought was that an APU unit was vibrating. But a glance at the gauges indicated they were running perfectly. It was not until later that I discovered the source of the noise. The cockpit of the X-15 is so small that when I lean forward to reach some of the controls my helmet wedges in the V-shaped canopy glass. The noise I heard was caused by the normal, healthy vibration of the X-15 machinery. My helmet, which is a kind of sound chamber, magnified this vibration manifold. I called this noise on the radio to my subsequent regret. All the vibration experts in the country have had a field day trying to solve this one. It would never have been noticed had not my helmet touched.

Two minutes after launch I reached 50,000 feet and pushed over in level flight. Then I dropped the nose slightly for a speed run, meanwhile maneuvering the ship through a series of turns and rolls, conscious of the deep rumbling noise of the rocket and a great rush of wind on the fuselage. It was obvious the black bird was in her element at supersonic speeds. She responded beautifully. I stared in fascination at the Mach meter which climbed quickly from 1.5 Mach to 1.8 Mach and then effortlessly to my top speed for this flight of 2.3 Mach or about 1,500 miles an hour. Then, because I was under orders not to take the X-15 wide open, I shut off three of the rocket barrels. As I slowed down, I recalled the agony at Edwards many years before when we had worked for months pushing, calculating, polishing, and who knows what else to achieve Mach 2 in the Skyrocket. Now with the X-15 we had reached that speed in three minutes on our first powered flight and I had to throttle back.

About four minutes (230 seconds, to be precise) after launch, the fuel tanks ran dry and the engines shut down. I got set for the fast dead-stick landing. As I swung into a turn to line up with the lake, the X-15's wedge-shaped tail bit the air and the nose turned sharply, causing me to comment on the radio: "Very powerful rudders on this little baby."

My altitude was dropping off rapidly. But now, with a total of nine or ten minutes flight time in the ship, including the first glide flight, I had complete confidence in her. I had probed her weaknesses and strengths and knew what would please her or make her angry. Routinely I called for a re-check of the winds on the lake bed. A comical exchange, no doubt arising from the tension on the ground, followed.

Sam Richter, parked on the lake in his van, consulted the readings from his anemometer and reported the winds as "four knots."

At the same moment Edwards tower reported the winds as "eighteen knots."

"Repeat, please," I said. The lake was growing larger by the second. I could see Sam's van, parked in the row of emergency vehicles. A crosswind of four knots was no problem. But a cross-wind of eighteen knots required sharp attention at touchdown.

Sam came back: "Four, repeat four, knots."

Edwards tower broke in: "Eighteen, repeat eighteen, knots."

Then on the radio circuit Sam and the Edwards tower lapsed into a debate about the winds. To relieve the mounting tension, I broke in: "Sambo, why don't you stick your head out of the van and see how bad the winds are?"

Sam stuck by his four-knot figure. Since he was stationed nearest the landing strip, though still several miles away, I accepted his estimate and lined up on the north-south runway, disregarding crosswinds. By now my chase pilots, Bob White and Joe Walker, had found me and were glued to my wingtips.

The winds at Edwards are often very variable and Edwards tower, it turned out, had correctly estimated them for my landing area. They were very strong from the west. When this fact was established, I was advised to shift to the east-west runway. But it was too late. The X-15, "gliding like a brick," was already too close to the ground. The men, concerned mainly for my personal safety, were still cluttering up the air with their debate. I cut them off sharply: "I'm committed. Let the chase have the radio."

During the turn on base leg I droned the readings on the panel gauges. I read off the APU bearing temperature as a disastrous 1700 degrees instead of 170, which is normal. Hearing this on the ground, Charlie Feltz nearly fell dead. He shouted at Sam: "Wha'd he say? Wha'd he say?" I quickly reassured him.

My speed fell off to 250 miles an hour when I crossed the edge of the lake bed and I blew off the ventral fin. Just at that moment I thought I heard chase Bob White report his plane had run into the fin. This would have been catastrophic.

I was concerned. With only a few seconds remaining before the X-15 would touch down on the lake, I spoke into the radio:

"You fouled the tail?"

"No," White replied. "The chute fouled. It failed to open."

It was a minor matter. Anyway, the chute did open a split second later. White dutifully reported this fact with the additional comment, "Isn't that nice?"

I was now beginning to feel the strong crosswind. To compensate, I aimed the X-15 to cross the marked lake-bed runway. My hope was that I would drift over between the black lines by touchdown. I commented on the radio: "That's a pretty good crosswind."

Chase White, who was "talking" me down, said: "Very nice."

As a matter of fact, the ship was flying smoothly. There was no sign of the violent porpoising I had experienced on the first glide flight. I held the nose high and seconds before touchdown, at 200 miles an hour, dropped the rear steel skids and nose wheel and flipped the flap switch.

Exactly ten minutes from launch by the X-15 clock the skids dug into the hard-packed surface and almost instantly the nose fell heavily, cushioned by the nose wheel. White repeated: "Very nice." As we skidded along throwing up dust, I joked: "What do you expect from the old pro, Daddy-O?" This comment was typical of the radio repartee of fighter pilots, who by nature will admit to no limitations whatever.

With God's help I had accomplished my mission as I was sure I would; the X-15 and I had not failed our friends, associates or, if you will, the nation. It was a great pleasure to confirm this triumph to myself. Involuntarily I voiced my feelings on the radio.

At that moment I became aware of a new danger looming in my path. The crosswind was stronger than I thought and the ship did not drift over onto the marked runway as I expected. I touched down outside the right boundary line and skidded at 150 miles an hour directly toward a deep drainage ditch about a mile ahead. If I coasted into that ditch, I knew that I could very well wipe out the X-15's landing gear or possibly damage the plane more seriously. The old pro, now feeling sheepish, pushed hard on the rudder pedal, hit the speed brakes, and dropped the elevators full down, desperately trying to steer the plane to the left and stop it all at once, to avoid another F-100 through the hangar wall. I snapped into the radio: "Hollered too soon, didn't I? I'm going to coast into that ditch." I thought: that's the way it will always be at Edwards—hero one minute, bum the next. As it turned out, I was only fifty feet off the marks and fortunately stopped a hundred yards short of the ditch.

After reporting with relief to Q. C. Harvey, who could no longer see the X-15, that everything was okay, I tried to open the canopy, but the release was stuck fast. While waiting for the ground crews to arrive and let me out, I proceeded with the post-flight chores, shutting down various systems and taking final readings. The decision on the coolant gas had been right and all systems looked good.

Unknown to me, a new and far more serious crisis was developing in the X-15. A pump casing had ruptured. Alcohol was flowing into the after engine bay and a furious though not yet visible fire had broken out. We later calculated that it started just after I blew the ventral, when I was still fifty feet in the air.

Sam Richter and Charlie Feltz arrived with the fire trucks, official observers, and ground-support equipment. The crewmen opened the canopy from the outside and removed my helmet. I climbed out into the stiff desert breeze to meet half a dozen outstretched hands.

Our mutual admiration society was in full flower when Sam spotted the fire. Dismayed, we all ran to look. Sam waved the fire trucks toward the tail section. The firemen unreeled the hoses and showered the tail section with fog. There was still a considerable quantity of alcohol on board. The X-15 at that moment was like a bomb with a lighted fuse. We chased the official observers back while the firemen, with no display of concern for their personal safety, put out the fire.

When I got a close look at the rear of the plane I realized again for the millionth time over the past twenty years that airplanes are not for the impatient. We would have to retrench and try again and again. The fire had burned through a large area, melting aluminum tubing, fuel lines, valves, and other machinery. Before the X-15 could fly again I knew we would have to rebuild the damaged section completely, and it would take time.

The fire was one more delay. The plane was built for the specific purpose of ferreting out such weaknesses. Our job was to correct these weaknesses one by one until an irreducible minimum remained, so that we could then move ahead. The X-15 was earning her way showing us how to advance. There was a little matter, however, for which we could all be thankful; if the alcohol fire had broken out one minute earlier, it is quite likely that the X-15 and the old pro at the controls would have been blown to oblivion.

40: Bad News with the Good

"Coming up on 40,000 feet."

Jack Allavie in the B-52 called our altitude. It was about fifteen minutes before launch, October 10, twenty-three days after the first powered flight and the fire, my ninth trip up in the X-15. The rear of the ship had been rebuilt in record time; some additional fixes had been made on the airplane while it was torn down. A new hydrogen peroxide tank had been installed.

There were two new faces in the B-52 crew. Charlie Bock was off to Fort Worth, Texas, to help conduct experimental flight tests on Convair's B-58 Hustler bomber, then undergoing its final shake-down. The B-52 co-pilot, Jack Allavie, moved over to the left-hand seat. Fitz Fulton, a longtime Edwards mother-plane and chase pilot, got the right-hand seat. This was Fulton's third tour at Edwards. He had launched Yeager, Everest, Murray, Crossfield, Kincheloe, and Mel Apt, among others.

The North American launch-panel operator in the B-52, Bill Berkowitz, bowed out of the flight-test program. One reason was that he was not able to get adequate life insurance to protect his wife and growing family. My old friend and cohort from NACA-Skyrocket days, Jack Moise, the lad who was sprayed by hydrogen peroxide on the day of my record Mach 2 flight in 1953, took Bill's place.

I admired Moise. He was a go-getter, a short man with a swarthy complexion and a cool, even disposition in the air. As an NACA hand, Moise pulled Joe Walker out of the burning X-1-A at 30,000 feet just before they threw it away. For this he was given a citation praising his courage, and a near-absolute guarantee that he would never be fired from the government, no matter what turn his life might take. But he decided to forego this big chunk of security to join the X-15 team. We were glad to have him. With Moise and Fulton in the B-52 it was like Old Home Week.

Moise was then struggling with the B-52 Lox top-off panel. "I can't pressurize the B-52 Lox tank," he reported. "Something is wrong."

Murphy's Law? Not again, I thought, not on Moise's and Fulton's first flight.

"I've tried the emergency by-pass," Moise reported. "Tank pressure will not rise." The critical Lox had stopped flowing to the X-15 tank, unbalancing the airplane. There was nothing Moise could do. We were finished.

"Abort," Q.C. announced with stark finality. It was October 14, my tenth flight in the X-15, my fifteenth hour airborne in my nest beneath the B-52 wing. After the Lox top-off failure the ground crews had prepared the ship for flight in the amazingly brief time of four days. We were ready.

When we passed 35,000 feet, the X-15 ram-air door open, the full-pressure suit came into play, holding the flesh of my body in a glove-like grip. At 41,000 feet I strained forward to close the ram-air door so that the cabin pressure would build to its normal level of 35,000 feet and relieve the pressure in the suit.

When I closed the ram-air door the nitrogen gas, as designed, built up in the cockpit at a rapid rate. The cockpit 'altitude' dropped to 35,000 feet and the pressure suit relaxed. Allavie and Fulton steered the mother plane toward launch point. My eyes swept back and forth across the instrument panel, routinely checking gauges. I noted then that the cockpit altitude was falling rapidly. It was down to 30,000 feet. Something was wrong. There was a regulator in the cockpit which was supposed to allow the flowing nitrogen gas to escape, maintaining a constant 35,000-foot altitude in the cockpit.

I kept my eye fixed on the cockpit pressure gauge. As the nitrogen built up inside the cockpit, the altitude dropped to 29,000, then to 25,000 and below. We were courting possible disaster. As the cabin altitude dropped toward an earth-like level, it became far more dense than the thin air outside the plane at 41,000 feet. If the difference became too great, I knew that the dense gas inside, seeking to equalize the pressure to the thin air outside, would cause the cockpit to explode for the same reason that an over-inflated rubber balloon pops. I opened the ram-air door to relieve the pressure.

"Delay the countdown," I radioed, asking Jack Allavie to circle the B-52. Then I added: "Hey, Q.C., I've got something bothering me. The cabin goes from 41,000 down through 20,000 and I don't dare let it go any further because it'll bust it. There's too big a pressure difference here."

Q.C. consulted his team of experts and relayed some technical suggestions. I recycled the pressurization and asked Allavie to make another turn.

"Oh, boy!" I radioed. "That thing pressurizes like mad. I don't dare let it go below 20,000 feet, do I? Let's think about this a minute." I was very much concerned. A cockpit explosion of the X-15 could inflict irreparable damage on the X-15 and her pilot and very probably drastically damage the mother plane. I re-cycled the system, again to no avail. I knew then, once again, we were finished. I had planned to fly the ship to 60,000 or 70,000 feet. With the cabin pressure on the blink this was out of the question.

"Abort," I radioed.

Later on the ground we discovered that somehow moisture had accumulated in the cabin regulator and frozen it shut. One more preflight item to check was added to the growing list.

"One minute to drop," Jack Allavie intoned.

"X-15 oxygen ON," I said. Then: "Data burst."

It was October 17. The X-15 ground crew had shattered its own record: it had made the ship ready for flight in three days. It was a beautiful fall day in the desert. The sky was deep blue and clear. Far to the north of us a few feathers of wispy cirrus reached toward the heavens. In the X-15 cockpit all gauges were in the green.

"40 seconds."

"Engine master switch ON."

"Both primes coming on NOW."

"Five. Four. Three. Two. One."

"DROP."

"Kerchunk." And for the third time the X-15 fell away from the B-52. My left hand was resting on two of the rocket-barrel switches. As soon as I heard the shackles rattle, I flicked the switches. Then my hand moved rapidly to the other six. Within five seconds all eight barrels were running wide open. An amber light flashed on near my knee. It was the roll damper, the automatic device which would help stabilize in roll, help to prevent severe, unexpected, or violent roll. It was out. No matter. I would simply be careful in roll control.

"Roll damper out," I said.

The ship felt a little sluggish. I missed the powerful punch of the Sky-rocket.

"Going uphill."

I moved the side-arm control ever so slightly with my right hand. The nose came up gently. The altimeter and Mach meter climbed. Following an item on the flight plan, I then pulled the nose up steeply until the plane shuddered in protest. It was a check of the 'buffet' point. I repeated this maneuver twice.

"Buffet at Mach .8," I said. "Going uphill. Supersonic."

The X-15 Mach meter approached Mach 1.6 and locked there. One minute had gone by. The recovery maneuver caused my check-list, mounted in spiral rings on a pad on my knee, to flip ahead several pages.

I knew the list by heart. But I always tried to follow each page, just to be doubly sure.

"I've lost my place," I said. I flipped back through the pages. "Never mind. Found it again."

"Going through 40,000 feet."

The roll damper was still out. Now I would see how much I needed that roll damper. I moved the side-arm control. The right wing flipped up sharply. I reversed the control. The right wing dropped and the left came up swiftly. With a little more control I could whip the ship horizontally through the air like a spinning bullet. In level flight I balanced on a knife edge.

"It's very sensitive to roll," I radioed.

"Pulling to a 1.8 G turn. Yaw." I kicked the nose to one side in an attempt to define the ship's sideslip characteristics. "Pushing over at 55,000." I leveled the nose. The pages of my spiral notebook flipped again. "Lost my place again."

"What's that?" It was Q.C. I could almost hear Charlie Feltz muttering: "Wha'd he say? Wha'd he say?"

"Never mind," I said.

I banked and dived. The G meter registered two. Then I deliberately side-slipped. I leveled out. The Mach meter climbed steadily: 1.6, 2.0, 2.4, or about 1,600 miles an hour. I had edged over my 2.0 restriction for a few seconds. Only three other men had flown that fast. Yeager had, and he almost died in the try. Pete Everest had. Mel Apt had gone to Mach 3. But he died in the X-2. The temptation to forge ahead and smash Apt's record, which I could easily do in the X-15, was very great. The plane was running like a dream. All I had to do was let the rocket engines burn a little longer, build up a little more speed and then. . . . Crossfield, the first man to fly at twice the speed of sound and the first man to fly at three times the speed of sound . . . and live. But no, that was reserved for someone else, for Joe Walker and Bob White or, if they died, their back-ups. I was an engineering test pilot. It was necessary that I adhere to plan in the air. If I deviated from plan, violated the discipline, then my value as an engineering test pilot was zero.

Dependability, perfection, these are the prerequisites of the test pilot. Too many airplanes and pilots have paid for violating the intelligence of planning. The X-15 would not.

I shut down several of the rocket barrels. I pulled the nose up and climbed quickly to 67,000 feet, my maximum planned altitude for the flight. Then as the remaining rocket barrels burned out, I nosed the X-15 into a steep, supersonic dive to check her stability going downhill at Mach 1.5 without rocket power.

"Burnout," I said.

At 50,000 feet I leveled out and my speed abruptly fell off to subsonic. It was time to begin thinking about the landing. At that moment my eye caught a blur flashing across my nose, dead ahead. It was NASA chase pilot Joe Walker in an F-104, joining up fast to escort me back to the lake bed. He was close.

"There goes my chase—right across my bow!" I called on the radio.

"About eight per cent fuel remaining. Going to jettison." I pushed the lever and a long trail of white vapor flowed into the sky in my wake.

"260 knots. 30,000."

"I'm going to land a little long this time," I said. I laid out my approach for the dry-lake landing strip, reporting my choice of direction by radio to the chase. At 8,000 feet, I turned on my final leg and for the third time got set to put the X-15 on the ground. Just then I thought I saw an airplane on the lake near the spot I had picked to land. I snapped in the radio: "There's an airplane down on the lake." I was committed. There could be no further maneuvers. At the X-15's glide speed on final, 280 miles an hour, I would touch down in twenty seconds. The 'airplane' turned out to be the emergency helicopter which hovers near the landing area. It was almost directly below me when I dropped the ventral fin. I radioed: "Hope that helicopter doesn't get hit."

Luckily it didn't. As I pulled the X-15 nose high, feeling for the ground, chase White reported: "You're looking good, buddy."

The flaps were slow in extending. I landed with 28 degrees of flaps instead of 40, which made the touchdown a little faster than usual. Even so, I judged it the best X-15 landing I had made. As was his custom, Q.C. radioed: "Everything all right?"

For once everything was all right. No fire, no porpoising near the ground, no other major malfunctions. It was judged a near-perfect flight from a mechanical standpoint.

"No sweat," I replied.

I called the gauges and opened the ram-air door to relieve the cockpit of nitrogen gas pressure so that I could open the canopy without undue strain. The ground crews arrived. The men lifted the X-15 onto its special trailer and towed it back to the North American hangar. Captain Richardson met me in his support van with a full-blown martini.

Not many days after that flight I received a startling piece of news. I had been promoted, or more precisely I had been granted a clearly defined slot in North American. No longer just a consultant for the X-15 and its demonstration pilot out on a limb, I was made Chief Engineering Test Pilot of the division, working directly for George Mellinger, long-time manager of North America's Engineering Flight Test. Here was one more handhold to insure the building of airplanes so that a pilot can fly them.

Slowly but surely the trend that started in 1942 with the deaths of Eddie Allen and Jimmy Taylor, of airplane design growing foreign to pilots' needs, was reversing. It now takes legions of engineers to build an airplane, and then in hindsight there is a pitifully slow and expensive stewing by the test pilot to make the fruit of this endeavor palatable.

In my life, it seems, bad news usually comes with the good. Shortly after my promotion, or assignment, we received the stunning word that the B-70, the last of the Air Force future combat airplanes, had been severely cut back. According to the Air Force, North American would build only one prototype, a gutless shell with no armament or weapons system. All the major sub-contracts were canceled. North American would make the complete airplane on much the same pattern by which we had built the experimental X-15. In the aircraft trade this 'cutback' was interpreted as stage-setting for complete cancellation of the project in the following Air Force budget. The cut left North American without any airplanes in production except a few twin-jet executive-type T-39s. The last of the advanced manned airplanes was all but gone.

The news left me bewildered. Now at last I was on the point of achieving my dream of being an engineering test pilot in a position to do some substantial good. But there would be no airplanes to fly. We were all dismayed at this incredible break in history. We were almost finished debugging the X-15. But there would be no airplanes to benefit from the data we collected in the flights. The dire prediction of one of my fellow pilots at NACA years before—that the X-15 would be the last of the manned aircraft—seemed to be coming true. We were not opening a new era in aviation at all. We were closing one. Unless...

The briefing room was crowded with Air Force and NASA brass. Stormy was holding forth with his limitless energy, in his persuasive, articulate, prophetic way. On the blackboard behind him was a drawing of Saturn, the giant booster rocket under development by Wernher von Braun and his team of ex-German rocket experts at the Army's Ballistic Missile Agency in Huntsville, Alabama. Perched atop Saturn, a cluster of eight Jupiter rocket engines generating a staggering 1.5 million pounds of thrust, was an ICBM-type second stage, and on top of that a familiar shape, the X-15.

"We figure the X-15, carrying two pilots on a maximum shot, could be put into orbit hundreds of miles above the earth. Or with a scientific or military payload of thousands of pounds, not including the weight of two X-15 pilots, the ship could be put into a lower orbit. The target date is, say, three or four years. By then our current X-15 will have accumulated more than one hundred powered flights. The ICBMs should be fully operational. Saturn itself will have been fired many times. We believe this is the logical, thoughtful, and economic approach to manned space travel. Many improvements to the X-15 will be required, of course, but we will begin from a firm foundation of experience. Many of the present X-15 systems are adaptable for true space flight. We will have amassed considerable flight-test experience, which is not acquired overnight, as you know quite well. We have an active flight-test team in being today."

Much later I asked Stormy: "What do you think?"

"I don't know, Scotty. NASA is pretty much absorbed with the Project Mercury capsule approach. The Air Force is reluctant to move because of the ill-defined lines of authority and maybe because the X-15 is NASA-inspired and NASA-controlled, and you know the President's directives in this area. The Air Force, I think, will probably award study contracts for specific kinds of orbiting vehicles yet to be invented. We'll keep trying. But I think politically our idea is neither fish nor fowl and because of that—certainly not for technical reasons—we may be left out in the cold."

"We can't let this thing just wither and die right on the verge of success," I said. "Too much has gone into it, too much can come out of it."

"But it's hard to get a point like that across, Scotty. People are too busy. Too many committees. Too many phone calls. Too many investigations. Too many specialists in details are growing up, building empires around special theories, turning their backs on the hard facts of operations."

"Well, maybe I'll write a book and try to get all this across," I said.
"Go ahead," Stormy said. "But I'll tell you that's a big job in itself."
And, as usual, Stormy was right.

41: "You Have a Fire!"

Five days after the second successful powered flight we were airborne again. On this flight we deliberately loitered at altitude over Edwards to simulate the long trip to the X-15's ultimate launch point over Utah. We spent the time on several launch rehearsals. Then we moved into the real thing, ticking off the items on the check-list with the precision of long practice.

"One minute to launch," Jack Allavie called.

The X-15 was humming to perfection. The APUs were churning out electricity and hydraulic power. My left hand reached for the valve to shift my oxygen supply from B-52 to X-15. I flicked my wrist, but nothing happened. The valve was jammed.

Involuntarily I made some unintelligible comment on the radio. Q. C. Harvey came back instantly: "What's the matter, Scott?"

"I can't switch over the oxygen. I've got to hold. Hold the countdown."

Seldom in my flying career had I been so thoroughly disgusted. That an elaborate, expensive flight might be canceled by the seizing of a fifty-cent valve seemed just too much. I worked it back and forth to try to loosen it.

"This one's got me stumped, Q.C.," I said, trying to think of some way to free it. With both hands I tried to turn it by main strength and ripped a seam in my left glove from the pressure.

Using my knee-pad as a lever, I tried to crack it free by hitting the pad with the heel of my hand. My tape recorder picked up the thud of this futile pounding. The gloves I was wearing on that flight were made of an experimental material, since discarded. When I tore them, I had to give up. We could not fly the X-15 without full-pressure suit protection.

"Q.C.," I grumbled, "I'm afraid we're dead."

A few minutes later the windshield frosted over, a trouble we had not experienced since the first captive flight. It was solid ice. No amount of scrubbing with my ripped gloves, no amount of de-fogging heat would remove it. If the oxygen valve had worked and we had launched, I would have found myself in serious trouble indeed, strapped in the X-15 flying blind. I wondered: Is Someone looking after us?

In late October the capricious desert weather led us a merry chase. The rainy season, unpredictable but usually falling in December, came early. Black clouds towered out of the Edwards basin. Scattered showers pelted the parched dry lakes, dampening and slicking the surface. We waited, hoping until the last moment, before canceling each flight. Much of the time the X-15 was kept mated to the B-52. With December's heavy showers, which could close the lake for several months, drawing ever closer, many of us were anxious, on the eve of continued success, to keep the team in training.

While chasing the weather during the last week in October, a situation arose that was obviously ridiculous, yet one that could not be completely ignored. Security informed us they had received a tip that Wernher von Braun and I would be assassinated on October 29. Some people wanted to cancel the flight scheduled for the next day. I objected. To protect our bird, however, we doubled the guard on the B-52 and the X-15. The North American Security Force offered me a bodyguard which I declined. I was worried only that some maniac might harm Alice and the children. On the afternoon of October 28 I flew down to Los Angeles and spent that evening and the next at my home in the community of Westchester, bordering the Los Angeles International Airport.

October 29 passed with no assassination attempt and we heard nothing more about the 'plot.' Weather again forced a cancellation of the flight that day and on October 30.

On Saturday, October 31—Halloween—the weather was marginal but we scheduled a flight. The meteorologists doubted that it would clear for at least twenty-four hours. But we have all long since learned that meteorology, like psychology, in aviation is a loosely organized superstition and that it is foolhardy to schedule flights according to weather predictions, especially in the desert. Stormy and I flew from Los Angeles to Edwards in my Bonanza and toured the area, intently observing the cloud formations. A warm-weather front was moving in from the east, a rare occurrence in the desert. It was indeed a marginal situation. I felt it was worth a gamble and after our survey Stormy agreed.

If nothing else, even a captive flight would be useful and would not waste the efforts and spirits of our ground crew; they had worked almost continuously for two weeks keeping the X-15 primed.

We took off late—0940—and by the time we reached launch altitude the freak easterly front had closed Cuddeback Lake emergency landing strip. This was our intended launch point. We pressed on. Nearby Rosamond Lake was still clear. I radioed Q. C. Harvey.

"I recommend we go as quickly as possible into a launch and that I make a subsonic local flight." My thought was that as long as we had come this far, a slow flight of the X-15 was better than no flight at all and we needed the data.

There were murmurs of protest on the radio. But I voted to continue. I was not being foolhardy. It's just that I have an inherent fear of 'cancelitis,' an insidious disease which, as we have seen, has afflicted many experimental airplane programs. When it sets in, the program loses its sense of urgency, and apathy seeps clear through the ranks from pilot to mechanic.

We could not afford to let this happen. When the ground command post agreed to my idea for a slow-speed flight, I radioed Q.C. again: "Now I want you to do something for me. Keep an eye on that front. If it gets one bit farther west, I've got to cancel this flight."

We began the launch procedure with all hands keeping a sharp eye on the front. A few moments before launch the ground station detected a rapid cloud advance. I radioed chase Al White:

"Al, do you think you could see the west edge of the lake from about 15,000 feet downwind?" In other words, I was asking if it would be possible for me to see to land the X-15.

"Scotty, I can just barely see the lake through the edge of the clouds." When I heard Al's reply I knew we were finished. The front had moved in.

Sam Richter came on the radio: "We strongly recommend we cancel this flight." Sam knew I would read "we" as "Stormy," who never used the radio. It was clear that he was anxious. A strong recommendation from Stormy was, of course, an order. "Okay," I replied glumly, even though I certainly agreed. We shifted to a launch-rehearsal procedure. Just before the simulated drop I radioed for the wind speed and direction on the lake, an ironic gesture. Some people on the ground thought I might still be seriously considering an actual drop.

Q.C. quickly came on and said: "No launch, of course, Scotty."

After the rehearsal I radioed again in a voice heavy with irony: "Beautiful launch."

We jettisoned fuel and Lox and landed. Three hours later, as if nature were deliberately mocking us, defying us to penetrate the secrets of space, the lake bed was unpredictably clear. By then it was too late for a second try.

So far we had conducted most of the X-15 flights—circular patterns—within about twenty miles of the Edwards base. Now as we advanced in our flight-test program, we planned to drop the ship farther out, to enable me to fly in a straight line and subject the X-15 to high-speed and high-altitude maneuvers to define her safe-flying limits. We selected the new, more distant launch points so that a flight would always begin over one of the dry lakes. If the engine failed or some other malfunction occurred, I could land. If it performed as expected, I could fly back to Edwards on my own steam and land on Rogers.

Two launching points that appealed to us were Cuddeback and Three Sisters Dry Lakes, about seventy miles from Edwards as the crow, or rather the X-15, flies. But our plan to launch over these lakes was complicated by the rapidly changing and generally deteriorating desert weather. Rain dampened Cuddeback and Three Sisters. Some 'experts' said that an emergency landing on these lakes would be like landing in a marsh.

Everyone who has ever flown at Edwards has his own unscientific and usually inaccurate method for testing the 'dampness' and strength of the dry-lake beds. One system is to poke a rod in the sand. I flew up to Cuddeback in a light plane to make my own test. It was damp but adequate, and since I would land there only in an emergency and I really did not anticipate an emergency, I proposed the longer-range launch at Cuddeback, rather than continue to idle around Edwards and delay the program.

Roy Ferren, North American's Chief Flight Test Engineer, was against launching over Cuddeback. He argued for more experience with launches closer in, over Bouquet Canyon Reservoir, say, which was within glide distance of Lake Rosamond, then in better shape than Cuddeback. Ferren made a good case and I conceded he had a point. In light of the near-disaster that followed, it was probably fortunate for both me and the X-15 program that he prevailed.

There was nothing in the take-off and pre-launch routine that day, November 5, to indicate a new and formidable crisis was in the making. The X-15 and B-52 were tight as ticks: no valves or regulators were leaking, the nitrogen pressure, APUs, Lox top-off system, pressure suit—everything—all perfectly tuned, so much so that I reported by radio:

"Take out the X-15 handbook, Q.C. See what the instrument-panel gauges should read. That's what I've got."

We bore down on the Bouquet Canyon Reservoir launch point at Mach 0.82 and 45,000 feet. After thirteen flights in the X-15, including the launches, I worked almost routinely in the cockpit.

I turned on the rocket-engine master switch, shifted to X-15 oxygen, and finally flashed the green launch-light in Jack Allavie's cockpit in the B-52. I was hoping that day, if all went well, to inch the X-15's speed to Mach 2.6 or about 1700 miles an hour, and to fly to 80,000 feet. At higher speed it was easier and safer to make our demonstration points and because of this neither NASA nor the Air Force seemed intent on enforcing the Mach 2.0 speed restriction on North American.

"DROP."

For the fourth time I heard the familiar "kerchunk." The X-15 fell away in free flight. Striving for a fast light-off I leveled the ship with my right hand and flicked the rocket switches with my left. I lighted number two and number four barrels on the lower motor first. Then I flicked number two and number four barrels on the upper motor. Then number three and number one on the upper. When I threw the toggle on number three and number one of the lower motor, the last two barrels, I felt a tremendous jar. The whole airplane shook violently, an explosion that seemed to be right behind me. My first thought was that the APU had blown again.

The ship was picking up speed. My eye swept to the APU gauges. They were in the green. The APU had not failed. I was puzzled. Then I noticed that the pump for the lower rocket motor was over speeding and shutting down, indicating a malfunction. An amber warning light flashed on in the cockpit. The flight was done before it began. I shut off the four switches for the lower motor. About five seconds had ticked by. At that instant chase pilot Bob

White, who was flying his F-104 close by the tail of the X-15, snapped on the radio: "Looks like you had an explosion in the rocket motor." Almost simultaneously a fire-warning light flashed on my instrument panel. For a rocket-plane pilot this is a pure and simple moment of truth.

In the past, four rocket planes had exploded and caught fire: the X-1-A, X-1-D, X-2, and 'Queenie.' Each was demolished. Two choices lay open: to pull the ejection-seat handle and bail out, or to ride the ship out and try to save her. The thought of a bail-out never occurred to me. I'm paid to bring airplanes back, not throw them away. My course was set when I first stepped in the airplane.

Working swiftly to minimize the chance that the fire might spread, and to prevent the ship from flying beyond reach of Rosamond Dry Lake, I shut down the rocket engines and closed the fuel lines. All the while I held the ship in level flight. Chase White, his voice rising with concern, said: "You have a fire!" From his position in the F-104 he could see the flames streaming from the rear of the X-15.

I had completed the shut-down and was thinking ahead to the emergency jettison when Bob White, now very worried for me, radioed: "You have a fire! Please shut down."

With no thrust to maintain her air speed, the X-15 was sinking rapidly. I glanced at the altimeter: 32,000 feet. In two minutes I would be on the ground. I spoke on the radio:

"Going to jettison NOW."

The heavy stream of Lox and Wale and hydrogen peroxide trailed through the sky behind me. The fire-warning light flickered out. I radioed White: "Bob, I'm going to put down on Rosamond. Please let me know when we have reached the center of the lake." I was thankful then that Roy Ferren had vetoed the Cuddeback launch. It might have been a mess.

"Jettison looks good," White reported. "I don't see any sign of the fire now."

"Where'd it come from? Could you see?" I asked.

"I think it was the lower engine."

"Thank you," I said. That fact tied in with the over-speed and shutting down of the lower pump. In my mind I envisioned the complex plumbing system, trying to guess what might have happened. How long would it take to fix it? How much more delay would these supposedly reliable engines, with so much time on them, cause us?

The jettison was completed in 114 seconds. There was still a little fuel left in the tanks. The powerful suction of the rocket engine usually burns them bone dry. In the less efficient jettison it is not possible to get all the fuel out. The X-15, I knew, would come in more than a thousand pounds heavier than the previous three landings. My thoughts turned to the landing gear. We had been planning to beef it up following this flight, to give us an added margin of safety. However, I was confident that the gear would hold.

Chase White radioed: "We're almost to the east edge of the lake now."

I was surprised. We should have been approaching the lake from the south. In another fifty seconds I would be touching down.

"Almost where?"

"Pardon me. Almost to the edge of the lake."

"Thank you." I could tell from White's radio transmissions and from others, that the entire X-15 flight-test group was frozen in tension. Every man was aware of the potential danger of fire in a rocket plane. Many of them no doubt expected to see an explosion smear across the sky at any second. To put them at ease, as I turned on downwind I cracked on the radio: "Sorry. I'm going to miss getting the data coming in here."

Chase White chanted my decreasing altitude on the radio: "8,000 . .. 7,000 . . . 6,000 . . . 5,000 ..."

I blew the ventral fin and got set for the approach, holding the X-15 nose high. I keyed my radio mike so that I could no longer receive radio transmissions which might be distracting. I lowered the tail skids and nose wheel, pulled the flaps, and felt for the lake bed. The skids dug in gently. The nose slammed down hard and the ship plowed across the desert floor, slowing down much faster than usual. Then she came to a complete stop within 1500 feet instead of the usual 5000 feet. Something was wrong; the skids failed, I was sure. Not knowing the cause of the trouble and with the fire still very much in my thoughts, I remained buttoned up in the fireproof cockpit.

My radio was dead. I sat alone, waiting in silence.

The emergency helicopter reached the X-15 first. I saw North American's flight surgeon, Toby Freedman, and Brian Lauffer jump out of the chopper and run toward the ship. A good sign, I thought. She wasn't on fire. I opened the canopy and removed my helmet.

Toby was the first to speak. "The plane's busted in two," he said. "What?" I asked. I couldn't believe it. Quickly I scrambled out of the cockpit. What I saw almost broke my heart. The fuselage had buckled immediately aft of the cockpit, two hundred and thirty inches back from the nose. Her belly had dragged in the sand, causing the abrupt deceleration on the lake. The rocket chambers which had exploded at launch were a shambles. When Stormy and Sam Richter first heard the report of fire on the radio, they jumped into a light plane at Edwards and flew immediately to Rosamond Lake, landing alongside the broken bird. They ran up, staring in disbelief. A minute later the fire trucks arrived. One of the firemen, an old friend who had probably met me on the lake in his truck a hundred and fifty times, cried quietly as he sprayed the broken plane with water. I felt like crying myself. At first look it seemed to all of us that that obstinate filly would never break to bit and was mocking our efforts in the grand plan for space flight.

I flew back to Edwards in the light plane. There was not much talk. I changed out of the pressure suit into street clothes. Toby Freedman examined me briefly for the record. Then we all flew back to the airplane again. By then the wreckers were there and, sad to say, some newspaper photographers. It was silly, but when they took their pictures I smiled. It was a vain attempt to laugh away our anguish, to tell anybody who might care that we were not defeated—not by a long shot. And the truth of the matter was, we weren't. Our course was set on the stars.

In the investigation immediately following the accident, the explosion was laid to an engine-ignition failure. This was a relief. At least it was no fundamental weakness in our pioneering airplane, no design fault. It was simply a piece of bad luck that could have happened at any time to any rocket airplane, regardless of meticulous grooming. In retrospect, there was nothing we could have done about it. But now we would plug this weakness and hope there were no more like it hidden away.

That flight proved one thing: the X-15 is a tough bird. When we trucked X-15 number two to the plant in Los Angeles for a close factory look at her, she was not so badly damaged. The rocket engine had to be completely replaced and the shattered engine bay rebuilt. We put a patch—called a doubler plate—inside the fuselage where she had cracked, and in thirty days, after a lot of additional work, she was better than ever. This was an airplane repair record, in any man's league. Meanwhile, we rolled out X-15 number one, which I had not flown since the first glide test. Since then we had been making her ready for a powered trip into the sky before the rains closed the lakes. We were ready for flight with X-15 number one in the week following the near-disaster with ship number two.

But there was an unanswered question gnawing at us. Why did the fuselage buckle? My touchdown had not been hard. The plane, with off-breed engines, NASA instrumentation, and excess fuel, weighed an additional several thousand pounds. But none of these factors added up to a broken fuselage, unless we had goofed terribly in the structure of the ship, something no one could believe. We postponed flight operations to conduct an agonizing reappraisal, checking and rechecking the data, probing, thinking, talking.

It was Charlie Feltz, with his wonderfully intuitive engineering sense, who came up with an answer that turned out to be correct.

He believed there was something happening in the nose-wheel shock absorber which denied the airplane the 'cushion' it required. Thus, he said, the strut was unduly rigid at touchdown and that was why it broke. The laboratory engineers confirmed his theory in a hundred tests of the nose wheel in the factory. The defect was caused by the rapid extension of the telescoped nose gear. The gear came down so fast that the oil in the shock absorber foamed or turned to vapor which has no shock-absorbing value. Unknowingly, up to then we had in effect been landing the ship with little or no nose-wheel shock absorber at all. It was just pure luck that the ship hadn't broken before.

We corrected the defect. To be doubly sure, Charlie asked me to lower the gear a little bit sooner to give the oil time to 'settle down.' But really, I think, his request was to save wear and tear on his own frazzled nerves while watching the landings.

X-15 number one had been ready for days. But now the rainy season had set in at Edwards, delaying all flights indefinitely. The first week of December passed and then the second. The rain thinned out; the lake beds dried. On December 16, forty-one days after the fire and explosion, we scheduled our fifteenth flight. My intent was to make a simple, brief powered flight—the first in that airplane. Then we would turn the craft over to NASA, approximately three and a half months behind schedule.

It was cold in the desert. The ground crews were bundled in heavy jackets. Stormy, Sam Richter, and I huddled in Sam's van, while I read through the carry-over list. One piece of navigating equipment, installed for the deep-space probes, was out. But this would in no way affect our demonstration flight.

After I put on my pressure suit I sprinted from the van to the X-15 boarding ladder, a vain attempt to instill some life and enthusiasm in our operation. The morale of the X-15 ground crew was sagging. A rumor had gotten around that our participation in the flight program was short-lived. A lot of Monday-morning experts could do it better. Our highly professional team, they thought, would soon be disbanded. Many of the men would be looking for other jobs.

We were airborne by 0830, climbing for altitude, intending to launch over Rosamond. On take-off my radio went out. The others could hear me key the mike, but not my voice. Routinely Q. C. Harvey shifted to the mike-clicking system to run through the countdown. One click from me meant yes; two clicks meant no.

While we had this tenuous but effective communications link, there was no need to cancel. It was a beautifully clear day. We pulled thick white contrails at altitude. At 0931 we reached 40,000 feet. Q.C. said: "If all okay, Scott, give me one click."

I keyed the mike one click.

Double-checking, Q.C. radioed: "Scott, if you wish to go ahead and launch without communications, please give me one click."

I keyed the mike one click.

Again rechecking, Q.C. said: "Do you desire to cancel the launch?"

I keyed the mike two clicks. It's not possible, of course, but I tried to transmit a feeling of urgency with those electronic clicks.

They were hard, firm clicks, at least. Why did I need a transmitter? Its main purpose was to keep people on the ground from getting lonesome.

Approaching the launch point I prepared the rocket engine for its first flight. Four minutes from launch time I turned the valve to pressurize the main fuel tanks, eyes glued to the gauge. The gauge indicated a rapid rise and then a sudden fall of pressure in the tanks. The helium regulator was erratic again. I pressed hard for a launch: we had a job to do and would get it done, if permitted.

Two minutes before launch the fuel-tank pressure began to climb slowly. Hope!

Q.C. said: "Scott, we understand you still want to launch. If this is correct, give me one click."

I keyed the mike once, firmly.

"One minute to launch."

I tested the flaps and controls. Chase reported they were operating satisfactorily. I was ready to go. The tank pressure was hanging within limits, though barely—it would need watching. But at the last second the tank pressure again began to sag. If I launched, I would endanger the ship.

Q.C. came on the radio for a final check: "Scott. Reaffirm that it is okay to launch. If so, give me one click."

With the greatest reluctance I keyed the mike twice.

"You do not want to launch, is that correct?"

I keyed the mike once. Then I saw a face in the new hemispherical window of the B-52. I drew my index finger under my throat indicating we were finished. We jettisoned and returned to base. The Monday morning quarterbacks sharply criticized us for attempting to launch without a transmitter. The same quarterbacks had declared a year earlier that only one transmitter was necessary, and even this one was not essential to the X-15 pilot's mission.

42: Minor Miracles

The year 1959 was a shake-down ride for the X-15. In her first year at Edwards the ship was carried aloft fifteen times. Two of these trips were planned captive flights with no intent to launch. The other thirteen were serious attempts to fly. On nine of these thirteen trips some part of the X-15 failed and the attempt was called off. Of the remaining four trips one was the first glide test.

The other three were rocket-powered flights. Of the three rocket-powered flights only one was completely successful. The other two began or ended in serious emergencies, traceable to the 'proven' X-1-type rocket engine. Moreover, a fire on the ground during a routine grooming gutted the engine of one airplane. One X-15 cracked and split open on landing.

These failures, heartbreaking as they are, are common to all new high-performance airplanes. In the case of the X-15 we, as old hands, had long since learned to live with them. They laid the foundation for a razzle-dazzle success story which immediately followed in 1960. The X-15 suddenly came out of the mire, flexed her wings, and took off with a speed and reliability that startled even us. We more than doubled her flight-test rate and at the same time almost eliminated all aborts. From January to late May—less than six months—the X-15 was carried aloft sixteen times. Of these sixteen tries only three were canceled. The remaining thirteen flights were rocket-powered runs, with only minor technical difficulties or none at all. On one of these flights our bird flew faster than any other plane in history.

For a little while, though, in early 1960 it looked as if we would never get off the ground. Both number one and number two X-15S had been repaired. New and stronger landing gear was installed. The birds were tuned to perfection, as were the two B-52 mother planes. But heavy rains flooded the Edwards dry lakes. For a time we believed the lakes might be closed for several months. Impatient to roll, we investigated the possibility of launching at a distant lake near Tonopah, Nevada. For some reason this lake seemed immune to the capricious desert weather. It was dry as a bone. We moved some of the X-15 ground crew and communications team to Tonopah. When the rain at Edwards fell off and the lakes began to dry, we canceled the Tonopah emergency plan.

On our first flight in 1960—January 23—we took off very late in the afternoon, having been delayed several hours by an airplane which crashed and tied up the main runway. I was riding X-15 number one, which I had yet to fly under power. The launch—at 45,000 feet—was rough. I rolled hard right and then left and was slow lighting the engine. But once I got it going, the ship took off like a jack rabbit, pushed along by a hundred-mile-an-hour tailwind. The airplane felt cranky and ill at ease. I kept a tight grip on both control sticks to hold her steady. Even so, she flew like the wind. Tracing a huge circle of rocket exhaust over the Edwards base, I performed some special maneuvers laid out in the flight plan. She pushed up to Mach 2.6—1700 miles an hour—and the chase lost me completely. Only Everest and Apt had flown faster and we were reigning even with low-powered engines.

I was exhilarated. Seventy-nine days had passed since my last previous X-15 powered flight. The ground crews felt happy, too, I knew, because the strict radio-circuit discipline was observed by no one. I keyed my mike in flight and sang: "Back in the saddle again!" Letting down on final, I radioed Q. C. Harvey and asked him if he'd like me to drive the X-15 up on the NASA ramp. When he replied, "Sure," someone else cut in on the circuit and said: "You'd better get someone to open the hangar door!" A friendly needler, recalling my near-disaster with the F-100, cracked: "Yes, at both ends." The landing was the best I'd ever made. I came in at 220 miles an hour with a 7 V2 degree nose-up angle. Because of the delays, I had spent eight hours in the pressure suit. In more ways than one, it was a relief to shuck it.

Only the unusual, uneasy feel of the airplane marred the flight, and not even this dampened our customer's eagerness to take possession of the airplane. On investigation we found that the problem was caused by a minor maladjustment of the SAS system. This was quickly fixed, and at NASA's request after this single powered flight we formally turned X-15 number one over to the customer-lagging five months on a five-year-old schedule. Captain Richardson forgot my martini that day, but NASA director Paul Bikle made up for it. At the post-flight briefing he presented me with a fifth of Old Taylor. Everybody was quite happy. The time had come to put the black bird to work.

The North American flight-test team then turned its complete attention to X-15 number two, the plane I had cracked on the November 5 landing. Under our contract terms we had to perform a series of required demonstration points with the airplane. We would show that the ship was capable of withstanding heavy G forces in a turn, pull-up or roll. I would dive the ship from extreme altitude to prove that it would recover satisfactorily. We would test the ballistic control system, the jet nozzles on the nose and wing which would be used later to steer the ship in airless space.

Our first attempt with X-15 number two on February 4 was a dismal failure, perhaps attributable to 'hangar fever.' The plane had not been in the air for ninety-one days. Everything seemed to go wrong. The cabin would not pressurize. My radio went out. An APU failed for the first time in almost a year. The Wale tank-pressure sagged. Even the jettison was feeble. We landed—the X-15 in its nest under the B-52 wing—with a great deal of the Lox, Wale, and hydrogen peroxide still on board.

After one week of intense fixing we got back into the air again on February 11. We loitered at altitude, simulating the long ride to the ultimate Utah launch point. The countdown revealed no malfunctions and, as still another test, I launched myself from the B-52. The eight barrels of the engine blazed and I zoomed easily to 90,000 feet, almost eighteen miles into the sky. I leveled out, rockets still blazing, to about 2.5 Mach. At burnout I pushed the ship into a very steep powerless dive, simulating a re-entry from space to earth. On Murray's 1954 altitude flight, the X-1-A had tumbled wildly at this crucial point, but the X-15 held stable. In the dive my speed held at Mach 2.0, or 1320 miles an hour. At that speed the desert floor comes up mighty fast. It took me only twenty seconds to dive from 90,000 to 55,000 feet—almost seven miles. The ship was a little slow in the dive recovery. Although I pumped in full 'up' stabilizer, she did not pull out until I reached about 50,000 feet.

Following the dive recovery I made several highly technical demonstration points. Then because I was curious I popped the dive brakes at Mach .9. The effect was startling, like hitting a brick wall. Inadvertently I said "Wow!" over the radio. This set off Charlie Feltz: "Wha'd he say? Wha'd he say?"

On the landing not many seconds later I caused a little more excitement. I had forgotten to arm the ballistic charge in the ventral fin. When I pushed the switch to blow the ventral at 6,000 feet on final, nothing happened. We all had visions of 'the world's fastest plow' digging a furrow in the lake bed. I quickly noted my oversight, armed the charge, and blew the fin before touchdown. On down-wind leg before landing, the oxygen regulator failed and it became extremely difficult to breathe. By the time the ship stopped I was not able to suck any oxygen at all. But this was no great emergency. I simply opened the ram-air door and the visor on my helmet. This flight was considered a whopping success.

We were rolling hard now, and it is difficult to recall the high points of the individual flights. On February 17 the upper rocket-engine unaccountably shut down halfway through the run and I finished the demonstration on one engine. We lost a little ground. But on the March 17 flight I doubled the number of in-flight data points and regained what we had lost. The ship flew beautifully, so well that I exclaimed on the radio: "The best airplane I ever flew." On the landing I felt so happy that I did a side-slip to lose a little excess altitude. This well-known maneuver is not recommended in modern high-performance airplanes, especially in one like the X-15, but it indicated our complete confidence in the black bird.

Our ground turn-around time was now amazingly brief. In fact on the very next day, March 18, the crew had the airplane ready again for flight. About ten seconds before I was to cut myself loose (by then self-launching was adopted as standard procedure in the North American operation), my chase pilot, Al White—bless him—noticed a faint trickle of alcohol pouring out of a drain from the engine bay. He called out, and I instantly canceled the drop.

Alcohol spilling in the engine bay spelled real potential trouble. If I had dropped and lighted off the engine, it would probably have exploded. The alcohol leak was traced to a cracked fitting in the maze of engine plumbing.

On March 25, sixty-two days after we turned X-15 number one over to NASA, test pilot Joe Walker made his first flight. This time the old pro, feeling oddly misplaced, flew in a chase plane. Joe took his time for his first launch. The B-52 made several circles while Joe held the countdown. But then he cut away cleanly for a brief run. During the long delay my chase plane ran low on fuel and I had to return to base. So I missed seeing another man land the X-15 for the first time. Walker danced a jig on the lake bed to show his elation.

In the next fifty-five days Walker and Air Force pilot Bob White made five additional powered flights in X-15 number one. This was an average of about one flight every ten days, a sustained turn-around time that beat most previous NASA records, except those we had established with the Skyrocket in the old days. Bob White experienced little difficulty in his first rocket-powered flight.

He did a beautiful job, in my opinion. On his third flight, May 19, he zoomed to an altitude of 107,000 feet. Later, on August 12, he reached 136,500 feet.

Walker made additional flights. On his third, May 12, he left all the rocket barrels on for the entire flight and added half a Mach number to the highest speed I had achieved in the plane. He reached almost the limit with the small engines, Mach 3.2, or about 2,110 miles an hour, a world's speed record. Later, on August 4, he flew the ship Mach 3.3, 2,196 miles an hour, breaking his own record.

X-15 number one was performing like the champion she was bred to be. Walker's speed run was made on X-15 number one's seventh consecutive powered flight with no intervening aborts. No experimental airplane in history—for that matter, very few conventional airplanes—have operated so well so soon after delivery from the manufacturer. This pleased us greatly and almost compensated for the year of frustration we had been through.

On March 29, four days after Joe Walker's first flight, I took X-15 number two into the air again for additional demonstrations. Most of these are too complicated to describe in detail. In essence I subjected the ship to severe strain in a variety of positions and angles of attack to prove that she would hold together in flight even under extraordinary circumstances. One of these maneuvers was an abrupt pull-up which put about six G's on the ship. The newspapers made a lot of this flight—the fact that by pulling six G's I weighed six times my normal weight, or almost half a ton—but a six-G maneuver is routine for a fighter pilot. Two days later, on March 31, I repeated these maneuvers and performed others.

During April we delayed our flight program temporarily to install and ground-test the ballistic control system. In principle, the little hydrogen-peroxide jets are quite simple. However, the installation is complicated. Both the jets and the APUs use the same source of hydrogen peroxide. Thus it was necessary to establish a careful balance between the two—meaning more regulator valves and other devices which leak. Ultimately this installation and test spun into another around-the-clock routine, with Stormy prodding us to the limit. By May 5 we were ready.

All the difficulties we feared, plus a few more, took place—just like the early days. At fifteen minutes to drop I operated the ballistic-control-system lever with my left hand. When I pushed the lever to the 'up' and 'down' positions, the hydrogen peroxide squirted through the jets in the nose. The system was not designed for operation at low altitude while the X-15 is cold. Thus when the undecomposed peroxide from the nose jets sprayed back and struck the windshield, a thick coating of ice was formed. I was sealed in blind. No amount of defogging gas helped. During the launch rehearsal an APU turned erratic and shut itself off. We had not yet achieved the necessary delicate balance in combining all the systems. This abortive flight touched off another night-and- day work regime that went on for about three weeks. We were ready again on May 26.

We took off on schedule. Jack Allavie was flying in the left seat of the B-52. Fitz Fulton, who had made most of the drops in 1960 as co-pilot, was replaced by Charlie Bock, back for his first mother-plane flight in seven months. I was in a flippant, cocky mood. It was my twenty-fifth flight in the X-15. I had never added the figures but I suppose by then I had spent some forty hours in the air under the B-52 wing.

I had some additional equipment in the X-15 cockpit that day, a so-called 'physiological package,' the type that will be sent aloft with the Project Mercury Astronauts when and if they orbit the earth. I was wired like a chimpanzee, with devices to measure my skin temperature, rate of breathing, heartbeat, blood pressure—everything but a 'rectal probe,' for reference temperature, and that I refused to buy. All these devices telemetered a constant flow of physiological data to a group of aero-medical officers on the ground. I consider this information rather personal, and it seemed an indignity to have it broadcast so freely. Besides, I question its usefulness. The roots of capability are in a man's spirit—a difficult measurement to get.

So while we loitered at altitude waiting to launch, I cooked up a plot to tease the aero-medical officers. For a period of about thirty seconds I breathed at a heavy rate and wriggled violently in the cockpit, driving their gauges almost to the limit, I'm sure.

Then I sat rigid—almost yoga-like—and held my breath for a full minute, during which time the gauges should have sagged to zero. In theory, I was dead. The aero-medical officers flashed no warning, a subtle proof that their faith lies in the man, not the equipment. A fine point can be made here.

A second trick occurred to me. I knew from long experience in altitude chambers with aero-medical devices that if I flexed my muscles violently for a few moments it would drive my EKG (heart wave trace) right through the ceiling. I planned to do this and then to pull the plug on the 'physiological package' tele-metering. The reading on their gauges would be a rapid heart acceleration and then a total, mysterious blank. I changed my mind about this at the last minute because I was afraid I might give Charlie Feltz real heart failure.

The launch—my eleventh in the X-15—was beautiful. For the tenth time my left hand flicked across the rocket-barrel toggles. My right hand gripped the side-arm control, which I intended to use throughout the flight and on the landing. I had not used this control on landing since the first glide-flight. During the early stages I was concerned that if anything dire happened on landing, it would probably be blamed on that very fine, but new and controversial, piece of equipment.

The X-15 zoomed toward the heavens, all eight barrels going wide open. At 42,000 feet I kicked the rudder and the ship yawed severely—another demonstration maneuver. I recovered easily and roared about the sky, turning, twisting, rolling, and spinning like a bullet, subjecting the plane to unusually heavy strains. My speed climbed up to Mach 2.7, considerably beyond my Mach 2.0 restriction. I had let the rocket engines burn a little longer because I needed the extra power to reach the lake bed. Also the demonstration points were safer to make at higher speed.

After engine burnout I coasted silently toward the desert lake, testing the ballistic control system. I squirted the hydrogen peroxide through the nose jets, calling 'nose up' and 'nose down' on the radio. This was simply a test to see whether the system functioned properly. In the thick atmosphere at 50,000 feet, where I began the test, the weak nozzles have no effect whatsoever on the X-15 flight attitude. The North American altitude restriction was still in force. Thus I could not make the test above 100,000 feet where a gentle squirt from the jets would considerably change the airplane attitude. We had corrected the cause of the liquid bath, and the windshield did not ice over.

I chose a runway and for the eleventh time brought the ship in for a landing. I used the side-arm control all the way. It is a little more sensitive than the center-control stick, but with practice I believe pilots will find it superior to the old-fashioned 'ax-handle' control. The X-15 touched down smoothly, concluding the last flight with the two smaller engines. It was time to take her to the 'barn' for the big-engine conversion.

With the conclusion of that flight, the box score on both airplanes was a total of thirty-one flights. A little over half of these—sixteen, to be precise— were made under rocket power, and one was the first glide test. These were completed five years almost to the day from the time Hugh Elkin and his Advanced Design group at North American first submitted the X-15 conception.

This time was about one year less than it took to design, build, and fly the Skyrocket, the most successful, after the X-1, of the early era of rocket airplanes. It was about two years less than the time it usually takes to design and build a modern jet fighter such as the F-100. It was about three or four years less than the time it took to build the hangar-loving X-3. It was five years less time than it took to build and fly the jinxed X-2 in which Everest, Kincheloe, and Apt set their world speed and altitude records.

Considering that the X-15 was not only the most advanced aircraft ever conceived by man, but also a ship designed to fly into the fringes of space, I do not believe it is immodest to claim that we had pulled off a minor miracle. We did this in spite of the false starts, frustrations, and malfunctions, those events that naturally cling to the memory and upon which I have probably dwelt too long in this account.

About this time a second minor miracle took place in Washington, D. C. The Congress and the new Secretary of Defense, Thomas S. Gates, took another look at the gutted B-70 bomber program. Gates announced publicly that he was ready to 're-consider' the craft as a weapons system. Then the Congress voted $285 million to restore about half the original program. There was, of course, no direct connection between this turnabout and the success of the X-15 flight-test program. But perhaps in some indirect way the fact that the X-15 had flown like a champion at Mach 3—the B-70 cruising speed—and routinely to the B-70 cruising altitude of 70,000 feet, influenced some people to think twice. The restoration of the B-70 now made each flight of the X-15 more meaningful. The data we collected from the X-15 would be used to advantage on the B-70.

Actually, I believe, the decision to restore the B-70 was inevitable. The United States simply could not abandon the manned aircraft altogether and survive as the pillar of freedom in the West. Now that wisdom prevailed, we hoped that the powers that be would take a careful look at the total manned-aircraft spectrum. Our current fleet of Air Force planes is approaching obsolescence. As yet there is still no advanced fighter aircraft in the works. In fact, as we look into the future, the B-70, which may be ready to fly a few years from now, stands very much alone, a single piece of hardware. Between the current, aging Air Force fleet and the B-70, amazingly enough, there is only one craft in existence, the X-15, and only one Air Force pilot, Bob White, who has ever flown it. Our United States Air Force should have a thousand rocket pilots. By contrast, the Soviet Union has never stopped building airplanes. Each year they turn up with ever-faster fighters and bombers, as well as a force of missiles. By default, the United States arrived at a point of imbalance that would be ludicrous if it were not so potentially dangerous. The U.S. must produce manned aircraft to match the Soviet Union. Missiles alone are not enough.

As I have said before, bad news usually comes with the good. The B-70 was restored but our efforts to persuade high circles in Washington that we should capitalize on the X-15 concept and the vast experience of our construction and flight-test teams for the exploration of space fell on deaf ears. Within NASA the Project Mercury capsule dominated. Within the Air Force there was still justifiably much uncertainty about the use of a space craft for a military mission, and the effort in that service was restricted largely to paper studies. Firmly believing that in the conquest of space the nation would ultimately swing to an X-15 concept—a craft that could go into space and then return to earth to land with dignity—we pressed on, proposing a two-seater version of the X-15, a trainer to check out large numbers of Air Force pilots. We urged manned concepts in the belief that to rely solely on automatic concepts presupposes a mathematical certitude not found in war, peace, or the quests of men. We made few converts.

43: 'THE REAL SIGNIFICANCE'

THE BIG SINGLE-BARREL XLR-99 ROCKET ENGINE designed to blast the X-15 on its ultimate mission to the fringes of space arrived in California in April, 1960, about a year and a half behind schedule. It was shipped to Edwards and bolted to the ground-test stand. During May the North American and Reaction Motors engineers ran the engine in a series of exhaustive tests. It was a sight to see: that small barrel spewing smoke and flame, thrust almost four times as great as the combined thrusts of the two smaller X-1-type engines then powering the X-15. The rocket-engine noise boomed across the desert for thirty miles.

In late May the first big engine was installed in X-15 number three, the ship we had specifically reserved for this first engine. And in early June X-15 number two, after my ninth and final powered flight in that craft, was torn down and the two smaller engines removed in preparation for the arrival of the second big engine. Meanwhile, we got set to ground-test the big engine which was installed in number three.

The ground tests of this engine, which has as much power as an Army Redstone missile and almost three times the power of the Navy's Vanguard missile, were elaborate for Edwards (though stark compared to the blank-check missile operations).

We had made some improvements on the ground-test stand. The engineers had built special steel clamps to hold the X-15 to the concrete apron. They had installed underground concrete observation bunkers, which looked like Maginot-Line pill-boxes. The telemetry engineers rigged elaborate equipment to transmit a record of everything happening in the X-15 during the engine run to a master console in the NASA administration building. For this big moment in the history of our craft, nothing would be left to chance.

Late in the afternoon of June 8, I arrived at the ground-test area wearing street clothes. X-15 number three, with her powerful new engine, was clamped in place on the stand. She was brimming with Lox and new fuel for the big engine—ammonia, more powerful or 'exotic' than the Wale used in the two smaller engines. A thick coating of ice had formed on the fuselage around the Lox tank. Wispy Lox vapor trailed off into the afternoon sky. A snarl of electrical power connections—the umbilical cords—ran from a hole in the concrete to the ship's side tunnels.

Harry Gallanes, North American's power-plant test boss, greeted me: "Looks like we're all set, Scotty." He and his crews had been working without let-up since dawn. They had pretty much kept to this dawn-to-dusk (sometimes later) schedule since the day the big engine arrived, another manifestation of that curious enthusiasm for things mechanical which seemed to infect all members of the flight-test team.

I climbed into the cockpit and donned a Scott Airpack breathing device similar to the unit skin divers wear underwater. It would supply my oxygen, pumped into the airplane from an external connection. The simple airpack was more comfortable and far less bother than the X-15 full-pressure suit, which I did not need on the ground. I closed the canopy and turned on the nitrogen gas flow, to cool the electronic equipment in the cockpit and to build up a pressure which would block out possible ammonia fumes or other toxicants, should something go wrong during the engine run.

On this ground test—my second in this airplane—we intended to simulate all the events of a real drop from the mother plane with rocket-engine light-off. If all went well, we hoped to make an actual flight a month later, perhaps sooner. Harry Gallanes and his men retired to the bunkers. Gallanes manned the radio circuit as test director. Q. C. Harvey took up his post in the forward bunker. Soon we were well through the countdown.

At six minutes to 'drop' I turned on the APUs. X-15 number three was completely on her own. It was time for the big test. A siren whined a warning. The mechanics, protectively dressed in hooded clothing, evacuated to the bunkers. They had been hanging around checking for leaks or other possible malfunctions until the last moment. A group of fire trucks, parked about two hundred yards away, were ready to rush to the rescue, if needed.

Otherwise there was no sign of life. Alone in the cockpit I checked the gauges. As we approached the time for engine light-off, three movie cameras, mounted outside and aimed at the rear of the X-15, began to roll. Inside the cockpit I turned on the data recorders.

I called each step of the engine-start procedure on the radio, pausing briefly after each item on the check-list.

"Master switch coming on NOW."

"Prime."

"Pre-cool."

"Pump idle."

"Igniter idle."

I then moved the main engine throttle from its stowed position to the engine-start position. The engine is designed to light off at half-thrust. When I moved the throttle, in effect opening the main fuel and Lox lines, the engine cracked to life with a tremendous roar. The ship vibrated powerfully in her steel mounts. The engine ran smoothly as designed. Slowly I opened the throttle to full power. The noise was terrific.

The North American X-15 Mach 2.0 speed and 100,000-foot altitude restrictions are still technically in force. If I allowed the big barrel to run full-bore in flight, I would quickly exceed those limits by a great margin and perhaps go hurtling off to the fringes of space. Thus for my big-engine 'demonstration' flights we had worked out a system whereby in the air I would shut down the engine periodically and restart it after the speed and altitude fell off. Now simulating my actual flight plan, I pulled the throttle back and shut down the engine. As prescribed, I waited fifteen seconds and then restarted the engine at fifty per cent thrust.

Rocket engines are equipped with special engine safety devices. If these devices 'sense' anything abnormal in burning or engine operation, they automatically shut the engine off and 'safety' all the electrical circuits. Evidently after my restart one such device 'sensed' a vibration. Almost immediately after I moved the throttle to half-thrust, the engine shut down automatically. There was no sign of trouble in the cockpit, so I prepared to restart the engine once again.

To restart the engine after an automatic shut-down, the pilot must push a special switch which 'unsafeties' the engine, or in effect resets all the circuits the automatic device has closed down. If these can be reset, the engine is again ready for start.

Beginning the restart procedure, I put the throttle in the stowed position and pressed the reset switch.

It was like pushing the plunger on a dynamite detonator. X-15 number three blew up with incredible force. The rear section of the airplane, from the trailing edge of the wing aft, was instantaneously demolished. The front section of the airplane, including the cockpit and the pilot, hurtled twenty feet across the concrete ramp at indescribable speed, the shortest and fastest rocket ride in history, subjecting me to an acceleration force of maybe fifty G's. Fortunately, my head was reclining in the headrest on the seat; otherwise my neck might have been broken.

Nine hundred gallons of ammonia and sixty gallons of hydrogen peroxide, a total of 16,000 pounds of powerful liquid, had ignited simultaneously. I knew, of course, that there had been a tremendous explosion, but I had no way of knowing precisely what happened. All I could think of was the possibility of a second explosion that might hurl my part of the airplane half-way across Edwards and through the main hangar and workshop.

In the cockpit I moved swiftly to do what I could to prevent this. I turned off the APUs and all external power supply and shifted from external oxygen to X-15 oxygen supply. Then I braced my feet on the instrument panel and put my arms across my face, waiting. There was no panic, no fear. I was concerned primarily for the safety of the other people—those outside—and I thanked God that He had given us the time to install the concrete pillbox bunkers, which were being used tonight for only the second time.

Half a minute later I watched a mass of red approaching the X-15. It was the fire truck. Its hoses pumped a great spray of water over the ship, smothering the fire still raging in the shattered rear section. A few seconds later I saw Art Semone and another mechanic hunched outside the cockpit. They were trying to pull the canopy handle to let me out. At that point I would have preferred to remain inside the cockpit, one of the safest places in the world in the event of fire. But I could see that no amount of hand-signaling would dissuade Semone, and rather than expose him to possible danger I helped open the canopy and leaped out.

Semone must have thought I was injured. When I jumped from the cockpit, he caught me in mid-air and tried to carry me out of the smoke and flames. I whopped him on the shoulder to let him know I was all right and then we all ran quickly to a spot about a hundred feet distant and I checked the bunkers. Everyone, it seemed, had survived, and for this I was very grateful. As it turned out, no one, including me, was even slightly injured. I had someone relay that fact to Alice as soon as possible, knowing the news would be on the radio before the fire was out.

The documentation of that explosion, like everything else about the X-15, was first-rate. In fact it was probably one of the best documented airplane accidents in history. Immediately afterwards, Q.C. gathered all of us in a room, and there we recalled in detail all that we could remember while it was still fresh in our minds. These eye-witness accounts, added to the miles of telemetry data and the film strips from the three movie cameras, would enable us to establish the cause of the explosion very quickly. It was not the fault of the engine. A sequence of coincidences, again hidden in the mysteries of Murphy's Law, had trapped us. We moved rapidly to avert any possibility of a recurrence in X-15 number two, meanwhile accelerating our efforts to install the big engine in that ship. NASA prudently grounded X-15 number one until we could do everything possible to make sure a similar disaster could not happen.

The fate of number three was quickly decided. She would be rebuilt. Some parts—nose, cockpit, wings—might be salvaged. This was obviously a major task requiring more time and money. The destruction of this airplane is simply part of the price man must pay for progress. Measured against the loss of fifty or so Atlas, Titan, and Polaris missiles at Cape Canaveral, each costing more than a single X-15, was a drop in the bucket, although a painful one because it temporarily reduced our complete air fleet by thirty-three and one-third per cent.

Inevitably the newsmen got on my trail. When they called, I was ready with the wisecrack I knew they wanted. "The only casualty," I said, "was the crease in my trousers. The firemen got them wet when they sprayed the airplane with water." Too late I realized how this might be interpreted.

"Are you sure it was the firemen?" the reporter asked.

"Yeah, I'm sure," I said. I pictured the headline:

SPACE SHIP EXPLODES; PILOT WETS PANTS!

"Mr. Crossfield," the reporter went on. "What is the real significance of all this?"

"The real significance?" I asked. "Have you got about ten or fifteen hours, maybe?"

"No," he said. "I've got about two minutes to meet a deadline. Just tell me what's going to happen now? Where does this leave the program?"

"We're not sure yet. There will naturally be some investigations. In all probability we'll accelerate putting the big engine in X-15 number two. A little later we'll put the big engine in NASA's X-15 number one."

"Does this affect your role in the program? Will you still go ahead and make a demonstration flight with the big engine?"

"I don't know," I said. "I was only supposed to make one or two low-speed demonstration flights with the big engine and then that was the end of my participation in the project. Bob White and Joe Walker would take it from there. They might change that now. I have no reason to believe there will be any change. There could be. I might not make the big-engine demonstration flights. I honestly don't know. It's all very indefinite."

"Well, thanks. Someday I'd like to talk to you about the real significance. But not now."

It was always the same: hurry, impatience, no time for thoughtful reflection. Move on quickly to the next story, the next pilot, or missile, or space vehicle, for a bigger and better headline.

"Okay," I said. "I'll be seeing you."

The real significance of the X-15, I hope, has come through in the foregoing pages. It is not just another airplane, another headline. It is another of man's restless attempts at perfection, and in the aviation world the greatest ever mounted. The X-15 sprang from a deep pool of aeronautical knowledge, the end product of fifty years, and more, of probing this frontier. It was created and built at tremendous cost in terms of money and sweat by some of the most skilled engineers in the free world. As always, we did not achieve our dream of perfection. Only God, I believe, can create the perfect. But in reaching out, we provided some water for man's never-ending thirst. We learned a great deal. We had set man on his path toward the stars.

Someday, I believe, he will get there. Not so quickly as one might think from reading the newspapers. The speed of this massive scientific effort is like that of the convoy, geared to the pace of the slowest vessel. Thus this daring adventure is regulated not so much by grandiose plans emanating from the increasing layers of scientific administrators in Washington as by the simple function of a valve, an APU unit, or a radio plug. Our tale of adversity with the X-15 is not unique; rather, it is typical of our age. Similar stories, many with fewer points of success, were taking place at the same time in our nation with Atlas, Polaris, Titan, Mercury, Minuteman, a dozen others I cannot recall. Someday, too, perhaps these stories will be written. In time, our splendid engineers will de-bug the big X-15 engine. I may or may not be allowed to make one or two low-speed flights. Then in the months ahead, depending on the speed or the scientific convoy, Bob White or Joe Walker or perhaps someone else will begin the first, tentative 'space' flights in the X-15. They will launch over the designated point in Utah, light off the powerful rocket barrel, and roar heavenward. With God's help they may reach a speed of 4,000 miles an hour and an altitude of perhaps 100 miles. I hope that many, many pilots will have the opportunity to make these pioneering voyages into space.

Ultimately our work, and the work of the tens of thousands of other engineers in this nation, will be merged to form a more advanced space machine. The bottom of this machine might not look like an Atlas or Saturn. The top might not look like an X-15. But the complete vehicle will be the sum product of all the work of all the engineers in this country. This machine will not rise effortlessly and gracefully from the earth on the first day. Dedicated people such as Charlie Feltz and Harrison Storms must first expend limitless sweat and tears. The machine may crash and explode. So might the second and third, perhaps the fourth and fifth. Congressional committees will investigate, and new layers of scientific administrators will grow atop the old in Washington. But the engineers will prevail in spite of them.

Someday this machine will rise from the face of the earth. It will take man into an orbital path about the earth. It will enable him to build a space station. From there he will shove off to the moon. Then he will go to the nearest planets in our solar system. A hundred years from now, if we have not destroyed our own planet in an ideological war, man may enter the solar system of the nearby stars. He will go there because he must. He is curious and intelligent. He is seeking answers—about himself, his universe, and his God. Because man is a creature of God and the instrument of God, he will not be denied. There will always be another dawn.

44: 'Prophecies of the Next Age'

THE EXPLOSION OF X-15 NUMBER THREE HAD A curious impact on me personally. For the first time in my flying career I was foggy-minded. I could not recall immediately exactly what happened, although in aerial emergencies in the past my mind always ticked on, recording even the most obscure gauge readings. Locked in the room with Q.C. and the others during the post-accident investigation, it took me fully ten minutes of thoughtful reconstruction to lay out the exact sequence of events that took place in the X-15 cockpit.

Flying home from Edwards late that night, I found my thoughts taking another unusual turn. Although I seldom think about death, my mind recreated in vivid detail the one death that stands out in my mind more than all others, that of my father.

He died on October 21, 1954, during the time I was flying for NACA at Edwards, six weeks or so after I drove the F-100 through the hangar wall. He had sold the farm at last, for a handsome profit, and moved to the California desert to be near his children and grandchildren. He dreamed of touring the United States in a trailer in the evening of his life. But it was too late. The more than nineteen years of hard physical labor on the farm drained his body of strength. After examining my father, one doctor told me: "He is the most worn-out man of sixty-three that I have ever seen."

Soon he fell quite ill. My mother was just recovering from a stroke, and we brought in a nurse to help out. Toward the end, I spent almost every night in his house, sleeping on a cot next to his bed. I was there primarily out of love, to do what I could for him. But there was another reason. I was curious to see whether in his final hours this unwavering, iron-willed man would reveal any weakness. If I saw the slightest hint, I would find a way to head it off, or at least obscure it from him. For sixteen years or more I had been searching for a break in his strength. I never found it. I didn't really expect him to ask for quarter now.

When I saw him on the morning of the 21st, I felt that he would not last the day. I was scheduled for a Skyrocket flight that morning and was on the verge of putting through a call to Walt Williams to cancel it when my father called for me.

"What were you supposed to be doing today?" he asked. "Why haven't you gone to work?"

"Oh, nothing," I said. "Just a routine flight. I can cancel it with no problem."

"I want you to go ahead and do your job." His voice was low but firm. His request was a command. There was no hint of quarter. "Okay. But will you wait for me?" We both knew what I meant.

"Yes."

I drove to the field and made the flight. My father waited, as he promised. As I soon learned from a telephone call, he died at the exact moment the Skyrocket's wheels touched down on the lake at the conclusion of my flight. He died quietly and bravely, without a single compromise on his conscience. That he found what he sought in the next life I have no doubt, for he was an honorable man and a Christian.

Returning home that night after the X-15 explosion, the real significance of my own life, which I had pondered for so many months at Edwards, came to me as though crystallized by the accident. My own life, in a different setting in time and circumstance, was an imitation of my father's, a striving toward unattainable perfection. As nature had sealed Bill Young's eyes and then mysteriously opened his ears to sounds beyond the experience of other men, so nature wounded me in childhood and then mysteriously endowed me with a special spirit that put fear beyond my experience and spurred me to improve everything that crossed my path. Who can presume to know why?

Nature and God are one. If there is an imperfection, it is not there by accident. Perhaps He intended that by my example the wounds of others lacking in this special spirit might be healed.

I honestly cannot believe that my being present at the birth and growth of the X-15 was an accident. This blending of man and machine in a common cause must be a part of His grand design.

My father may have fallen short of his goal. I have fallen short of my goal, probably I always shall. It may be that only ignorant men reach goals. The important thing, I think, as with the X-15, is the striving itself. Each of us who strives toward the unattainable contributes to man's ever-growing reservoir of knowledge and fact. Each drop, however small, is vital for those who follow behind us. Without it man must inevitably atrophy. Thus, as Emerson says, "Men walk as prophecies of the next age."

I realized that night that my new circle, the meaning of which I had so intensively probed during the long months at Edwards, was boundless. It was, in a few words, more of the same on a grander scale. The details were not important. The ultimate end was not a fixed slot, which I imagined in my youth to be the satisfying end, a life devoted not to the specific but to the infinite, to the collection of a few drops for that vast and wonderful pool.

A small contribution which would ease my children's way, or perhaps in time open men's eyes to a part of the grand mystery. It was quite late when I pulled into our driveway in Westchester. I strode briskly to the front door and entered quietly.

The children were asleep. I mixed a drink and Alice and I relaxed in the living room.

"Well, you look all right to me," she said.

"There's nothing wrong with me."

"So what's next?" It was many years since she had put that question to me.

"I don't know." A thousand thoughts flashed through my mind. A thousand imperfections, a thousand horizons, a thousand Mount Everests, the story of man since time began. I was in a strange mood.

"Well," Alice said, "they say life begins at forty. You've got a full year and a half to make up your mind."

"You know what I've been thinking," I said absently. "This house is getting pretty crowded with five kids. Maybe we ought to add a new wing. Then there's another thing I'd like to do. Maybe we could build a little summerhouse out in the back yard—you know, one of those lattice-work things—with a tower, or cupola, on top. If we built one tall enough, we could see over the shrubbery and the fence. We could sit up there and watch the airplanes taking off and landing at the airport. We could see the sky and the horizon unobscured."

The tower is not yet begun. But that is a new story, another dawn.

THE END